PUFFIN BOOKS
THE PUFFIN FACTFINDER

Derek O'Brien was born in Kolkata. He began his professional career as a journalist for *Sportsworld* magazine but soon shifted to advertising. After working for a number of very successful years as Creative Head of Ogilvy, Derek decided to focus all his energy and talent in his passion—quizzing.

Today, Derek O'Brien is Asia's best-known quizmaster and the CEO of Derek O'Brien & Associates Pvt. Ltd. He is the host of the longest-running game show on Indian television, The Cadbury Bournvita Quiz Contest, for which he was voted the Best Anchor of a Game Show at the Indian Television Academy Awards three years in a row. He also hosts the longest-running corporate quiz show, The Economic Times Brand Equity Quiz. Derek conducts quizzes across India, in the Gulf, Pakistan, Nepal, Sri Lanka, Singapore and the US. He is also credited with having conducted the first quiz on Twitter.

Derek O'Brien has also authored more than thirty reference and quiz books for Penguin, making him Penguin India's highest-selling reference author. He is also the author of two extremely successful school textbook series with Pearson Education: *Know and Grow with Derek* and *Be a GK Champ*.

In 2011, Derek O'Brien was voted to the Rajya Sabha as a Member of Parliament (MP). He is the Chief Whip of the Trinamool Congress in the Rajya Sabha, and had the honour of addressing the UN General Assembly in 2012.

To know about Derek and his company, visit the website www.derek.in. You can also follow Derek on Twitter (@quizderek).

# THE PUFFIN FACTFINDER

## EDITED AND COMPILED BY
# DEREK O'BRIEN

**PUFFIN BOOKS**

An imprint of Penguin Random House

PUFFIN BOOKS

USA | Canada | UK | Ireland | Australia
New Zealand | India | South Africa | China | Singapore

Puffin Books is part of the Penguin Random House group of companies
whose addresses can be found at global.penguinrandomhouse.com

Published by Penguin Random House India Pvt. Ltd
4th Floor, Capital Tower 1, MG Road,
Gurugram 122 002, Haryana, India

Penguin
Random House
India

First published in Puffin by Penguin Books India 2012

Content provided by Amit Ghosh, Ammar Hamid, Anik Ghosal, Ayashman Dey,
Natasha Gasper, Nilanjana Basu, Shalini Chaudhury and Srirupa Roy.

10 9 8 7 6 5 4 3 2

ISBN 9780143332534

Typeset in Frutiger by InoSoft Systems, Noida

Printed at Manipal Technologies Limited, India

www.penguin.co.in

MIX
Paper | Supporting
responsible forestry
FSC® C043100

# CONTENTS

HISTORY 01

COMPUTER 107

ENVIRONMENT 119

GEOGRAPHY 141

INDIA 221

LANGUAGE AND LITERATURE 269

MUSIC & ENTERTAINMENT 290

SPORT 301

SCIENCE 318

MATHEMATICS 347

INDEX 352

# CONTENTS

HISTORY

COMPUTER

ENVIRONMENT

GEOGRAPHY

INDIA

LANGUAGE AND LITERATURE

MUSIC & ENTERTAINMENT

SPORT

SCIENCE

MATHEMATICS

INDEX

# AUTHOR'S NOTE

Twenty years. Yes, that's how old, or should I say young, we are now. And over these past two decades we have enjoyed, with fair success, bowling yorkers, bouncers and googlies (if you'd excuse the cricket analogy) to our audience and readers. From shows in auditoriums and stadia, to TV networks to books and newspapers—*making knowledge interesting to help people grow* is our mission.

Through these very satisfying years, we have interacted with students from diverse backgrounds across our great nation. So, when Puffin asked us to research and edit a fun, fact-filled book for the youth, we dived straight ahead and took the catch.

We have had an enjoyable innings putting together this ready reckoner. To take my cricket analogy a little further, if our other reference books are five day Test matches and ODIs, this Factfinder is Twenty20 cricket: exciting, concise yet exhaustive, and easy to follow.

The toil of net practice is over and the match is in full swing. Now get bowled over by *The Puffin Factfinder*.

# AUTHOR'S NOTE

# HIST⬥RY

---

## UNDERSTANDING TIME

BC is an abbreviation for Before Christ. It is used to indicate that a given date occured the specified number of years before Christ was born.

AD is an abbreviation for Anno Domini. It is used to indicate that a given date comes the specified number of years after the accepted date of Christ's birth.

In recent years, some writers have started using the abbreviations CE (of the Common Era) in place of AD, and BCE (before the Common Era) in place of BC.

## STONE AGE TO IRON AGE

The Stone Age was a prehistoric cultural stage in human evolution. It was characterized by the creation and use of stone tools. The Stone Age is usually divided into three separate periods, based on the degree of sophistication in the fashioning and use of tools. These periods are: Paleolithic Period (Old Stone Age), Mesolithic Period (Middle Stone Age), and Neolithic Period (New Stone Age). The Neolithic Period was followed by the Chalcolithic or Bronze Age, which gave way to the Iron Age.

| PALEOLITHIC PERIOD | MESOLITHIC PERIOD | NEOLITHIC PERIOD | CHALCOLITHIC AGE | IRON AGE |
|---|---|---|---|---|
| Also called Old Stone Age, appeared between 500,000–6000 BC (approx.). | Appeared between the 8th and 4th millenniums BC; transitional stage between Paleolithic and Neolithic periods. | Appeared between 9000 and 6000 BC; final stage of cultural evolution or technological development among prehistoric humans. | Also known as Copper Stone Age between 6000 and 1500 BC; also known as Bronze Age because metals like copper and bronze were introduced. | Between 1200 and 1000 BC; widespread export of knowledge of iron metallurgy and iron objects. |
| First ancestors of modern human beings appeared; rudimentary chipped tools made of flint, stone, bone, and antlers came into use; most important weapon—the pointed wooden spear. | Mesolithic hunters achieved greater efficiency than the paleolithic. Exploited a wider range of animal and vegetable food sources. | Stone tools sharpened by polishing or grinding. Domestication of plants and animals. | Invention of the wheel and the ox-drawn plough. Bronze Age declined in circa 1000 BC, as heating and forging iron became feasible. | Large-scale production of iron implements, catalyzing new patterns of permanent settlement began. |
| Food gathering and hunting prevailed; people collected wild fruits, nuts and berries, and hunted wild animals and birds. | New forms of chipped stone tools called microliths introduced. | Permanent villages appeared. Practice of crafts such as pottery and weaving began. | Age witnessed in India during the Indus Valley Civilization. | Utilization of iron for weapons, resulting in arms in the hands of the masses for the first time. |
| Small sculptures and paintings made; designs and reliefs incised on cave walls. Fire discovered. | | | | |

The Puffin Factfinder

## DID YOU KNOW?

- ❖ The chipped stones of the Paleolithic Period were usually made of a kind of hard rock called 'quartzite'. Owing to this, the Paleolithic people in India are also known as Quartzite Men.
- ❖ It has been suggested that the Paleolithic men belonged to the Negrito race, like the modern people of Andaman Islands, and were characterized by short stature, dark skin, woolly hair, and flat noses.
- ❖ The Neolithic men sometimes put their dead bodies in large urns. These tombs were known as Dolmens.
- ❖ Carbon-14 Dating is a method of dating the past. It is based on the fact that carbon is continuously produced in the atmosphere and is a part of all living organisms.
- ❖ The earliest evidence of settled agriculture in India comes from Mehrgarh, now in Pakistan.
- ❖ Excellent cave paintings of the Mesolithic Age are found at Bhimbetka, Madhya Pradesh.

## PROFILE OF CIVILIZATIONS

### CHINESE CIVILIZATION

**Location:** The Chinese civilization, which developed along the Hwang Ho and the Yangtze Kiang rivers, is regarded as the oldest continuous civilization of the world.

**Society:** The society was divided into three classes: a) the emperor, occupying the highest rank on the social ladder, b) the nobles, traders, farmers, and c) the slaves.

**Economy:** Agriculture was the main occupation of the people of this civilization. They were the first to cultivate tea and silk, and develop the art of making coloured pottery using ceramics and porcelain. They carried on trade with India, Mesopotamia and Egypt, and exported silk, chinaware, tea, and paper.

**Art and architecture:** They developed a script in the form of pictures. The Great Wall of China is one of their finest architectural legacies. They also constructed stupa-style temples known as pagodas.

**Scientific developments:** Some of the notable inventions include the manufacture of gunpowder, kites, umbrellas, the mariner's compass, and the lunar calendar. Acupuncture and other forms of treatment were also discovered by the Chinese.

**Religion:** In ancient times, the Chinese mostly worshipped nature and their ancestors, but later turned to Confucianism, a philosophy based on moral conduct and named after Confucius.

## DID YOU KNOW?

◇ While it was being made, the Great Wall was called 'the longest cemetery on earth' because many people died during its construction. Reportedly, it cost the lives of more than a million people.

◇ It is believed that a helpful dragon laid out the course of the Great Wall of China and the builders just followed the tracks.

## EGYPTIAN CIVILIZATION

**Location:** The Egyptian civilization flourished along the banks of the Nile river, stretching from the Mediterranean down to present-day Sudan in Africa.

**Time span:** It is divided into three periods: Old Kingdom (2575–2130 BC), Middle Kingdom (2000–1700 BC), New Kingdom (1600–1100 BC).

**Society:** Society was divided into three distinct classes: Upper class (pharaoh, priests, high-ranking officials), middle class (traders), lower class (slaves).

**Economy:** Though the Egyptians were mainly agriculturists, there were several skilled craftsmen such as potters, goldsmiths, carpenters, weavers, sculptors, and painters as well.

**Religion:** The ancient Egyptians worshipped many gods. While their main god was the sun god called Re (or Ra), each city had its own pantheon.

**Science:** The Egyptians knew a great deal about the human body and preserved the dead in pyramids through mummification. Some of the most outstanding contributions of the Egyptians were the pyramids, hieroglyphics (writing in picture form) and paper (from papyrus). They observed the stars and prepared calendars based on the phases of the moon and the solar year.

**Polity:** Some of their important rulers were Khufu, Khafra, Queen Hatshepsut, Tutankhamen and Rameses II, External invasions and internal revolts weakened and ended the civilization.

## DID YOU KNOW?

❖ The people of ancient Egypt believed that the pharaoh, after death, became Osiris—king of the dead; and the new pharaoh became Horus—god of the heavens and protector of the sun god. The rising and setting of the sun was symbolic of this cycle.

❖ A part of a dead pharaoh's spirit, his *Ka,* was believed to remain within his body. It was also thought that if the corpse did not receive proper care, the former pharaoh would not be able to carry out his new duties as king of the dead. If this happened, the cycle would be broken and disaster would befall Egypt. To prevent such a catastrophe, each dead pharaoh was mummified.

### INDUS VALLEY CIVILIZATION

**Location:** The Indus Valley civilization developed along the Indus and Saraswati rivers in present-day Pakistan.

**Excavation:** Evidence of the civilization was first uncovered in 1921 by Dayaram Sahni and, in 1922–23, by Rakhaldas Banerjee. The two important cities of the civilization were Harappa and Mohenjo-daro. In fact, some historians use the name Harappa for the civilization as it was the first region to be unearthed by archaeologists. There were at least sixty smaller settlements spread along the coast of the Arabian Sea and on the Indus floodplain.

**Town planning and architecture:** The Indus Valley people were great builders. The most important features of the civilization were the dockyard, the Great Bath (public water tank) and the Great Granary (used for storing foodgrains). Houses were built according to a grid pattern. Toilets and baths were backed by an advanced drainage system.

**Economy:** Agriculture and domestication of animals were the main occupations.

**Religion:** People mostly worshipped nature, but seals resembling the Hindu god Shiva and terracotta figurines of a Great Mother resembling Shakti indicate that they prayed to idols too. They believed in life after death. Graves found in the region often had pottery and other objects inside them.

**Decline:** Some historians believe that the cities were destroyed by Western invaders, probably a group known as the Aryans. However, climatic changes, floods and epidemics may also have caused the downfall of the civilization.

## DID YOU KNOW?

◇ Some of the important sites of the Indus Valley Civilization are Harappa, Mohenjo-daro, Lothal, Kalibangan, Dholavira and Surkotada.

◇ Mohenjo-daro, located in the Larkana district of Sind in Pakistan, is situated on the right bank of the Indus.

◇ Harappa, located in present-day Pakistan, is situated on the left bank of the Ravi river.

## MESOPOTAMIAN CIVILIZATION

**Etymology and location:** The name Mesopotamia is derived from the Greek words *mesos* meaning 'middle' and *potamos* meaning 'river', indicating 'land between the rivers'. It was located between the Tigris and Euphrates rivers (in modern Iraq) and included the cities of Sumer, Akkad, Babylonia and Assyria.

**Town planning:** The cities were divided into three parts—sacred area, walled city, and outer town comprising temple towers called *ziggurats*. People lived in the walled city and the outer town, and each city had its own patron deity.

**Society:** The Mesopotamian society was patriarchal, and was divided into three classes—upper class (royal family, priests, other high officials), middle class (farmers, artisans, traders), and lower class (slaves). Some of their important kings were Gilgamesh, Hammurabi and Nebuchadnezzar.

**Economy:** Agriculture was their main occupation, and they invented the seeder plough and the ox-drawn plough.

**Art and culture:** They invented the first form of writing known as cuneiform—engraved pictures on wedge-shaped clay tablets. The region was the centre of a culture which influenced the Middle East and extended as far as the Indus valley, Egypt and the Mediterranean.

**Decline:** Rain, floods and shifting sands led to the eventual burial of the mud-brick cities and temples of Mesopotamia, leaving only the shapeless mounds that still stand across Iraq today. Repeated invasions resulted in the collapse of the kingdoms, bringing an end to the civilization. It was during this period that the Neolithic Revolution germinated.

## DID YOU KNOW?

Over 5,000 years ago, people living in Mesopotamia developed a form of writing to record and communicate different types of information. The earliest writing was based on pictograms. Pictograms were used to communicate basic information about crops and taxes. Over time, writing evolved and the signs developed into a script that we call cuneiform.

## VEDIC AGE

The Vedic Age began in India in about 1500 BC with the coming of the Aryans. The Rig Vedic period derived its name from the Rig Veda, the oldest Vedic literature, and was followed by the Later Vedic Period.

**Society:** Vedic society was based on the patriarchal joint family system where the master of the family was the father, the *grihapati*. Though women enjoyed equal status, their position deteriorated during the Later Vedic Period. The political system consisted of a clannish set-up. Several clan-based assemblies such as *sabha*, *samiti*, *vidatha*, and *gana*, exercising military and religious functions, have been mentioned in the Rig Veda. The Later Vedic Period witnessed significant changes in the political structure. The *sabha* was gradually converted into the king's court.

**Economy:** The Aryans were originally nomadic and pastoral people. Their chief occupation was cattle rearing, and agriculture was a secondary means of subsistence. In the Later Vedic Period, *srenis* or trade guilds came into existence, based on the barter system. Grouped according to their craft and profession, smiths, carpenters, physicians, potters, weavers, tanners and grinders of corn often worked together.

**Religion:** All their gods were manifestations of various natural forces like the sun, rain, wind, storm, and thunder. They worshipped them through reciting prayers and offering sacrifices. They believed in life after death.

**The Vedas:** The word *veda* is derived from the Sanskrit word *vid*, which means 'to know' or 'knowledge'. The Vedas are divided into four parts: Rig Veda, Sama Veda, Yajur Veda and Atharva Veda. Of the four, the Rig Veda is the oldest religious text in the world. Every Veda has several Brahmanas (explanations and discussions) attached to it. The Aranyakas are generally called 'Forest Books' and are the concluding portions of the Brahmanas. The Vedas are followed by Upanishads, also called Vedantas, meaning 'the end of the Vedas'.

**Varna:** The term *varna*, literally meaning 'colour', played an important role in formation of the social structure during the Rig Vedic period. The Purushasukta of the Rig Veda clearly mentions the four-fold division of the society, namely the Brahmins, the Kshatriyas, the Vaishyas and the Sudras, who were said to have sprung from the mouth, arms, thighs and feet, respectively, of god Brahma. The Brahmins emerged as the most important class. They conducted rituals and sacrifices. The Kshatriyas had supremacy in temporal affairs. The Vaishyas constituted the common people associated with agriculture and cattle breeding. The Sudras, who belonged to the lowest rung, were required to serve the Brahmins and Kshatriyas.

**Ashrama system:** A member of each of the three higher castes, wishing to live an ideal life, had to pass through the rigorous discipline of the *ashramas* or the four stages of life, namely *brahmacharya* (live the life of a student), *grihastha* (lead a domestic life), *vanaprastha* (live the life of an ascetic in a forest) and *sanyasa* (give away all of one's possessions and wander from place to place begging for food).

## DID YOU KNOW?

- ◇ The Rig, Yajur and Sama Vedas are together known as Trayi Veda.
- ◇ The Hittites were the oldest known group of the Aryans.
- ◇ In the Rig Vedic period, the treasurer was known as *samgrahitri*, the collector of taxes was known as *bhagadugha*, the royal herald or charioteer was known as *suta*, the chamberlain was known as *kshattri*, the courier was known as *palagala* and the chaplain was known as *purohit*.

## JANAPADAS AND MAHAJANAPADAS

The tribal political organization of the Rig Vedic phase gave way to the rise of territorial states, referred to as *janapadas*, towards the end of the Vedic period. The political process among the ancient Indo-Aryans started with semi-nomadic tribal units called *janapada*. The term is composed of *jana* meaning 'tribe' and *pada* meaning 'foot'. *Janapada* primarily means a place where people live. The territorial idea, however, gradually strengthened at the beginning of the 6th century, in places where there was no paramount power. North India, then, was divided into a large number of independent states. In the post-Vedic period, the entire northern territory, mostly situated north of the Vindhyas and extending from the north-west frontiers to Bihar, was divided into the three kingdoms of Magadha, Kosala and Vatsa, along with Kuru, Panchala, Surasena, Kasi, Mithila, Anga, Kalinga, Asmaka,

Gandhara, and Kamboja. These states were autonomous clans with a non-monarchical form of government, not ruled by the kings but forming petty republics, or oligarchies. They were known as *sodasha mahajanapadas* meaning 'sixteen mahajanapadas'. They were Kasi, Kosala, Anga, Magadha, Vatsa, Avanti, Gandhara, Kamboja, Matsya, Kurus, Panchala, Surasena, Chhedi, Vajis, Malas, and Assaka.

---

**MAHAJANAPADAS AND THEIR PRESENT LOCATION (ROUGH) IN MODERN INDIA**

East Bihar–Anga

South Bihar–Magadha

Benares–Kasi

Oudh–Kosala

North Bihar–Vriji

Gorakhpur district–Malla

Area between the Yamuna and the Narmada–Chedi

Bareilly, Badaun, Farrukhabad districts–Panchala

Jaipur–Matsya

Mathura–Surasena

Region on the Godavari–Asmaka

Malwa–Avanti

Peshawar and Rawalpindi districts–Gandhara

South-west Kashmir–Kamboja

---

# KINGS AND QUEENS OF THE WORLD

## ALEXANDER THE GREAT (356 BC–323 BC)

Alexander the Great was also known as Alexander III. He was the King of Macedonia who conquered and ruled over a large part of the world, giving a new direction to history. His parents were Philip II and Olympias. Alexander was born in Macedonia, a Greek kingdom, in 356 BC. During his early years, he was taught by the great philosopher Aristotle. When his father was assassinated in 336 BC, Alexander was given the responsibility of an unstable state. During his reign, Alexander fiercely fought his enemies, strengthened the Macedonian power in Greece and expanded it.

By the age of twenty-five, Alexander had become the emperor of Asia Minor, leader of the Greeks, Pharaoh of Egypt and the 'Great King' of Persia. His empire flourished for the next eight years, during which he founded over seventy cities and created an empire that stretched across three continents.

He was an outstanding and dynamic general. Two of his greatest victories were at the Battle of Gaugamela (where he defeated Darius III of Persia) and the Battle of Hydaspes (where he overpowered the Indian king Porus).

Alexander died of a fever in Babylon in 323 BC. He was thirty-three. The three centuries after the death of Alexander are together known as the Hellenistic Age, from the Greek word *hellenizein*, meaning 'to act like a Greek'.

## DID YOU KNOW?

◇ Legend has it that the temple of Artemis burned on the night on which Alexander the Great was born. The Persian magi foretold great disaster for the Persian empire.

◇ In 326 BC. Alexander founded a city named Bucephala, on the bank of the Hydaspes, in honour of his favourite horse which died there.

## ATTILA THE HUN (AD 410–AD 453)

Attila was the king of the Huns (nomadic people) from AD 434 until his death in AD 453. He was a ferocious warrior who attacked the Roman empire, invading the southern Balkan provinces and Greece. He then went on to strike Gaul and Italy.

Attila acquired a vast empire that stretched through parts of what are now Germany, Russia, Poland, and much of south-eastern Europe. He helped unite the Hun kingdom, in an area that is now Hungary.

He came to be known as the 'Scourge of God', because of the devastation he brought upon the Roman empire. Atilla died in AD 453.

## DID YOU KNOW?

Of Attila it is said that 'the grass never grew on the spot where his horse had trod.'

## BONAPARTE, NAPOLEON (AD 1769- AD 1821)

Napoleon Bonaparte was a French general, first consul (1799–1804), and Emperor of France (1804–1815).

He was one of the greatest military leaders of all time who revolutionized military organization and training. He not only established the Napoleonic Code (the prototype of later civil law codes) but also formed the Continental System, a method of economic warfare against Britain.

Napoleon was born on 15 August 1769 in Corsica. He became a consul in 1799. He was most interested in the policy of territorial expansion. He defeated the Austrians at Marengo and annexed Prussian lands to strengthen his control over Europe.

In 1804, he was made emperor but soon met with numerous defeats. His forces were defeated by the English at Trafalgar in 1805. Later, the Peninsular Wars and his failure in the Russian invasion of 1812 drained the French forces of all its resources.

As a result, Paris fell into the hands of the opposition in 1814. Napoleon went into exile on the Mediterranean island of Elba. However, his adventures were not over. In March 1815, Napoleon escaped from prison and marched to the French capital.

Once out, Napoleon engaged with the other European powers during his Hundred Days of Restoration. Soon, this too came to an end with his defeat at the Battle of Waterloo. This ended his brief second reign. The English imprisoned him on the remote Atlantic island of St Helena, where he died on 5 May 1821.

## DID YOU KNOW?

Although Napoleon is now known as 'the little corporal', he actually was of average height. His height was mentioned by doctors—including his own physician, Francesco Antommarchi, who carried out his autopsy—as 5 feet 2 inches by French measurement. At the time, the French foot was slightly longer than the English foot, corresponding to Napoleon being 5 feet 6.5 inches tall—the average height of men in those days!

## CATHERINE THE GREAT (1729-1796)

Catherine II was the empress of Russia from 1762 to 1796. She was born Sophie Friederike Auguste von Anhalt-Zerbst in 1729 in a German royal family. At the early age of fourteen she was married to Peter, the heir to the throne of Russia.

In 1762, Catherine overthrew her husband, declared herself Empress and began a reign spanning thirty-four years. She gave herself the title of Catherine II. During her reign she extended the Russian empire southwards and westwards, adding territories which included Crimea, Belarus and Lithuania. She presented the legislative commission with her *Nakaz* (or Instruction), a strikingly liberal document that presented the empress' vision of an ideal government. Being a progressive ruler, she encouraged book publishing, journalism, architecture and theatre, and sponsored the first school for girls in Russia. She built about a hundred new towns, renovated old ones, and improved trade and communication. These measures, combined with successful military campaigns and expansion programmes, won Catherine a celebrated place in history.

Catherine the Great died on 17 November 1796.

## CHARLEMAGNE (AD 747–AD 814)

Charlemagne, meaning 'Charles the Great', became King of the Franks in AD 768. He united almost all the Christian lands of Western Europe into one state, which became known as the Holy Roman Empire.

Son of Pippin the Short and Bertrade, he belonged to the Carolingians, a particularly powerful branch of the Franks. Once he became the sole ruler of the Franks in AD 771, he tried to strengthen his kingdom culturally, socially and economically. To make trading and other business transactions simpler, he set up money standards.

Charlemange also tried to build a Rhine–Danube canal, in order to improve agriculture. In AD 772, he launched a thirty-year campaign that conquered and brought Christianity to the powerful Saxons in the north. By AD 800, Charlemagne was the undisputed ruler of western Europe.

His vast realm covered what is modern France, Switzerland, Belgium and the Netherlands. It also included half of present-day Italy, Germany and Austria. By establishing a central government over western Europe, he paved the way for the development of modern Europe. His coronation at St Peter's Basilica in Rome was the foundation of the Holy Roman Empire. Even though Charlemagne did not use the title, he is considered the first Holy Roman Emperor.

## HENRY VIII (1491–1547)

Henry VIII was the second Tudor monarch of England who reigned from 1509 to 1547.

He was born on 28 June 1491 in Greenwich, and became monarch when he was not even eighteen. He is chiefly remembered for breaking away from the Roman Catholic Church and establishing the Church of England. This brought forth the English Reformation, an important era in the history of England.

Henry broke away from the Catholic Church because the pope, at that time, refused to grant him permission to marry Anne Boleyn, a maid of honour at court. Henry was then already married to Catherine of Aragon and the Pope saw remarriage as unacceptable according to Catholic teachings and practices.

The Archbishop of Canterbury's decision to permit Henry's second marriage severed all ties between England and the Roman Catholic Church. Henry then took control of the nation's churches, reformed the services and published an English translation of the Bible to make it accessible to the common people.

This revolutionary step marked the establishment of the Church of England, or the Anglican Church, with the English monarch as its head. Henry severely punished those who followed Catholic beliefs. Henry VIII married four more times in the hope of begetting a male heir to the throne. He died on 28 January 1547.

## NERO (AD 37–AD 68)

Nero, also known as Lucius Domitius Ahenobarbus, was the fifth Roman emperor and the last of the Julio–Claudian dynasty. He was born near Rome in AD 37. Mainly remembered as an infamous and brutal leader, he ruled from AD 54 to AD 68.

The first five years of his reign were exemplary. He banned capital punishment, reduced taxes and strengthened the power of the Roman Senate. Nero's religious obsessions, his artistic pretensions, lack of attention to government, and extravagant spending, however, alienated many of his countrymen. When Rome was destroyed in a fire, Nero was blamed.

In AD 68, revolts broke out in parts of the empire, and the Senate condemned Nero to death, but he fled the city. He is believed to have killed himself the same year.

## SHI HUANGDI (259 BC-210 BC)

Shi Huangdi, also known as Zhao Zheng, was the emperor of the Qin dynasty and creator of the first unified Chinese empire. Born in 259 BC, he served as the emperor during 221–210 BC. As emperor, he initiated a series of reforms. He abolished territorial feudal power and divided the country into thirty-six military districts, each with its own military and civil administrator. He constructed a network of roads and canals. On his death, he was buried in the Qin tomb, a complex designated as a UNESCO world heritage site in 1987. The unified Chinese empire collapsed less than four years after his death.

## TUTANKHAMEN (LIVED 14TH CENTURY)

Tutankhamen was a king of ancient Egypt who reigned from AD 1333 to AD 1323. In 1922, archaeologists Howard Carter and George Herbert discovered his tomb—completely intact and not violated by gravediggers. This brought the dead pharaoh under the limelight. The remarkable artefacts from the tomb, including a beautiful golden mask, are on display at the Egyptian Museum in Cairo.

Born Tutankhaten, he became king at a very early age. He changed his name to Tutankhamen and issued a decree restoring the temples, images, personnel, and privileges of the old gods.

## VICTORIA (1819-1901)

Queen Victoria, was born in London on 24 May 1819. She went on to become the longest-reigning British monarch, and the figurehead of a vast empire. Victoria was eighteen years old when she became queen of the UK, upon the death of her uncle William IV in 1837. She was a very active ruler. After the First War of Indian Independence in 1857, the government of India was transferred from the East India Company to the Crown. In 1877, Victoria came to be known as 'Empress of India'.

Her vast empire also included Canada, Australia, New Zealand and large parts of Africa. Her rule witnessed remarkable developments in the fields of science, literature and the arts. She made the Crown a symbol of both 'private virtue and public honour'.

Even though she died on 22 January 1901, the Victorian Age is considered to have continued until 1914, when Europe was plunged into World War I.

> ## DID YOU KNOW?
>
> ◇ On her accession, Victoria adopted Prime Minister Lord Melbourne as her political mentor.
>
> ◇ Warm-hearted and lively, Victoria had a gift for drawing and painting. Educated in her childhood by a governess at home, she was a natural diarist and kept a regular journal all her life.
>
> ◇ Victoria was the first reigning monarch to use trains; she made her first train journey in 1842.

## MAJOR WARS AND BATTLES OF THE WORLD

### AMERICAN CIVIL WAR (1861–1865)

The American Civil War was fought between the twenty-three Northern and eleven Southern states of the USA. The Northern states supported the federal government, while the Southern states wished to withdraw from the Union and form an independent government called the Confederate States of America. After President Abraham Lincoln issued the Emancipation Proclamation in 1862 with the goal to abolish slavery, the problem became critical. The Northern states supported the abolition of slavery whereas the Southern states were in favour of its continuation. The North fought to preserve the Union while the South fought to win recognition as an independent nation.

The Northern states won the war and slavery was finally put to an end. The defeated states were gradually taken back into the Union after they agreed to the terms set by the Federal government. Federal troops remained in the South for more than a decade after the war. Buildings and properties in the South were severely damaged and its economy had to be rebuilt.

### AMERICAN REVOLUTION (1775–1783)

Thirteen colonies of North America revolted against their British rulers in 1775, which began the American Revolution. It ended with a peace treaty in 1783. Many events led up to this war. The enforcement of the Navigation Acts (laws requiring the colonies to trade mostly with Britain), the Stamp Act (law requiring the colonists to attach stamps purchased from the British government to legal documents and other items), the Townshend Acts (placing taxes on tea, lead, paint, paper, and glass imports entering colonial ports) and the Tea Act were the primary reasons.

On 16 December 1773, a group of colonists in Boston, dressed like Native Americans, boarded some ships and threw the tea into the harbour. This rebellious act came to be known as the Boston Tea Party.

The British government responded by closing the port of Boston until the colonists paid compensation for the ruined tea. Anger in the colonies reached new heights, directly catalysing the American Revolution. War began on 19 April 1775, when British regulars fired on the Minutemen of Lexington, Massachusetts. The fighting ended with the surrender of the British and the signing of the Treaty of Paris in 1783. The treaty recognized the US as an independent nation and set the western boundary of the new nation at the Mississippi river.

The first president of America, George Washington, led the colonists and played a very important role in the revolution.

## BATTLE OF WATERLOO (1815)

Napoleon's troops and the combined forces of the Duke of Wellington's Allied army (with British, Dutch, Belgian, German and Prussian units) fought at the Battle of Waterloo. The battle marked Napoleon's final defeat, ending twenty-three years of recurrent warfare between France and the other powers of Europe.

Napoleon's forces included 72,000 troops while the opponent army was 1,13,000-strong. Because of heavy rain on the night of 17 June, Napoleon's artillery could not move. He delayed the attack until nearly midday, a decision that cost him the battle.

On 22 June 1815, four days after the battle of Waterloo, Napoleon signed his second abdication in Paris.

## CRIMEAN WAR (1853–1856)

The Crimean War, named after the Crimean peninsula (now in Ukraine), was the direct result of a religious conflict. In 1853, Czar Nicholas I of Russia demanded the right to protect Christian shrines in Jerusalem, then part of the Turkish empire. When the Turkish sultan refused the demands, the Russian troops moved into the Turkish Balkans. War began and by August 1854, Turkey, with the help of Britain, France and Sardinia, had driven the Russian forces out of the Balkans.

To bring the war to a decisive end, the allied fleets proceeded to the Crimean peninsula. These troops landed on 16 September 1854 and laid siege to the Russian fortress of Sevastopol. Severe battles were fought in Crimea at the Alma river, at Balaklava and at Inkerman.

During the siege of Sevastopol, disease ravaged the French and British troops. Florence Nightingale's heroic work as head of the hospital service did much to improve conditions and heal the injured.

In 1856, the powers signed a treaty at Paris. The new czar, Alexander II, withdrew all claims to Balkan territory. The Black Sea was neutralized. Turkey was admitted to the family of European powers with the sultan promising to treat his Christian subjects according to the public law of Europe.

## THE CRUSADES (1095–1291)

The Crusades, or the Holy Wars, were fought between the Christians and the Muslims. Jerusalem, a holy city of the Muslims, Jews and Christians was under the control of the Muslims before the Seljuk Turks, a new Muslim group, took over the control in 1071.

The Seljuks ill-treated the Christian pilgrims and destroyed their sacred places. In 1071, they captured Byzantine, seat of the Christian church in the East, and started extending their territories. The Byzantine emperor requested the Western Christians to fight a holy war for the sake of the pilgrims. His appeal had an impact on popes, knights and common men, who set out to battle for their religion.

Over 196 years, as many as eight Crusades were fought due to the continuous unrest. In the end, the Christians retreated from engaging in any more holy wars. The Muslims assumed control of the last of the crusader states in the Holy Lands. The Crusades brought a significant cultural contact between the East and the West, and made a deep impact on the fields of architecture, medicine and warfare. This cultural contact stimulated the flowering of the Renaissance in Europe.

## FRENCH REVOLUTION (1787–1799)

The French Revolution shook France between 1787 and 1799 and reached its first climax there in 1789. Among the many causes for this revolt, the primary one was inequality among the classes. Members of the Third Estate (the class including peasants, artisans, merchants and professionals) had to pay many taxes that the nobles and clergy were exempt from. In addition to this, there were many social inequalities too.

Writers and thinkers of the age inspired commoners to demand their political, social and economic rights. The French government, headed by King Louis XVI and Queen Marie Antoinette, spent a lot of money to help American colonists in their revolution against Britain, which led the government to the brink of bankruptcy. To make up their losses, the government tried to squeeze the money out of the common people.

The civilians took the Oath of the Tennis Court on 20 June 1789, pledging not to go back until they had written a constitution. The slogan of 'Liberty, Equality, Fraternity' resounded across the country. On 14 July, a mob stormed the Bastille, an old royal prison in Paris that was a symbol of the king's power. When King Louis XVI refused to obey the constitution of limited monarchy, a mob invaded the royal residence and took Louis XVI and Marie Antoinette prisoners on 10 August 1792.

The National Assembly officially ended the practice of feudalism in August 1789 and France was declared a republic in September 1789.

## HUNDRED YEARS' WAR (1337–1453)

Believed to be the longest war in recorded history, the Hundred Years' War was a struggle between France and England for 116 years. It lasted through the reigns of five English kings (Edward III to Henry V) and five French kings (Philip VI to Charles VII). The causes for disputes were many, but the right of succession to the French crown was the major cause.

The English king Edward III wanted to occupy the French throne as his mother was a sister of the late French king Louis X, while Philip VI (who went on to become the king) was only a cousin. Philip VI was opposed to this as the law in France stated that no woman could inherit the throne and that the crown could not be inherited through a woman.

In 1346, King Edward III clashed with Philip VI at Normandy and defeated him. In the following years, the French were defeated at various places. When the French king, Charles VII, was about to lose Orléans, his last considerable stronghold, Joan of Arc appeared on the battlefield.

Inspired by her patriotism, the French forced the English to raise the siege of Orléans. Victories followed in rapid succession. By 1453, France had defeated England and the French king acquired power over his kingdom. Instead of winning the French throne for the English king, the Hundred Years' War lost for him the possessions that once belonged to Henry II.

This conflict fostered in the French a patriotism that came to characterize France later.

## RUSSIAN REVOLUTION (1917)

The Russian Revolution of 1917 was a watershed in the history of Russia. It was a revolt by the people of Russia against the oppression of the czars.

After Russia suffered a terrible loss in World War I, the major cities suffered shortages of food and fuel that the government failed to provide. The civilians flared up and the first riots took place in the capital city of Petrograd (now St Petersburg). During the Revolution, the Bolsheviks became one of the strongest parties of the Soviet and went on to win the revolution.

Czar Nicholas II was forced to step down and a provisional government was formed. The authority of the government was soon challenged, making way for the rise of the Bolsheviks, led by Vladimir Lenin.

In October 1917 (November according to the Western calendar), the Bolsheviks took over the government with Lenin as the commander-in-chief of the army.

## SPANISH CIVIL WAR (1936–1939)

The Spanish Civil War was perhaps the most gruesome conflict in the first half of the 20th century. It was a clash between the Nationalists under Francisco Franco (helped by Italy and Germany) and the Republicans (helped by the Soviet Union and individuals from many countries, including the US and Great Britain).

Between World War I and 1936, Spain had become almost ungovernable. There were so many factions and divisions within the country that no political party could cater to all of them. Besides, these political parties also wanted to overthrow the government and there were numerous other problems.

The murder of the former finance minister of Spain, José Calvo Sotelo, was the immediate cause of the war. After an ensuing struggle for two years and 254 days, the Republicans were defeated and General Franco became the undisputed leader.

The ruthlessness and violence of the Spanish Civil War shocked the world. The Nationalists' bombing of Guernica on 26 April 1937 is depicted in a painting by Pablo Picasso.

## VIETNAM WAR (1954–1975)

The Vietnam War was the result of a conflict between the communist government of North Vietnam (along with their allies in South Vietnam, the Soviet Union and China) and the Republican government of South Vietnam (assisted by the US).

The core of the conflict was the desire of the North Vietnam government to unify the entire country under a single communist regime modelled after those of the Soviet Union and China. The South Vietnam government, on the other hand, fought to preserve a Vietnam more closely aligned with the West.

In the war that followed, South Vietnam fell to a full-scale invasion by the North. Ho Chi Minh, President of North Vietnam from 1945 to 1969, played a pivotal role in this conflict. The war caused mass devastation disrupting agriculture, business and industry.

A mass exodus of people loyal to the South Vietnam cause took place in 1975. Meanwhile, the US began a process of coming to terms with defeat in its longest and most controversial war. The two countries resumed formal diplomatic relations in 1995.

## WORLD WAR I (1914–1918)

A major international conflict from 1914 to 1918, World War I was fought between the Central Powers (Germany, Austro-Hungarian empire, Turkey, Bulgaria) and the Allied Powers (England, France, Belgium). The immediate cause was the assassination of Archduke Ferdinand of Austria–Hungary on 28 June 1914.

Other causes included economic rivalries. Germany's rise as a military and industrial power that mounted from the naval arms race between Britain and Germany alarmed its neighbours. The war sparked off when Austria–Hungary declared war on Serbia. In the end, Germany was defeated and forced to surrender. The war ended on 11 November 1918, after an armistice was signed.

The Treaty of Versailles was signed on 28 June 1919 and the population and territory of Germany was reduced by about 10 per cent. In addition, they were made to pay a huge amount of money as compensation.

The League of Nations was then formed as an international body to provide nations with diplomatic means to solve their differences and to avoid war in the future.

## WORLD WAR II (1939–1945)

Two decades after the end of World War I, lingering disputes erupted in an even larger and bloodier conflict—World War II. The struggle took place between the Axis Powers (Germany, Italy, Japan) and the Allied Powers (Britain, France, Russia, US, Poland). One of the important reasons of the war was the rise of Adolf Hitler and his Nazi Party. The Nazis, committed atrocities on Jews and tortured them in concentration camps.

The war also saw the rise of Italy and Japan as imperialist powers. Germany, devastated after World War I, invaded the port of Danzig, Poland on 1 September 1939. When Germany refused to withdraw its troops, Britain and France declared war on Germany.

In 1941, Japan launched a sudden attack on Pearl Harbour, an American Naval base. The US Pacific fleet was completely crushed. The devastation was countered by US when they dropped the first atomic bombs on Nagasaki and Hiroshima in Japan in 1945. The entire population of the two cities perished as a consequence.

On 2 September 1945 Japan surrendered and World War II came to an end.

World War II brought an end to Nazism and Fascism. Germany was divided into East Germany (controlled by the Soviet Union) and West Germany (controlled by the US, Britain, and France). The emergence of the US and the Soviet Union as two major world powers followed. Later, these two powers were involved in the Cold War that came about after World War II. The Cold War was waged on political, economic and propaganda fronts and had only limited recourse to weapons. After World War II, the United Nations (UN) was founded by fifty-one nations in 1945, with the aim to maintain international peace.

# LEADERS OF THE WORLD

## ATATÜRK, MUSTAFA KEMAL (1881–1938)

Founder and first President of the Republic of Turkey, Kemal Atatürk was born in Salonika, Greece, in 1881. He attended a military secondary school, where he was given the nickname Kemal—Arabic for 'perfection'.

Kemal opposed the presence of foreign powers in Turkey and, in 1920, as leader of a national resistance movement, he set up a rival government in Ankara. He expelled the Greek forces from Asia Minor and proclaimed the end of the Ottoman empire in 1922. He became President of Turkey the following year and held the office until his death.

During his presidency, Kemal proclaimed Turkey as a secular republic and closed down all Islamic religious institutions. In his effort to align Turkey with the customs of the Western nations, he urged the people to adopt a European way of life, write Turkish in the Latin alphabet and adopt European-style names.

He also modernized the legal system and adopted a new civil and penal code. Later, he took the name Atatürk, meaning 'Father of the Turks'. Kemal died in Istanbul in 1938.

## BANDARANAIKE, SIRIMAVO (1916–2000)

Credited with being the world's first female prime minister, Sirimavo Ratwatte was born in 1916 into a wealthy family in Ceylon, now Sri Lanka. She married S.W.R.D. Bandaranaike, a member of Ceylon's cabinet and the country's prime minister (1956–1959) in 1940. Sirimavo became politically active after her husband was assassinated in 1959. She belonged to the Sri Lanka Freedom Party and was a remarkable stateswoman. Upon her party's victory in the 1960 general elections, she took over as prime minister.

During her term, she replaced English with Sinhalese as the nation's official language, declared a new constitution that created an executive presidency, and made Ceylon into a republic named Sri Lanka. She left office in 1965 but returned to serve two more terms (1970–977, 1994–2000) as prime minister. Sirimavo retired from politics in August 2000 and died later that year in Colombo.

## BISMARCK, OTTO VON (1815–1898)

Otto Eduard Leopold von Bismarck, also known as the Iron Chancellor, was the founder and first Chancellor (1871–1890) of the German empire. Born in 1815 into an aristocratic family in Berlin, he began his political career in the Prussian legislature in 1847. Bismarck was appointed prime minister of Prussia in 1862.

Soon, he led a war against Denmark and, along with a few regions including Schleswig and Holstein, formed the North German Confederation. After Prussia's victory in the Franco–Prussian War, Bismarck was declared Chancellor in 1871.

During his term, Bismarck concentrated on building a powerful state with a unified national identity. For most of the latter half of the 19th century, his policies controlled the destinies of most of the countries of Europe. In 1890, Bismarck resigned after disagreeing with the new Emperor, Wilhelm II. He retired to his estate near Hamburg and died there on 30 July 1898.

### DID YOU KNOW?

In 1889, Germany became the first nation in the world to adopt social insurance for old age. The policy was designed by Chancellor Otto von Bismarck.

## BOLIVAR, SIMON (1783–1830)

Simon Bolivar, also known as the George Washington of South America, was a statesman and revolutionary general who liberated Venezuela, Colombia, Panama, Ecuador, Peru and Bolivia from the rule of Spain.

Simon was born in 1783 in Venezuela into a noble Spanish family. He was educated in Europe. While on the continent, he absorbed the spirit of revolution and later dedicated himself to the cause of Venezuela's liberation.

When Napoleon Bonaparte laid siege on Spain, its colonies revolted. Venezuela first declared its independence in 1811 and the struggle for independence continued for the next nineteen years. Bolivar led the revolt with his limited resources, through both victories and defeats.

Between 1825 and 1828, he was President of Gran Colombia (now Venezuela, Colombia, Panama, and Ecuador), Peru and the newly-formed Bolivia. Bolivar believed in equality and liberated all his slaves, years before the law abolishing slavery was passed. Bolivia was named after Simon Bolivar. He died in Colombia in 1830.

## CAESAR, JULIUS (100 BC–44 BC)

Julius Caesar is considered one of the greatest politicians who largely extended the Roman empire and, by becoming its dictator, paved the way for the imperial system of government.

Caesar was born in 100 BC into a wealthy family. He served in several offices of the Roman political system before he was elected as a consul in 59 BC. After a year as consul, he was sent to govern a Roman province in Gaul (France). While there, he conquered the rest of Gaul and made several raids into Britain and Germany.

Following a successful campaign in Egypt, he placed Cleopatra on the throne of Egypt. It was after an easy victory in Asia Minor that he wrote the famous words 'I came, I saw, I conquered'. Caesar now made himself consul and dictator of Rome.

In March 44 BC, a group of Republican Senators, led by Cassius and Brutus, who had been offended when Caesar set up his statue alongside the statues of the early kings of Rome, assassinated him on the Ides of March (15 March according to the Roman calendar).

The assassination sparked the final round of civil wars that ended the republic. It also brought about the elevation of Caesar's great nephew Octavius, as Augustus, to the position of first emperor of Rome.

## DID YOU KNOW?

- ◇ Julius Caesar was born in Rome on 12 or 13 July 100 BC into the prestigious Julian clan. His family was closely connected with Roman politics.
- ◇ The Roman month Quintilis, in which Caesar was born, was renamed July in his honour.
- ◇ Julius Caesar was assassinated on 15 March 44 BC in the Forum Magnum in Rome, by a group of around sixty members of the Roman Senate.

## CASTRO, FIDEL (b. 1926)

Fidel Castro, a political leader of Cuba, served as premier of the country from 1959 until 1976. Born in 1926 into a wealthy family, he studied law at the University of Havana. In 1952, he was a candidate for the Cuban Congress, but General Fulgencio Batista, the President, cancelled the elections.

Deciding to act against the Batista regime, Castro, along with his brother, Raoul, attacked the army barracks in 1953 and was sent to prison. Out of this revolt came the name of Castro's organization, the 26th of July Movement.

Following his release in 1955, they reorganized their army and waged guerrilla warfare along with Argentinean revolutionary Che Guevara. Batista fled from Cuba in 1959 and Castro became premier.

Castro introduced socio-political reforms that were heavily influenced by communist ideas. Through the 1970s and 1980s, Castro emerged as one of the leaders of the non-aligned nations. He remained in firm control of the country into the 21st century. In 2008, just days before the National Assembly were to vote for the country's leader, Fidel Castro officially declared that he would not accept another term as president.

## CHURCHILL, WINSTON (1874–1965)

One of the greatest statesmen of the world, Sir Winston Churchill was the prime minister of Great Britain. Born in 1874 into an influential family, he graduated from Sandhurst, a famous military college. In 1895, Churchill became a sub lieutenant in a distinguished cavalry regiment and also began to write. Later, while covering the Boer War as a correspondent for *The Morning Post*, he was captured. However, he made an extraordinary escape. On his return to London, Churchill was treated as a hero and elected to Parliament.

As Lord of Admiralty, he formed the Royal Naval Air Service in 1911. In the phase between the two World Wars, he wrote his famous book *Life of Marlborough* and painted under the name Charles Marin.

In 1940, Churchill replaced Neville Chamberlain as prime minister. When the powerful German forces were trying to beat the English, Churchill made his famous declaration: 'I have nothing to offer but blood, toil, tears, and sweat.'

In 1953, he was knighted by Queen Elizabeth II and also awarded the Nobel Prize for Literature. He finally resigned from the office of prime minister in 1955 and died in London in 1965.

## DID YOU KNOW?

Winston Churchill was the first commoner since 1852 to receive a state funeral.

## CONFUCIUS (551 BC–479 BC)

Confucius, born Kong Qiu, was the most famous teacher, philosopher and political theorist of China. He is known as the first teacher in China whose ideas have influenced East Asia and shaped the cultural history of China.

Born in 551 BC, Confucius began working in minor government posts at a young age and later became a brilliant teacher. Though Confucianism, founded by him, is commonly called a religion, it is actually a code of moral conduct. His *Analects* are wise sayings similar to the Book of Proverbs in the Bible. After years of teaching and travel, he settled in the province of Shandong. At the age of fifty-two, Confucius was appointed governor of the province of Chung-tu. He later went into exile when a neighbouring governor plotted to overthrow him, but returned to Lu at the age of sixty-nine and died there three years later. After his death, temples were erected in his honour across China. His grave at Qufo (Shandong) is a place of pilgrimage.

## DID YOU KNOW?

Confucius' teachings, conversations and exchanges with his disciples are recorded in the *Lunyu* or *Analects*, a collection that probably achieved its current form around the 2nd century BC.

## CROMWELL, OLIVER (1599-1658)

Oliver Cromwell was an English soldier and statesman. He helped establish England as a republic. He ruled as Lord Protector from 1653 to 1658.

Cromwell was born in 1599 into a family of landowners. He became a radical Puritan at the age of twenty-seven and led the Puritan Revolution in England. Cromwell played a very important role in the Civil War of 1642. He organized the cavalry called the 'Ironsides' and convinced the Parliament to establish a professional army. This led to a victory over the king's forces at Naseby in 1645. Cromwell served as the Lord Protector of UK and helped to develop an effective foreign policy. In 1658 Cromwell died and was buried in Westminster Abbey.

## HITLER, ADOLF (1889-1945)

One of the most infamous dictators in history, Adolf Hitler was the leader of the Nazi Party from 1920–21 and Chancellor and Führer of Germany from 1933–1945. Born in 1899 in Braunau am Inn, on the Austrian–German border, he did not complete schooling. In his youth he tried to earn his living as a painter in Vienna, where he developed his political ideologies. He served in the German army during World War I and later became a member of the fascist German Worker's Party.

By 1921, the Nationalist Socialist German Workers' Party (NSDAP or Nazi Party) had been consolidated with Adolf Hitler as their leader. He was arrested for provoking an armed uprising in Munich in 1923. While in prison, he dictated the book *Mein Kampf*, explaining his political ideology.

Soon after his release, Hitler started to reorganize the Nazi Party using new means of mass communication, such as films like the *Triumph of the Will*, for his campaigns. He believed the greatest enemy of humanity to be the Jews. Hence he launched anti-Jewish campaigns, which culminated in the extermination of millions of Jews.

Hitler became Chancellor of a coalition government in 1933, with his Nazi Party gaining power. The rise of Hitler and his powerful territorial expansion resulted in World War II. When Germany was defeated in the war, Hitler killed himself in 1945.

## DID YOU KNOW?

- ❖ In 1914, on being screened for Austrian military service, Adolf Hitler was declared unfit because of inadequate physical vigour and enthusiasm.
- ❖ Though he was good at painting, he failed to get an entry into the Academy of Fine Arts in Vienna twice. For a short period, he painted postcards and advertisements to make ends meet.

## JOAN OF ARC (1412–1430)

Joan of Arc, also known as the Maid of Orléans, was a national heroine of France. Believing that she was acting under divine guidance Joan led the French army to a momentous victory at Orléans. It repulsed an English attempt to conquer France during the Hundred Years' War.

Born in 1412 to a poor farmer, Joan was a religious girl. During her childhood, France and England were engaged in the Hundred Years' War. To help the French king Charles VII, who had lost one territory after another, she went to Chinon to meet him.

Convinced by her passion, Charles VII provided her with armour, attendants and horses to save the Fortress of Orleans. Joan commanded several attacks against the English forces, finally driving them out of the city. The French army entered the city of Reims, and Charles was crowned king.

Joan was separated from her soldiers during a raid into Burgundy, captured and sold to the English who ordered her death. She was accused of being a heretic, was held in chains and tortured during her trials. Joan asserted her innocence but was burned to death at the stake on 30 May 1431 when she was only nineteen.

On 16 May 1920, the Roman Catholic Church declared Joan of Arc a saint.

## KING, MARTIN LUTHER, JR (1929–1968)

Martin Luther King, Jr was one of the most outstanding leaders in the US who aroused whites and blacks alike to protest against racial discrimination, poverty and war. Born in Atlanta to Martin Luther, Sr, pastor in the Ebenezer Baptist Church, Luther encountered racism from a very early age and this inspired him to fight against the evil. Luther's energetic personality and powerful oratory helped unite many blacks in a search for peaceful solutions to racial oppression

His brief career greatly advanced the cause of civil rights in the US and paved the way for the Civil Rights Act of 1964 and the Voting Rights Act of 1965. He was awarded the Nobel Peace Prize in 1964 for his championing of non-violent resistance.

In 1968, he travelled to Memphis to support a strike of poorly paid sanitation workers. There, on 4 April, he was assassinated by a sniper, James Earl Ray. In 1977, he was posthumously awarded the Presidential Medal of Freedom for his battle against racism. In 1986, the US Congress established a national holiday in his honour to be observed on the third Monday in January as the Martin Luther King, Junior, Day.

## LINCOLN, ABRAHAM (1809–1865)

Abraham Lincoln, one of the greatest American leaders, was the sixteenth president of the US. He played a pivotal role in the American Civil War. Born into a poor family in 1809 in Kentucky, he was mostly self-educated. After becoming a lawyer, he sat in the state legislature and, in 1846, was elected to the Congress, representing the Whig Party. Later, as member of the new Republican Party, he ran for the Presidential elections in 1860. After Lincoln's victory, seven Southern states left the Union to form the Confederate States of America since he opposed the practice of slavery.

However, Lincoln was determined to preserve the Union. Civil War broke out in April 1861. In January 1863, he issued the Emancipation Proclamation, which freed all slaves in areas still under Confederate control. In his efforts to win the war, Lincoln declared martial law and suspended all legal rights.

In July 1863, the Union defeated the Confederate forces at Gettysburg. On 19 November 1863, Lincoln delivered his famous Gettysburg Address at the dedication of a national cemetery at the battlefield of Gettysburg. In 1864, he won the re-election and proposed reconciliation with the southern states.

Just a few days after the Confederates surrendered, Lincoln was shot at while attending a performance at Ford's Theatre in Washington, DC and he died the next morning, on 15 April 1865.

### DID YOU KNOW?

◇ At 6 feet, 4 inches, Abraham Lincoln was the tallest US president.

◇ Abraham Lincoln was the first American President to be assassinated. The whole country mourned his death. As the nine-car funeral train carried him home to Springfield, Illinois, for burial, people showed up at stations all along the way to pay their respects.

## MANDELA, NELSON (b. 1918)

Nelson Rolihlahla Mandela, a South African leader and statesman, was the President of South Africa from 1994 to 1999. Born into the royal family of the Tembu in 1918, he enrolled to study law. However, he was suspended from the University College of Fort Hare in 1940 for taking part in a student protest.

In 1944, Mandela joined a black liberation organization called African National Congress (ANC) and founded its influential Youth League. He gave up the policy of non-violence and established the ANC's military wing, Umkhonto we Sizwe or 'The Spear of the Nation'.

In 1963, Mandela and other ANC leaders were tried for plotting to overthrow the government by violence. The following year, Mandela was sentenced to life imprisonment. He was first held in Robben Island, and later in Pollsmoor Prison on the mainland. Mandela's release in 1990 was one of the most celebrated events in modern history. He was awarded the Nobel Peace Prize in 1993. Mandela has become a worldwide symbol of victory against the apartheid system.

## DID YOU KNOW?

◇ Mandela was given the African name Rolihlahla by his parents after his birth. Later, his teacher, Miss Mdingane, gave him the English first name Nelson, as the name he should respond to in school.

◇ In 1990, Mandela was awarded the Bharat Ratna, India's highest civilian award. He became one of the only two non-Indians (Khan Abdul Ghaffar Khan being the other) to be given the award.

## MARX, KARL (1818–1883)

Karl Marx was a German revolutionary, sociologist, historian and economist. Born to a Jewish lawyer in 1818 in West Germany, he studied law in Bonn and Berlin, where he was introduced to the ideas of Hegel and Feuerbach.

Later, after moving to Paris, Marx became a revolutionary communist and was introduced to Friedrich Engels who became a lifelong friend. They co-authored *The Communist Manifesto*, which, when published in 1848, became the foundation of the ideology of communism. He fought for social equality and for the upliftment of the proletariat or the working class. In 1849, Marx moved to London, where he was to spend the rest of his life. He suffered from poverty but was supported by Engels and his family. His most acclaimed work is *Das Kapital*, considered to be the 'Bible of the Working Class'.

In his final years, Marx's health and creative work declined. He was affected by the death of his wife and one of his daughters. He died on 14 March 1883 and is buried at Highgate Cemetery in London.

## DID YOU KNOW?

Marx's father wanted him to become a lawyer. Marx, however, was more interested in philosophy and literature. He wished to be a poet and dramatist. As a student, he wrote a great deal of poetry, most of which is preserved.

### MINH, HO CHI (1890–1969)

Ho Chi Minh, born Nguyen Sinh Cung, was the leader of the Vietnamese nationalist movement for more than thirty years. Born in 1890 in central Vietnam, then a French colony, he was inclined towards the communist ideology from as early as 1923. In 1930, he founded the Indo–Chinese Communist Party and, after the Japanese invaded Indo–China in 1941, he initiated the Viet Minh, a communist-dominated independence movement. At the end of World War II, the Viet Minh announced Vietnamese independence but the French refused to liberate the colonies. War broke out and the French were forced to initiate peace talks in Geneva. Vietnam was divided into communist North and non-communist South; Ho became President of North Vietnam. He worked to reunite Vietnam. Ho Chi Minh passed away in 1969. When the communists won over the South Vietnamese capital of Saigon in 1975, they renamed it Ho Chi Minh City in his honour.

### MUSSOLINI, BENITO (1883–1945)

Benito Mussolini, also known as Il Duce, meaning the leader, was the prime minister of Italy from 1922 to 1943 and the first of fascist dictators of 20th-century Europe. Born in Italy in 1883, he left Italy for Switzerland at an early age and became a popular political journalist and public speaker. On his return, during World War I, he went against most of the socialists and advocated Italy's support of the Allies. Mussolini formed an army of supporters with discontented socialists and others who joined him on his March on Rome to seize the government. In 1922, Mussolini became the youngest-ever prime minister of Italy. As premier, his policies initially endeared him to the masses. However, they turned against him when he banned opposition parties, trade unions, and the free press. He then turned into a dictator. Despite all his successful campaigns, his harsh rules created enemies at home, and his international policies paved the way for World War II. After the Allies invaded Sicily in 1943, Mussolini was forced to resign. He was shot dead by Italian partisans in 1945 when trying to escape in disguise.

## DID YOU KNOW?

Mussolini was spotted heading towards Switzerland by an Italian customs guard at Dongo, near Lake Como. He was driving a car in a column of other German cars, wearing a German greatcoat over his uniform.

### NIGHTINGALE, FLORENCE (1820–1910)

Florence Nightingale, also known as the Lady with the Lamp, was an English nurse and the founder of trained nursing as a profession.

Born in 1820 into an upper-class family in Florence, she grew up in London. She wanted to study nursing despite her parents' objections. Florence visited hospitals in England and continental Europe. After a few years, she joined the Institution of Protestant Deaconesses at Kaiserswerth in Germany.

Nightingale's most important role came to light during the Crimean War of 1854–1856 in Scutari, where more soldiers were dying from infectious diseases like typhoid and cholera (due to unhygienic conditions and lack of basic amenities) than from injuries incurred in battle.

Her efforts resulted in a major decline in the number of deaths. By 1856, Nightingale had gained across the world. She established the Nightingale School for Nurses in 1860. Her efforts and fame made nursing a respectable profession for women. Nightingale died in 1910, in London. Her birth anniversary is celebrated across the world as International Nurses Day.

## DID YOU KNOW?

◆ Nightingale used statistical data to create her Polar Area Diagrams or 'coxcombs' as she called them. These were used to give graphical representations of the mortality figures during the Crimean War.

◆ She was the first woman to receive the Order of Merit from Edward VII, the king of England in 1907.

### ROOSEVELT, FRANKLIN D. (1882–1945)

Franklin Delano Roosevelt, thirty-second President of the US, was elected to the office four times. He led the US through two of the greatest crises of the 20th century: the Great Depression and World War II.

Born in 1882 in New York, Roosevelt was elected to the New York Senate in 1910, and gradually became a prominent Democrat. In 1928, he was elected governor of New York and, in 1932, he was voted president by a landslide victory.

Roosevelt steadily safeguarded his country during his tenure, and was elected for a second term in 1936, followed by a third in 1940. While he devised policies to keep America out of World War I, he also helped Britain with financial support and equipment. After Japan devastated Pearl Harbour, America declared war by joining the Allied powers. Roosevelt later worked on brilliant post-war strategies such as the establishment of the UN. He died while in office on 12 April 1945.

## DID YOU KNOW?

- ◆ In 1921, Roosevelt suddenly contracted polio and was unable to walk without braces or a cane. However, with the support of his wife Eleanor, he was able recover and return to work.
- ◆ He was the first president to have his own aeroplane.

## ROOSEVELT, THEODORE (1858–1919)

Theodore Roosevelt, the twenty-sixth President of the US, was born in 1858. He studied at Harvard and Columbia Law College. Elected as a Republican to the New York State Assembly at the age of twenty-three, he made a name for himself as an enemy of corrupt politics.

In 1884, after the death of his mother and his wife, he spent two years as a cattle rancher in Dakota and then became a writer. He published a four-volume history of America's westward expansion. He also served in prestigious political ranks—as a member of the US Civil Service Commission, as President of the New York City Police Board and as lieutenant-colonel of the Rough Rider Regiment during the Spanish–American War.

Theodore became President of the US after William McKinley was assassinated in 1901. He designed anti-monopolistic reforms to curb the power of large corporations. In foreign affairs, Roosevelt declared that the US should 'speak softly and carry a big stick'. He brought an end to the Russo-Japanese war. He was awarded the Nobel Peace Prize in 1906. Roosevelt retired in 1908 and passed away on 6 January 1919.

## STALIN, JOSEPH (1879–9153)

Joseph Stalin, born Iosif Vissarionovich Dzhugashvili, was secretary-general of the Communist Party of the Soviet Union from 1922 to 1953 and Premier of the Soviet state from 1941 to 1953. Born on 18 December 1879 in Georgia, he was actively involved in the revolutionary movements against the Russian monarchy. He was arrested and exiled to Siberia several times.

In 1922, Stalin became the general secretary of the Communist Party and, after Lenin's death in 1924, established himself as the dictator of the Soviet Union. Stalin's policy of rapid industrialization brought about remarkable increase in productivity and gave a boost to the economy. A period of great terror prevailed during the 1930s, when millions were killed and exiled to slave labour camps by Stalin's policy of purging the party of the 'enemies of the people'. The huge loss of life weakened the army, yet he emerged victorious in the attack made by Hitler in 1941. This conflict ended in mass destruction.

At the end of World War II, the Soviet Union had control over the entire Eastern European empire. Faced with increasing challenges, Stalin died of a stroke in 1953.

## TERESA, MOTHER (1910–1997)

Born Agnes Gonxha Bojaxhiu, Mother Teresa founded the Order of the Missionaries of Charity, a congregation of women dedicated to the poor, especially active in India. Born at Skopje (Macedonia) in 1910, she went to Ireland in 1928 to join the Sisters of Loreto at the Institute of the Blessed Virgin Mary. Barely six weeks later, she sailed to India. She taught for about seventeen years at the order's school in Calcutta. In 1946, Sister Teresa experienced her 'call within a call', and founded her own order—the Missionaries of Charity. In 1952, she established Nirmal Hriday ('Place for the Pure of Heart'), a hospice where the terminally ill could spend their last days with dignity.

Under Mother Teresa's guidance, the Missionaries of Charity built a leper colony called Shanti Nagar ('Town of Peace'), near Asansol in India. For her great humanitarian work, she received the Nobel Peace Prize in 1979 and the Bharat Ratna in 1980. She died in 1997, and was beatified in 2003.

## DID YOU KNOW?

On 17 August 1948, dressed for the first time in a blue-bordered white sari Mother Teresa passed through the gates of her beloved Loreto Convent to serve the poor.

## THATCHER, MARGARET (b. 1925)

Margaret Thatcher, nicknamed the Iron Lady, was the first woman prime minister of Great Britain and is the only British prime minister in the 20th century to have won three consecutive terms, from 1979 through 1990. At the time of her resignation, she was Britain's longest continuously serving prime minister since 1827.

Thatcher was born in 1925 to a grocer's family. She studied at Oxford University and became a research chemist. Her political career started when she entered the House of Commons, winning the Conservative seat of Finchley in northern London in 1959. From 1964 to 1970, she served in a number of positions in Edward Heath's shadow cabinet. She became prime minister in 1979.

During her term, she implemented the policy of privatization of state-owned industries and utilities, reformed trade unions, lowered taxes, and reduced social expenditure across the board. Her policies succeeded and she won a landslide victory in the 1983 general election. She won a third term in office in 1987. However, controversial policies led to a fissure in the party, and she agreed to resign in 1990.

## WASHINGTON, GEORGE (1732–1799)

George Washington, also known as Father of the Nation in the US, was an American General and commander-in-chief of the colonial armies in the American Revolution and subsequently the first President of the United States of America. Born in 1732 in Virginia, into a family of prosperous farmers, he joined the Virginia militia in the early 1750s. He was greatly appreciated for his duties during the Seven Years' War.

In 1759, Washington entered the Virginia House of Burgesses, where he strongly opposed what he saw as unfair British taxes. In 1775, he was appointed commander of all colonial forces. Soon, he assumed control over the Continental Army and, during the American Revolution that lasted for six years, fought against many odds. For instance, he was leading a force of untrained, unpaid men who often left the army. Despite the challenges, in 1781, they forced the British to surrender and sign a peace treaty.

In 1789, Washington was unanimously elected president. Again, he faced huge challenges in welding together the individual states to establish a new nation. Washington wanted to retire after his first term but was re-elected in 1792. He finally retired from public life in 1797, and died at Mount Vernon on 14 December 1799.

## DID YOU KNOW?

◇ Ice cream was one of George Washington's favourite foods.

◇ He was the only president who did not live in Washington, D.C.

## ZEDONG, MAO (1893–1976)

Mao Zedong, a Chinese Marxist theorist and statesman, was the Chairman (chief of state) of the People's Republic of China (PRC) from 1949 to 1959. He led the communist revolution in China. Zedong was born in 1893. He was inspired by the works of Marxist philosophers. He founded the Chinese Communist Party (CCP) in 1921. Later, he allied with the Kuomintang (KMT) nationalist party to defeat the warlords in northern China.

After the warlords were defeated, the KMT tried to eliminate the members of CCP. Following World War II, civil war broke out between the two parties. Mao's party emerged victorious. He formed the PRC and introduced significant social reforms. He introduced the policy of 'cultural revolution' in 1966, aimed at removing 'impure elements' from China and bringing about a reawakening of the revolutionary spirit.

As a result, more than a million people perished and several cultural heritage sites were destroyed. By September 1967, many cities were breaking into anarchy, and Mao had to send armed forces to restore order. During his later years, he tried to build political ties with the US, Japan and Europe. Mao died on 9 September 1976.

# SOME CONTEMPORARY LEADERS OF THE WORLD

## CAMERON, DAVID (b. 1966)

David Cameron became the prime minister of the United Kingdom in 2010. Born in London, he was educated at Eton. He later studied philosophy, politics and economics at Oxford University. In 1988, he joined the Conservative

Research Department and in 2001 was elected Member of Parliament for Witney, Oxfordshire. His election as prime minister in 2010 makes him the youngest person to hold the office since Lord Liverpool in 1812. It also marks the the first coalition government since World War II.

## CLINTON, HILLARY RODHAM (b. 1947)

A former first lady (1993–2001),Clinton was appointed the US Secretary of State in 2009. The eldest child of Hugh and Dorothy Rodham, she graduated from Wellesley College and finished her post-graduation from Yale Law School. In 1974, she participated in the Watergate inquiry. Later she moved to Arkansas and in 1975 married Bill Clinton, who was to be the 42nd President of the United States. In 2000, she started her political career by defeating her Republican rival in the US Senate seat from New York. In 2007, she initiated her campaign to be the the Democratic Party's presidential candidate. Although she began as a front-runner in her quest, she eventually lost out to Barack Obama. In December 2008, Obama selected Clinton to serve as the Secretary of State.

## GILLARD, JULIA (b. 1961)

Julia Gillard is the 27th prime minister of Australia. Born in Barry, Wales, she grew up in Adelaide. She began studying law and arts at the University of Adelaide. In 1982, she moved to Melbourne where she served as president of the Australian Union of Students and continued her studies at the University of Melbourne. Julia Gillard first contested the Federal seat of Labor for the Australian Labor Party in 1998. From 1998 to 2001, she served the House of Representatives Standing Committee on Employment, Education and Workplace Relations. Following the Australian Labor Party's victory at the 2007 Federal Election, she was sworn in as deputy prime minister and minister for education, employment and workplace relations and social inclusion. Julia Gillard is the first woman to hold the offices of the leader of Australian Labor Party and the prime minister of Australia.

## HOLLANDE, FRANOIS (b. 1954)

Franoise Hollande was elected as the twenty-fourth President of France on 6 May, 2012. Hollande was born in the north-western city of Rouen and attended the ENA (National School of Administration), and another elite institution, Sciences Po. Having been active in student politics, he joined the Socialist party in 1979 and was an economic adviser in the Mitterrand presidency. Hollande is the first Socialist president to win a French election since François Mitterrand's re-election in 1988.

## JINTAO, HU (b. 1942)

Hu Jintao became the general secretary of the Chinese Communist Party in 2002 and the President of China in 2003. He was born in Taizhou and received his primary education there. In 1965, he graduated from the Tsinghua University with a degree in Hydraulic Engineering. He joined the communist party during the cultural revolution. In 1987, he was named as a member of Central Committee of the party and was sent to Tibet, where he imposed martial law in 1989 to quell unrest. In November 2002, he succedded Jiang Zemin as the general secretary of the party and was elected as the president of the country in March 2003.

## JONG-UN, KIM (b. 1980)

Born in the early part of 1980s, Jong-Un Kim is the youngest of the three sons of the late North Korean leader Kim Jong Il. He received his education from the International School of Berne and the National War College in Pyongyang. Around 2009, it was rumoured that he was being groomed as his father's successor. In April 2009, he was drafted into the National Defence Commission. After his father passed away in December 2011, he was declared the head of North Korea's government and military forces. In 2012, he became the head of the Korean Worker's Party, chairman of the Central Military Commission, and chairman of the National Defence Commission.

## KYI, AUNG SAN SUU (b. 1945)

Aung San Suu Kyi became the leader of the Opposition of the Parliament of Myanmar in 2012. Born in Rangoon to Aung San and Daw Khin Kyi, she received her early education in Burma and India. After obtaining a BA in philosophy, politics and economics from Oxford University, she worked for the UN Secretariat. She lived and worked in Japan and Bhutan, and later in the UK. She went back to Rangoon in 1988 to look after her critically-ill mother and was soon propelled into leading the revolt against the then-dictator, General Ne Win. In 1989, she was put under house arrest. She was finally released in 2010. She was awarded the Nobel Peace Prize in 1991 for her non-violent struggle for democracy and human rights.

## LAGARDE, CHRISTINE (b. 1956)

Christine Lagarde created history when she became the first woman managing director of the International Monetary Fund in 2011. Born in Paris, France, she graduated in 1974 and then studied at the Law School of the University of Paris X-Nanterre. Later she worked for an American law firm handling labour and competition law cases. In March 2004, she received to France's highest order, the Legion of Honour, from the then President Jacques Chirac, She was also the first woman to be in charge of economic policy in France. In 2007, she became France's first woman Finance Minister.

## LAMA, DALAI (b. 1935)

The 14th Dalai Lama, Tenzin Gyatso, was born into a farming family in Tibet. He was recognized as the reincarnation of the 13th Dalai Lama, Thubten Gyatso, in 1937 and enthroned in 1940; when he was vested with full powers as head of state in 1950. He fled to India in 1959 and set up a Government of Tibet-in-exile in Dharmsala. Tibetans normally refer to him as *Yeshin Norbu*, the Wish-fulfilling Gem, or simply, *Kundun*, meaning The Presence. He has been honoured with numerous awards, including the 1989 Nobel Peace Prize and the 2012 Templeton Prize. In 2011, the Dalai Lama stepped down as the political head of the Tibetan government-in-exile.

## MERKEL, ANGELA (b. 1954)

Angela Merkel, Germany's first woman chancellor, was born in Hamburg in 1954. In 1978, Merkel received a physics doctorate at the University of Leipzig and then worked as a quantum chemist at the Academy of Sciences in East Berlin. Merkel joined the Christian Democratic Union in 1990 just two months before German reunification, and was the deputy speaker of the first freely elected East German government. In April 2000, Merkel was chosen to lead the CDU, becoming the first woman and the first non-Catholic to lead the party. Since 2005, she holds the position of the Chancellor of the Federal Republic of Germany, the first woman to hold the office.

## MONTI, MARIO (b. 1943)

Mario Monti is the fifty-fourth prime minister of Italy. Born in Varese, Italy, he served for ten years as member of the European Commission, in charge first of the internal market, financial services and taxation, and then of competition. He was the chairman of the Italian Treasury's committee on the banking and financial system and member of the committee which drafted Italy's first Competition Law. On 9 November 2011, he was appointed a Senator for Life in the Italian Senate by President Napolitano. Following the resignation of Silvio Berlusconi, he was appointed prime minister of Italy and minister of economy and finance.

## NETANYAHU, BENJAMIN (b. 1949)

Benjamin Netanyahu, the ninth prime minister of the State of Israel was born in Tel Aviv and grew up in Jerusalem. Son of the historian Benzion Netanyahu, he moved with his family to Philadelphia in the United States in 1963. He did his MBA from the Massachusetts Institute of Technology. Netanyahu held several positions as ambassador before being elected to the Knesset (Israeli Parliament) as a Likud member in 1988. In the elections of 1996, the first in which the prime minister was directly elected, Netanyahu became the youngest person ever to serve as Israel's prime minister. He lost the premiership to Ehud Barak in 1999. In 2009, following the elections to the 18th Knesset, Benjamin Netanyahu formed the next government, and was sworn in as prime minister. Benjamin Netanyahu has written and edited a number of books, including *Terrorism: How the West Can Win* (1986) and *A Durable Peace: Israel and Its Place Among the Nations* (2000).

## OBAMA, BARACK (b. 1961)

Barack H. Obama is the forty-fourth President of the United States of America. Born in Honolulu, Hawaii, to Ann Dunham and Barack Obama Sr., he received his early education in Hawaii and in Jakarta (Indonesia). After receiving a BA from Columbia University, he studied law at Harvard University, where he became the first African-American president of the *Harvard Law Review*. He became a member of Illinois senate in 1997. In 2004, he was elected to the US senate and served from 3 January 2005 to 16 November 2008, when he was elected president of the United States of America. He has won numerous awards, including the 2009 Nobel Peace Prize, for his extraordinary efforts to strengthen international diplomacy and cooperation between peoples.

## PUTIN, VLADIMIR (b. 1952)

Vladimir Vladimirovich Putin was elected president of the Russian Federation for the third time in 2012. He was born on 7 October 1952 in Leningrad, which is now St Petersburg. In 1975, he graduated from the Law Department of Leningrad State University and started working for the State Security Committee (KGB). He was elected president in 2000, and for a second term in 2004. In 2007, he was named *Time* magazine's Person of the Year.

## SHINAWATRA, YINGLUCK (b. 1967)

Yingluck Shinawatra was born on 21 June 1947. Elected in August 2011, she is the present prime minister of Thailand, the first woman to hold the post.

Youngest of the nine children of Lert Shinawatra and Yindi Ramingwong, she is the sister of former prime minister Thaksin Shinawatra. She is a businesswoman and politician, and holds a master's degree in political science and business administration from Kentucky State University.

# MAJOR MOVEMENTS AND REVOLUTIONS OF THE WORLD

## RENAISSANCE IN EUROPE

Renaissance, a French term, is derived from the Latin word *renascor* meaning 'rebirth'. It was primarily an age of the revival of classical learning and wisdom after a long period of cultural decline and stagnation.

The Renaissance began in Italy during the 14th century, swept across Europe after the Middle Ages and reached its height in the 15th century.

During this period, people of Europe took a renewed interest in the ancient classical ideas of Greece and Rome. Inspired by these thoughts they developed their own ideas. Humanism was the basis of Renaissance.

The Humanists were classical scholars who gave more attention to the study of classical literature, grammar, history and poetry. The movement first flourished in Italy, because after the crusades, people from Rome and Greece migrated there, making Italy a centre for exchange of ideas and culture. The invention of the printing press in 1450 by Johannes Gutenberg helped spread these ideas across Europe.

The spirit of self-discovery and enquiry led to a revival in science, with path-breaking inventions and discoveries. Inspired by the quest for knowledge, Christopher Columbus and other explorers from Spain and Portugal travelled in search of places.

Francesco Petrarch, also known as the father of humanism, was one of the first thinkers who initiated Renaissance in the field of literature. Some important men of this period were Erasmus, Copernicus, Galileo, Newton, Leonardo da Vinci, Michelangelo, Botticelli and Raphael. The age thus broadly marked an era of looking at the world and one's self with a new perspective.

## ENLIGHTENMENT IN EUROPE

The Enlightenment that started in Europe during the 1700s inspired people to use their faculty of reason and to challenge flawed beliefs and superstitions which had come down the ages. Thomas Paine called this period of intellectual flowering 'The Age of Reason'.

The monarchs and the Catholic church used to declare that their power was gifted by God and thus they held absolute authority. The nobility, churchmen and the rich enjoyed all kinds of privileges, while the common man was exploited. The Enlightenment led people to question the government and demand the responsibility of governance. The ideas of the Renaissance inspired many thinkers like Voltaire, Rousseau, Adam Smith and John Locke to question the unreasonable impositions of orthodox religion.

Three primary premises in history that led to the Enlightenment were the ideas of the ancient Greek philosophers, the Renaissance, and the scientific revolution of the late Middle Ages. While the Enlightenment made the role of education very significant, the Roman Catholic Church and monarchs tried to ban books and works of philosophers. Learning triggered an awakening among the masses. This awakening eventually led to the American and French revolutions, which brought about the end of monarchies.

With Enlightenment came Enlightened Despots—those autocratic emperors who brought about various reforms and tried to rule their people in the Light of Reason. Some famous Enlightened Despots were Federick II, King of Prussia the Great of Prussia, Catherine II of Russia, Maria Theresa and Joseph II of Austria, and Charles III of Spain.

## REFORMATION

The Reformation was a significant religious and social reform movement in Europe. It occurred during the 1500s, bringing with it profound changes in religious matters and affecting the social, political, intellectual and artistic lives of the people.

Europe was then suffering from the malpractices and corruptions of the Catholic church. In fact, the church was looked upon as an exploitative agency, causing the common people to hate its authorities, the Pope and the clergy. It is this strong feeling of anticlericalism which ultimately ushered in the Reformation.

The movement, originating in Western Europe, was begun by Martin Luther who was a priest and preacher in Germany, and propogated by John Calvin and Huldrych Zwingli. It spread to almost every part of Europe, marking a turning point in history. Luther questioned the absolute authority of the Catholic church in interpreting the Bible. He translated the Latin Bible into German, the language of the common people. With the help of the printing press, the Bible reached the homes of the common people and they recognized the wrongs of the Catholic church authorities.

Later, Luther established the Protestant church. To oppose this wave of Reformation, a Counter-Reformation was started in the 1540s by the Catholic church. An important development was the formation of the Society of Jesus whose followers were known as the Jesuits. They tried to check the spread of Protestantism and to regain the lost glory of the church. St Francis Xavier was a famous Jesuit. The Council of Trent, a Catholic body, decided to introduce the papal index or press censorship to prevent publication of any book contrary to the teachings of the Catholic church. The conflict between the Protestants and Catholics lasted for a long time. It had an impact deep into the 1600s when the Thirty Years' War sparked off and spread all across Europe.

## INDUSTRIAL REVOLUTION

The Industrial Revolution is the name given to the movement in which machines changed the lives of the people. This process began in England in the 18th century and from there, spread to other parts of the world. The invention of machines to do the work of hand tools, the use of steam (and later, of other kinds of power, in place of the muscles of human beings and of animals) and the adoption of the factory system led to the Revolution.

The Industrial Revolution started in the textile industry, with the invention of the flying shuttle in 1733. In 1770, James Hargreaves invented the spinning jenny that made weaving faster and easier. Muscle power was replaced with smoke power with the invention of the steam engine by James Watt. In 1830, the first railroad connecting Liverpool and Manchester was opened after George Stephenson built a type of steam engine that could move on rails.

The Industrial Revolution resulted in newer and faster means of manufacture and transport. New trade routes were found, trading firms were established, iron steam ships were built and populated industrial towns started to grow. This relatively sudden change in the way people live deserves to be called a revolution. It had a major impact on the life of the people.

## THE GREAT DEPRESSION

An acute economic crisis that arose in the US in 1929, affecting the entire world, popularly came to be called the Great Depression. It completely drained the US economy—banks went bankrupt, businesses collapsed and many people lost their jobs. Stock prices at that time were on a gradual decline and the immediate cause of the depression was felt on 29 October, also called Black Tuesday, when the stock market collapsed drastically and stock prices were reduced to a fraction of their original values.

Europe, attempting to recover from the losses after World War I, was severely affected because European countries were dependent on the US for loans and trade. In the US, the discontented people ousted President Herbert Hoover and elected Franklin D. Roosevelt to office. Roosevelt introduced the New Deal—a programme of economic reform that would generate new jobs for people.

In the aftermath of this economic crisis, all other countries placed high taxes on imported goods to restrict foreign trade. This was a period of acute poverty, lack of food and shelter. Writers and artists of the US based their works on the sufferings of people affected by the depression. John Steinbeck's famous novel, *The Grapes of Wrath*, is an apt depiction. The crisis ended with the beginning of World War II.

# PROMINENT LEADERS DURING INDIA'S FREEDOM STRUGGLE

## ALI, ARUNA ASAF (1908-1996)

Bharat Ratna awardee (1997) Aruna Asaf Ali was a legendary heroine of India's freedom struggle. Born in Punjab in 1908, she is chiefly remembered for hoisting the Congress tricolour in Bombay at the meeting in August 1942 where Gandhi asked the British to quit India. She gained importance in the underground revolutionary movement in 1942 and, after independence, moved between the Congress, Socialist, and Communist parties before returning to the Congress and being elected mayor of Delhi. She also published a newspaper, *Patriot*, and a magazine, *Link*.

## AMBEDKAR, BHIMRAO (1891-1956)

The undisputed leader of the Harijans ('untouchables' or low-caste Hindus), Ambedkar was the first law minister of independent India (1947–1951). Born into an 'untouchable' Mahar family of western India, he was often subjected to humiliation by his high-caste schoolfellows. He soon established his leadership among Harijans, founded several journals on their behalf, and succeeded in obtaining special representation for them in the legislative councils of the government. Contesting Gandhi's claim to speak for Harijans, he wrote *What Congress and Gandhi Have Done to the Untouchables* (1945). He was elected as the chairman of the committee that was set up by the Constituent Assembly to draft a Constitution for independent India. He was awarded the Bharat Ratna in 1990.

## DID YOU KNOW?

◇ On 24 May 1956, on the occasion of Buddha Jayanti, Ambedkar declared that he would adopt Buddhism. On 14 October 1956, he embraced this religion along with many followers. The same year, he completed his last work, *Buddha and His Dharma*.

◇ The period from 14 April 1990 to 14 April 1991 was observed as the 'Year of Social Justice', in memory of Babasaheb, a name he was popularly known by.

## AZAD, CHANDRA SHEKHAR (1906–1931)

Freedom fighter Chandra Shekhar Azad was born in 1906 in Uttar Pradesh. He was fascinated by and drawn to the great national upsurge of the non-violent, non-cooperation movement of 1920–1921 launched by Mahatma Gandhi. Azad joined the Hindustan Socialist Republican Army and was involved in the Kakori Conspiracy of 1926, the attempt to blow up the Viceroy's train, the Assembly bomb incident, the Delhi Conspiracy, the shooting of Saunders at Lahore in 1928, and the second Lahore conspiracy. In 1931, betrayed by an associate, he shot himself to evade arrest.

## DID YOU KNOW?

On one occasion, when he was arrested and produced before a magistrate, he gave his name as 'Azad', his father's name as 'Swatantra', and his residence as 'Prison'. The provoked magistrate sentenced him to fifteen lashes. The title of 'Azad' stuck on.

## AZAD, ABUL KALAM (1888–1958)

Independent India's first Union minister for education, Maulana Abul Kalam Azad was one of the foremost leaders of the Indian freedom struggle and a supporter of Hindu–Muslim unity. He was also an Indian Muslim scholar and a senior political leader of the Indian independence movement.

Born in Mecca, Abul Kalam was a descendent of a lineage of learned Muslim scholars or *maulanas*. During his days as a leader of the Khilafat movement, he came into close contact with Gandhi and became an enthusiastic supporter of his ideas of non-violent civil disobedience.

He worked actively to organize the non-cooperation movement in protest against the 1919 Rowlatt Acts. Abul Kalam committed himself to Gandhi's ideals, including promoting *swadeshi* products and the cause of *swaraj* for India. Abul Kalam became the youngest person to serve as the president of the Indian National Congress in 1923.

## DID YOU KNOW?

Kalam spent years in jail, where some of his prison mates thought of him as an 'extraordinarily interesting companion' who had an astonishing memory.

### BESANT, ANNIE (1847–1933)

Annie Besant was a prominent Theosophist, social reformer, political leader, women's rights activist, writer and orator. She was the president of the Theosophical Society from 1907 until her death.

Born in London in 1847, Besant had an unhappy childhood living in poverty after her father's death. However she received a good education. She became a member of the National Secular Society, which preached 'free thought', and also of the Fabian Society, the noted socialist organization. In 1875, she became interested in Theosophy, a religious movement. She first visited India in 1893 and later settled there, becoming involved in the Indian nationalist movement. In 1916, she established the Indian Home Rule League, of which she became president. She was also a leading member of the Indian National Congress. Although she was Irish, she made India her home, spending her life fighting for the rights of the Indians.

### BOSE, KHUDIRAM (1889–1908)

Khudiram was one of the youngest revolutionaries in the Indian independence movement. Born in 1889 at Midnapore in West Bengal, he became disillusioned after the Partition of Bengal in 1905 and joined Jugantar, the party of revolutionary activities. At the early age of sixteen, Bose defied the police by planting bombs near police stations and targeting government officials. In 1908 in Muzzafarpur, along with Prafulla Chaki, he threw a bomb at a carriage supposed to be carrying Judge Kingsford. Unfortunately, the carriage was carrying Mrs Kennedy, wife of barister Pringle Kennedy, their daughter and a servant, all of whom were killed immediately. Bose was hanged to death while Chaki shot himself.

## BOSE, SUBHAS CHANDRA (1897-1945)

Subhas Chandra Bose, popularly known as Netaji, was one of the greatest nationalist leaders of the freedom struggle of India. Born in 1897 into a wealthy family, Bose was deeply influenced by the intellectual and cultural milieu of Bengal at the turn of the century. Though he qualified for the Indian Civil Service, he resigned as he did not want to wear the 'emblem of servitude'. He believed India should become an independent federal republic. To this end, he joined the non-cooperation movement and became a journalist, an educator of the youth, and commandant of the Bengal Congress volunteers. He was arrested several times for his suspected role in revolutionary acts.

In 1938, Netaji was elected president of the Indian National Congress and formed a planning committee, which formulated a policy of broad industrialization. However, this idea did not go down well with Gandhian economic thought and Bose resigned.

Bose later founded the Forward Bloc, hoping to continue the struggle, but was imprisoned. He escaped to Germany and made regular broadcasts from the German-sponsored Azad Hind Radio, beginning in January 1942. On 4 July, he assumed leadership of the Indian independence movement in East Asia and proceeded, with Japanese aid and influence, to form a trained army of about 40,000 troops in Japan-occupied South-east Asia. On 21 October 1943, Bose proclaimed the establishment of a provisional independent Indian government and his Indian National Army (Azad Hind Fauj). With the support of Japanese troops Netaji's Indian National Army marched to Kohima. Here they were defeated and forced to retreat. Netaji is believed to have died in an air crash on his way to Tokyo.

### DID YOU KNOW?

- ◇ Subhas Chandra Bose was elected the mayor of Calcutta in 1930.
- ◇ Bose was arrested eleven times by the British, but finally escaped and went secretly to Nazi Germany via Afghanistan and the Soviet Union to seek support for an armed campaign against British rule.

## CAMA, MADAME BHIKAJI (1861-1936)

Madame Bhikaji Cama, an important figure in the Indian independence movement, actively participated in the struggle for freedom and gender equality. Born Bhikaji Rustom Cama into a Parsi family in Bombay in 1861, she received a good education. From an early age, she was a rebel and harboured strong nationalist sentiments. With a firm command over several languages, she could argue the country's cause in different circles. Cama is mainly remembered for raising the Indian flag at the International Socialist Conference in Stuttgart, Germany, in 1907. On 26 January 1962, the Indian Post and Telegraph Department issued a stamp in her honour. The Indian Coast Guard has a ship named after her—ICGS Bhikaji Cama.

## GANDHI, MAHATMA (1869–1948)

Mohandas Karamchand Gandhi, known as Father of the Nation, was one of the greatest leaders of the Indian nationalist movement. He is internationally known for his policy of non-violent protest to achieve political and social progress. Born in Porbundar, Gujarat, in 1869, he was married to Kasturba at the young age of thirteen. In 1888, Gandhi went to England to study law and was later called to South Africa by a merchant to fight a legal suit for him. During his stay in South Africa, he experienced racism at different levels. His life underwent a radical change and he developed most of his political ideas from his experiences there. After returning to India in 1894, he decided to dedicate himself completely to the service of humanity. From 1915 to 1918, Gandhi dominated Indian politics. He participated in two peasant movements in Champaran and Kaira, and also in the labour dispute involving mill workers in Ahmedabad. He introduced the concept of ahimsa and non-cooperation satyagraha as the only weapons to fight against the British. He also devoted himself to the propagation of what he regarded as the basic national needs, namely, Hindu–Muslim unity, abolition of untouchability, equality of women, popularization of the *charkha*, and reconstruction of the village economy.

Gandhi started the non-cooperation movement in 1920 and was elected president of the Indian National Congress four years later. On 12 March 1930, Gandhi started the historic Dandi March to break the law, which banned Indians from producing their own salt. This was followed by the civil disobedience movement. He opposed the Communal Award in 1932, gave minority groups separate electorates where only they could vote.

In 1942, Gandhi gave the call for the Quit India Movement for which he was arrested by the British along with other leaders. He also raised the slogan 'do or die', which became very popular at that time. He was assassinated by Nathuram Godse in New Delhi on 31 January 1948. His autobiography, *The Story of My Experiments with Truth*, throws light on his life and his philosophy. His birth anniversary, 2 October, is celebrated as the International Day of Non-Violence by the UN. In India we celebrate it as Gandhi Jayanti.

## DID YOU KNOW?

Initially, Mahatma Gandhi could not arrive at a proper name for satyagraha. Hence, he offered a nominal prize through the newspaper *Indian Opinion* to the reader who made the best suggestion on the subject. Maganlal Gandhi, his nephew, coined the word *sadagraha* (*sat* = truth + *agraha* = firmness) and won the prize. To make the meaning clearer, Gandhi changed the word to satyagraha. It became a buzzword for the freedom struggle.

### GHOSH, AUROBINDO (1872–1950)

Indian nationalist freedom fighter, poet, philosopher, and yogi, Aurobindo Ghosh was born on 15 August 1872. He launched a systematic criticism of moderate politics through a series of articles entitled *New Lamps for Old* (1893–1894), while serving as a lecturer in Baroda. In 1907, through a series of articles in *Bande Mataram*, of which he was an editor, Ghosh advocated the doctrine of passive resistance. He also played an important role in the anti-Partition movement of Bengal. He was arrested by the British in 1908 due to his involvement in the Kennedy murder case, following which he escaped to Pondicherry, where he devoted himself intensively to the exploration of the new possibilities it opened up to him. Supported by his spiritual collaborator, The Mother, he worked for the upliftment of India and concentrated on philosophical, spiritual and literary activities. He died in 1950.

### JINNAH, MUHAMMAD ALI (1876–1948)

Muhammad Ali Jinnah, also known as Qaid-e-Azam, was the founder and the first governor-general (1947–1948) of Pakistan. Born in 1876 in Karachi, he passed out from the University of Bombay and went to England, where he took keen interest in Indian issues and the matters of Indian students. After returning to India, he turned to active politics. Jinnah rose to prominence in the Indian National Congress (INC) by helping shape the 1916 Lucknow Pact between the Muslim League and the INC. He also became a key leader in the All India Home Rule League. He proposed a fourteen-point constitutional reform plan to safeguard the political rights of the Muslims in a self-governing India. After the creation of Pakistan, he became its first head of state.

## DID YOU KNOW?

Jinnah joined the Lincoln's Inn in 1893 and became the youngest Indian to be called to the Bar, three years later. He was also the first parliamentarian to have a Private Member's Bill passed at the Imperial Legislative Council of India.

## NAIDU, SAROJINI (1879–1949)

Political activist, feminist and writer, Sarojini Naidu, also known as the Nightingale of India, was born in 1879. She joined the Indian national Movement after the Partition of Bengal in 1906 at the insistence of Gopal Krishna Gokhale. She campaigned for the Montagu–Chelmsford Reforms, the Khilafat issue, the Rowlatt Acts, the Sabarmati Pact, and the Satyagraha Pledge, and played a very important part in Gandhi's civil disobedience movement of 1919.

In 1925, she became the first Indian woman president of the Indian National Congress. She was also a distinguished poet and was one of the great orators of her time. Some of her works include *The Golden Threshold* and *The Bird of Time.* In 1914, she was elected a fellow of the Royal Society of Literature. She passed away in 1949 in Lucknow while serving as governor.

## DID YOU KNOW?

After the court case in which Gandhiji was tried for sedition in regard to two articles he had written in his paper *Young India* in 1922, Naidu gave up her luxurious silks in favour of khadi.

## NAOROJI, DADABHAI (1825–1917)

Dadabhai Naoroji, also known as the Grand Old Man of India, was an important Indian nationalist leader and a strong critic of the British economic policy of India. Born in Bombay in a priestly Parsi family, he graduated in 1845 and initially marked in London as a business in the firm Cama & Co. He also taught at University College, London. He was elected as Member of Parliament for Central Finsbury, London, in 1892. He became widely known for his unfavourable opinion of the economic consequences of British rule in India and was appointed a member of the royal commission on Indian expenditure in 1895. He founded several magazines and journals such as *Rast Goftar* and *Voice of India*. He passed away in 1917.

> ## DID YOU KNOW?
>
> Educated at Elphinstone College, Naoroji was a professor of natural philosophy and mathematics.

## PAL, BIPIN CHANDRA (1858-1932)

Bipin Chandra Pal was popularly known as the father of revolutionary thought in India. He belonged to the extremist trio of Lal–Bal–Pal, the other two being Lala Lajpat Rai and Bal Gangadhar Tilak. They were called extremists because they did not want to use the traditional methods of prayer, plea, and petitions, and believed in direct action in the form of agitations and radical movements. Moreover, they wanted complete independence from the British rule as opposed to the dominion status as demanded by the moderates.

Born in 1858 in Bangladesh in a wealthy family, Bipin began his journalistic career when he started the weekly *Paridarsak* and later became assistant editor of *Public Opinion* and *Tribune*. Though he began his political career as a moderate, after the Partition of Bengal, he switched over to radical protest. He was recognized as one of the chief exponents of a new national movement revolving around the ideas of swaraj, swadeshi, boycott, and national education.

## PANDEY, MANGAL (1827-1857)

Mangal Pandey was a sepoy under the British East India Company. Believed to have been born in 1827 in Uttar Pradesh, he is chiefly remembered for his attack on a senior British officer, which triggered the First War of Independence in India. The reason behind this was a rumour that the cartridges provided to the Indian soldiers for use were greased with the fat of cows and pigs, and had to be bitten off to remove the cover prior to use. This practice went against the religious beliefs of the Muslims and Hindus. The general opinion was that the British had deliberately done this to hurt the sentiments of Indians. For this act of rebellion, Mangal Pandey was hanged at Barrackpore near Kolkata.

## PATEL, VALLABHBHAI (1875–1950)

Popularly known as the Iron Man of India, Sardar Patel was a prominent nationalist leader. He was the first deputy prime minister and home minister of independent India and played an important role in unifying the country.

Born in Gujarat in 1875, Patel studied law in London and became a leading barrister on his return to India. In 1917, he became deeply influenced by Gandhiji's philosophy and his life underwent a radical change. He first made his mark in 1918, when he planned a mass campaign of farmers and landowners of Kaira (Gujarat), against the decision of the Bombay government to collect the full annual revenue tax, despite crop failures caused by heavy rains. In 1928, he successfully led the landowners of Bardoli in their resistance against increased taxes. His efficient leadership of these campaigns earned him the title of *sardar* (leader).

After India's independence, Vallabhbhai tried his best to peacefully integrate the princely Indian states into the Indian Union, and thus unify India politically. After a prolonged illness, he passed away on 15 December 1950. He was posthumously awarded the Bharat Ratna in 1991.

## RAI, LALA LAJPAT (1865–1928)

Lala Lajpat Rai, popularly known as 'Punjab Kesari', was a politician and writer. Born in Jagraon in 1865, he studied law. It was during his years as a lawyer that he met Dayananda Saraswati, founder of the Arya Samaj, and became his follower.

Rai soon joined the Congress party and was deported to Mandalay, Burma, for taking part in a political agitation in the Punjab. However, he was set free due to insufficient evidence. In 1920, he led the special session of the Congress party that launched the non-cooperation movement. Imprisoned from 1921 to 1923, he was elected to the Legislative Assembly on his release. In 1928, he introduced the legislative assembly resolution for the boycott of the British Simon Commission on constitutional reform.

Shortly thereafter, while leading a protest procession against the Simon Commission, he was severely wounded. He died due to injuries. In his last moments, he is believed to have said: 'Every blow aimed at me is a nail in the coffin of British imperialism.'

## RAJAGOPALACHARI, CHAKRAVARTI (1879–1972)

Chakravarti Rajagopalachari, popularly known as Rajaji, was the only Indian governor-general of independent India. He was a very well-known lawyer, writer, statesman, and a prominent figure in the Indian National Congress during India's struggle for independence.

Born in 1879, he studied law and became a respected solicitor. However, he soon left his successful practice to participate in the struggle for freedom. He served as the member of the Congress Working Committee from 1919 to 1942 and from 1950 to 1955.

Rajaji pleaded strongly for the implementation of social reform schemes and passed numerous acts, including the Madras Temple Entry Act of 1939 to do away with untouchability. He became the founder and leader of the Swatantra Party in 1959. He was also the supreme leader of the civil disobedience movement in south India, and led the Salt Satyagraha as well.

After India's independence, he was made chief minister of Madras state. He was also a reputed writer, and won the Sahitya Akademi Award. He was awarded the Bharat Ratna in 1954.

## SAVARKAR, VINAYAK DAMODAR (1883–1966)

Popularly known as Veer Savarkar, V.D. Savarkar was a great revolutionary. Born in Maharashtra in 1883, Savarkar's revolutionary activities began in India and continued in England. He was associated with India House, and founded student societies, including Abhinav Bharat Society and Free India Society. He was the first person to refer to what the British termed the Sepoy Mutiny of 1857 as the First War of Indian Independence. He was one of the first to set fire to foreign clothes, and was rusticated from a government-aided school because of his patriotism. For his revolutionary activities, he was arrested and imprisoned in Cellular Jail from 1911 to 1924. He passed away in 1966. The airport at Port Blair, the capital of Andaman and Nicobar Islands, has been named in his honour.

### DID YOU KNOW?

Savarkar's book, *The Indian War of Independence*, could not be published in India and the manuscript was returned to him. It was first printed in Holland in 1909. It went on to become one of the most widely smuggled and circulated books among young Indians and future revolutionaries.

## SINGH, BHAGAT (1907–1931)

Bhagat Singh was one of the most influential revolutionaries of the Indian independence movement. Born in Punjab, he graduated in 1923 and joined the Hindustan Socialist Republican Association. In 1925, he founded the Nav Jawan Bharat Sabha at Lahore to inculcate a spirit of revolution among the youth.

Along with Rajguru and Chandra Shekhar Azad, Singh made an attempt to assassinate the superintendent of police, James A. Scott, believed to be responsible for the *lathi* blows given to Lala Lajpat Rai when he was leading a black flag demonstration against the all-White Simon Commission. Instead, the trio killed Saunders, assistant superintendent of police. Singh escaped to Calcutta thereafter.

In 1929, Singh and B.K. Dutt threw a bomb into the Central Legislative Assembly in Delhi to protest against the autocratic alien rule. Bhagat Singh was later arrested and hanged to death in Lahore Central Jail on 23 March 1931.

## DID YOU KNOW?

Bhagat Singh visited Jallianwala Bagh on the day following the massacre and collected a packetful of blood-soaked soil, which he kept at his home.

## TILAK, BAL GANGADHAR (1856–1920)

Bal Gangadhar Tilak, also known as Lokmanya, was a scholar, mathematician, philosopher and nationalist, who helped lay the foundation for India's independence. Born in Ratnagiri, he began his political career as a moderate but became an extremist at the beginning of the 20th century. He was a pioneer in the use of religious orthodoxy as a method of mass contact through his organization of the Ganapati festival (1893).

Tilak was also the first to organize the Shivaji festival (1895). He was a prominent member of the Deccan Education Society and helped establish the New English School, which later became Fergusson College. He was the editor of two newspapers—*Kesari* in Marathi and *Mahratta* in English. He founded the Home Rule League in April 1916 and declared: 'Swaraj is my birthright and I will have it.' He was imprisoned by the British for his nationalist activities and died in 1920.

## DID YOU KNOW?

◆ After earning his university degree, Tilak studied law but then decided to teach mathematics in a private school in Poona (now Pune). The school became the basis for his political career. He developed the school into a university college after founding the Deccan Education Society (1884), which aimed at educating the masses, especially in the English language.

◆ In tribute, Mahatma Gandhi called him the 'Maker of Modern India' and Jawaharlal Nehru described him as the 'Father of the Indian Revolution'.

## SOME FAMOUS THINKERS

### ARISTOTLE (384 BC–322 BC)

Aristotle, a follower of Plato, was one of the greatest Greek philosophers of all time. Born in 384 BC in Stagaria, he joined Plato's Academy in Athens and stayed there for twenty years. Aristotle became a teacher in a school in Asia Minor, and was later invited by the king of Macedonia to teach his son, Alexander the Great.

Aristotle made a significant contribution to the field of knowledge by classifying the various disciplines of study into broad, distinct branches like philosophy, rhetoric, poetics, physics, psychology, metaphysics, logic and others. His *Poetics* is a masterpiece of literature that particularly lays out the framework of modern drama. He died in 322 BC on the island of Euboea.

### ERASMUS (1466–1536)

Desiderius Erasmus was a celebrated humanist, thinker, scholar, and a leading figure of the European Renaissance. Born in 1466 in Holland, he wrote extensively on theology, religious issues, education and philosophy. Erasmus' publication of the Greek New Testament is a turning point in the perception of Christianity. Some of his best works are *Enchiridion militis Christiani* (1503) and *The Praise of Folly* (1509). Though Erasmus wanted to reform Christianity, he did not agree with the idea of a divided church.

### HIPPOCRATES (460 BC–377 BC)

Hippocrates, himself a physician, is regarded as the father of medicine. He has been revered for his ethical standards in medical practice, mainly for the Hippocratic Oath, though it is suspected that he did not write it. He is known for his writings and his scholarship. He was not only a reputed practitioner of medicine during his time, but also an acclaimed teacher. Hippocrates is known to be the first physician of the world. He was a great writer and it is believed that during the 3rd or 2nd century BC, some of the works were sent to the great library at Alexandria in Egypt. These were *Ancient Medicine*, *Regimen in Acute Diseases*, *Wounds of the Head*, *Aphorisms*, and *Epidemics*. He died at Larissa, Thessaly, in 377 BC.

## HOBBES, THOMAS (1588–1679)

Thomas Hobbes was an English philosopher, scientist and historian, best known for his political philosophy. Born on 5 April 1588, he graduated from Oxford University in 1608. He was drawn to mathematics before he engaged himself with the study of politics. Hobbes' first important work was his translation of Thucydides' *History of the Peloponnesian War* in 1629. In his masterpiece *Leviathan*, he laid out the principle of an ideal state in which all citizens must agree to a common law and live with equality. He also published translations of Homer's *Odyssey* and *Iliad* in 1675. He passed away in Derbyshire on 4 December 1679.

## PETRARCH (1304–1374)

Petrarch was an Italian scholar, poet and humanist whose poems contributed to the Renaissance flowering of lyric poetry. Born Francesco Petrarca in 1304, he was regarded as the greatest scholar of his age. While he was studying classical literature, he touched upon a connection between Christianity and ancient Greek and Roman writings. The most celebrated of all Petrarch's writings is his series of poems, *Rime,* dedicated to his idealized beloved Laura. Through the 317 love poems of the *Canzonniere*, Petrarch developed the sonnet form. Some of his other works include *Africa* and *My Secret*. He died in Arqua in Italy on 19 July 1374.

## PLATO (428 BC–348 BC)

Plato was an ancient Greek philosopher, the second of the great trio which included Socrates, Plato and Aristotle, who laid the philosophical foundations of Western culture. He was born in an aristocratic family of Athens, and grew up to become an ardent follower of Socrates. After his mentor's death in 387 BC, Plato opened his Academy at Athens. The precursor to the modern system of colleges and universities, the Plato Academy focused on mathematics, law, science and philosophy. Plato's philosophy had a deep impact on thinkers down the ages. His book on governance and the system of justice, *The Republic*, has attained the status of a classic. Plato passed away in Athens in 348 BC.

## ROUSSEAU, JEAN-JACQUES (1712–1778)

Swiss-born philosopher, writer and political theorist, Rousseau's treatises and novels inspired the leaders of the French Revolution. His writings on politics, literature, society and education had a deep impact on philosophers and thinkers in later years. Born in 1712 in Geneva, he fled to Italy, then France at an early age. He realized that the Parisian society only served the privileges of the aristocrats and had no consideration for the welfare of the common man.

Rousseau explained the origins of the government in a book called *The Social Contract* (1762). It stated that no law is fixed and compulsory unless accepted by the people. This idea played a pivotal role in the French Revolution about thirty years later. He died in Ermenonville, France, in 1778.

## SOCRATES (470 BC–399 BC)

Socrates was a Greek philosopher whose way of life, character and thought exerted a profound influence on ancient and modern philosophy. Born in Athens in 470 BC, he studied sculpture but later gave it up in pursuit of the 'truth'. Socrates urged people to search for truth in the inner core of one's conscience. According to him, the best way of learning was by knowing oneself properly.

Socrates never documented his teachings in writing. It was passed down from generation to generation through the words of his disciples, Plato and Aristotle. The details of his life are also preserved in *Memorablia*, a work by the historian Xenophon.

Socrates was tried by the court of Athens and convicted of the false charges of 'neglect of the gods' and 'corruption of the young' He was put to death by being made to drink hemlock.

## VOLTAIRE (1694–1778)

Acclaimed historian, essayist, playwright, storyteller, poet, philosopher and social reformer, Voltaire was born François-Marie Arouet in 1694. He is best remembered for championing of human rights. He challenged organized religion, and questioned royal authorities through stark satirical verses that he write from the age of sixteen. His *Philosophical Letters* was a path-breaking work in the field of thought. *Candide*, a comic novel, was Voltaire's most popular composition. Voltaire died on 30 May 1778.

## MAJOR KINGS AND QUEENS OF INDIA

### AIBAK QUTB-UD-DIN (d. 1210)

Qutb-ud-din Aibak was the founder of the Slave Dynasty. In his childhood, he was sold as a slave and raised at Nishapur. Muhammad Ghori bought him and put him in charge of the royal stables. Eventually Aibak was elevated to military command and, in 1193, given charge of strengthening the conquests in north-west India. When Ghori was assassinated, Qutb-ud-din was his logical successor but he faced opposition since he was still a slave. He married the daughter of Taj-ud-Din Yildiz of Ghazni, another logical successor of Ghori and, through other judiciously arranged alliances, consolidated his rule. Surviving inscriptions describe Qutb as *malik* ('king'). He died in 1210 owing to injuries received while playing polo.

### AJATASHATRU (d. 461 BC)

Ajatashatru was one of the early kings of Magadha who reigned from 492 to 462 BC (during Buddha's time). Born to King Bimbisara of Magadha (now Bihar), he eventually murdered his father to become the king. During his reign, he firmly established the predominance of the Magadhan empire in Eastern India. However, years of war and violence tormented him and he began searching for peace and truth. This search ultimately brought him closer to Buddha. Deeply influenced by Buddha's teachings, Ajatashatru subsequently built stupas all over the capital and renovated monasteries. Later, he organized the first Buddhist Council at Rajagriha. He is chiefly remembered as the great conqueror who laid the foundations of the future Magadhan empire, which included almost the whole of India, and also as one of the greatest patrons of Buddhism.

### AKBAR (1542–1605)

Jalaluddin Muhammad, popularly known as Akbar, was one of the greatest Mughal emperors of India. He reigned from 1556 to 1605 and extended the Mughal empire over most of the Indian subcontinent. Born in Umarkot in 1542 to Mughal emperor Humayun, he became the governor of the Punjab in 1556. In the same year, under the guardianship of Bairam Khan, he won the Second Battle of Panipat against Hemu, the Hindu general of an Afghan claimant, who had proclaimed himself independent. To preserve the unity of his empire, Akbar adopted certain measures including matrimonial alliances that won the loyalty of the non-Muslim populations of his region. He reformed and strengthened his administration and also centralized his financial system. He reorganized tax collection processes and introduced the *mansabdari* system, where ranks were bestowed on nobles who were given control over an area of land.

Although Akbar never renounced Islam, he was tolerant towards other religions. He took an active interest in organizing the *ibadat khana* (prayer hall for worship) where representatives of all religions engaged in discussions. In the late 16th century, he formulated a religious movement called Din-i Ilahi, which never really became popular. A patron of the arts and architecture, he built numerous monuments, including the famed Fatehpur Sikri. After his death in 1605, he was succeeded by his son Jahangir.

## DID YOU KNOW?

Akbar's court had *navratnas* ('nine jewels'), a group of nine extraordinary people:

- ◇ Abul Fazl (Akbar's chief advisor and author of *Akbarnama*)
- ◇ Faizi (Akbar's poet laureate)
- ◇ Mian Tansen (Hindu singer who converted to Islam)
- ◇ Birbal (a noble man known for his wit)
- ◇ Raja Todar Mal (Akbar's finance minister)
- ◇ Raja Man Singh (Akbar's trusted general)
- ◇ Abdul Rahim Khan-I-Khana (nobleman and renowned poet)
- ◇ Fakir Aziao-Din (mystic and advisor)
- ◇ Mullah Do Piaza (advisor)

## ALI HYDER (1722–1782)

Hyder Ali, a Muslim ruler of Mysore, played an important role in the wars in southern India in the mid-18th century. Born in 1722, he studied military tactics and became the ruler of Mysore in 1761. In 1766, the Marathas, the Nizam of Hyderabad, and the British entered into a triple alliance against Hyder but he defeated them. In 1780, he warred on the Carnatic, destroyed a British detachment of 2,800 men, and seized Arcot. The British defeated him three times successively in 1781. After the British fleet captured Nagappattinam, Hyder, who was then on his deathbed, urged his son Tipu Sultan to make peace with the British. Tipu Sultan did so and later assumed the title of Sultan of Mysore.

## ASHOKA (d. 283 BC)

Ashoka, also known as Devanampriya Priyadarshi ('Beloved of the Gods'), was the last great emperor of the Mauryan dynasty. His enthusiastic patronage of Buddhism during his reign consolidated its expansion throughout India. Among the events of Ashoka's reign, the one most frequently referred to by modern historians has been his conversion to Buddhism. This was linked to the famous military campaign in Kalinga. Around 260 BC, Ashoka campaigned against the Kalingans and defeated them. The destruction caused by the war filled the king with remorse and, in a dramatic turnaround, it compelled him to convert to Buddhism. He renounced armed conquest and adopted a policy that he called *dhamma* (a code of conduct for a righteous life). To gain wide publicity for his teachings and his work, Ashoka made them known by means of oral announcements and engravings on rocks and pillars. These inscriptions—rock edicts and pillar edicts (such as the Sarnath pillar, the Lion Capital of which has become India's national emblem)—contain statements about his thoughts and actions and provide information on his life and acts.

### DID YOU KNOW?

It is said that on his birth, Ashoka's mother exclaimed, 'I am now without sorrow.' It is from her statement that the child is believed to have got his name—Ashoka, meaning 'without sorrow'.

## AURANGZEB (1618-1707)

Aurangzeb, son of the Mughal emperor Shah Jahan, was the last great ruler of the Mughal dynasty. Born Muhi-ud-Din Muhammad in 1618, he reigned from 1658 to 1707. Under him, the Mughal empire reached its greatest extent, although it was his policies that ironically led to its dissolution.

Until 1680, he consolidated his power in northern India by safeguarding his domain from the Persians and the Central Asian Turks. After 1680, his reign underwent a change in both attitude and policy. The first clear sign of his religious non-tolerance had been the reimposition of jaziya (religious tax) on non-Muslims in 1679. This tax had been abolished by Akbar. Aurangzeb strictly imposed Islam during his rule. Much of the second half of his reign was spent in subduing rebellions in south India, particularly the Rajput revolt of 1680–81.

Aurangzeb's wars exhausted the imperial treasury, and he began to lose control of northern India. The most unfortunate aspect of his reign was his severe intolerance of other religions, mainly Hinduism. Aurangzeb maintained the empire for nearly half a century, but the Maratha campaign drained the resources, and the rebellion of the Sikhs and Jats weakened the empire. The failure of his successors to cope with the problems he had created led to the downfall of the Mughal empire. He died in 1707.

## DID YOU KNOW?

It is believed that Aurangzeb knitted *haj* caps and copied out the Quran all his life.

### BABUR (1483–1530)

Babur, the founder of the Mughal dynasty, was the emperor of India from 1526 to 1530. He was a descendent of the Mongol Timur or Tamerlane on his father's side and Changez Khan on his mother's. Born in Ferghana in 1483, his original name was Zahir-ud-Din Muhammad. He was an acclaimed military commander, a gifted poet and diarist, a statesman, and an adventurer. When Babur made his first raid into India in 1519, the Punjab was part of the dominions of Sultan Ibrahim Lodi of Delhi. In the First Battle of Panipat in 1526, he killed Lodi, marking a turning point in the history of medieval India. It helped lay the foundation of the Mughal dynasty, which ruled India for over 300 years.

The two major battles that helped him expand his kingdom were the Battle of Khanua with Rana Sanga and the Battle of Ghaghra against the allied Afghans of Bihar and Bengal. At the time of his death in 1530, his dominions were secure from Kandahar to the borders of Bengal, with the southern limit marked by the Rajput desert and the forts of Ranthambhor, Gwalior, and Chanderi. Babur was a gifted poet as well as a lover of nature, and constructed numerous gardens, including the Ram Bagh at Agra. His prose memoir, the *Babur-Nameh*, has been widely acclaimed.

## DID YOU KNOW?

In 1530, when Humayun fell ill, Babur is said to have offered his life to God in exchange for Humayun's, walking seven times around the bed to complete the vow. Humayun recovered and Babur's health declined. Babur died the same year.

## BAHADUR SHAH II (1775–1862)

Bahadur Shah Zafar was the last Mughal emperor of India, who reigned from 1837 to 1858. Born to Akbar Shah II in 1775, he was a poet, musician and calligrapher, more an artist than a political leader. He wrote several ghazals in Urdu under the pen name Zafar meaning 'victory'. For most of his reign, he remained a puppet king under the British, without real authority. During the First War of Independence in 1857, he was forced to accept nominal leadership of the revolt. At the age of eighty-two for fear of his life, Bahadur Shah acquiesced. After the rebellion was put down by the British, he was banished to Burma with his family. He died in exile on 7 November 1862. His death marked the end of more than three centuries of Mughal rule in India.

## BIMBISARA (558 BC–491 BC)

Bimbisara was the king of Magadha with his capital at Rajagriha or Rajgir. Born in 558 BC, he was crowned at the age of fifteen, and reigned for fifty-two years. His expansion of the kingdom, especially his annexation of the kingdom of Anga to the east, is considered to have laid the foundations for the later expansion of the Mauryan empire. He used marriage alliances to strengthen his position. He is also known for his cultural achievements and was a great disciple of Gautama Buddha. Bimbisara built the city of Rajagriha. He was killed by his son Ajatashatru, who ascended the throne in 492 BC.

## BINDUSARA (320 BC–272 BC)

Bindusara was the second Mauryan emperor. He succeeded his father Chandragupta Maurya around 297 BC, reigning till 273 BC. Greek sources refer to him as Amitrochates, the Greek equivalent of the Sanskrit word *amitraghata* meaning 'destroyer of foes'. During his reign, he consolidated his father's territories and extended his empire considerably till what is now Karnataka. At the time of Bindusara's death in 272 BC, a large part of the subcontinent had come under the Mauryas. One territory that remained hostile, possibly interfering with Mauryan commerce with the peninsula, was Kalinga. Its conquest was left to his son Ashoka. In foreign affairs, Bindusara maintained friendly relations with the Hellenistic West, established by his father and received as an ambassador, a Greek named Deimachos, in his court.

## BALBAN (1200–1287)

Ghiyas-ud-Din Balban was an important ruler of the Slave Dynasty of the Delhi Sultanate. He was one of the forty Turkish slaves of Iltutmish who descended from the Ilbari tribe of Turkestan. He became the sultan of Delhi in 1266 and ruled for almost twenty-two years. His career was one of struggle against internal troubles and external danger. He had, therefore, no opportunity to launch conquests to expand the limits of his dominions. He organized a separate department of the army called *Diwan-i-Arz* and reform military administration. He worked to restore the glory of the Delhi Sultanate. He organized his court on the model of the Old Persian kings and introduced Persian ceremonies such as *saijdah* (kissing the monarch's feet) and *paibos* (prostration). He also introduced the Persian Nauroz ceremony. He gave shelter to many exiled princes from Central Asia. He died in 1287.

## DID YOU KNOW?

◇ Balban's court was an austere assembly where jest and laughter were seldom heard.

◇ Famous poet Amir Khusrau, nicknamed 'Parrot of India', was a contemporary of Balban.

## CHANDRAGUPTA II [VIKRAMADITYA]

Chandragupta II was a powerful Gupta emperor, who ruled northern India from AD 375 to AD 415. He was the son of Samudragupta and grandson of Chandragupta I. During his reign, he carried on the policy of world conquest pursued by his predecessors. Although he took the title of Vikramaditya ('Sun of Valour'), his reign is associated more with cultural and intellectual achievements than with military campaigns. He encouraged education. The famous astronomer Varahamihira and the great Sanskrit poet and dramatist Kalidasa were part of his court. The Chinese Buddhist pilgrim Fa Hien, who spent six years in India during Vikramaditya's reign, praised his governance and benevolence.

## CHAUHAN, PRITHVIRAJ (c. 1149–1192)

Prithviraj Chauhan was a powerful Chauhan king of Delhi and Ajmer. In AD 1177, at the age of eleven, Prithviraj ascended the throne of a kingdom that extended from Thanesar in the north to parts of Mewar in the south. After Muhammad Ghori aquired Tabarhindh, a part of Prithviraj's kingdom, they clashed in the Battle of Terrain in 1191. Prithviraj completely crushed Ghori's troops. To avenge this defeat, Ghori organized his army and challenged Prithviraj in the Second Battle of Terrain in 1192. In this battle, Prithviraj was captured and killed.

### DID YOU KNOW?

Though Prithviraj was the rival of King Jaichand, the ruler of Kannauj, he fell in love with Jaichand's daughter, Sanyogita. Their swayamvara is epitomized in Chand Bardoi's epic *Prithviraj Rasau*.

## CHOLA I, RAJENDRA

Rajendra Chola was an able king of the Chola dynasty. He ruled jointly with his father Rajaraja I for two years, succeeding him in 1014. He made extensive overseas conquests, overran the Deccan and, in 1023, sent an expedition to the north that penetrated up to the Ganges river and brought its water to the new capital, Gangaikondacolapuram. He defeated Mahipala I of Bengal and vanquished the Chalukya king of the Deccan plateau.

## HARSHAVARDHANA (AD 590–AD 647)

Harshavardhana was the ruler of a large empire in northern India from AD 606 to 647. He ascended the throne of Thanesar and Kannauj after the death of his brother, Rajyavardhana. By 612, Harsha had consolidated his kingdom in northern India. His reign marked a transition from the ancient to the medieval period, when regional powers continually struggled for control.

Harsha was well known for his religious tolerance, able administration and diplomatic relations. He held quinquennial assemblies at the confluence of the Ganges and the Yamuna rivers at Prayag, at which he distributed the treasures that he had accumulated in the previous four years. The famous Chinese traveller, Hiuen Tsang, visited India during his reign. A poet himself, Harsha composed three Sanskrit works: *Nagananda*, *Ratnavali*, and *Priyadarsika*. A lively narrative of his life comes from *Harshacharita*, a biography written by Banabhatta.

## HUMAYUN (1508–1556)

Humayun, born Nasin al-Din Muhammad, was the second Mughal emperor of India. Born in 1508 to Babur, Humayun ruled from 1530 to 1540 and again from 1555 to 1556. Humayun inherited an empire that was ravaged by several conflicts. When Sher Shah Suri defeated Humayun at Chausa in 1539 and at Kannauj in 1540, Humayun became a homeless wanderer seeking support first in Sindh, then in Marwar, and then in Sindh again. His son Akbar was born there in 1542.

Reaching Iran in 1544, Humayun was granted military aid by Shah Tahmasp and went on to conquer Kandahar (1545) and to seize Kabul three times, the last being in 1550. Taking advantage of civil wars among Sher Shah's descendants, Humayun captured Lahore (now in Pakistan) in February 1555. After defeating Sikandar Suri, the rebel Afghan governor of the Punjab, Humayun recovered Delhi and Agra. Humayun died accidentally while descending the steps of a library in 1556.

## DID YOU KNOW?

Humayun was passionately devoted to the study of astronomy. He also loved painting and wrote Persian poetry.

## ILTUTMISH (d. 1236)

Iltutmish was the third and greatest sultan of the Slave Dynasty of the Delhi Sultanate. Born into the tribal community of Ilbari in Turkestan, he was sold into slavery to Qutb-ud-din Aibak, whom he succeeded in 1211. By dint of his merit, he was made the governor of Badaun and married to a daughter of Qutb-ud-din. After his accession, he strengthened and expanded the Muslim empire in northern India and moved the capital to Delhi. He defeated Taj-ud-Din Yildiz, the ruler of Ghazni. He built a strong administrative system and protected his empire against the ravages of Mongol invasions during his reign.

The *Adab-Muluk* (Conduct of Kings), an Indo-Muslim treatise on the art of government and warfare, was written for Iltutmish. Tolerant towards Hindus, Iltutmish built waterworks, mosques, and amenities in Delhi to make it an efficient seat of government. Iltutmish's eldest son died early and his other sons were incompetent. He provided excellent education to his daughter Raziya and nominated her as his heiress.

## DID YOU KNOW?

Though Iltutmish was the real consolidator of Muslim power in India, he commenced his career as a *sari-jandar* (head of the royal bodyguards) and controlled the region of Badaun. Iltutmish received the *mansur* (letter of investiture), which gave him legal status, from the Abbasid Caliph in 1229.

## JAHANGIR (1569–1627)

Jahangir, born Prince Salim at Fatehpur Sikri, was the Mughal emperor who ruled India from 1605 to 1627. The highlight of his reign was his victory over the Rajputs of Mewar, who had for long defied the might of the Mughals. He successfully continued the campaigns against Ahmadnagar, and achieved partial success when his son Shah Jahan captured Ahmadnagar in 1616. Another notable military success of Jahangir's reign was the capture of the fortress of Kangra in Punjab. Jahangir highly valued the opinions of his Persian wife Nur Jahan. Jahangir died while travelling from Kashmir to Lahore.

## DID YOU KNOW?

After his ascension, Jahangir tried to win the hearts of the people through various measures. He promulgated twelve edicts, which were ordered to be observed as rules of conduct in his kingdom, and set up the famous Chain of Justice at Agra.

## KANISHKA (d. AD 127)

Kanishka was the greatest king of the Kushan dynasty that ruled over the northern part of the Indian subcontinent, Afghanistan, and possibly areas of Central Asia, north of Kashmir. He is, however, chiefly remembered as a great patron of Buddhism and noted for having convened the fourth great Buddhist council in Kashmir. His accession is estimated to have occured between 78 BC and 144 BC, and his reign is believed to have lasted for twenty-three years. The year 78 BC marks the beginning of the Saka era, a system of dating that Kaniska might have initiated. During his reign, contacts with the Roman empire via the Silk Route led to significant increase in trade and exchange of ideas. Perhaps the most remarkable example of the fusion of Eastern and Western influences in his reign was the Gandhara School of Art, in which classical Greco-Roman lines are seen in images of the Buddha.

## KHALJI, ALA-UD-DIN (d. 1316)

Ala-ud-din Khalji, born Ali Gursap, was the second and the most powerful ruler of the Khalji dynasty of the Delhi Sultanate. He ascended the throne in 1296 and ruled till 1316. During his rule, he captured Ranthambhore (1301) and Chittor (1303), conquered Mandu (1305), and annexed the wealthy Hindu kingdom of Devagiri. He also repelled Mongol raids. Apart from his conquests, he is famous for the various reforms he made in military and economic fields, especially the market policy.

## DID YOU KNOW?

The Neelkanth Mahadev Temple in Jalore in Rajasthan is an ancient temple. According to a general belief, when Ala-ud-din Khalji's army attacked Jalore, they tried to destroy the *shivlinga* there but were attacked by black bees. Filled with terror , the soldiers fled. Khalji pleaded for Lord Shiva's mercy and promised to build a temple if he was forgiven. His prayers were answered. Khalji kept his promise and built the Neelkanth Mahadev Temple there.

## LODI, IBRAHIM (d. 1526 BC)

Ibrahim Lodi of the Lodi dynasty was the last Afghan sultan of Delhi. Son of Sikandar Lodi, he ascended the throne in 1517 after his father's death, and immediately faced disputes between the royal family and Afghan nobles. A noble, Daulat Khan Lodi, governor of the Punjab, invited Babur to invade India. Babur defeated Ibrahim in the First Battle of Panipat in 1526. This brought about the final collapse of the decadent Delhi Sultanate and led to the founding of the Mughal empire in India. Ibrahim Lodi died on 21 April 1526.

## MAHMUD OF GHAZNI (997–1030)

Mahmud of Ghazni is often referred to as the founder of Islamic rule in India. A sultan of the kingdom of Ghazni, a principality in Afghanistan, he reigned from 998 to 1030. He is mostly remembered for the raids he conducted in India while he was in power. He invaded India seventeen times between 1001 and 1025. Between 1009 and 1026, he conquered Multan, Thanesar, Kanauj, and Mathura and plundered the famous Somnath temple. The raids of Indian towns were largely for plunder; he wanted to destroy Hindu temples and loot the country's wealth to replenish the Ghazni treasury. His conquest of northern India helped the exchange of trade and ideas between the Indian subcontinent and the Muslim world.

The Puffin Factfinder

## DID YOU KNOW?

◇ Mahmud conquered Afghanistan and Persia, obtained the title *Yamin-al-Daula* ('Right Hand of the State') from the Caliph. He also exacted tribute from local rulers in seventeen raids across India.

◇ Mahmud used some of his wealth to support Al-Biruni, the master geographer who compiled a brilliant account of medieval India.

### MAURYA, CHANDRAGUPTA (340 BC–298 BC)

Chandragupta Maurya, founder of the Mauryan dynasty, succeeded to the Nanda throne in 321 BC. He was the first emperor to unify most of India under one central administration. In Greek and Latin accounts, Chandragupta is known as Sandrokuptos, Sandrokottos or Androcottus. Some of his most memorable achievements include his victory over Alexander's Macedonian Satrapies, his conquest of the Nanda empire, his victory over Seleucus Nicator, and the establishment of centralized rule across southern Asia.

Ranging from the Himalayas and the Kabul valley (in modern Afghanistan) to the southern tip of India, Chandragupta's Indian empire was one of history's most extensive. Its continuation for at least two generations, is attributable in part to his minister Chanakya and his style of politics, immortalized in the text *Arthashastra*.

## DID YOU KNOW?

◇ According to the Jaina tradition (*parisistaparvan*), Chandragupta embraced Jainism towards the end of his life, and stepped down from the throne in favour of his son Bindusara.

◇ Accompanied by Bhadrabahu and several other Jaina monks, he is said to have gone to Shravanabelagola near Mysore, where he starved himself to death in the approved Jaina fashion (*sallekhana*).

### GHORI, MUHAMMAD (d. 1206)

Muhammad of Ghur or Shihab-ud-Din Muhammad Ghori was the Ghurid conqueror of the north Indian plains and one of the founders of Muslim rule in India. Ghori invaded India for the first time in AD 1175 and after conquering Multan and Punjab, he advanced towards Delhi. The Rajput chiefs of northern India, headed by Prithviraj Chauhan, defeated him in the First Battle of Terrain in AD 1191. After a year, Ghori returned to avenge his defeat and a furious battle was fought again in Terrain in 1192 when the Rajputs were defeated and Prithviraj captured and put to death. The second battle, however, proved to be decisive and laid the foundations of Muslim rule in northern India.

## NANA SAHIB (1820–1859)

Nana Sahib, or Dhondu Pant, was an active leader in the First War of Indian Independence in 1857. In 1827, Baji Rao II, the last Maratha peshwa prince, adopted him and educated him as a Hindu nobleman. On the death of the exiled Baji Rao in 1852, he inherited Baji Rao's home and private property. The British, however, refused his claim on Baji Rao II's pension and, instigated by the sepoys' threats, Nana Sahib joined the rebellion of the sepoy battalions at Cawnpore (Kanpur) in June 1857. He had written to Sir Hugh Wheeler, commander of British forces at Cawnpore, warning him of the attack. He was declared peshwa in July 1857 by Tantia Tope and his followers, after the capture of Gwalior. Nana Sahib lacked knowledge of military tactics and was defeated by General Henry Havelock and, in 1857, by Sir Colin Campbell. In 1859, Nana Sahib was made to take refuge in the hills of Nepal, where he is believed to have died.

## RANI LAKSHMIBAI (1835–1858)

Rani Lakshmibai or Rani of Jhansi, born Manikarnika, has become a legend for fighting the British valiantly during the First War of Indian Independence in 1857. Growing up in the household of Peshwa Baji Rao II, she trained in martial arts and sword fighting. She was married to Maharaja Gangadhar Rao of Jhansi and the couple in 1851 had adopted a son, Damodar Rao.

When Lord Dalhousie annexed Jhansi, declining to recognize their adopted son as the heir (under the Doctrine of Lapse), Lakshmibai refused to cede Jhansi. Shortly after the War began, she was proclaimed the regent and ruled on behalf of the minor heir. She took charge of the rebels in Bundelkhand. In 1858, the British forces surrounded the fort of Jhansi, but Lakshmibai did not surrender. She escaped to Gwalior with another rebel leader Tantia Tope. She was killed in battle on 16 June 1858. General Sir Hugh Rose called her 'the best and the bravest' of all the rebel leaders.

## DID YOU KNOW?

Badal, was the name of Rani Lakshmibai's favourite horse.

### RAYA, KRISHNA DEVA (d. 1529)

Krishna Deva Raya was the greatest ruler of the Vijayanagar empire. During his reign (1509–1529), the kingdom became more powerful than ever because of internal consolidation. He defeated the Bahmani forces (who by this time were virtually separated into five states), captured Raichur fort, subdued both Gulbarga and Bidar and restored the imprisoned Bahmani sultan to his throne in 1512. During most of his reign, Krishna Deva maintained a mutually advantageous relationship with the increasingly powerful Portuguese powers. Krishna Deva Raya was a scholar and patron of Telugu and Sanskrit literature. Around 1524, Krishna Deva abdicated the throne in favour of his son.

### SHAH JAHAN (1592–1666)

Born in 1592, Shah Jahan was the son of Mughal emperor Jahangir. After Jahangir's death in 1627, Shah Jahan proclaimed himself emperor with the support of Asaf Khan and Nur Jahan. He ruled India from 1628 to 1658. His reign is remembered for his continuous success against the Deccan states. By 1636, Ahmadnagar was annexed and Golconda and Bijapur were forced to become his territories. Shah Jahan transferred his capital from Agra to Delhi in 1648, creating the new city of Shahjahanabad. He had a strong passion for architecture.

At his first capital, Agra, he had built two great mosques, Moti Masjid and Jami Masjid. He built the Taj Mahal in memory of his wife Mumtaz Mahal. At Delhi, he built the fortress-palace complex called the Red Fort. His reign was also a period of great literary activity, painting and calligraphy.

In 1657, Shah Jahan fell ill. This triggered a struggle for succession among his four sons. The victor, Aurangzeb, declared himself emperor in 1658 and confined Shah Jahan in the fort at Agra until his death in 1666.

### SHIVAJI (1627/1630–1680)

Shivaji, popularly known as Chhatrapati Shri Shivaji Maharaj, was the founder of the Maratha kingdom in India. Born to Shahji, a *jagirdar* in Shivner, Shivaji descended from a line of prominent nobles. At that time India was under strict Muslim dominance. Shivaji found this oppresive. He trained a group of followers in guerilla tactics and began to seize the weaker Bijapur outposts around 1655. His righteousness won him the support of the common man. In 1659, the Sultan of Bijapur sent an army of 20,000 under Afzal Khan to attack him. Shivaji managed to lure Afzal Khan to a meeting, where he killed the general with steel claws. Overnight, Shivaji had become a formidable warlord. He was the first Indian ruler in modern times to understand the importance of naval power, for trade as well as for defence. In 1674, Shivaji ascended the throne as an independent sovereign. He ruled for six years, through a cabinet of eight ministers known as the *ashtapradhan*. Shivaji died after an illness in 1680.

## DID YOU KNOW?

◇ After Shivaji defeated Aurangzeb's viceroy, the Muslim emperor, alarmed by his growing strength, launched an attack against him. Soon, Shivaji was sent to Agra and placed under house arrest. He fled from the palace hidden in a basket of fruits.

◇ On 6 June 1674, Shivaji formally crowned himself king at Raigarh with great pomp, and assumed the title of Chhatrapati ('Lord of the Umbrella' or 'King of Kings').

### SINGH, RANJIT (1780–1839)

Ranjit Singh, popularly known as the Lion of the Punjab, was the founder of the Sikh kingdom of Punjab. Ranjit Singh was the only child of Maha Singh, on whose death in 1792 he became the chief of the Shukerchakia Sikhs. His inheritance included Gujranwala and the surrounding villages, now in Pakistan. In the early 1800s, he seized Lahore and Amritsar but his later expeditions towards the east were resisted by the British, with whom he signed the Treaty of Amritsar in 1809, confirming the Sutlej river as the eastern boundary of his territories. By 1820, he had consolidated his rule over all of Punjab between the Sutlej and the Indus rivers. Shortly after annexing Ladakh, Ranjit Singh fell ill and died in Lahore in 1839.

### SIRAJ-UD-DAULAH (1729–1757)

Mirza Mohammad Siraj-ud-Daulah was the last independent Nawab of Bengal, Bihar, and Orissa (now Odisha). His defeat at Plassey marked the end of the last independent state in India, introducing the British East India Company's rule over Bengal.

When Nawab Ali Vardi Khan died without a male heir in 1756, Siraj was made the next nawab. He was against the political and military presence of the British in Bengal since he was aware of the British interest in colonization. He was unhappy with the British for having abused the trade privileges granted to them by the Mughal ruler and also the fortification around Fort William in Calcutta without his approval. When the British did not stop further enhancement of military preparedness at Fort William, Siraj captured Calcutta from the British in June 1756. This resulted in the Black Hole tragedy, in which many English captives suffocated to death in a jail cell. Siraj fought the British troops led by Robert Clive at the Battle of Plassey in 1757. Betrayed by his former army chief Mir Jafar, Siraj lost the battle and had to flee.

## SULTAN, RAZIYA (1205–1240)

Raziya Sultan, daughter of Iltutmish, was the queen of the Slave Dynasty of the Delhi Sultanate. She reigned from 1236 to 1240. When Raziya came into power, she had a tough task ahead as some of the nobles found it difficult to accept a woman as their sultan. Using tact and diplomacy, she overpowered her enemies. She marched in person against them, discarded the veil and conducted the affairs of her government with great efficiency, in the open darbar clad in male attire. During her reign, she elevated the Abyssinian slave Jalal-ud-din Yaqut to the post of master of the stables and that offended the Turkish nobles.

When Ikhtiyar-ud-din Altuniya, the governor of Sirhind, revolted, she tried to suppress the revolt but was defeated and imprisoned. While she was away, her brother Muiz-ud-din Bahram was proclaimed sultan. To escape the critical situation, she married Altuniya and marched back to Delhi with him. On the way, she was deserted by Altuniya's followers, defeated by Muiz-ud-din Bahram and put to death, along with her husband.

## DID YOU KNOW?

Raziya did not like to be addressed as sultana because it meant 'wife or mistress of a sultan'. She preferred the title 'sultan'.

## SULTAN TIPU (1750–1799)

Tipu Sultan, also known as the Tiger of Mysore, ruled Mysore from 1782 to 1799. Born to Hyder Ali in Devanhalli, he learnt military tactics from the

French officers employed by his father. During the Second Mysore War, he defeated Colonel John Brathwaite and succeeded his father as the ruler of Mysore in 1782. In 1784, he made peace with the British but then, in 1789, he provoked British invasion by attacking their ally, the king of Travancore. His defeat in the Third Anglo-Mysore War in 1792 forced him to sign the Treaty of Seringapatnam, by which he lost half his dominions. Burning with revenge, he decided to win back his lost territories and refused to accept the Subsidiary Alliance. This led to the Fourth Anglo-Mysore War in 1799. Tipu died defending Seringapatnam. Tipu was an able general and, despite being a Muslim, he was very tolerant towards his Hindu subjects.

## DID YOU KNOW?

Tipu Sultan had a fascination for tigers. Tiger symbols and motifs adorned most of his possessions—from his guns to the uniforms of his guards. 'Tipu's Tiger', a mechanical life-sized beast seized from Srirangapatnam in 1799, has been a popular attraction since the late 1800s, when it was first displayed in the East India Company's museum in London.

### SURI, SHER SHAH (1486–1545)

Sher Shah Suri was one of the most prominent rulers of the Sur dynasty. He was the emperor of north India from 1540 to1545. Born Farid Khan, he began his life in a humble way and rose to prominence by dint of personal merit. He later worked for the Mughal king of Bihar, who rewarded him for bravery with the title of Sher Khan.

After he defeated an army in Bengal, he took over as the ruler of Bihar. At the Battle of Chausa on 26 June 1539, he defeated the Mughal emperor Humayun. In 1540, he again crushed Humayun at Kannauj and drove his foes from Bengal, Bihar and the Punjab. Intent on expanding the sultanate of Delhi, he captured Gwalior and Malwa but was killed during the siege of Kalinjar in 1545.

Sher Shah was the architect of a brilliant administrative system. His brief reign of five years was marked by innovative changes in every branch of administration and a carefully planned revenue system. He built many roads, including the Grand Trunk Road, and several inns along these roads. His tomb at Sasaram is one of the most magnificent in India.

## TUGHLAQ, FIRUZ SHAH (1305–1388)

Firuz Shah Tughlaq was the ruler of the Tughlaq dynasty from 1351 to 1388. He ascended the throne amidst chaos after the sudden death of Muhammad-bin-Tughlaq. According to historians, he was weak and incapable and lacked the essential qualities of a good ruler. In critical moments during his campaigns, when almost on the verge of victory, he withdrew to avoid shedding the blood of co-religionists.

Though he met with failure in many campaigns, he was successful in conquering Sind in 1363. He had a great passion for building new cities and renaming old ones. He founded the towns of Jaunpur, Fatehabad, Hissar, Firuzpur and Firuzabad and laid out 1,200 new gardens near Delhi. He held the khalifah of Egypt in high regard and styled himself as his deputy. He also received robes of honour from him. His reign of almost four decades was a period of prosperity and happiness for the people.

### DID YOU KNOW?

◇ Factories or *karkhanas* were developed rapidly by the army of slaves recruited by Firuz through the newly created *diwan-i-bandagan* (department of slaves).

◇ During his reign, he developed the concept of free hospitalization and established marriage bureaus to help poor Muslim parents meet the wedding expenses for their daughters.

## TUGHLAQ, MUHAMMAD-BIN (1290–1351)

Muhammad-bin-Tughlaq, born in Delhi, was the second sultan of the Tughlaq dynasty. He reigned from 1325 to 1351 and extended the rule of the Delhi Sultanate over most of the subcontinent in a very short time. Muhammad confronted over twenty rebellions, from the time he ascended the throne till his death, within twenty-six years.

He tried to win over the Sufi saints and *ulemas* to his service, failing which he curtailed their powers. He transferred the capital in 1327 to Deogir to have a firm hold over the conquests in southern India. It helped to spread the Urdu language in the Deccan due to the migration of Muslims. He introduced several reforms in the monetary system; his coins were fascinating in design as well as workmanship. Muhammad died at Sonda in Sind in 1351during his last expedition against the rebel Taghi.

## DID YOU KNOW?

Muhammad was the first ruler to introduce crop rotation, establish state farms and set up a department of agriculture to improve artificial irrigation. When famine broke out in northern India during 1338–1340, he moved his residence to Swargdwari, to supervise famine relief measures himself.

# GROWTH OF NATIONALISM

## CHAMPARAN SATYAGRAHA (1917)

The Champaran Satyagraha took place in 1917 on the indigo plantations in the Champaran district of Bihar. The poor farmers of this region were excessively oppressed and exploited by the European planters. They were compelled to grow indigo on 3/20th of their land (the *tinkathia* system) and to sell it at prices fixed by the planters. In 1917 Gandhi began to conduct a detailed enquiry into the condition of the peasants at Champaran. The infuriated district officials ordered him to leave the district, but he defied the order and stayed on. Later, the government developed cold feet and appointed an enquiry committee in June 1917, with Gandhi as a member. This led to the Champaran Agrarian Act, which freed the tenants from the special taxes levied by the indigo planters.

## CIVIL DISOBEDIENCE MOVEMENT (1930–1931)

As evident in its name, the civil disobedience movement was a protest, through non-payment of taxes, against the unjust and tyrannical laws of the British government. The movement took place in two phases. The first phase started with Gandhi breaking the Salt Law at Dandi as a symbol of the refusal of Indians to live under British rule.

Soon it spread to other parts of India and people joined in *hartals*, demonstrations and campaigns to boycott foreign goods. They also refused to pay land revenue and rent and had their lands confiscated. A notable feature of the movement was the wide participation of women.

The second phase started after the Second Round Table Conference in 1932. As a result, the Congress was declared illegal by the government and most of its leaders were arrested. The movement lost momentum with the sudden announcement of the Communal Award and gradually waned away. The Congress officially suspended the movement in May 1933 and withdrew it in May 1934.

## FIRST WAR OF INDIAN INDEPENDENCE (1857)

British historians call it the Sepoy Mutiny. Nationalist historians such as V.D. Sarvarkar call it the First War of Indian Independence. History records it as an Indian uprising against the British in 1857.

There were many reasons for this rebellion, including the expansionist policies and economic exploitation by the British. However, military reasons were the immediate cause. The cartridges of the newly-introduced Enfield rifle had to be greased with the fats of cows and pigs and that sparked off a fire of discontent against the British in the form of a revolt. The first sign of unrest appeared in 1857 at Barrackpore in Bengal. Mangal Pandey, a sepoy, killed a senior officer on parade and triggered off the revolt, which spread to many places including Meerut, Kanpur, Lucknow, Jhansi and Bareilly.

In all these places, Indian soldiers killed senior officers and released Indian prisoners from jails. However, the British used superior forces, better resources and modern means of communications and transport to swiftly suppress the revolt.

Though the revolt was started by Indian soldiers who were in the service of East India Company, it spread across the country. Millions of peasants, artisans and soldiers fought heroically for over a year. Hindus and Muslims put aside their religious differences and fought together to free themselves from foreign rule.

The revolt failed due to lack of planning, organization and leadership. However, it was a milestone in the history of India, as it was the first time that Indians came together to fight against a foreign military power.

## GANDHIAN FORMS OF STRUGGLE (1919-1934)

The nationalist period of movement from 1919 to 1934 is called the Gandhian era. During this period, the Mahatma played a significant role in the political and social fields in India. He was an ardent follower of the concepts of truth and non-violence. He regarded non-violence not as the weapon of the weak but of the powerful. He attributed importance to morality in politics. He drew out the nationalist movement from the hands of militant extremists and revolutionaries and handed it over to the masses. The first satyagraha movement was launched by Gandhi at Champaran in Bihar in 1947. During 1920–1922, he launched the non-cooperation movement against the British government. In 1930, he launched the civil disobedience movement with his famous Dandi March. In 1940, he decided to launch individual satyagraha. In 1942, he asked the British to Quit India, failing which, he threatened to launch uncompromising agitation. At the same time, he gave the Indians the slogan 'do or die' which provided inspiration for nationalist struggle.

## HOME RULE MOVEMENT (1916)

The Home Rule Movement was a struggle by Indians to obtain for India a status equivalent to other colonies of the British empire. It was neither moderate nor thoroughly revolutionary. Two Home Rule Leagues were formed, one by Lokmanya Tilak in July 1916 (limited to Maharashtra) and the other by Annie Besant in September 1916 (functional across India). The objectives of both leagues were to educate the people and enable the Congress to put forward a strong demand for self-government. The activities consisted of holding public meetings, organizing discussions and distributing pamphlets. The movements left a deep impact on Indian politics and prepared the ground for the non-cooperation movement.

## INDIAN NATIONAL CONGRESS (1885)

The Indian National Congress, a major political party in India, played a very important role during the struggle for freedom. Founded in 1885 by a retired British civilian, Allan Octavian Hume, it comprised many important people, including Mohandas Karamchand Gandhi, Sardar Vallabhbhai Patel, Jawaharlal Nehru, Subhas Chandra Bose, Dadabhai Naoroji, Dinshaw Wacha, Womesh Chandra Bonnerjee, Surendranath Banerjee, Monomohun Ghose, Mahadev Govind Ranade, Bipin Chandra Pal, Bal Gangadhar Tilak and Lala Lajpat Rai. Though it was dominated by Hindus, it had members from virtually every religion, ethnic group, economic class and linguistic group. Hence it provided true representation of the masses of India in their struggle for freedom from the British.

## INDIGO REVOLUTION (1859–1960)

The Indigo Revolution of Bengal was directed against the British planters who forced peasants to grow indigo under terms that were not profitable to the farmers. They faced inhuman oppression if they refused to cultivate indigo. The planters were forced to grow indigo instead of food crops and were paid very little in return. The revolt began at Govindapore in Nadia district. It was led by Digambar Biswas and Bishnu Biswas who organized the peasants into a counter force to deal with the planters' *lathiyals* (armed retainers). In April 1860, all the cultivators of the Barasat subdivision and Pabna and Nadia districts refused to sow indigo. Soon, the strike spread to other places in Bengal. The problem was resolved with the appointment of an Indigo Commission in 1860, which passed a law directing the planters to stop forcing the farmers to plant indigo against their will. The Revolt received great support from the intelligentsia. It was vividly portrayed by Dinabandhu Mitra in his seminal play *Neel Darpan*.

## KHILAFAT MOVEMENT (1919–1922)

The Khilafat Movement was a significant Islamic movement in India during the British rule. Its main objective was to force the British government to change its attitude towards Turkey and restore the Turkish sultan (khalifa) to his former position. With this aim, a Khilafat committee was formed under the leadership of the Ali brothers, Maulana Azad, Hakim Ajmal Khan, and Hasrat Mohani. On 9 June 1920, the Khilafat Committee of Allahabad asked Gandhi to lead the movement. Congress leaders, including the Mahatma, viewed the agitation as a golden opportunity for cementing Hindu–Muslim unity and bringing the Muslim masses into the national movement. In 1920, the movement was marred by the exodus of Muslim peasants from India to Afghanistan. It was also tarnished by the Muslim Moplah rebellion in south India in 1921. Gandhi's suspension of the movement and his arrest in March 1922 weakened the Khilafat movement further. Finally, the caliphate was abolished in 1924.

## NON-COOPERATION MOVEMENT (1921–1922)

The non-cooperation movement was a significant phase of the Indian struggle for freedom from British rule. The struggle was led by Gandhi with the support of the Indian National Congress. The main demands of the faction were the annulment of the Rowlatt Act and an apology for the Jallianwala Bagh massacre. Boycott of government schools, colleges, courts, war and foreign goods were encouraged. Many people surrendered their titles and honorary offices and resigned from nominated seats in local bodies. They refused to work on foreign assignments. The concept of swadeshi was popularized through khadi and *charkha*. This developed closer unity between Hindus and Muslims, bringing about a positive change in Indian society.

## QUIT INDIA MOVEMENT (1942)

The Quit India Movement or 'Bharat Chhoro Andolan' was a non-violent mass struggle in 1942 under Gandhi's leadership. The failure of the Cripps Mission, rising prices, wartime shortages, and the Japanese threat forced the Congress to take active steps to compel the British in accepting the Indian demand for independence. But before the Congress could start a movement, the government arrested Gandhi and other Congress leaders on 9 August 1942. Bereft of leadership and lacking in organization, the masses reacted in a chaotic manner. All over the country there were *hartals*, strikes in factories, schools and colleges, and demonstrations which were lathi-charged and fired upon. People took to violence and attacked the symbols of British authority—police stations, railway stations and other buildings. In general, students, workers and peasants provided the backbone of the 'revolt' while the upper classes and the bureaucracy remained loyal to the government. In the end, the government succeeded in crushing the movement.

## ROWLATT SATYAGRAHA (1919)

The Anarchical and Revolutionary Crimes Act, popularly known as the Rowlatt Act, was a law passed by the British in colonial India in 1919 to control public unrest. This act authorized the government to imprison, even without trial, any person suspected of terrorism. It was met with protests across the country. An all-India hartal was organized on 6 April, 1919. Also, meetings were held all over the country to signify popular disapproval of the Act. Unfortunately, there were several violent incidents in the Punjab, Gujarat and Bengal. Deeply upset, Gandhi decided to call off the movement. The Rowlatt Satyagraha is significant because it set into motion a chain reaction culminating in the Jallianwala Bagh massacre.

## SWADESHI MOVEMENT (1905)

The Swadeshi Movement was a strong protest against the decision of the British to partition Bengal. The partition plan infused a sense of nationalism among the Indians and gave birth to this movement. People took up the solemn vow of using swadeshi or Indian manufactured goods, thus boycotting foreign clothes. Their ideology was 'Be swadeshi, buy swadeshi'. This movement was instrumental in the establishment of many Indian textile mills, national banks, soap factories, tanneries, chemical works, and insurance companies. Many swadeshi stores were also opened. Moved by patriotism, people preferred costlier indigenous goods to cheaper foreign products. On the day of the Partition of Bengal, 16 October 1905, people fasted, bathed in the Ganga and walked barefoot in processions singing *Vande mataram*. They tied rakhis to each other, as a symbol of unity between the two halves of Bengal. Thus this movement helped the Indians take a stand aginst the British and to participate in new forms of political activity.

# MAJOR WARS AND BATTLES OF INDIA

## ANGLO-AFGHAN WARS (1839–1842; 1878–1880; 1919)

Also called the Afghan Wars, these were three conflicts in which Great Britain, from its base in India, sought to extend its control over neighbouring Afghanistan and to oppose Russian influence there. The first war demonstrated the ease of overrunning Afghanistan and the difficulty of holding it. The second war proved to be a victory that was offset by massive losses for the British. Though unable to occupy Afghanistan permanently, the British controlled its foreign affairs until the last war established full Afghan independence.

## ANGLO-MARATHA WARS (1775-1882, 1803-1805, 1817-1818)

The Anglo-Maratha Wars were three conflicts between the British and the Maratha confederacy, resulting in the destruction of the confederacy. The first war was caused by the interference of the British in the internal affairs of the Marathas, which included struggle for power among the Marathas. The British were defeated at Talegaon, resulting in the signing of the Treaty of Salbai (1782). This bought peace to both sides for the next twenty years. The second war was caused by Peshwa Baji Rao II's defeat by the Holkars (one of the leading Maratha clans) and his acceptance of British protection by the Treaty of Bassein in 1802. The Sindhia and the Bhonsle families contested the agreement, but they were defeated. Then Holkar joined in and the Marathas were left with a free hand in the regions of central India and Rajasthan. The third war was chiefly the result of internal quarrels about the succession to the kingdom of Nagpur, which gave the English the opportunity to bring the kingdom under their influence. In the course of operations against the Pindari robbers, Lord Hastings invaded the Maratha territory.

The peshwa's forces, followed by those of the Bhonsle's and Holkar's, rose against the British (November 1817) but the Sindhias remained neutral. Defeat was swift, followed by the pensioning of the peshwa and annexation of his territories, thus completing British supremacy in India.

## ANGLO-MYSORE WARS (1766-1799)

A series of armed conflicts between the rulers of Mysore and the British came to be termed as the Anglo-Mysore Wars. Hyder Ali wanted to drive the British away from the Carnatic and from India, and this caused the first war in which the British were defeated. It ended with a defensive treaty and promises of mutually working together. The British, however, did not keep their promise and seized the port of Mahe, which was very useful to Hyder, thus triggering off the second war. During this war, Hyder was killed and his son Tipu Sultan continued the fight. Unfortunately, he was no match for the mighty powers of the English and was defeated. He was compelled to sign a treaty at Mangalore in 1784.

The third war began in 1790, when Governor-General Lord Cornwallis dropped Tipu's name from the list of the company's 'friends'. The battle ended with Tipu's defeat in 1792. The Treaty of Seringapatam was signed, and Tipu lost almost half of his territory. The fourth war was undertaken by

Governor-General Lord Mornington on the plea that Tipu was receiving help from France. British troops stormed Seringapatam in May 1799; Tipu died fighting and his troops were defeated.

## ANGLO-SIKH WARS (1845–1846; 1848–1849)

The Anglo–Sikh Wars were two campaigns fought between the Sikhs and the British. The first war was caused by the Sikh army's apprehension of a British attack on the Sikh territory, at a time when the East India Company had been pursuing a policy of annexation. Alarmed by the British preparation, the Sikh troops crossed the Sutlej on 11 December 1845 and attacked the English troops commanded by Sir Hugh Gough. Four battles were fought at Mudki, Ferozeshah, Buddewal, and Aliwal. The final Battle of Sobraon (1848) proved decisive. The English army occupied Lahore and dictated peace terms by the Treaty of Lahore. However, a few months later, intrigues again cropped up between the English and the Sikhs. The discontentment of the Sikh sardars with the British control over Punjab, the desire of the Sikh army to avenge their humiliation of the first war, and the treatment of Rani Jindan by the British were the main causes for the second war. However, the Multan revolt, caused by various reasons, served as the immediate cause. The Sikhs lost the war and Punjab was annexed in 1849.

## BATTLE OF BUXAR (1764)

The Battle of Buxar was fought in 1764 between Mir Qasim, the Nawab of Bengal, and the British. Qasim wanted to recover Bengal from the British and sought help from Mughal emperor Shah Alam II and Nawab Shuja-ud-Daulah of Oudh. This alarmed the British and they immediately took steps to curb his powers, causing an armed conflict. The combined forces of Qasim, Shuja-ud-Daula, and Shah Alam II could not win over the British, due to lack of coordination. The victory consolidated the English as a great power in northern India and contenders for the supremacy of the whole country. With victory in this battle, the British became the de facto rulers of Bengal, Bihar, and Orissa.

## BATTLE OF CHAUSA (1539)

This battle was fought between Afghan chief Sher Shah Suri and Mughal emperor Humayun. Sher Shah was expanding his dominion in the east and Humayun attacked with the aim of bringing the latter's province under Mughal control. The two met on the field of Chausa. Humayun was crushed by Sher Shah, who captured Bengal and Bihar. After this victory, Sher Shah assumed the title of Farid al-Din Sher Shah.

## BATTLE OF GHAGHRA (1529)

The Battle of Ghaghra was fought between Babur and the allied Afghans of Bihar and Bengal on 6 May 1529 at Ghaghra, near the junction of the river of the same name with the Ganges near Patna. It was a part of Babur's expansionist policy in northern India. Babur's victory in this battle established him as a major power in north India.

## BATTLE OF HALDIGHATI (1576)

The Battle of Haldighati was fought between Akbar and Rana Pratap. Akbar wanted to annex the Rajput provinces and consolidate his rule over India but Rana Pratap would not let this dream of the Mughal emperor be fulfilled. What followed was a decisive battle on the 'yellow' battlefield of Haldighati. The battle lasted for barely four hours. Led by Man Singh of Amber and Asaf Khan, the Mughal forces defeated Rana Pratap, who barely escaped with his life, riding his horse Chetak. The impact of the battle was significant; it is considered to be the first major Rajput counterattack against the Mughals.

## BATTLE OF HYDASPES (326 BC)

This was the fourth and the last major battle fought by Alexander the Great during his campaign of conquests in Asia. It was fought between him and Porus, the Indian ruler of the territory between the Jhelum and the Chenab rivers (now in Pakistan). Alexander won a decisive victory but, impressed by Porus, he formed an alliance with him and allowed him to remain king. After the battle, Alexander left for Macedonia, never to return.

## BATTLE OF KHANUA (1527)

The Battle of Khanua was fought between Babur and Rana Sangram Singh of Mewar, popularly known as Rana Sanga. When Rana Sanga realized that Babur did not intend to return home after the First Battle of Panipat (as his ancestors had done), he advanced with a huge force. They met at Khanua, west of Agra, on 16 March 1527. After ten hours of fighting, Babur's forces were victorious and Rana took flight. The victory at Khanua secured Babur's position in the Delhi–Agra region.

## BATTLE OF PLASSEY (1757)

The Battle of Plassey was fought between the then Nawab of Bengal, Siraj-ud-Daula and the British. The misinterpretation of the Mughal *farman* of 1717 by the British and their misuse of *dastaks* (free passes) forced the nawab to come into an open conflict with the British, led by Robert Clive, at a village named Palashi or Plassey. The English conspired with the generals and nobles of the Nawab's court and defeated him. The Battle of Plassey helped pave the way for the British acquisition of Bengal.

## BATTLES OF TERRAIN (1191, 1192)

The first battle was fought between Muhammad Ghori and the Rajput king of Ajmer and Delhi, Prithviraj Chauhan, in 1191. Ghori's expansionist ambitions and conquests were the main reason of the battle. Prithviraj defeated Ghori and sent him back, but Ghori resurfaced after a year and attacked him in 1192 in the second battle, which was fought in the north of Delhi. Prithviraj was defeated and the kingdom of Delhi fell into the hands of Ghori, who captured it along with other Rajput capitals. As a result, Ghori was able to control northern Rajasthan and the northern part of the Ganga–Yamuna Doab.

## FIRST BATTLE OF PANIPAT (1526)

Fought between Babur and Ibrahim Lodi in 1526, this battle marked a turning point in the history of medieval India. It was a part of Babur's expansionist policy. Babur killed Lodi, defeated his army and established the Mughal dynasty, which ruled over India for more than 300 years.

## SECOND BATTLE OF PANIPAT (1556)

The second battle was waged in 1556 between Akbar and Hemu, the Hindu general of an Afghan claimant who had proclaimed himself independent. With Akbar's win, it marked the restoration of Mughal power. Earlier Humayun had been overthrown by Sher Shah Suri, the Afghan, in 1540.

## THIRD BATTLE OF PANIPAT (1761)

Fought between Ahmed Shah Abdali and the Marathas in 1761, it ended the Maratha attempt to succeed the Mughals as rulers of India and marked the virtual end of the Mughal empire. The Maratha army, under Bhao Sahib, uncle of the peshwa, was defeated by the Afghan chief Ahmad Shah Durrani. It began forty years of anarchy in north-western India and paved the way for later British supremacy.

## KALINGA WAR (260 BC)

The Kalinga War was fought by Ashoka to control the routes to south India both via land and sea. Though Ashoka emerged victorious, he was heartbroken after witnessing the resultant devastation. The thirteenth major rock edict of Ashoka vividly describes the horrors and miseries of the war and the deep anguish it caused to Ashoka. The battle dramatically changed Ashoka and he adopted Buddhism and the path of ahimsa.

# MAJOR RELIGIONS OF INDIA

## BUDDHISM

Buddhism is a religion and philosophy that developed from the teachings of Gautama Buddha, in northern India between the 6th and 4th centuries BC. The main principles of Buddhism are contained in the teachings of Buddha, which are the Four Noble Truths. According to Buddha, to attain Nirvana, one should follow the Eightfold Path. Buddha preached in Pali, the language of the common man, about *ahimsa* or non-violence. The simplicity of the religion, the establishment of monasteries and its order (sangha or assembly), the patronage of kings like Ashoka, and the establishment of universities like Nalanda popularized it not only in India but also in other countries like China, Japan, Burma and Sri Lanka.

## CHRISTIANITY

Christianity is the world's most widespread religion. Its largest groups are the Roman Catholic Church, the Eastern Orthodox churches, and the Protestant churches. It originated and is based on the teachings of Jesus of Nazareth, called Christ, meaning messiah or saviour. It is generally believed that Jesus lived between 4 BC and AD 30. The Holy Bible is the sacred book of the Christians. Christianity became the formal religion of the Roman empire after Emperor Constantine converted in AD 313.

## HINDUISM

Hinduism is one of the most ancient religions of the world, supposed to have developed some 5,000 years ago. It is a diverse system of thought which has developed over time and has no distinct founder. According to Hinduism, three lords rule the world—Brahma the Creator, Vishnu the Preserver and Shiva the Destroyer. There are a host of mother goddesses like Durga, Kali, Laxmi and Saraswati. Hinduism believes in reincarnation.

## ISLAM

Islam is a major world religion. It was started by Prophet Muhammad in Arabia in the 7th century AD. The Arabic term Islam, meaning 'surrender', focuses on the fundamental religious idea of the religion—that the believer, accepts 'surrender to the will of Allah'. Allah is viewed as the sole God—creator, sustainer, and restorer of the world. The will of Allah, to which man must submit, is made known through the Islamic sacred scripture, the Quran, which Allah revealed to his messenger, Muhammad.

## JAINISM

Jainism originated around the 6th century BC in the Gangetic basin of north India. The last and twenty-fourth *tirthankara*, Vardhamana Mahavira, is regarded as the founder of Jainism. He was born in 599 BC near Vaishali. Though he was a Kshatriya prince, he left home at the age of thirty in search of truth. After about twelve years of meditation, he gained Enlightenment. Mahavira preached in Prakrit, the language of the common man. Jainism follows the principle of the 'Three Jewels' (*ratnatraya or triratna*) of Right Knowledge, Right Faith and Right Practice. The highest goal of a person's life is to attain *moksha* (salvation) by following these three jewels. The rulers of Magadha, Bimbisara and Ajatashatru, were his followers. After Mahavira's death at the age of seventy-two, Jainism was divided into two sects—Digambaras and Svetambaras.

## SIKHISM

Sikhism was founded in 15th-century Punjab by Guru Nanak Dev. The word Sikh is derived from the Pali *sikkha* or Sanskrit *shishya*, both meaning 'disciple'. Sikhs are the disciples of their gurus. According to this religion, god is one and unique without any form or gender. Their holy book is called the Adi Granth. The duties of a Sikh include *sewa*, *kirtan* and *satsang*. They organize *langars* to provide training to the Sikhs in voluntary service and to help banish all distinction of high and low, touchable and untouchable from their minds. Among their customs, the most important are the five Ks that denote their five emblems—*kesha* (hair), *kara* (steel bracelet), *kanga* (wooden comb), *kachcha* (cotton underwear), and *kirpan* (steel sword). Sikhs pray in gurudwaras, the most significant of them being Amritsar's Golden Temple, which houses the Adi Granth.

## ZOROASTRIANISM

Zoroastrianism is one of the oldest religions in the world based on the belief of monotheism (belief in one god). It was founded by the Prophet Zoroaster (Zarathustra) in ancient Iran, approximately 3,500 years ago. It was the official religion of Persia (Iran) from 600 BC to AD 650. In Zoroastrianism, Ahura Mazda (Lord of Life and Wisdom) rules the universe through his divine entities called Amesha Spenta (immortal shining ones). The sacred texts are collectively called the Avesta. The book of daily prayers is called Khordeh Avesta. After Zarathstra's death, his teachings spread slowly into Bactria and Persia. Today, it is one of the world's smallest religions, followed in India by the community known as Parsis.

# SOCIO-RELIGIOUS REFORM MOVEMENTS

## ARYA SAMAJ

The Arya Samaj was founded in Bombay in 1875 by Mulshankar, popularly known as Swami Dayanand. It opposed untouchability and caste discriminations, and advocated widow remarriage and more rights for women in society. However, its most distinguished achievement was in the field of education. To spread education, a DAV school was started at Lahore under the leadership of Lala Hansraj in 1886, while Swami Shradhan started a gurukul at Haridwar in 1902 to revive Vedic ideas. The Arya Samajis established a girls' school known as Arya Kanya Pathshala. The movement inculcated pride, self-confidence and self-reliance in the Hindus and undermined the belief in the superiority of the white race and Western culture. As a disciplined Hindu organization, it succeeded in protecting Hindu society from the onslaught of Islam and Christianity. It always remained in the forefront of political movements and produced leaders of eminence like Lala Hansraj, Pandit Guru Dutta and Lala Lajpat Rai.

## BRAHMO SAMAJ

The Brahmo Samaj was one the earliest movements to be greatly influenced by Western ideas. Founded by Raja Ram Mohan Roy in Calcutta in 1828, it played a notable role in the Indian Renaissance. The Samaj opposed polytheism (worship of more than one god), idol worship, priesthood, and any kind of religious sacrifices. It stressed on prayers, meditation, and readings from the Vedas and the Upanishads. It took no definite stand on the doctrine of karma and transmigration of the soul. It spoke against many dogmas and superstitious beliefs prevalent in Hindu society. It worked for the upliftment of the status of women in the society, condemned the practice of sati, advocated the abolition of the *purdah* system, and discouraged child marriage. The Samaj also fought for widow remarriage and attacked casteism and untouchability. After Raja Ram Mohan Roy's death in 1833, Maharshi Debendranath Tagore and Keshab Chandra Sen infused new life into the Samaj. In 1865, Keshab left and founded a new organization known as the Brahmo Samaj of India. Dependranath's organization came to be known as Adi Brahmo Samaj.

## PRARTHANA SAMAJ

An offshoot of the Brahmo Samaj, Prarthana Samaj was founded in Bombay in 1867 by Atmaram Panduranga, under the guidance of Keshab Chandra Sen. It stood for social reform and monotheism. Its two great leaders were R.G. Bhandarkar and M.G. Ranade. The Samaj started to reform Hindu religious thoughts and practices in the light of modern knowledge. It laid stress on the abolition of the caste system, introduction of widow remarriage, encouragement of female education, abolition of the *purdah* system and child marriage, and upliftment of the depressed classes. The activities of the Samaj spread to south India due to the efforts of the Telugu reformer Virasalingam.

## RAMAKRISHNA MISSION

Swami Vivekananda, a disciple of Ramakrishna, founded the mission to preach the Vedanta philosophy of his guru in the country and abroad. Swamiji realized that there is truth in every religion and there are different paths to reach one goal. The mission was basically revivalist in nature. It upheld pure Vedanta doctrines as its ideal and recognized the value and utility of idol worship. Ramakrishna Mission, thus founded on 5 May 1897, stood not only for religious reform but also for social reform.

## THEOSOPHICAL SOCIETY

The Theosophical Society was founded in New York in 1875 by Madame H.P. Blavatsky and Colonel M.C. Olcott. In 1882, they shifted their headquarters to Adyar, on the outskirts of Madras. The society had three main objectives: (1) to establish a nucleus of the universal brotherhood of humanity; (2) to promote the study of comparative religion and philosophy; and (3) to make a systematic investigation into occultism. Later, Annie Besant, who settled in India in 1893, assumed leadership of the society.

## YOUNG BENGAL MOVEMENT

The Young Bengal Movement was started by Henry Vivian Derozio, a teacher at Hindu College between 1826 and 1831. His followers, the Derozians, attacked old traditions and decadent customs. They also advocated women's rights and education and educated the public on the current socio-economic and political questions through the press, trial by jury, protestation of peasants, and so on.

# MAJOR REFORMERS OF INDIA

### BHAVE, VINOBA (1895–1982)

Vinoba Bhave, born Vinayak Narahari Bhave, was one of India's best-known social reformers and founder of the Bhoodan Yojana ('Land-Gift Movement'). Born into a Brahmin family, he was a spiritual visionary and developed a deep bond with Gandhi. In 1923, he was imprisoned at Nagda Jail and Akola Jail for taking a prominent part in the Flag Satyagraha at Nagpur. In 1932, he raised his voice against British rule and was arrested again. He started several social reform movements such as the Bhoodan Yojana and the Sarvodaya Movement. For his contribution to the society, he was awarded the Bharat Ratna in 1984. He died on 15 November 1982.

## DID YOU KNOW?

In 1958, Acharya Vinoba Bhave became the first Indian to receive the Ramon Magsaysay Award for Community Leadership.

## DAYANAND SARASWATI, SWAMI (1824–1883)

Dayanand Saraswati, a Hindu ascetic and social reformer, was the founder of the Arya Samaj (1875), a Hindu reform movement. Born Mula Shankara in 1824 in the town of Tankara in Gujarat, he spent fifteen years as a wandering ascetic and later received education from Swami Birajananda at Mathura. He founded the Arya Samaj in 1875. He considered the Vedas as eternal and infallible, and was against idolatry and priesthood. He preached against child marriage and caste system based on birth, and encouraged inter-caste marriages and widow remarriage. He started the Shuddhi movement for the purification of the souls of Hindus. He passed away in 1883.

## NIVEDITA, SISTER (1867–1911)

Sister Nivedita was an Anglo-Irish social worker, author, teacher and disciple of Swami Vivekananda. Born Margaret Noble, she became popular as Sister Nivedita, a name given to her by Vivekananda. Arriving in India at the invitation of Vivekananda, she devoted herself to social service and promotion of the education of women. In 1898, she established a school for girls deprived of basic education. Her aim was to help improve the lives of Indian women of various social classes and castes, and thereby end class distinction. Later, she became involved in activities that promoted the cause of India's independence.

## PARAMHANSA, RAMAKRISHNA (1836–1886)

Ramakrishna Paramhansa was a Hindu religious leader, founder of the school of religious thought that became the Ramakrishna Order, and the most renowned Hindu saint of the 19th century. Originally known as Gadadhar Chattopadhhyay, he was born in 1836 in Kamarpukur village in Hooghly district of West Bengal. He became a priest in the temple of Goddess Kali at Dakshineshwar near Calcutta and sought religious salvation in the traditional way through renunciation, meditation and devotion. He preached that there were several roads to God and salvation, and that service to man was service to God. He wished to effect a synthesis among divergent faiths. Vivekananda, his disciple, later founded the Ramakrishna Mission.

### DID YOU KNOW?

Sri Ramakrishna attained *Nirvikalpa Samadhi*, one of the the highest spiritual experiences mentioned in the Hindu scriptures, under the guidance of a wandering monk Totapuri.

## PANTULU, VIRESHALINGAM (1848-1919)

Kandukuri Vireshalingam Pantulu is considered to be the Father of Modern Telugu Literature. He was also a prominent social reformer of south India in the second half of the 19th century. He founded the Rajamundri Social Reform Association in Andhra Pradesh in 1878 with the principal objective of promoting widow remarriage. He was the first person to use literature as a means of eradicating social evils. His creation, *Harishchandra*, is considered to be the first important dramatic treatise in Telugu.

## ROY, RAJA RAM MOHAN (1772-1833)

Raja Ram Mohan Roy was a religious, social and educational reformer. Born in Radhanagar in West Bengal, he was a pioneer of several socio-religious and political reform movements. He established the Atmiya Sabha in Calcutta in 1815 to fight evil customs and practices in Hinduism. Later, in 1828, he established the Brahmo Samaj to purify Hinduism and to preach monotheism. He led a lifelong crusade against the practice of *sati* and finally succeeded in persuading Lord William Bentick, then governor-general of India, to abolish it in 1829. He championed women's rights including the right to inheritance of property and abolition of polygamy. He fought for the spread of modern education through the medium of English. He also pioneered Indian journalism, thus educating the public on current issues to enable them to represent public opinion before the British government. He passed away at Bristol in England in 1833.

## DID YOU KNOW?

A walk by the house in Stapleton, Bristol, where Raja Rammohan died, is named Raja Ram Mohan Roy Walk.

## VIDYASAGAR, ISHWAR CHANDRA (1820–1890)

Pandit Ishwar Chandra Vidyasagar contributed to the upliftment of Indian women by working towards widow remarriage, by opposing child marriage and polygamy and by campaigning in favour of the education of women. He evolved a new technique of teaching Sanskrit and a modern prose style in Bengali. He became the principal of Sanskrit College in Calcutta in 1851. He introduced the study of Western thought in the college and initiated the admission of non-Brahmin students.

## DID YOU KNOW?

Ishwar Chandra received the title Vidyasagar, meaning 'ocean of learning' from the authorities of the Sanskrit College, Calcutta, in recognition of his erudition.

## VIVEKANANDA, SWAMI (1863–1902)

Swami Vivekananda was a famous Hindu spiritual leader and reformer of India. Originally known as Narendranath Dutta, he was born in 1863 in Calcutta. He was an ardent follower of Ramakrishna Paramhansa. He established a monastery at Baranagar (1887) after the death of his guru. He also extensively toured India which brought him into close contact with the people and enabled him to realize the true condition of India. He attended the World Parliament of Religions (1893) at Chicago and raised the prestige of India and Hinduism. He popularized his guru's religious message and tried to put it in a form that would suit the needs of contemporary Indian society. Further, he condemned casteism and the Hindu focus on rituals. He urged people to imbibe the spirit of liberty, equality and free thought. He proclaimed the essential oneness of all religions.

## DID YOU KNOW?

- ◇ Fond of food from his childhood, Vivekananda organized an association of gluttons—the Greedy Club. When a disciple asked his opinion about consuming non-vegetarian food, Swamiji asked him to eat fish and meat as much as possible in order to become healthy and courageous
- ◇ Every year, Swami Vivekananda's birth anniversary, 12 January, is celebrated as National Youth Day in India.

# THE CONSTITUTION OF INDIA

India, is a sovereign socialist democratic republic with a Parliamentary system of government. It is governed in accordance with the terms of the Constitution of India, which was adopted by the Constituent Assembly on 26 November 1949 and came into force on 26 January 1950.

## CONSTITUENT ASSEMBLY OF INDIA

During the Indian freedom struggle, it became clear that the people of India wanted a democratic form of government. This, in turn, led to the demand for a constitution. To frame such a constitution, Jawaharlal Nehru proposed the formation of a Constituent Assembly. Even though such a proposal was accepted by the Indian National Congress in 1934, it took seven years before the Constituent Assembly of India became a reality.

The Constituent Assembly met for the first time in New Delhi on 9 December 1946 in the 'Constitution Hall' now known as the Central Hall of Parliament House. A total of 207 representatives, including nine women, were present. Some of its important members were Jawaharlal Nehru, Maulana Abul Kalam Azad, Vallabhbhai Patel, Acharya J.B. Kripalani, Dr Rajendra Prasad, Sarojini Naidu, Hare-Krushna Mahatab, Govind Ballabh Pant, Dr B.R. Ambedkar, Sarat Chandra Bose, C. Rajagopalachari and M. Asaf Ali.

The Constituent Assembly took two years, eleven months and seventeen days to complete the task of drafting the Constitution of independent India. During this period, it held eleven sessions covering a total of 165 days.

The Constitution of India was finally adopted on 26 November 1949 and the members signed it on 24 January 1950. In all, 284 members actually signed the Constitution. Finally, it came into force on 26 January 1950. On that day, the Assembly ceased to exist, transforming itself into the Provisional Parliament of India until a new Parliament was constituted in 1952.

The original edition of the Constitution of India took nearly five years to complete. It is signed by the framers of the constitution, most of whom are regarded as the founders of the Republic of India. It is kept in a special helium-filled case in the library of the Parliament of India. The illustrations represent styles from the different civilizations of the subcontinent, ranging from the prehistoric Mohenjo-daro, in the Indus Valley to the 1940s. The calligraphy in the book is done by Prem Behari Narain Raizada. It is illuminated by Nandalal Bose and other artists.

## INSPIRATIONS FROM OTHER CONSTITUTIONS OF THE WORLD

The Constitution of India has the unique distinction of being the lengthiest and most detailed constitutional document in the world. The framers of the Constitution tried to incorporate aspects from different constitutions of the world. They also included detailed provisions about the organization of the judiciary. This was done to make the Indian Constitution free from loopholes and defects.

- The concept of fundamental rights is taken from the American Constitution.
- The Parliamentary system of government is adapted from the British Constitution.
- The idea of directive principles of state policy is taken from the Irish Constitution.
- Provisions relating to emergencies are taken from the Constitution of the German Reich and the Government of India Act, 1935.
- While the US Constitution deals only with the federal government, leaving the states to draw up their own form of government, the Indian Constitution provides the Constitutions of both the Union and the states.
- Under the special status enshrined in the Constitution, Jammu and Kashmir has a separate Constitution.
- The fundamental rights are lengthy because the framers of the Indian Constitution had to include certain matters relating to peculiar problems of India, such as untouchability and preventive detention.
- The Constitution is partially flexible. In the first forty-two years of its working, it was amended only seventy times.

# ORGANS OF THE INDIAN GOVERNMENT

The Union government is the highest in India. The headquarters of the Union government are at New Delhi. It consists of three organs: the executive, the legislature, and the judiciary. The president is the constitutional head, assisted by the Parliament in the execution of his duties. The Parliament is divided into two houses: the Rajya Sabha and the Lok Sabha. The vice-president is the ex officio chairman of the Rajya Sabha. The speaker and the deputy speaker are the presiding officers of the Lok Sabha. The leader of the Lok Sabha is the prime minister. Normally, three sessions of Parliament are held in a year: (1) budget session (February–May); (2) monsoon session (July–August); and (3) winter session (November–December). The Union judiciary consists of the Supreme Court.

**Executive:** The Union executive consists of the president, the vice-president, and the council of ministers, with the prime minister as the head to aid and advise the president. All of them are elected for terms of five years.

**President:** He is the first citizen of the country and the head of state. His official residence is the Rashtrapati Bhavan, New Delhi.

**Vice-President:** He is the ex officio chairman of the Rajya Sabha, who acts as president when the latter is unable to discharge his functions due to absence, illness or any other cause, or till the election of a new president (to be held within six months when a vacancy is caused by death, resignation or removal).

**Prime Minister:** He is the leader of the majority party. He selects other ministers to form his cabinet ministry to be appointed by the president. He is the link between the president and the cabinet and is also the chairman of the Planning Commission.

**Council of Ministers**: Headed by the prime minister, it aids and advises the president in the exercise of his functions. The council is collectively responsible to the Lok Sabha. It comprises ministers who are members of the cabinet, ministers of state (independent charge), other ministers of state and deputy ministers.

**Legislature:** The Legislature of the Union, also called the Parliament, consists of the president and two Houses: Council of States (Rajya Sabha) and House of the People (Lok Sabha).

## RAJYA SABHA

The Rajya Sabha is the Upper House of Parliament. Its maximum strength is 250, of which 238 members are elected and twelve are nominated by the president. Members are elected by the legislative assemblies of various states and Union Territories. Every state and UT is allotted a certain number of seats based on population. The twelve nominated members are persons who have earned distinction in the fields of literature, art, science, sports and social service. The minimum age of a member is thirty years. The Rajya Sabha is a permanent body. It is not subject to dissolution, but one-third of its members retire every two years. It was duly constituted for the first time on 3 April 1952 and held its first sitting on 13 May that year. The vice-president is the ex officio chairman. Dr S. Radhakrishnan was the first chairman of the Rajya Sabha and is the only chairman to have served two terms.

## LOK SABHA

The Lok Sabha, as the name itself signifies, is the body of representatives of the people. Its members are directly elected, normally once every five years, by the adult population of the country that is eligible to vote. The minimum qualifying age for membership is twenty-five years. The maximum strength of the house, according to the Constitution, is 552–530 members representing the states, twenty members representing the Union Territories, and not more than two members of the Anglo-Indian community to be nominated by the President if, in his opinion, the community is not adequately represented. The ratio of the population to the number of elected members is almost the same for all states and Union territories. The Lok Sabha elects one of its own members as its presiding officer, called the speaker. The conduct of business is the responsibility of the speaker. Meira Kumar was the first woman to be appointed speaker of the Lok Sabha.

## JUDICIARY

The judiciary is the third organ of the government, comprising the Supreme Court and other lower courts of justice. It plays an important role in protecting the rights of the citizens. It analyses and interprets the provisions of laws and the Constitution. In addition, there are high courts at the state level, district courts, and tribunals.

**Supreme Court**: It is the apex court of India. According to the Constitution, its roles are that of a federal court, guardian of the Constitution and highest court of appeal. The Supreme Court consists of the chief justice and twenty-five other judges. The chief justice is appointed by the president, and the other judges are appointed by the president in consultation with the chief justice.

## STATE ADMINISTRATION

The state legislature consists of the governor and one or two houses. While all states have the Legislative Assembly (Vidhan Sabha), some have two houses, adding on the Legislative Council (Vidhan Parishad). The Legislative Assembly is headed by the chief minister. Members of the Legislative Assembly (MLAs) are directly elected while members of the Legislative Council (MLCs) are elected indirectly. The governor is akin to the nation's president. The role of the chief minister and the cabinet within the Vidhan Sabha is similar to the Lok Sabha, while the Vidhan Parishad is much like the Rajya Sabha.

## LOCAL SELF-GOVERNMENT

### RURAL INDIA

The Constitution (73rd Amendment) Act, 1992, has institutionalized panchayati raj at the district, intermediate and village levels, as the third tier of governance, after the Union and state administration levels. In May 2004, the Ministry of Panchayati raj was formed as the nodal agency looking after the empowerment of panchayati raj institutions in the country. The basic unit in this system is the gram sabha. The gram panchayat is the executive committee of the gram sabha and is elected by its members. The elected chairperson of the gram panchayat is called the pradhan. Pradhans of several villages make up the panchyat samiti (block council). The small law courts of the panchayati raj system are called the nyaya panchayat. A nyaya sahayak is attached to every nyaya panchayat, appointed in a manner prescribed by the state government.

### URBAN INDIA

The Constitution provides three types of municipalities: nagar panchayats for areas in transition from rural to urban, municipal councils for smaller urban areas, and municipal corporations for large urban areas.

### ELECTIONS

The Election Commission of India is a permanent constitutional body, entrusted with the responsibility to conduct, supervise and control elections to parliament and legislature of every state and to the offices of president and vice-president of India. It was established on 25 January 1950. Originally, it had only a chief election commissioner (CEC). It currently consists of the CEC and two election commissioners appointed by the President for six years (or up to the age of sixty-five years).

For elections, the country is divided into 543 Parliamentary constituencies, each electing one member. Voting is by secret ballot, normally done by electronic voting machines. Polling stations are set up in public institutions, such as schools and community halls.

Every citizen aged eighteen years and above is eligible to vote. To prevent electoral fraud, the commission has been issuing electors' photo identity cards since 1993.

Every year, 25 January is celebrated as National Voters' Day across India.

## FACTS ON ELECTIONS IN INDIA

- In 1951, the villagers of Chini in Himachal Pradesh became the first Indians to cast votes in the first general election of independent India.

- About 18,000 candidates were running for 4,412 seats: 497 in the Lok Sabha and the rest in state governments.

- During the first general election, 17.6 crore Indians, 85 per cent of whom couldn't read or write, formed the electorate. Symbols were used on ballot papers for each party and independent candidate, so that the illiterate would know where to cast their vote. Voters were not even required to mark their ballot papers; they simply had to put them into boxes marked with the symbol of their favoured candidate.

- There were 2,24,000 polling booths and as many policemen pressed into service during the first general election.

- When results came in for the first general election, the Congress led by Nehru swept into power, winning 364 of the 489 seats in Parliament.

- Sukumar Sen was the first chief election commissioner of India.

- As many as 3,89,816 phials of indelible ink were used in the first election.

- The highest number of candidates that an electronic voting machine can support is sixty-four. If the number exceeds this, manual ballots are used.

- There were 1,033 candidates for a single seat in the Modaurichi assembly constituency in Tamil Nadu in 1996.

- In the 2009 general election, on 30 April, the lone voter Mahant Bharatdas Guru Darshandas, cast his vote at the Banej Tirthdam polling booth (India's only single-voter polling booth) in the Gir lion sanctuary, Junagadh.

- In 1996, the Bharatiya Janata Party government lasted only thirteen days, the most short-lived government in the history of India.

- An indelible ink, manufactured by Mysore Paints and Varnish Ltd, is applied to the left index finger of the voter as an indicator that the voter has cast his vote.

- Women voter turnout increased from 38.8 per cent in the 1950s to nearly 60 per cent in the 1990s, whereas the increase in the turnout of men in the same period was only 4 per cent. In the 1984 general election, for instance, as many as 128 seats in twenty-three states were contested by 173 women, of whom forty-three got elected.

↯ In 1989, thought a constitutional amendment through the Parliament reduced the minimum voting age from twenty-one to eighteen. For the first time, as many as 35.7 million voters in this age group exercised their right to vote. Their inclusion in the electoral list raised the strength of the total electorate by 7.71 per cent.

↯ At the 2009 general election, authorities of a Pune school declared that students would be awarded two grace marks in civics if they ensured that their parents voted.

## ELECTIONS OF THE WORLD

↯ When a person running for public office in ancient Rome greeted voters in the Forum (the centre of judicial and public business), he wore a toga whitened with chalk. As a result, the Latin word for someone seeking office became *candidatus*, literally 'clothed in white'. It has been adopted into the English language as candidate.

↯ The highest-ever voter turnout in a democratic general election was in the 2003 presidential election in Armenia, when 99.98 per cent of the electorate voted, while the lowest ever was in Poland during the EU Parliamentary elections, when only 20.87 per cent of the electorate turned out to vote.

↯ According to the *Guinness Book of World Records 2008*, the highest-ever personal majority for any politician was 4,726,112 in the case of Boris Nikolayevich Yeltsin, the people's deputy candidate for Moscow, in the Parliamentary elections held in the Soviet Union on 26 March 1989. Yeltsin (later President of the Russian Federation) received 5,118,745 votes out of the 5,722,937 cast in the Moscow constituency. His closest rival obtained just 392,633 votes.

↯ Also according to the *Guinness Book of World Records 2008*, the names of most candidates on a ballot paper appeared during the November 1994 municipal elections in Prague, Czech Republic. There were 1,187 candidates on the ballot for the single-city constituency. The ballot paper measured 101.5 × 71.5 cm and was delivered to all 1,018,527 eligible, registered voters, who could nominate up to fifty-five candidates for the fifty-five available seats.

↯ The first Republican president of the US was Abraham Lincoln, elected in 1860 and 1864. The first Democrat president was Andrew Jackson, elected in 1828 and 1832.

✤ In March 2007, Estonia in Eastern Europe became the first country to allow Internet voting in parliamentary elections.

✤ In 1940, Khertek Anchimaa-Toka, a leading politician in her native Tuva (now in Russia), became the chairperson of the Presidium of the Little Khural (Parliament), and thus the world's first non-royal female head of state of a republic.

✤ The first two countries to grant women the rights to vote and to stand for election were New Zealand in 1893 and Australia in 1902, but those granted the right were a specific minority category of women—those of European descent.

# UNION BUDGET

The Union Budget is presented in the Lok Sabha by the finance minister. It takes into account a period of one financial year, from 1 April to 31 March. The budget is an official statement by the government of the country's income from taxes and how it will be spent in that financial year. It has to be passed by the Lok Sabha before it can come into effect on 1 April. In India, by convention, the budget is presented on the last working day of February.

The budget of the Indian Railways is presented separately to the Parliament by the railway minister, although the receipts and expenditure of the railways form part of the Consolidated Fund of India, and relevant figures are included in the Annual Financial Statement.

## A LITTLE ABOUT BUDGETS

✤ The word budget comes from the French word *bougette*, meaning 'little bag'.

✤ For a long time, the Union Budget was announced at 5 p.m. on the last working day of February. It was changed to 11 a.m. in 2001.

✤ On 26 November 1947, R.K. Shanmukham Chetty presented the first budget of independent India.

✤ Budget papers began to be prepared in Hindi from 1955–1956.

✤ As finance minister, Morarji Desai has presented the maximum number of budgets so far—ten.

✤ Morarji Desai was the only finance minister to have had the opportunity to present budgets twice on his birthday—in 1964 and 1968.

✤ So far, Indira Gandhi has been the only female finance minister.

✤ In India, we often see the finance minister pose for cameras with a briefcase containing the budget speech. Long before this became a practice, Chancellor George Ward Hunt arrived at the Commons in 1869 and opened the Budget Box to find that he had left his speech at home! The story goes that his goof-up resulted in the practice of the chancellor showing the assembled crowd the budget box by holding it aloft before leaving for the House of Commons for his speech.

# SOME PRIME MINISTERS AND PRESIDENTS OF INDIA

### GANDHI, INDIRA (1917–1984)
**Term: 24 January 1966–24 March 1977; 14 January 1980–31 October 1984**

Indira Gandhi, Jawaharlal Nehru's daughter, was the first and only female prime minister of India who served from 1966 to 1977 and then again from 1980 to 1984. She was actively involved in the freedom struggle and her first term as prime minister witnessed the Green Revolution and the White Revolution. During her tenure, India also liberated Bangladesh and conducted nuclear tests in the 1970s. She declared a National Emergency when, in 1975, the Allahabad High Court ordered her removal for election fraud. She came back to power in 1980 with a strong majority. Indira Gandhi was assassinated by her own bodyguards in 1984. She won many awards during her lifetime, including the Bharat Ratna in 1972.

### GANDHI, RAJIV (1944–1991)
**Term: 31 October 1984–2 December 1989**

Rajiv Gandhi became India's youngest prime minister (aged forty-four years) when he came to power after the death of his mother, Indira Gandhi. He was a licensed commercial pilot but was drawn into politics, and elected to the Parliament in 1981. As prime minister, he worked towards the advancement of science and technology and launched the Ganga Action Plan. During his tenure, telephone booths to facilitate telecommunication within the country and overseas were set up across India. He introduced the panchayati raj system to empower the rural people. He was assassinated in 1991.

### KALAM, A.P.J. ABDUL (b. 1931)
**Term: 25 July 2002–25 July 2007**

Dr A.P.J. Abdul Kalam, sometimes referred to as the Missile Man of India, was the 11th president of our country. Born on 15 October 1931, he specialized in aeronautical engineering from Madras Institute of Technology. He worked in the Indian Space Research Organization for two decades and was responsible for the evolution of its launch vehicle programme, particularly the Polar Satellite Launch Vehicle configuration. He was the scientific advisor to the defence minister and secretary of the Department of Defence Research and Development from July 1992 to December 1999. During this period, he led the famous Pokhran-II nuclear tests. He has written many books including *Wings of Fire, India 2020: A Vision for the New Millennium, My Journey* and *Ignited Minds*. Recipient of numerous awards, he was conferred the Bharat Ratna in 1997.

## MUKHERJEE, PRANAB (b. 1935)
### Term-25 July 2012–till date

Shri Pranab Kumar Mukherjee became the 13th president of India on 25 July 2012. Born in Mirati in West Bengal on 11 December 1935, he acquired a master's degree in history and political science and also a degree in law. After serving as a teacher and a journalist, he plunged into politics in 1969 following his election to the Rajya Sabha. He has held different portfolios at different times: external affairs, defence, commerce and finance. He was elected to the Upper House of the Parliament (Rajya Sabha) five times from 1969 and twice to the Lower House of the Parliament (Lok Sabha) from 2004. He served as a member of the Congress Working Committee, the highest policymaking body of the party, for over twenty-two years. He has won numerous awards, including the Padma Vibhusan in 2008, the Best Parliamentarian Award in 1997 as well as the Best Administrator in India Award in 2011.

## NEHRU, JAWAHARLAL (1889–1964)
### Term: 15 August 1947–27 May 1964

Born in 1889, Jawaharlal Nehru was a great political leader and India's first prime minister. After receiving his early education at home, he joined Cambridge University. He was later called to the Bar from Inner Temple. He returned to India in 1912 and joined politics. His first meeting with Mahatma Gandhi, in 1916, thoroughly inspired him. Nehru became the secretary of the Home Rule League in 1919. He organized the first Kisan March in Pratapgarh, Uttar Pradesh, in 1920. He faced imprisonment several times for participating in various movements including the non-cooperation movement and the Salt Satyagraha. In 1929, Nehru was elected president of the Lahore Session of the Indian National Congress, where complete independence for India was adopted as the goal. He was elected president of the Congress for the fourth time on 6 July 1946 and again for three terms from 1951 to 1954. A prolific author, he wrote several books, including *Discovery of India* and *Letters from a Father to his Daughter*. His birthday, 14 November, is celebrated as Children's Day in India.

## PATIL, PRATIBHA DEVISINGH (b. 1934)
**Term: 25 July 2007– 25 July 2012**

Born in Jalgaon district of Maharashtra, Pratibha Devisingh Patil was the first woman president of India. She has masters' degrees in both economics and political science as well as a degree in law, and initially practised at Jalgaon District Court. Patil successfully contested her first election to the Maharashtra legislature from Jalgaon at the young age of twenty-seven. She served as a Member of Parliament in the Rajya Sabha from 1985 to 1990. In 1991, she was elected as a Member of Parliament to the 10th Lok Sabha from Amravati constituency. From November 2004, she served as governor of Rajasthan.

## PRASAD, RAJENDRA (1884–1963)
**Term: 26 January 1950–13 May 1962**

Dr Rajendra Prasad was the first president of India. Born in Bihar, he was influenced by Gandhian ideals while he was in college and soon became a follower of the Mahatma. In 1920, he joined the Indian National Congress and was elected to the All India Congress Committee. Thereafter, he became its president several times and served prison terms for anti-British activities. In 1950, with the proclamation of the Indian republic, he became the president. His autobiography, *At the Feet of Mahatma Gandhi*, is one of his notable writings. He received the Bharat Ratna in 1962.

## RADHAKRISHNAN, SARVEPALLI (1888–1975)
**Term: 13 May 1962–13 May 1967**

Dr Radhakrishnan served as president from 1962 to 1967. Initially a professor at Mysore and Calcutta universities, he also served as the vice-chancellor of Andhra University, Benares Hindu University and chancellor of Delhi University. He taught eastern religions and ethics at the University of Oxford (1936–1952) also and served as India's ambassador to the Soviet Union (1949–1952). Through his innumerable speeches and books, he tried to interpret Indian thought for Westerners. He received the Bharat Ratna in 1954. His birthday, 5 September, is observed as Teachers' Day throughout India.

## SINGH, DR MANMOHAN (b. 1932)
**Term: 22 May 2004–till date**

Dr Manmohan Singh is the current prime minister of India. He was first elected to the post in 2004. He was a professor at Punjab University and Delhi University and also served with the UN, International Monetary Fund, and other international bodies. He joined the Indian government as an economic advisor and was India's finance minister from 1991 to 1996. He also served as the governor of Reserve Bank of India from 1982 to 1985. He introduced the concept of service tax as finance minister and is widely acclaimed as the architect of India's original economic liberalization programme implemented in 1991.He has won many awards for his work and contribution to society, including the Padma Vibhushan (1987), the Euro Money Finance Minister of the Year (1993) and the Asia Money Finance Minister of the Year (1993).

## VAJPAYEE, ATAL BIHARI (b. 1924)
### Term: 16 May 1996–1 June 1996 and 19 March 1998–22 May 2004

Born in 1924, Vajpayee shares credit with Jawaharlal Nehru for becoming prime minister for two successive mandates. His was introduced to Indian politics through his participation in the Quit India Movement in 1942. Later, in 1951, he joined the Bharatiya Jana Sangh, the forerunner of today's Bharatiya Janata Party. He was remarkably elected to the Lok Sabha nine times, and to the Rajya Sabha twice. As India's prime minister, foreign minister, chairperson of various standing committees of Parliament and also leader of the Opposition, he contributed hugely in shaping India's post-Independence domestic and foreign policies. Besides being an avid political personality, he was a great supporter of women's empowerment and social equality. For all his achievements, he was awarded the Padma Vibhushan in 1992. He is a prolific author and his works include *Meri Ikyavana Kavitaen* and *Bindu-Bindu Vichara*.

## DID YOU KNOW?

- Dr Rajendra Prasad was the only president to serve two complete terms in office, from 1950 to 1962.
- Dr S. Radhakrishnan was the first president to receive the Bharat Ratna (1954) before he became president (1962).
- Dr Zakir Hussain was the first governor to become president. He was the governor of Bihar from 1957 to 1962, and became president in 1967.
- Neelam Sanjiva Reddy was the youngest president at sixty-five years.
- Neelam Sanjiva Reddy was also the first chief minister to become president. He was the chief minister of Andhra Pradesh from 1956 to 1960 and from 1962 to 1964.
- In 1998, K.R. Narayanan became the first serving president to cast his vote in a general election.

## FACTS ON INDIAN PRIME MINISTERS

❧ Jawaharlal Nehru was the longest serving prime minister, from 1947 to 1964.

❧ Former prime minister Atal Bihari Vajpayee is the only parliamentarian to be elected from four different states: Uttar Pradesh, Gujarat, Madhya Pradesh and Delhi.

❧ Rajiv Gandhi was the youngest person to become prime minister at the age of forty-four years, and Morarji Desai the oldest at eighty-one.

❧ In 1977, Desai became the first non-Congress prime minister. He represented the Janata Party.

❧ Lal Bahadur Shastri was the first prime minister to receive the Bharat Ratna posthumously, in 1966.

❧ Indira Gandhi has been the only female prime minister till date.

❧ Morarji Desai was the first chief minister of independent India to become prime minister. He became the chief minister of Bombay from 1952 to 1956, and prime minister from 1977 to 1979.

❧ Dr Manmohan Singh is the first and only prime minister to sign currency notes, as governor of Reserve Bank of India from 1982 to 1985.

## PRIME MINISTERS OF INDIA

| NO. | NAME | TENURE | PARTY |
|---|---|---|---|
| 1 | Jawaharlal Nehru | 15 August 1947–27 May 1964 | Congress |
| 2 | Gulzari Lal Nanda | 27 May 1964–9 June 1964 | Congress |
| 3 | Lal Bahadur Shastri | 9 June 1964–11 January 1966 | Congress |
| 4 | Gulzari Lal Nanda | 11 January 1966–24 January 1966 | Congress |
| 5 | Indira Gandhi | 24 January 1966–24 March 1977 | Congress |
| 6 | Morarji Desai | 24 March 1977–28 July 1979 | Janata Party |
| 7 | Charan Singh | 28 July 1979–14 January 1980 | Janata Party |
| 8 | Indira Gandhi | 14 January 1980–31 October 1984 | Congress(I) |
| 9 | Rajiv Gandhi | 31 October 1984–2 December 1989 | Congress (I) |
| 10 | V.P. Singh | 2 December 1989–10 November 1990 | Janata Dal |
| 11 | Chandra Shekhar | 10 November 1990–21 June 1991 | Janata Dal (S) |
| 12 | P.V. Narasimha Rao | 21 June 1991–16 May 1996 | Congress (I) |
| 13 | Atal Bihari Vajpayee | 16 May 1996–1 June 1996 | BJP |
| 14 | H.D. Deve Gowda | 1 June 1996–21 April 1997 | Janata Dal |

| 15 | I.K. Gujral | 21 April 1997–19 March 1998 | Janata Dal |
| 16 | Atal Bihari Vajpayee | 19 March 1998–22 May 2004 | BJP |
| 17 | Manmohan Singh | 22 May 2004–till date | INC |

## PRESIDENTS OF INDIA

| NO. | NAME | TENURE |
|---|---|---|
| 1 | Rajendra Prasad | 26 January 1950–13 May 1962 |
| 2 | Sarvepalli Radhakrishnan | 13 May 1962–13 May 1967 |
| 3 | Zakir Hussain | 13 May 1967–3 May 1969 |
| 4 | Varahagiri Venkata Giri | 3 May 1969–20 July 1969 |
| | | 24 August 1969–24 August 1974 |
| 5 | Fakhruddin Ali Ahmed | 24 August 1977–11 February 1977 |
| 6 | Neelam Sanjiva Reddy | 25 July 1977–25 July 1982 |
| 7 | Giani Zail Singh | 25 July 1982–25 July 1987 |
| 8 | R. Venkataraman | 25 July 1987–25 July 1992 |
| 9 | Shankar Dayal Sharma | 25 July 1992–25 July 1997 |
| 10 | K.R. Narayanan | 25 July 1997–25 July 2002 |
| 11 | A.P.J. Abdul Kalam | 25 July 2002–25 July 2007 |
| 12 | Pratibha Devisingh Patil | 25 July 2007-25 July 2012 |
| 13 | Pranab Mukherjee | 25 July 2012 - till date |

## FORMS OF GOVERNMENT

❧ **Dictatorship** is a form of government where one person or a small group has absolute power without any constitutional limitations. Adolf Hitler (Nazi Germany), Joseph Stalin (Soviet Union), and Benito Mussolini (Italy) were all dictators.

❧ **Monarchy** is a political system based on the rule of a single person. The term applies to states in which supreme authority rests with the monarch, an individual ruler who functions as the head of state and achieves his position generally through heredity.

❧ **Oligarchy** is a form of government run by a small and privileged group of people for corrupt or selfish purposes. Aristotle used the term *oligarchia* to designate the rule of the few when it was exercised not by the best but by bad men unjustly. In this sense, oligarchy is a debased form of aristocracy, which denotes government by the few in which power is vested in the worst individuals.

- **Anarchy** may refer to an absence of government or a state of lawlessness or political disorder due to the absence of governmental authority.

- **Presidential** government is a system where the president is both the chief executive and head of state. The president is unique in that he or she is elected independently of the legislature. Such a form of government is followed in the US.

- **Communism** is a political and economic set-up where all people are meant to enjoy an equal share of a country's property and wealth.

- **Democracy** is a form of government in which the power rests in the people and is exercised by them directly or indirectly through voting /universal adult suffrage (a system of representation usually involving periodic free elections). This system is followed in India.

- **Federal Republic** is a form of government in which the powers of the central government are restricted and where the component parts (states, colonies, or provinces) retain a degree of self-government. Ultimate sovereign power rests with the voters who choose their governmental representatives.

- **Democratic Republic** is a form of government in which the supreme power rests in the body of citizens entitled to vote for officers and representatives responsible to them.

- An **emirate** is a government in which the supreme power is in the hands of an *emir* (the ruler of a Muslim state). The *emir* may be an absolute overlord or a sovereign with constitutionally limited authority. It is similar to a monarchy or sultanate.

## SOME OTHER CONSTITUTIONS OF THE WORLD

### CONSTITUTION OF THE UNITED STATES OF AMERICA

The constitution of the US is one of the oldest written constitutions still in use by any nation. It is the supreme law of the US. The members of the Constitutional Convention signed the United States Constitution on 17 September 1787 in Philadelphia, Pennsylvania. The new federal government came into existence in 1789. The Constitution provides the rules and powers of the three branches of government: a legislature, a bicameral Congress, the executive leaded by the president and the federal Judiciary.

### CONSTITUTION OF THE UNITED KINGDOM

The Constitution of the UK is the set of laws and principles under which UK is governed. The country has no written Constitution. Instead, Britain has a mixture of various statutes, conventions, judicial decisions, and treaties which collectively can be referred to as the Constitution. It is thus more accurate to refer to Britain's Constitution as an 'uncodified' Constitution, rather than an 'unwritten' one. It provides for a constitutional monarchy which includes hereditary succession. Amendments to the Constitution of UK can be made with majority support in both houses of Parliament followed by royal assent.

| COUNTRY | NAME OF THE PARLIAMENT |
| --- | --- |
| Australia | Parliament of the Commonwealth of Australia |
| Bangladesh | Jatiyo Sangsad (Bangladesh Parliament) |
| Brazil | National Congress |
| China (Mainland) | National People's Congress |
| France | Parlement (Parliament of France) |
| Germany | Bundestag (Lower House), Bundesrat (Upper House) |
| Iran | Majlis |
| Japan | Diet (National Parliament of Japan) |
| UK | Parliament (House of Commons and House of Lords) |
| US | Congress (House of Representatives and Senate) |

# INTERESTING FACTS

### 10, DOWNING STREET, UK

King George II offered the house on Downing Street to Sir Robert Walpole, who held the title First of Lord of the Treasury and also effectively served as the first prime minister, as a personal gift. Walpole refused and instead asked the king to make the house available to him, and future First Lords of the Treasury, in their official capacity. To this day, prime ministers occupy Number 10 in the role of First Lord of the Treasury. The brass letter box on the black front door is still engraved with this title.

### RASHTRAPATI BHAVAN, INDIA

The Rashtrapati Bhavan was scheduled to be built in four years but took seventeen years to complete. On the eighteenth year of its completion, India became independent.

## WHITE HOUSE, US

At various times in history, the White House has been known as the President's Palace, the President's House, and the Executive Mansion. In 1901, President Theodore Roosevelt officially gave the White House its current name.

## THE PRESIDENTIAL PALACE, FINLAND

The Presidential Palace in Helsinki was, at the beginning of 19th century, a salt storehouse named J.H. Heidenstrauch.

# COMPUTER

## TIMELINE

**1930:** American engineer Vannevar Bush develops the differential analyser, the first modern analog computer, at Massachusetts Institute of Technology.

**1938:** German engineer Konrad Zuse invents Z1, the first programmable binary computing machine in the world.

**1940:** George Stibitz demonstrates the CNC (Complex Number Calculator) in US, which is considered to be the first demonstration of remote access computing. Alan Turing and others design the codebreaking machine, Bombe, in England. It helped decipher German ciphers during World War II.

**1944–1945:** Konrad Zuse develops the first high-level computer programming language, Plankalkul ('Plan Calculus').

**1946:** The ENIAC (Electronic Numerical Integrator and Computer), built by John Mauchly and J. Presper Eckert, is unveiled to the public. It improves on the speed of its contemporaries by 1,000 times.

**1948:** The world's first stored-program electronic digital computer, the Manchester Small Scale Experimental Machine, nicknamed 'The Baby', successfully executes its first program.

**1950:** Engineering Research Associates of Minneapolis build ERA 1101, the first commercially-produced computer. Their first customer is the US Navy.

**1954:** IBM 650 magnetic drum calculator establishes itself as the first mass-produced computer, with the company selling 450 units in one year.

**1957:** FORTRAN (short for FORmula TRANslator), a programming language, is developed by John Backus. With the help of this program, a computer can perform repetitive tasks from a single set of instructions, by using loops.

**1958:** SAGE (Semi-Automatic Ground Environment) links hundreds of radar stations in the US and Canada, in the first large-scale computer communications network. Jack Kilby invents the integrated circuit, or the 'chip', made of germanium.

**1960:** The precursor to the minicomputer, PDP-1 (Programmed Data Processor), is launched. It includes a cathode ray tube and graphic display, functions without air conditioning and needs only one operator. The large scope of the microcomputer inspires the early hackers at MIT, to write the first computerized video game, SpaceWar for it.

AT&T designs Dataphone, the first commercial modem.

**1963:** ASCII (American Standard Code for Information Interchange) permits machines from different manufacturers to exchange data.

**1964:** The 6600 supercomputer, designed by Seymour Cray, performs up to 3 million instructions per second, making it the fastest computer in the world. Thomas Kurtz and John Kemeny create BASIC (Beginner's All-purpose Symbolic Instruction Code), an easy-to-learn programming language.

**1966:** Hewlett-Packard manufactures HP-2115, offering a computational power formerly found only in much larger computers. It supported a wide variety of languages, among them BASIC, ALGOL (ALGOrithmic Language), and FORTRAN.

**1967:** Seymour Papert designs LOGO as a computer language for children.

**1970:** Xerox opens Palo Alto Research Centre (PARC), which produces many inventions that transform computing: the personal computer graphical user interface (Ethernet), the laser printer, and object-oriented programming.

**1971:** John V. Blankenbaker designs Kenbak-1, the first personal computer, advertised in the magazine *Scientific American* and selling at a cost of 750 dollars. The first e-mail is sent by Ray Tomlinson. Tomlinson, who is also credited with deciding on the @ sign for use in e-mail, sends his message over the military network, ARPANET (Advanced Research Projects Agency NETwork). The email simply read 'QWERTYUIOP'.

An IBM team, originally led by David Noble, invents the 8-inch floppy diskette, with which users can easily transfer floppies in protective jackets from one drive to another.

**1972:** Pong, a video game on ping-pong or table tennis, is released. Pong goes on to revolutionize the arcade industry and launch the modern video game era.

**1973:** Robert Metcalfe devises the Ethernet method of network connection.

**1974:** Alto, the first workstation with a built-in mouse for input is designed at Xerox Palo Alto Research Center. Some of the features of the Alto include storing several files simultaneously in windows, offering menus and icons and offering the option of linking to a local area network.

**1975:** Microsoft Corporation is founded by Bill Gates and Paul Allen. The Altair 8800 computer goes on sale. Gates and Allen license BASIC as the software language for the Altair. 8800 inventor Ed Roberts coins the term 'personal computer' (PC) to describe it.

**1976:** Apple Computer Inc. is founded by Steven Wozniak, Steven Jobs, and Ron Wayne. Apple I, a computer designed and hand-built by Wozniak, is launched.

**1977:** Apple II is released and is an instant hit. Atari releases the Atari Video Computer System, later renamed Atari 2600. The first widely successful video game system, it sells over 20 million units.

**1979:** Seymour Rubenstein and Rob Barnaby create WordStar word processing software. John Shoch and Jon Hupp discover the computer 'worm', a short program that searches a network for idle processors. Initially designed to provide more efficient use of computers and for testing, the worm has the unintended effect of invading networked computers, and develops as a type of virus.

**1981:** IBM introduces its PC, igniting a fast growth of the PC market. The first PC uses Microsoft's MS-DOS (Microsoft Disk Operating System). Adam Osborne completes the first portable computer, Osborne I, weighing 24 pounds. Sony introduces 3½-inch floppy drives and diskettes.

**1982:** Mitch Kapor develops Lotus 1-2-3, writing the software directly into the video system of the IBM PC. By bypassing DOS, it runs much faster than its competitors. Elk Cloner, written by the fifteen-year-old Richard Skrenta in 1982 for Apple II, is the first computer virus known to have spread in the wild (outside the computer system or lab in which it was written).

**1983:** Apple introduces Lisa, the first PC with a graphical user interface (GUI). Microsoft announces Word, originally called Multi-Tool Word.

**1984:** Apple launches Macintosh, the first successful mouse-driven computer with a GUI. With the capacity to hold 550 MB of pre-recorded data, CD-ROMs (Compact Disc Read-Only Memory) grow out of music compact discs (CDs).

**1985:** Microsoft introduces the Windows operating system. The C++ programming language emerges as the dominant object-oriented language in the computer industry.

**1988:** Apple co-founder Steve Jobs, who had left Apple to form his own company, unveils NeXT, the first PC to incorporate a drive for an optical storage disk (for instance, a CD), a built-in digital signal processor allowing voice recognition, and object-oriented languages to simplify programming.

**1990:** The World Wide Web (WWW) is born when Tim Berners-Lee develops HTML (HyperText Markup Language). He allows the Internet to expand into the WWW, using specifications such as URL (Uniform Resource Locator) and HTTP (HyperText Transfer Protocol). A browser, such as Netscape or Microsoft Internet Explorer, follows links and sends a query to a server, allowing a user to view a site.

**1991:** The WWW is made available to the general public. The US National Science Foundation (NSF), through its NSFNET (linking five supercomputer centres at five US universities), allows commercial use of the Internet for the first time. Linux operating system, designed by Finnish student Linus Torvalds, is introduced.

**1994:** Netscape Communications Corporation is founded and delivers its first Internet browser in October. Yahoo is founded by Stanford graduate students Jerry Yang and David Filo and quickly becomes one of the most popular search engines.

**1996:** The Internet World Exposition is the world's first fair to be held on the Internet.

**1996:** Sabeer Bhatia, along with Jack Smith, launches the e-mail service Hotmail, the first web-based e-mail service.

**1997:** Larry Page and Sergei Brin create the search engine BackRub, later changed to Google in 1998.

## TYPES OF COMPUTERS

**Mainframe Computers:** Used in the early days of computing, these were huge data processing machines that took up a lot of space, sometimes an entire room. Though the size of computers have drastically reduced, these are still used in some large companies, to process massive transactions every day.

**Personal Computers:** A personal computer (PC) is one which is used typically by a single user for general purpose. Most people tend to relate a PC with a computer running the Windows operating system. However, a Mac is technically a PC. PCs were also known as microcomputers initially, as they were much smaller than the huge computers used in businesses.

**Desktop Computers:** A PC that is designed to be kept in a permanent location is known as a desktop. It is divided into separate components such as the CPU, monitor, keyboard, and mouse that are to be assembled for the entire system to work. Desktops are generally synonymous with bigger screens, more power and more storage space than portable computers.

**Laptop:** A portable computer that integrates the various components of the computer into one whole unit is a laptop. Laptops provide the option to carry them around as they are usually lightweight and small, and are also known as notebooks.

**Personal Digital Assistants:** PDAs are even smaller than laptops and more often than not, they depend on flash memory to store data, rather than a hard drive. They are generally operated using 'touch screen' technology.

**Wearable Computers:** These are integrated miniature electronic devices that are worn by people under with or on top of clothing. Common computer applications (e-mail, database, multimedia, and calendar/scheduler) are integrated into watches, cell phones, visors and even clothes. Google has started Project Glass, focused around augmented-reality glasses.

**Video Games:** We have come a long way from 8-bit video games that needed cartridges to be attached to play. In the age of the X-box and the Playstation, video games have become a rite of passage for every kid. Computers play an integral part; almost every game can be played on the computer just as well. Here are some of the types of games:

- **Beat 'Em Up and Hack-and-Slash:** These games have an emphasis on one-on-many close-quarter combat, beating large numbers of computer-controlled enemies. Gameplay involves the player fighting through a series of increasingly difficult levels. The sole distinction between these two genres are that beat 'em ups feature hand-to-hand combat, while hack-and-slash games feature melee weaponry, particularly bladed weapons. Some popular titles are Street Fighter, Mortal Kombat, and Tekken.

- **First Person Shooter:** This is a video game genre that centres the gameplay on gun and projectile weapon-based combat through first person perspective; the player experiences the action through the eyes of a protagonist. Doom was the breakthrough game of the genre, and other popular games are Halo, Call of Duty, and Counter-Strike.

- **Role-playing Games**: These draw their gameplay from traditional role-playing like Dungeons & Dragons. Most cast the player in the role of one or more 'adventurers' who specialize in specific skill sets (melee combat, casting magic spells) while progressing through a predetermined storyline, like Final Fantasy, Fallout, and Grand Theft Auto.

- **Simulation Games**: There are two broad spectrums in which simulation games are divided. Vehicle simulation games are those which attempt to provide the player with a realistic interpretation of operating various kinds of vehicles, like Flight Gear and NASCAR. Then there are life simulation games involve living or controlling one or more artificial lives. A life simulation game can revolve around individuals and relationships, or it could be a simulation of an ecosystem, as in Sims and Spore.

- **Strategy Games:** They focus on gameplay requiring careful, skilful thinking and planning to achieve victory. 4X refers to a type of strategy video game with four primary goals: eXplore, eXpand, eXploit, eXterminate. A 4X game can be turn-based or real-time. Some examples are Warcraft, Age of Empires, and Command and Conquer.

❧ Batman: Arkham Asylum holds the Guinness World Record for being the 'Most Critically Acclaimed Superhero Game Ever Released'.

Apart from proper video games, there has been a recent upsurge of apps that one can play on smartphones. Among *Time*'s list of the top apps for the iPhone are Angry Birds, Scrabble, Doodle Jump, Fruit Ninja and Cut the Rope.

## SOCIAL NETWORKING

**Orkut:** Launched in 2004. This was the website that started the trend of social networking. Named after Orkut Buyukkokten, a Google employee, it gained massive popularity in its early days, though it has hit a slump after the rise of Facebook. It has faced problems in countries like Saudi Arabia, Iran and the United Arab Emirates, where it has been banned.

**Facebook** Launched in February 2004, Facebook allows users to share ideas, thoughts, images and videos amongst themselves and their social circles. The credit for creating Facebook is given largely to Mark Zuckerberg, who designed it while still a student at Harvard. *The Accidental Billionaires* is a book based around the birth of Facebook, on which film the *The Social Network* was made. In February 2011, an Egyptian couple named their baby Facebook to commemorate the vital role played by Facebook and other social media in Egypt's revolution.

**Twitter:** Created by Jack Dorsey and launched in July 2006, it is a new-age microblogging site that allows members to upload text messages of up to 140 characters and images. As of May 2012, Twitter has around 140 million users worldwide, generating over 200 million tweets and handling over 1.6 billion search queries every day. It has also played a vital role during times of emergencies and social unrest, with people raising awareness or voicing dissent via tweets.

## VIRUS

A virus is a computer program that can use a network to replicate itself and spread from one computer to another, without the user being aware of it. The term 'virus' is commonly, but mistakenly, used to refer to different types of malware like worms and Trojan horses, adware and spyware. Fred Cohen's paper 'Computer Viruses: Theory and Experiments', written in 1984, was the first paper to call a self-reproducing program a virus, a term introduced by Cohen's mentor Leonard Adleman.

**Trojan Horse:** Named after the legendary wooden horse left in Troy by the Greeks, it is a code fragment that hides inside a program and performs a disguised function. It hides in an independent program and while the program runs normally, the Trojan penetrates the defences of the system and gains unauthorized information.

**Worm:** A worm is a program that makes and facilitates the distribution of copies of itself; from one disk drive to another or by copying itself by using e-mail or another transport mechanism. It normally damages and compromises the security of a computer.

**Overwrite Virus:** One of the more dangerous kinds of viruses, they work by infecting executable files. They overwrite some of the code of the original program, thus the program slowly stops working while the virus runs and eventually infects other programs as well.

**FAT Virus:** The File Allocation Table (FAT) is a file system that keeps track and helps access all the files on a disk, which may often be scattered due to fragmentation. A FAT virus works by infecting this table which leads to the computer being unable to locate certain files, making them unusable. Due to this data, or even entire directories, can be permanently lost.

**Sparse Infectors:** For a virus to spread in a computer, it is essential for it to avoid detection. To that end, some viruses use any number of different techniques to minimize the chances of them being discovered. They can run every 20th time a program is executed, or only affect files that have a specified size.

## ARTIFICIAL INTELLIGENCE

This a branch of study that deals with the simulation of intelligent human behaviour in computers. John McCarthy coined the term in 1956 at the Massachusetts Institute of Technology, and defined it as 'the science and engineering of making intelligent machines.' Thus it is basically the development of computer systems that are able to perform tasks which require human intelligence.

Artificial Intelligence is used for data mining, financial systems, logistics, medicine and software designed to help people with impairments, such as voice command and character recognition. The greatest advancement has come in the role of gameplaying, and the best computer chess programs are capable of beating humans, as was evidenced on 11 May 1997, when Deep Blue became the first computer chess-playing system to beat a reigning world chess champion, Gary Kasparov. In 2005, a Stanford robot won the DARPA Grand Challenge by driving autonomously for 210.82 km along an unrehearsed desert trail. In February 2011, in a *Jeopardy!* quiz show exhibition match, IBM's question answering system, Watson, defeated the two greatest *Jeopardy!* champions, Brad Rutter and Ken Jennings, by a huge margin.

In fiction, AI has fulfilled many roles, including that of a servants (R2D2 and C3PO in the *Star Wars* franchise), a law enforcer (K.I.T.T. in *Knight Rider*), a comrade (Lt. Commander Data in *Star Trek: The Next Generation*), a conqueror/overlord (Mr Smith in *The Matrix* trilogy), an assassin (*Terminator*), a sentient race (*Transformers*), and a menace due to divided loyalties (HAL 9000 in *2001: A Space Odyssey*).

## P2P SHARING

In simple terms, P2P sharing refers to computer systems which are connected via the Internet so that files can be shared directly from each other, without the need of a central server. The basic requirement to engage in P2P sharing is an Internet connection and a P2P software, like BitTorrent or Limewire. These can be used to share content such as audio, video, images, data or anything in digital format.

The first peer-to-peer application was the file-sharing system Napster, originally released in 1999. Since then, other applications like BitTorrent, Limewire, Skype, and Spotify have become household names.

This has also come under a lot of controversy, as many critics point out that P2P networks walk hand in hand with the growing threat of piracy. In fact, one can download movies, songs, games and most types of digital content without paying. In October 2007, Comcast, one of the US' largest broadband Internet providers, started blocking P2P applications such as BitTorrent. Kim Dotcom, founder of the site Megaupload, which allowed users to download most types of digital content, was arrested in 2012 for copyright infringement, and the site was shut down by the US Department of Justice.

## HACKING

Hacking means detecting weaknesses in a system and exploiting them. There are many reasons why a person may hack, such as for profit, as a sign of protest, or as a challenge. Hackers who try to gain unauthorized access to other computers via the Internet, breaking past the security measures installed, are known as Black Hat Hackers. Then there are those who legitimately try to break into computers or servers to ensure the security measures are adequate and debug or fix problems. They are known as White Hat Hackers. However, there is often a fine line between the two, resulting in a group of people with a morally ambiguous stand, known as Grey Hat Hackers.

There is another group of people who approach programming in a spirit of playful cleverness. This is far removed from computer security and deals with innovation, associated with free software and open source. Thus, from a technical point of view, greats like Tim Berners-Lee, Steve Jobs, Linus Torvalds and Bill Gates were also hackers who revolutionized the computing industry.

Ethical hackers are people who are hired by an organiztaion to test the entire security of an organization's computer network, to check for any flaws and help the organiztaion take pre-emptive measures against malicious attacks. Ankit Fadia is probably one of the best-known hackers in India who, at the age of fifteen, released his book on ethical hacking, and now helps many government agencies curtail cyberterrorism.

## CLOUD COMPUTING

Cloud computing basically consists of a network of computers in an organization which are connected to a 'cloud', which can be accessed through the Internet. Thus, instead of loading applications or softwares to every single computer individually, one can access them directly from the cloud. A simple example of this would be e-mail accounts in Gmail or Yahoo-mail, where your personal data is not stored in your computer, but can be accessed by logging into your account via the Internet. Thus, one can store their data in the cloud, instead of a particular computer, and access it from any system over the world.

## COMPUTER GLOSSARY

**Bit:** Claude E. Shannon first used the word *bit* in a 1948 paper. Shannon's bit is a portmanteau word for **b**inary and dig**it**. He attributed its origin to John W. Tukey.

**BASIC:** In computer programming, BASIC (Beginner's All-purpose Symbolic Instruction Code) is a family of high-level programming languages designed to be easy to use.

**Bug:** This is a fault in a computer program, which prevents it from working correctly. The term is often credited to Grace Hopper. In 1946, she joined the Harvard Faculty at the Computation Laboratory where she traced an error in the Harvard Mark II to a moth trapped in a relay. This bug was carefully removed and taped to the iBook.

**Cookie:** This is a packet of information that travels between a browser and the web server. The term was coined by web browser programmer Lou Montulli after the term 'magic cookies' used by UNIX programmers.

**Cache:** This is an auxiliary memory from which easy and high-speed retrieval is possible.

**Hardware:** This comprises multiple physical components of a computer, on which can be installed on operating system and many types of software to perform desired functions.

**Mouse potato:** A person who spends all of his time at a computer, surfing the net or playing games, is a mouse potato.

**Spam:** Unwanted repetitive messages, such as unsolicited bulk e-mail, are termed spam.

# PIONEERS

### BABBAGE, CHARLES (1791-1871)

Known as the Father of the Computer, Babbage was a mathematician, mechanical engineer, philosopher and inventor. While studying in Cambridge, he and his friends started the Ghost Club, where they tried to resolve supernatural phenomena. He designed the analytical engine, the first programmable mechanical computer. He was a founding member and a gold medal winner of the Royal Astronomical Society.

### GATES, BILL (b. 1955)

William Henry Gates III is the chairman of Microsoft. During his career, he was the chief executive officer and chief software architect. He now devotes a greater part of his time at the Bill and Melinda Gates Foundation, a charity that helps various causes all around the world. He has been consistently ranked amongst the richest people in the world by *Forbes*.

### JOBS, STEVE (1955-2011)

Founder, chairman and former CEO of Apple, he was also the former CEO of Pixar Animation Studios. Along with his partners, he successfully founded the first line of commercially viable personal computers. He was the man behind the hugely famous products Macintosh, the iPad, the iPhone, and the iPod. He was also the largest individual shareholder of Walt Disney Company.

### LEE, TIM BERNERS (b. 1955)

Credited with inventing the World Wide Web, he is the first person to have implemented successful communication between a Hypertext Transfer Protocol (HTTP) and a server via the Internet. He was working at CERN at that time and the first website address he created was info.cern.ch. He has

The Puffin Factfinder

been knighted by the Queen, been awarded an Order of Merit, and is a fellow of the Royal Society.

### LOVELACE, ADA (1815–1852)

Augusta Ada King, Countess of Lovelace, was a writer best known for her work on Babbage's analytical engine. She was the daughter of the famous poet Lord Byron. Her notes on the analytical engine included an algorithm to be processed by the machine. She is known as the world's first computer programmer.

### PAGE, LARRY (b. 1973)

An internet entrepreuner and computer scientist, he is the co-founder of Google along with Sergei Brin. During the research stage of Google, the project was nicknamed BackRub. In 2002, the World Economic Forum named Page a Global Leader for Tomorrow. He is the eleventh richest person in the US.

### STIBITZ, GEORGE (1904–1995)

Stibitz is recognized internationally as one of the fathers of the modern computer. When he was working at Bell Laboratories, he designed a machine he named Model K (K for kitchen table), which could calculate numbers using binary. He was the first to design a computing machine that could be remotely used by a phone line, which he unveiled at a public exhibition in New York.

### TURING, ALAN (1912–1954)

Considered the father of computer science and artificial intelligence, he created the Turing machine, which formalized the concepts of computing and algorithms, the basis of modern computers. During World War II, he was head of Britain's codebreaking centre that dealt with German naval ciphers. Since 1966, the Turing Award has been given by the Association for Computing Machinery for technical excellence in computing.

### ZUCKERBERG, MARK (b. 1984)

Named by *Time* as Person of the Year in 2010, he is the co-founder and president of Facebook. The film *The Social Network* revolves around his life and the birth of the networking site. Like Bill Gates and Warren Buffet, he has pledged to give away around half his wealth to charity. *Vanity Fair* named Zuckerberg number one on its 2010 list of '100 Most Influential People of the Information Age'.

# DID YOU KNOW?

◇ The first mouse, made by Doug Englebart and his lead engineer Bill English, was encased in a wooden block, with wheels in the underbelly.

◇ Steve Jobs drew a salary of 1 dollar in 2010 as the CEO of Apple.

◇ MacQuariums are aquariums made to sit inside Macintosh computer shells, which makes the fish moving inside look like a screensaver.

◇ In computing, a Three-finger-salute is when one presses the keys Ctrl-Alt-Del.

◇ The Apple logo originally had Newton sitting under an apple tree, with an apple about to fall on his head, but it was later changed to the now iconic graphic of a bitten apple—a reference to the Bible, where the apple was the fruit of knowledge.

◇ Sony changed the size of the CD from 8 cm to 12 cm, which is its existing size, so that it could incorporate Beethoven's Ninth Symphony.

◇ A byte consists of 8 bits, and 4 bits make up a nibble.

◇ The word spam, used for unwanted e-mail, was actually the name of a variety of brand of tinned meat served to the US army during World War II.

◇ 'Hole in the Wall' was a project started all over India where computers were placed in niches in walls of slums and government schools, so children could work out basic computing skills on their own.

◇ *The Dark Knight* was the first movie available for rent from Facebook.

# ENVIRONMENT

Our environment includes all living and nonliving things around us. The nonliving components are land, water and air. The living components are plants, animals and humans. All animals and plants adjust to the environment into which they are born. Any change in it may cause discomfort and affect their normal life. Any unfavourable change or degeneration in the environment is known as environmental pollution.

## ENVIRONMENT CALENDAR

**2 February:** World Wetlands Day

**21 March:** World Forestry Day

**22 March:** World Water Day

**23 March:** World Meteorological Day

**22 April:** Earth Day

**5 June:** World Environment Day

**11 July:** World Population Day

**16 September:** World Ozone Day

**28 September:** Green Consumer Day

**First Monday of October:** World Habitat Day

**4 October:** World Animal Day

**1–7 October:** World Wildlife Week

**13 October:** International Day for Disaster Reduction

# ENERGY

Energy is defined as the ability or the capacity to do work. We need energy to do work and for movement. When we eat, our bodies transform the food into energy. When we run or walk or do some work, we 'burn' energy in our bodies. Cars, planes, trolleys, boats, and machinery also transform energy into work. There are many sources of energy, which are broadly divided into two major groups: renewable and nonrenewable.

**Renewable energy**: Renewable energy resources are those natural resources that are not depleted by use (forests, fish). Theoretically, the supply of these natural resources can never be exhausted because they are continuously produced. Under this category are sources such as the sun, wind, water, agricultural residue, firewood, and animal dung. Energy generated from the sun is known as solar energy whereas energy derived from water is hydel energy. Biomass refers to energy-sources like firewood, animal dung, biodegradable waste from cities, and crop residues. Geothermal energy is derived from hot dry rocks, magma, hot water springs, and natural geysers. Ocean thermal is energy derived from waves and tidal waves.

**Nonrenewable energy:** Nonrenewable resources are those natural resources that are depleted and not naturally replenished once harvested. Metal ores and fossil fuels (coal, natural gas, oil) are some of the examples of nonrenewable sources. Fossil fuels are formed over millions of years by the action of heat from the Earth's core and pressure from rock and soil on the remains ('fossils') of dead plants and creatures. Another nonrenewable energy source is the element uranium, whose atoms we split (through nuclear fission) to create heat and electricity.

# POLLUTION

## AIR POLLUTION

The contamination of air by the discharge of harmful substances in such quality and for such duration as is injurious to human health or welfare, animal or plant life is called air pollution. Industries, vehicles, increase in the population, and urbanization are the major factors responsible for air pollution. Agencies that emit considerable pollutants into the air are thermal power plants, cement and steel industries, refineries, petrochemical industries, and the mining industry.

## MAJOR AIR POLLUTANTS AND THEIR SOURCES

**Carbon monoxide** (CO) is a colourless, odourless gas produced by the incomplete burning of carbon-based fuels including petrol, diesel and wood.

It is also produced by the combustion of natural and synthetic products, such as cigarettes. It lowers the amount of oxygen that enters our blood. It can slow our reflexes and make us sleepy.

**Carbon dioxide** ($CO_2$) is the most important greenhouse gas, emitted as a result of human activities such as the burning of coal, oil, and natural gases.

**Chlorofluorocarbons** (CFC) are gases that are released mainly from air conditioning systems and refrigeration. When released into the air, CFCs rise to the stratosphere, where they come in contact with few other gases, which lead to a reduction of the ozone layer that protects the earth from the harmful UV rays of the sun.

**Lead** is present in petrol, diesel, lead batteries, paints, hair dye, etc. It affects children adversely. It can cause damage to the nervous system and digestive problems and can also lead to cancer.

**Nitrogen oxides** (NOx) cause smog and acid rain. They are produced from burning fuels including petrol, diesel and coal. During winter, NOx can lead to respiratory diseases.

**Ozone** ($O_3$) occurs naturally in the upper layers of the atmosphere. This important gas shields the earth from the harmful UV rays of the sun. However, at the ground level, it is a pollutant with highly toxic effects. Vehicles and industries are major sources of ground-level ozone emissions. Ozone makes our eyes itch, burn and water. It lowers our resistance to colds and pneumonia.

**Suspended particulate matter** (SPM) consists of solids in the air in the form of smoke, dust and vapour that can remain suspended for extended periods. It is also the main source of haze, which reduces visibility. The finer of these particles, when breathed in, can lodge in our lungs and cause lung damage and respiratory problems.

**Sulphur dioxide** ($SO_2$) is a gas produced by burning coal, mainly in thermal power plants. Some industrial processes, such as production of paper and smelting of metals, produce $SO_2$. A major contributor to smog and acid rain, it can also cause lung diseases.

## WATER POLLUTION

Water pollution is the deterioration in the quality of water caused by toxic substances that enter lakes, streams, rivers, oceans, and other waterbodies, making them unfit for use and adversely affecting aquatic ecosystems. Pollutants can also seep down and affect the groundwater deposits.

Water pollution has many sources. The most polluting of them are the city sewage and industrial waste discharged into the rivers. Facilities to treat waste water are not adequate in India. Due to this, pollutants enter groundwater, rivers, and other waterbodies. Such water, which ultimately ends up in our households, is often highly contaminated and carries disease-causing microbes. Agricultural run-off is another major water pollutant, as it contains fertilizers and pesticides.

## SOIL POLLUTION

Soil pollution is caused when toxic compounds, chemicals, salts, radioactive materials, or disease-causing agents are built up in the soil, adversely affecting plant growth and animal health. Soil pollution is caused by man-made chemicals or other changes in the natural soil environment. Application of pesticides, fuel dumping, leaching of wastes from landfills or direct discharge of industrial wastes to the soil are some of the ways in which soil is contaminated. The most common chemicals involved are petroleum hydrocarbons, solvents, pesticides, lead and other heavy metals.

## NOISE POLLUTION

Increasing ambient noise levels in public places from various sources, industrial activity, construction activity, generator sets, loudspeakers, public address systems, music systems, vehicular horns and other mechanical devices have adverse effects on human health and the psychological well-being. It is necessary to regulate noise sources to maintain the ambient air quality standards with respect to noise. The state government may categorize areas into industrial, commercial, residential or silence areas/zones for the purpose of implementation to noise standards for different areas. An area comprising not less than 100 m around hospitals, educational institutions and courts may be declared as a silence area. If the noise level exceeds the ambient noise standards by 10 dB(A) or more, complaints can be lodged.

## GLOSSARY OF ENVIRONMENT TERMS

**Acid rain:** Strong acids fall from the atmosphere in the form of rain, snow, fog or dry particles. The acid is the result of pollution caused mostly by sulphur oxides and nitrogen oxides that are discharged into the atmosphere. It is also created by burning coal and oil, by smelting industries and vehicles. In the atmosphere, these gases combine with water vapour to form acids, which then fall back on the Earth. The result often kills forests and sterilizes lakes.

**Afforestation:** Planting trees where there were none before.

**Algae:** Simple rootless, flowerless plants belonging to a large group that include seaweeds and many single-celled forms. They grow in sunlit waters and are food for fish and small aquatic animals. They lower the dissolved oxygen in the water leading to deterioration of water quality.

**Atmosphere:** The envelope of air surrounding the Earth. Most of the total mass of the atmosphere lies within the troposphere and the stratosphere. Most weather events are confined to the troposphere, the lower 8–12 km of the atmosphere. The ozone layer is found in the stratosphere, which typically extends 10–40 km above the Earth.

**Biodegradable:** That which is capable of being broken down by living organisms into inorganic compounds. Ideally all waste should be biodegradable.

**Biological diversity:** The variety of different living organisms from all sources including terrestrial, marine and other aquatic ecosystems and the variety of different ecosystems that they form. This includes diversity within species, between species and ecosystems, and the genetic variability of each species.

**Biomass**: The total amount of living organisms in a given area.

**Biosphere**: The global ecosystem; that part of the Earth and atmosphere capable of supporting living organisms.

**Climate change**: The slow variation of climatic characteristics over time at a given place. It usually refers to the change of climate which is attributed directly or indirectly to human activity that alters the composition of the global atmosphere and which is, in addition to natural climate variability, observed over comparable periods.

**Climate system**: The totality of the atmosphere, hydrosphere, biosphere, and geosphere and their interactions that characterize the average and extreme conditions of the atmosphere over a long period at any one place or region of the Earth's surface.

**Conservation**: The long-term protection and sustainable management of natural resources in accordance with principles that ensure socio-economic benefits.

**Deforestation:** The felling of trees, usually for commercial purposes.

**Desertification**: Land degradation in arid, semi-arid and dry sub-humid areas resulting from various factors, including climatic variations and human activities.

**DDT**: Dichloro-diphenyl-trichloroethane is generally used as an insecticide. It has been banned since 1969 in most developed countries because it is a probable cause of cancer. However, it is still widely used in developing countries.

**Drought:** A naturally-occurring phenomenon that occurs when precipitation is significantly below normal levels, causing water levels to drop and vegetation to die. This extended period of dry weather usually lasts longer than expected and leads to measurable losses. (crop damage, water supply shortage).

**Ecosystem:** A dynamic and complex system of plant, animal and microorganism communities and their nonliving environment, all interacting as a functional unit within a defined physical location. The term may be applied to a unit as large as the entire ecosphere, but usually refers to a division thereof.

**Emissions:** The release of greenhouse gases and/or their precursors into the atmosphere over a specified area and period.

**Endangered species:** A species threatened with extinction.

**Erosion:** The wearing away of land surface by wind, water, glaciers, chemicals, and exposure to the atmosphere. Erosion occurs naturally but can be intensified by land-clearing practices related to farming, residential or industrial development, road building or deforestation.

**Extinct species:** A species that no longer survives anywhere in the world.

**Global warming:** Global warming and global cooling actually refer to the natural warming and cooling trends that the earth has experienced all through its history. The term, though, is usually applied to the gradual rise in the Earth's temperatures that could result from the greenhouse effect caused by increased levels of carbon dioxide, chlorofluorocarbons, and other pollutants.

**Greenhouse effect:** Warming of the Earth's atmosphere due to the presence of certain gases such as water vapour, carbon dioxide, methane, and nitrous oxide. These gases, collectively called greenhouse gases, absorb radiation emitted by the Earth and reduce the loss of energy to space. The greenhouse effect is responsible for maintaining the Earth's surface at a temperature that makes it habitable for human beings. When the concentration of these gases increases to a high degree, the natural greenhouse effect is enhanced, causing a large and rapid rise in average global temperatures

**Greenhouse gases**: Those gaseous constituents of the atmosphere, both natural and artificial, that absorb and re-emit infrared radiation and that are responsible for global warming. The most potent greenhouse gas, carbon dioxide, is rapidly accumulating in the atmosphere due to human activities.

**Groundwater**: The supply of fresh water found beneath the earth's surface (usually in aquifers), often accessed through wells and springs.

**Habitat:** The geographical location(s) and the associated set(s) of environmental conditions that is necessary for the flourishing of a particular type of plant or animal.

**Hydrochlorofluorocarbons (HCFCs):** Organic substances composed of hydrogen, chlorine, fluorine, and carbon atoms. These chemicals are less stable than CFCs, and are therefore less damaging to the ozone layer.

**Hydrofluorocarbons (HFCs):** Chemicals with fluorine but no chlorine, and therefore not likely to damage the ozone layer. However, HFCs are potent greenhouse gases.

**Hazardous waste:** Refuse that could present dangers through the contamination and pollution of the environment. It requires special disposal techniques to make it harmless or less dangerous.

**Hydroelectricity:** Electric energy produced by water-powered turbine generators.

**Inorganic**: Matter other than plant or animal, and not containing a combination of carbon, hydrogen and oxygen, which all living things contain.

**Integrated resource planning:** The management of two or more resources in the same general area, such as water, soil, timber, grazing land, fish, wildlife, and recreation.

**Land degradation:** The reduction or loss of the biological or economic productivity from rainfed cropland, irrigated cropland or range, pasture, forest and woodlands. Land degradation usually results from unsustainable land use.

**Natural resource:** Resources whose supply can essentially never be exhausted, usually because they are continuously produced. Eg: tree, biomass, freshwater fish.

**Nuclear fission:** The splitting of uranium isotopes to produce heat, which is then harnessed to produce electricity.

**Nuclear fusion:** The fusing together of elements to produce either electrically-charged particles or heat, which is then harnessed to produce electricity. This technology is currently being researched but thus far is not cost-effective. Some scientists believe that it is possible to produce non-radioactive nuclear power with this type of technology.

**Organic compounds:** Compounds composed of carbon and hydrogen. They form the basic building blocks of living tissue.

**Organic:** Referring to or derived from living organisms. In chemistry, organic refers to any compound containing carbon.

**Pesticide**: A substance or mixture of substances intended to prevent, destroy, repel, or mitigate any pest. Pesticides can accumulate in the food chain and contaminate the environment if they are misused.

**Photosynthesis**: Manufacture of carbohydrates and oxygen by plants from carbon dioxide and water in the presence of chlorophyll, using sunlight as an energy source. Plants absorb carbon from the atmosphere with this process.

**Precipitation**: Any and all forms of water, whether liquid or solid, which fall from the atmosphere and reach the Earth's surface. A day with measurable precipitation is a day when the water equivalent of the precipitation is equal to or greater than 0.2 mm.

**Recyclable**: Refers to products such as paper, glass, plastic, oil and metals that can be reprocessed into products instead of being disposed of as waste.

**Reforestation**: The process of re-establishing a forest on previously cleared land.

**Resource**: A person, thing, or action that is used to produce a desired effect or product, usually for meeting human needs or improving the quality of life.

**Septic tank:** A tank (usually underground) used to hold domestic waste when a sewer line is not available to carry it to a treatment plant. It stores the solid waste until bacteria breaks it down and the relatively clean water is absorbed by the ground.

**Smog (photochemical smog):** Derived from the words 'smoke' and 'fog', it is the colloquial term used for photochemical fog, which includes ozone and numerous other contaminants. Smog usually adds a brownish haze to the atmosphere.

**Sustainable development:** Development that ensures that use of resources and the environment today does not compromise their availability in the future.

**Troposphere**: Layer of the atmosphere that contains about 95 per cent of the earth's air and extends 6–17 km up from the earth, depending on latitude and season.

**Ultraviolet (UV) radiation:** Electromagnetic radiation in the wavelength range of 200 to 400 nanometres, also known as UV light.

**Waste water:** Water that carries wastes from homes, businesses, and industries. It is usually a mixture of water and dissolved or suspended solids.

**Waste water treatment plant:** A facility containing a series of tanks, screens, filters, and other processes by which pollutants are removed from water.

**Water quality**: A term used to describe the chemical, physical and biological characteristics of water with respect to its suitability for a particular use.

**Wetlands**: Lands where water saturation is the dominant factor that determines the nature of soil development and the types of plant and animal communities living in the surrounding environment. Wetlands are also called bogs, ponds, estuaries or marshes.

## SOLID WASTE AND ITS DISPOSAL

### SOLID WASTE

Items that we no longer need, or do not have any further use for, fall in the category of solid waste. Solid waste can be classified into different types depending on the source: (1) household waste or municipal waste, (2) industrial or hazardous waste, and (3) biomedical or hospital waste.

Municipal solid waste consists of household waste, construction and demolition debris, sanitation residue, and waste from streets. This garbage is generated mainly from residential and commercial complexes.

Industrial and hospital waste are considered hazardous as they may contain toxic substances. Certain types of household waste are also hazardous. Hazardous wastes could be highly toxic to humans, animals and plants. They are corrosive, highly inflammable or explosive, and react when exposed to certain things such as gases. India generates around 7 million tonnes of hazardous wastes every year, most of which is concentrated in four states: Andhra Pradesh, Bihar, Uttar Pradesh and Tamil Nadu.

Hospital waste is generated during the diagnosis, treatment or immunization of human beings or animals, or in research activities in these fields. It may include wastes like soiled waste, disposables, anatomical waste, cultures, discarded medicines, chemical wastes. This waste is highly infectious and can be a serious threat to human health if not managed in a scientific manner. It has been roughly estimated that of the 4 kg of waste generated in a hospital, at least 1 kg would be infected.

### THE FOUR RS (REFUSE, REUSE, RECYCLE, REDUCE) OF WASTE MANAGEMENT

1. **Refuse:** Instead of buying new containers from the market, use those that are in the house. Refuse to buy new items though you may think they are prettier than the ones you already have.

2. **Reuse:** Do not throw away soft drink cans or bottles; cover them with home-made paper or paint on them and use them as pencil stands or small vases. Use shopping bags made of cloth or jute, which can be used over and over again.

3. **Recycle:** Segregate your waste to make sure that it is collected and taken for recycling. Recycling involves the collection of used and discarded materials, processing these materials and making them into new products.

4. **Reduce:** Reduce the generation of unnecessary waste; for instance, carry your own shopping bag when you go to the market.

# FORESTRY

The forest is a complex ecosystem consisting mainly of trees that buffer the earth and support life. The Food and Agriculture Organization has defined forest as 'land with tree crown cover (or equivalent stocking level) of more than 10 per cent and area of more than 0.5 hectares'. The trees should be able to reach a minimum height of 5 m at maturity in its original spot. Forests are subdivided into plantations and natural forests. Natural forests mainly comprise indigenous trees, not deliberately planted. Plantations are forests established by planting or seeding, or both, in the process of afforestation or reforestation.

## USES OF FORESTS

**Fuelwood:** Wood is an important source of energy for cooking and heating.

**Fodder:** Fodder from the forest forms an important source for cattle and other animals in hilly and arid regions and during droughts.

**Fencing:** Fences created with trees and shrubs are preferred in developing countries as they are cheap to maintain yet give protection. Species that have thorns or are prickly, and have stiff branches and leaves that are not edible, are preferred. These species should be fast growing, hardy, and long-lived.

**Windbreaks and shelter belts:** Trees grown for windbreaks should be bushy and sturdy to withstand strong winds, both hot and cold. Along the Saurashtra coast in India, casuarina has successfully been planted to check degradation due to salt-laden coastal winds. A species of prosopis, called *P. juliflora*, planted along the desert border in Haryana and Gujarat, has successfully halted the advance of the desert.

**Soil erosion check:** Tree roots bind the soil and prevent erosion by wind or water. Leaf fall also provides a soil cover that further protects the soil. Casuarina planted along the coastal region in Saurashtra has helped in binding the sand and stabilizing the sand dunes in the area.

**Soil improvement:** Some tree species can fix or return nitrogen to the soil through root decomposition or fallen leaves. Such trees are planted to increase the nitrogen content of the soil.

# FORESTS AND INDIA

## THE BISHNOIS

The Bishnois are members of a Vaishnavite sect who live in western Rajasthan, on the fringe of the Thar Desert. They have, for centuries, been conserving the flora and fauna to the extent of sacrificing their lives to protect the environment. In the 15th century, Jambhoji, a resident of a village near Jodhpur, had a vision that the cause of the drought which had hit the area and the hardship that followed was caused by people's interference with nature. Thereafter, he became a *sanyasi* and was known as Swami Jambeshwar Maharaj. This was the beginning of the Bishnoi sect. He laid down twenty-nine tenets for his followers, including a ban on killing animals, a ban on felling trees (especially khejri, which grows extensively in these areas), and on using material other than wood for cremations. The underlining feature of the sect was the protection of nature. Since then, the sect has religiously followed these tenets.

## CHIPKO MOVEMENT

In the 1970s, an organized resistance to the destruction of forests spread throughout India and came to be known as the Chipko Movement. The name of the movement comes from the Hindi word for 'embrace', as the villagers hugged trees to prevent the contractors from felling them. The first Chipko action took place in April 1973 in Mandal village in the upper Alaknanda valley and, over the next five years, spread to many Himalayan districts of Uttar Pradesh. It was sparked off by the government's decision to allot a plot of forest area in the Alaknanda valley to a sports goods company. This angered the villagers because their similar demand to use wood to make agricultural tools had been denied. With encouragement from Dasoli Gram Swarajya Sangh, an NGO, the women of the area—under the leadership of activist Chandi Prasad Bhatt—formed a circle around the trees, blocking off the woodcutters. The Chipko protests achieved a major victory in 1980 with a fifteen-year ban on green felling in the Himalayan forests of that state, by order of Indira Gandhi, the then prime minister. Since then, the movement has spread to many states in the country. During the movement, Sunderlal Bahuguna coined the slogan, 'Ecology is permanent economy'.

## VAN MAHOTSAV

Van Mahotsav is a week-long festival of tree planting organized every July all across India. It was launched in 1950 by Kanhaiyalal Munshi, the then Union minister for agriculture and food, to enthuse the common men to preserve forests and plant trees, as 'trees mean water, water means bread, and bread is life'.

# PEOPLE ASSOCIATED WITH THE ENVIRONMENT

## ALI, SALIM ABDUL (1896-1987)

Dr Salim Moizuddin Abdul Ali, better known as the 'Birdman of India', was a famous Indian ornithologist and naturalist. He was among the first Indians to conduct systematic bird surveys across India, and his books are the foundation of ornithology in India. Dr Ali authored numerous books, including the *Book of Indian Birds* and *Handbook of the Birds of India and Pakistan*. He was awarded the Padma Vibhushan in 1976. Dr Ali passed away in 1987 at the age of ninety-one, after a prolonged battle with prostate cancer.

## AMTE, BABA (1914-2008)

Baba Amte, born Murlidhar Devidas Amte, was a social worker and activist. Born in 1914 in Maharashtra, he is chiefly remembered for his efforts towards the rehabilitation of poor people suffering from leprosy. Anandvan, a leprosy rehabilitation centre, which he founded in 1949, houses thousands of inmates. In his effort to promote national integration, he launched two *Bharat Jodo* movements, in 1985 and 1988. He established an ashram called Nijibal, to protest against the building of the Sardar Sarovar Dam on the Narmada River. He received the Rashtriya Bhushan (1978), Padma Vibhushan (1986), Magsaysay Award (1988) and Gandhi Peace Prize (1999).

## BAHUGUNA, SUNDERLAL (b. 1927)

Sunderlal Bahugana is an environmentalist. He led the Chipko Movement to preserve the forests in the Himalayas, and later spearheaded the Anti-Tehri Dam Movement. From 1981 to 1983, he led a 5,000-km march across the Himalayas ending in a meeting with Prime Minister Indira Gandhi, who then passed a legislation to protect certain areas of the Himalayan forests. He also championed the cause of women's rights and rights of the poor. He was awarded the Padma Vibhushan on 26 January 2009.

## BORLAUG, NORMAN ERNEST (1914-2009)

Norman Borlaug was an American agronomist, humanitarian and Nobel laureate who has been called the 'Father of the Green Revolution'. By cranking up a wheat strain containing an unusual gene, Borlaug created the so-called 'semi-dwarf' plant variety—a shorter, stubbier, compact stalk that supported an enormous head of grain without falling over from the weight. This curious principle of shrinking the plant to increase the output from the same acreage resulted in Indian farmers eventually quadrupling their production of wheat, and later rice. It heralded the Green Revolution. He received the Nobel Peace Prize in 1970.

## CARSON, RACHEL (1907-1964)

Rachel Carson was a writer, scientist and ecologist. She was the editor-in-chief of all publications for the US Fish and Wildlife Service. She wrote *The Sea Around Us* (1952) and *The Edge of the Sea* (1955), both attempts to produce a biography of the oceans. In *Silent Spring* (1962), she challenged the practices of agribusiness, and called for a change in the way people viewed the natural world.

## FOSSEY, DIAN (1932-1985)

Dr Dian Fossey founded the Karisoke Research Center in Rwanda's Virungas Mountains in 1967, to protect and study endangered mountain gorillas. Fossey's objectives were to study gorilla ecology, demography, and social organization. Her book, *Gorillas in the Mist,* was published in 1983.

## GOODALL, DAME JANE (b. 1934)

Dame Goodall is a British primatologist, anthropologist, and UN Messenger of Peace. Considered to be the world's foremost expert on chimpanzees, she is best known for her study of social and family interactions of wild chimpanzees in Gombe Stream National Park, Tanzania. She is the founder of the Jane Goodall Institute and has worked extensively on conservation and animal welfare issues.

## GORE, ALBERT, JR (b. 1948)

Al Gore served as the forty-fifth vice-president of the US (1993–2001), under President Bill Clinton. He is an author, businessman, and environmental activist. He is a founder of the Alliance for Climate Protection. Gore has received several awards, including the Nobel Peace Prize in 2007 (along with the Intergovernmental Panel on Climate Change) and a Grammy Award for Best Spoken Word Album (2009) for *An Inconvenient Truth.*

## HILLARY, EDMUND (1919-2008)

Edmund Hillary, the New Zealand beekeeper who conquered Mount Everest, was one of the 20th century's greatest adventurers. He spent decades pouring energy and resources from his own fundraising efforts into Nepal through the Himalayan Trust, which he founded in 1962. He helped set up hospitals, health clinics, airfields, and schools. A strong conservationist, he demanded that international mountaineers clean up thousands of tonnes of discarded oxygen bottles, food containers, and other climbing debris that litter the lower slopes of the Everest. He was honoured by the UN as one of its Global 500 conservationists in 1987.

## MAATHAI, WANGARI (1940–2011)

Wangari Maathai was an environmentalist, a civil society and women's rights activist, and a former parliamentarian. She was the founder of the Green Belt Movement. In 1976, while she was serving the National Council of Women, Prof. Maathai introduced the idea of community-based tree planting. She continued to develop this idea into a broad-based grassroots organization whose main focus was poverty reduction and environmental conservation through tree planting. With the organization, which became known as the Green Belt Movement, she assisted women in planting over forty million trees on community lands including farms, schools, and church compounds. She received the Nobel Peace Prize in 2004 for her 'contribution to sustainable development, democracy and peace'.

## PACHAURI, DR RAJENDRA K (b. 1940)

Dr Pachauri chairs the Intergovernmental Panel on Climate Change (IPCC) and is the Director-General of The Energy and Resources Institute. He has taught at numerous academic and research institutes and authored twenty-three books and several papers and articles. It was during his tenure as chairman that the IPCC was awarded the Nobel Peace Prize in 2007. He was awarded the Padma Bhushan in January 2001 and the Legion of Honour by the Government of France in 2006. He received the Padma Vibhushan in 2008 and the Mexican Order of the Aztec Eagle in 2012.

## PATHAK, BINDESHWAR (b. 1943)

Bindeshwar Pathak is a humanist and social reformer. He founded Sulabh International, a social service organization that works to promote human rights, environmental sanitation, non-conventional sources of energy, waste management and social reforms through education. Sulabh International has also developed a safe and hygienic on-site human waste disposal technology; generation of biogas and low maintenance waste water treatment plants of medium capacity for institutions and industries. Dr Pathak has received several awards like the International St. Francis Prize for the Environment (1992) and the Padma Bhushan in 1991.

## PATKAR, MEDHA (b. 1954)

Reputed social activist Medha Patkar is the founder of the Narmada Bachao Andolan (NBA) and the National Alliance of People's Movements (NAPM). After earning a degree in social work, she worked with voluntary organizations in Bombay slums as well as in tribal districts of Gujarat. She abandoned her doctoral studies to dedicate herself to the work of tribal and peasant communities in Maharashtra, Madhya Pradesh and Gujarat, eventually organized as the NBA. The NBA continued as a fight for just rehabilitation for the lakhs of people to be ousted by the Sardar Sarovar Dam and other large dams along the Narmada river. Patkar has received numerous awards, including the Mahatma Phule Award, Right Livelihood Award (Alternative Nobel Prize), Goldman Environment Prize, Green Ribbon Award for Best International Political Campaigner by BBC, and the Human Rights Defender's Award from Amnesty International.

## RATHORE, FATEH SINGH (1938–2011)

Fateh Singh Rathore, former field director of Ranthambore National Park, was India's best-known tiger conservationist. His name was synonymous with Project Tiger. After retiring from the forest department, Rathore headed Tiger Watch, an NGO, in Sawai Madhopur. Widely acknowledged as 'Tiger Guru' for his legendary knowledge of the big cat, he had the uncanny ability to predict a tiger's whereabouts. His single-minded drive to protect Ranthambore National Park made him an enemy of poachers. In 1983, Fateh Singh received the International Valour Award for his contribution to conservation.

## SHIVA, VANDANA (b. 1952)

Vandana Shiva is a physicist, philosopher, environmental activist, eco-feminist, and author. In the 1970s, she participated in the Chipko Movement to protest against the felling of trees. In 1982, she founded the Research Foundation for Science, Technology and Ecology dedicated to addressing significant ecological and social issues. Navdanya is an important organic farming programme of this foundation. Some of her important books are *Water Wars, Biopiracy: The Plunder of Nature and Knowledge* and *Stolen Harvest: The Hijacking of the Global Food Supply, The Violence of Green Revolution,* and *Monocultures of the Mind.* She received the Right Livelihood Award (Alternative Nobel Prize) and the UNEP Global 500 Award in 1993, and the Golden Plant Award (International Award of Ecology) of Denmark in 1997.

## THAPAR, VALMIK (b. 1952)

Valmik Thapar is a respected natural historian, wildlife expert and conservationist of India. He is chiefly associated with tiger conservation. He has authored a large number of books and made documentaries on India's natural habitat for leading TV channels. His documentary *Kalbelias: Nomads of Rajasthan* was widely appreciated. His passion for the tiger helped set up the Ranthambore Foundation in 1987. He was appointed a member of the Tiger Task Force in 2005.

## WHITAKER, ROMULUS EARL (b. 1943)

Romulus Earl Whitaker is a herpetologist (a person who studies amphibians and reptiles), wildlife conservationist, and founder of Madras Snake Park and The Andaman and Nicobar Environment Trust (ANET). In 1976, he co-founded Madras Crocodile Bank, after realizing that three Indian species of crocodiles were on the verge of extinction. He has published widely and made dozens of films. He set up India's first rainforest research station in Agumbe, for which he was rewarded the Whitley Fund for Nature Award in 2005 and the Rolex Award for Enterprise in November 2008.

# MAJOR ORGANIZATIONS AND INSTITUTIONS

## THE EUROPEAN ENVIRONMENTAL AGENCY (EEA)

The EEA is a body under the European Union. Its principle objectives are to help the community and member countries make informed decisions about improving the environment (by considering environmental issues while framing economic policies) and to coordinate the European Environment Information and Observation Network. It came into force in 1993 and currently has thirty-two member countries.

## INTERGOVERNMENTAL PANEL ON CLIMATE CHANGE (IPCC)

The IPCC is a leading scientific international body, formed in 1988 by the United Nations Environment Programme (UNEP) and the World Meteorological Organization (WMO). It assesses the most recent scientific, technical and socio-economic information about climate change. It is open to all member countries of the UN and WMO. The IPCC shared the Nobel Peace Prize with Al Gore in 2007.

## UNITED NATIONS ENVIRONMENT PROGRAMME (UNEP)

The UNEP was established in 1972 to provide leadership and encourage partnership in caring for the environment by inspiring, informing and enabling nations and people to improve their quality of life without compromising that of future generations. It works with many partners: UN entities, international organizations, national governments, NGOs, business, industry, media and civil society. Its headquarters are in Nairobi, Kenya.

## GREENPEACE

Greenpeace is an NGO whose goal is to 'ensure the ability of the Earth to nurture life in all its diversity'. It works on universal concerns such as global warming, deforestation, overfishing, commercial whaling, and anti-nuclear issues. It was started in 1971. Based in Amsterdam, Greenpeace now has 2.8 million supporters worldwide, and national as well as regional offices in forty-five countries.

## WORLD METEOROLOGICAL ORGANIZATION (WMO)

The WMO is a designated UN agency that deals with issues of the Earth's atmosphere, its interaction with the oceans, its climate and the distribution of water resources. Established in 1950, the WMO became a specialized agency in 1951 for meteorology, operational hydrology and related geophysical sciences. Under its leadership, National Meteorological and Hydrological Services works towards the protecting of life and property against natural disasters, safeguarding the environment, and developing economic and social well-being in the areas of food security, water resources and transport. The WMO facilitates free, unrestricted exchange of data, products and services on matters relating to social security, economic welfare and environmental protection. The WMO had a membership of 189 states and territories as on 4 December 2009.

## THE INTERNATIONAL UNION FOR THE CONSERVATION OF NATURE (IUCN)

Founded in 1948, IUCN is the world's oldest and largest global environmental organization that addresses the most pressing environment and development challenges. The IUCN Red List provides comprehensive information on the status of wildlife to convey the urgency and scale of conservation problems to the public and policymakers, and to motivate the global community to work together to reduce extinction of species. The IUCN's headquarters are in Gland, near Geneva, Switzerland. It is a democratic membership union working with over 1,000 government and NGO member organizations, and comprises almost 11,000 volunteer scientists in more than 160 countries.

## FAST FACTS ABOUT GLOBAL WARMING

- The earth is showing many signs of worldwide climate change. According to NASA's Goddard Institute for Space Studies, average temperatures have climbed 0.8 °C around the world since 1880. The rate of warming is increasing too. The 20th century's last two decades were the hottest in 400 years. The IPCC reports that eleven of the past twelve years have been among the dozen warmest since 1850.

- Average temperatures in Alaska, western Canada, and eastern Russia have risen at twice the global average, according to the *Arctic Climate Impact Assessment* report compiled between 2000 and 2004. Arctic ice is fast disappearing, and the region may have its first completely ice-free summer by 2040 or earlier. Wildlife, including polar bears and indigenous human cultures, are already suffering from the impact.

❧ Glaciers and mountain snows are rapidly melting. Montana's Glacier National Park now has only twenty-seven glaciers as against 150 in 1910. In 1998, coral reefs (highly sensitive to small changes in water temperature) suffered the worst bleaching or die-off.

❧ Extreme weather events, such as wildfires, heatwaves and violent tropical storms, are also attributed in part to climate change.

❧ Industrialization, deforestation and pollution have greatly increased atmospheric concentrations of water vapour, carbon dioxide, methane and nitrous oxide, all greenhouse gases that help trap heat near the Earth's surface. Human beings add carbon dioxide into the atmosphere much faster than plants and oceans can absorb it.

❧ A follow-up report by the IPCC (April 2007) warned that global warming could lead to large-scale food and water shortages and have catastrophic effects on wildlife. Sea levels could rise between 7 and 23 inches by the end of the century. Rises of just 4 inches could flood many South Sea islands and swamp large parts of south-east Asia.

❧ Glaciers around the world could melt, causing sea levels to rise while creating water shortages in regions dependent on run-off for fresh water.

❧ Strong hurricanes, droughts, heatwaves, wildfires, and other natural disasters may become common in many parts of the world. The growth of deserts may also cause food shortages.

❧ More than one million species face extinction owing to disappearing habitats, changing ecosystems, and adding acidity to oceans.

❧ The ocean's circulation system—the ocean conveyor belt—could be permanently altered, causing a mini-Ice Age in Western Europe.

❧ At some point in the future, warming could become uncontrollable by creating a so-called positive feedback effect. Rising temperatures could release additional greenhouse gases by unlocking methane in permafrost and undersea deposits, freeing carbon trapped in sea ice, and causing increased evaporation of water.

❧ The United Nations General Assembly declared 2011 as the International Year of Forests to raise awareness on sustainable management, conservation and sustainable development of all types of forests, including fragile forest ecosystems, for the benefit of current and future generations.

❧ John Harte, an ecosystem sciences professor at University of California, Berkeley, has artificially heated sections of a Rocky Mountain meadow by about 3.6°F (2°C) for fifteen years to study the projected effects of global warming. He has documented changes in the meadow's plant community. Soils in test plots have lost about 20 per cent of their natural carbon. If similar carbon loss were repeated on a global scale, it could double the amount of carbon in the atmosphere.

## INTERESTING FACTS ON RECYCLING

- One tree can make 15,000 sheets of A4 paper. Every tonne of paper recycled saves fifteen average-size trees, as well as their surrounding habitat and wildlife.

- A recycled aluminium can saves enough energy to run a TV for two hours. Recycling aluminium saves up to 95 per cent of energy and produces 95 per cent less greenhouse gas emissions than if raw materials are used.

- If we collected the 90 million mobile phones that we no longer use, they could be recycled for the metal inside them. This would equal 18 tonnes of copper, 428,000 ounces of silver, and 85,000 ounces of gold.

- Recycling just one plastic bottle can save the same amount of energy needed to power a 60-watt light bulb for six hours.

## INTERESTING FACTS ON WATER

- Human brain is 75 per cent water, bones are 25 per cent water, and human blood is 83 per cent water.

- Drinking too much water too quickly can lead to water intoxication, which occurs when water dilutes the sodium level in the bloodstream and causes an imbalance of water in the brain. It occurs during periods of intense athletic performance.

- By the time a person feels thirsty, his or her body has lost over 1 per cent of its total water amount. The weight a person loses directly after intense physical activity is weight from water, not fat.

- As much as 75 per cent of the Earth is covered with water, and 97 per cent of Earth's water is in the oceans. Only 3 per cent of this water can be drunk. Also, 75 per cent of the world's fresh water is frozen in the polar ice caps.

- Sources of water pollution include oil spills, fertilizer and agricultural run-off, sewage, storm water, and industrial waste.

- Ancient Egyptians treated water by siphoning it from the top of huge jars after allowing the muddy water from the Nile to settle. Hippocrates, known as the father of medicine, directed people in Greece to boil and strain water before drinking it.

## DID YOU KNOW?

- The Amazon rainforest has been described as the 'lungs of our planet' because it provides the essential environmental service of continuously recycling carbon dioxide into oxygen. More than 20 per cent of the world's oxygen is produced there. It works like a great air conditioner, as it cools down the temperature of the entire world by 1°C or 2°C, and balances humidity and rain in several parts of the globe.

- The Nepalese government requires a 4,000-dollar deposit from climbers of Mount Everest that it refunds only if the mountaineers bring down the same amount of gear and supplies that they took up.

- According to the Constitution of Bhutan, 60 per cent of the country has to be under forest cover in perpetuity.

- The Delhi Metro Rail Corporation has become the first railway project in the world to earn carbon credits. The UN has registered the metro under the clean development mechanism, enabling it to claim carbon credits.

- The wildlife law in India has a long history. The earliest codified law can be traced back to the 3rd century BC, when Emperor Ashoka enacted a law in the matter of preservation of wildlife and environment.

- The ozone hole was first discovered in Antarctica by Joseph Farman and his colleagues at the British Antarctic Survey in 1985.

- To increase consumer awareness, the Government of India launched the eco-labelling scheme known as 'Ecomark' in 1991 for easy identification of environment-friendly products. Any product made, used or disposed of in a way that significantly reduces the harm it would otherwise cause the environment can be considered environment-friendly.

- The Taj Mahal is being saved from the corrosive effects of industrial pollution by an ancient face pack recipe: *Multani mitti* (Fuller's earth). Archaeologists hit upon the idea when examining ancient records of Indian buildings. They discovered that in the 16th century it was common to use a mud mixture to clean and preserve marble. There was no record of the recipe, so they adapted the formula for *multani mitti*. The mud, brushed on in layers until it is an inch deep, draws out the polluting sulphates and carbonates. It is then washed with distilled water.

## ENVIRONMENTAL AND INDUSTRIAL DISASTERS

### BHOPAL GAS TRAGEDY

By all accounts, the methyl isocyanate gas leak from the American-owned Union Carbide plant in Bhopal, Madhya Pradesh, on the night of 2–3

December 1984, is the worst chemical disaster in Indian history. It took a heavy toll of human life. Poisonous fumes killed hundreds of people there and then, and maimed thousands in the ensuing months. The effects on health (deaths and diseases) continued well after the accident. Many children were born deformed. Officially, 578,000 people were affected, though the actual toll could be higher.

## MINAMATA BAY MERCURY POISONING

In the 1950s, one of the most severe incidents of industrial pollution and mercury poisoning occurred in the small seaside town of Minamata, Japan. Chisso Corporation dumped an estimated 27 tonnes of methylmercury, a by-product in the production of plastics, into the Minamata Bay over thirty-seven years. This highly toxic waste contaminated the local fish, on which the residents of the town were highly dependent for food. The methylmercury ingested through the highly contaminated fish caused severe neurological damage and killed more than 900 people. Many babies in the area were born with gnarled limbs. Similar mercury poisoning was also detected in two other places in Japan. Till 2010, more than 2,000 victims were identified in all, of which around 1,700 had already died.

## CHERNOBYL NUCLEAR DISASTER

The Chernobyl nuclear power plant accident occurred on 26 April 1986, near Pripyat in the then Soviet Union (now in Ukraine). The accident at the Unit 4 reactor at 1.24 a.m. was the result of a combination of basic engineering deficiencies in the reactor and faulty actions of the operators. It resulted in a series of explosions and consequent fires that completely destroyed the reactor and caused the release of massive amounts of radioactive materials over a ten-day period. The Chernobyl accident is the most serious nuclear power plant accident ever. The radioactive materials released deposited in the greatest density in Ukraine and Belarus, and also in Lithuania, Poland and Moldova. There is no particular figure as to how many died because of the accident. Quite a few died directly because of the incident, and many have since died or have developed disorders, including cancers. A report, published in 2005, found that around fifty people had been killed from direct exposure to the radiation at the site. Over twenty lakh people suffered from its consequences later.

## EXXON VALDEZ OIL SPILL

The spill occurred in Prince William Sound, Alaska, on 24 March 1989, when *Exxon Valdez*, an oil tanker of Exxon Mobil Corp. bound for Long Beach, California, struck Prince William Sound's Bligh Reef and spilled 260,000–

750,000 barrels (41,000–119,000 m³) of crude oil. The 11 million gallons spill (unofficial estimates are much higher), which landed on almost 2,100 km of Alaska coastline, killed thousands of birds and otters, hundreds of seals and eagles, and damaged the livelihood of many fishermen.

## GULF WAR OIL SPILL

One of the worst oil spills in history, the Gulf War spill spewed about 8 million barrels (13,60,000–15,00,000 tonnes) of oil into the Persian Gulf after Iraqi forces opened valves of wells and pipelines or set them ablaze as they retreated from Kuwait in 1991. The oil slick reached a maximum size of 162.54 km by 67.59 km and was 12.7 cm thick. Plumes of black smoke billowed for hundreds of miles downwind of the burning wells, and debris rained down on the Kuwaiti population. Caught in the gulf's currents, the oil spread to Saudi Arabian shores. It also sank into the land and contaminated the country's drinking water. Vegetation and wildlife were destroyed throughout the fragile desert ecosystem and in the waters of the gulf itself. Thousands of migrating and indigenous birds, mistaking the oil lakes' surfaces for water, landed on them and drowned. Almost two decades later, both countries still suffer the consequences.

## GULF OF MEXICO OIL SPILL

The Gulf of Mexico oil spill started when the drilling rig *Deepwater Horizon* caught fire after an explosion on 20 April 2010 and sank. The explosion killed eleven men working on the platform and injured seventeen others. Initially, 1,000 barrels of oil a day spilled into the sea, and was still 53,000 just before the leak was capped. The spill is by far the world's largest accidental release of oil into marine waters. Sea birds landed on the oil-covered water for catching fish and got drenched. Many died because their oil-covered wings became heavy and did not allow them to fly. Marine creatures like fishes and dolphins were also affected, as they were unable to find fresh water over a large area. Studies are continuing on the effects of this oil spill on the environment.

## FUKUSHIMA DAIICHI NUCLEAR DISASTER

This was a series of equipment failures, nuclear meltdowns, and releases of radioactive materials at the Fukushima I Nuclear Power Plant, following the Tohoku earthquake and tsunami on 11 March 2011. It is believed to be the largest nuclear disaster since the Chernobyl disaster of 1986.

# GEOGRAPHY

## SPACE

### MILKY WAY

The Milky Way is a collection of roughly 100 billion stars. It is the galaxy in which our solar system is located. It has three general components: a thin disc consisting of young and intermediate age stars, a bar of older stars, and an extended dark halo whose composition is unknown.

### SOLAR SYSTEM

The Solar System has eight planets, about 170 moons, thousands of asteroids and comets, gas and dust, all orbiting around the Sun, held together by its force of gravity. The four planets closest to the Sun—Mercury, Venus, Earth, Mars—are called the terrestrial planets because they have solid rocky surfaces. The four large planets beyond the orbit of Mars—Jupiter, Saturn, Uranus, Neptune—are called gas giants. The Sun has a magnetic field, the heliosphere, which envelops our entire solar system.

## PLANETS OF THE SOLAR SYSTEM

### MERCURY

Mercury is the innermost planet. Nearest to the Sun, it revolves once every 88 Earth days and rotates once almost every 59 Earth days—a rotation slower than that of any other planet except Venus. Mercury is the smallest planet in terms of both mass and diameter and is the densest with a large metallic core. With no known satellite, it has a dry, rocky, and heavily cratered surface. It is named after the swiftest ancient Roman god.

## VENUS

The second planet from the Sun, Venus is the closest planet to the Earth and also, most similar to it in size, mass, volume, and density. It is the third smallest planet and appears before sunrise as a 'morning star' and in the evening as an 'evening star' at various times of the year. It is the only planet that takes longer to rotate once about its axis (243 earth days) than to travel once around the Sun (225 Earth days). Venus, like Uranus, rotates counterclockwise. With no known satellite, Venus is covered by a thick, rapidly spinning atmosphere, maintaining a temperature hot enough to melt lead. Venus is named after the ancient Roman goddess of love and beauty.

## EARTH

Earth is the third planet from the Sun and the fifth largest in our solar system. Being the ocean planet, 70 per cent of its surface is covered by water. The Earth's axis of rotation is tilted at 23.45° with respect to the plane of its orbit, and this causes the change of seasons. The 23 hours 56 minutes 4.09 seconds that it takes for one rotation is called a solar day. The 365 days 6 hours 9 minutes 9.54 seconds taken to complete one revolution is called a sidereal year. The atmosphere enveloping the Earth's surface consists of 78 per cent nitrogen, 21 per cent oxygen and 1 per cent of other ingredients. The rapid rotation and molten nickel–iron core form the Earth's strong magnetic field. The moon is its only natural satellite. Unlike all other planets, named after the Greek and Roman deities, Earth takes its name from an English/German word meaning 'the ground'.

## MARS

The fourth planet from the Sun, Mars is the second smallest planet in the solar system, after Mercury. Viewed from the Earth, Mars appears bright reddish-orange due to iron-rich minerals in its soil. Temperatures at its surface vary from as low as about −195 °F near the poles during the winter to as much as 70 °F at midday near the equator. Mars completes a solar day in 24 hours 39 minutes 35 seconds. It revolves around the Sun once every 687 Earth days. Named after the ancient Roman god of war, Mars has two small moons, Phobos and Deimos.

## JUPITER

Jupiter, the largest planet, is fifth distant from the Sun. Its magnetic field is nearly 20,000 times as powerful as that of the Earth. Its most prominent feature is the Great Red Spot. It has more than sixty moons—the four larger ones being Io, Europa, Ganymede, and Callisto. Jupiter's atmosphere is composed mostly of hydrogen and helium. It has many rings composed of tiny dust particles that orbit the planet. Jupiter rotates faster than any other planet taking 9 hours 56 minutes to spin around once on its axis. It completes one orbit in 4,333 Earth days, or almost 12 Earth years. Ancient astronomers named Jupiter after the king of Roman gods.

## SATURN

Saturn is the second largest planet of the solar system. Seven thin, flat rings surround its equator. Saturn spins around only once in only 10 hours 39 minutes and travels around the Sun in an elliptical orbit in about 10,759 Earth days. Saturn has the lowest density though it has a greater mass than any other planet except Jupiter. The largest among Saturn's twenty-five satellites is Titan, the second-largest moon in the solar system. Ancient astronomers named it after the Roman god of agriculture.

## URANUS

Uranus, discovered by William Herschel in 1781, was the first planet discovered with the aid of a telescope. Being seventh from the Sun, it takes eighty-four Earth years to complete one orbit. Its rotational axis is tilted almost parallel to its orbital plane, so it appears to be rotating on its side. Its atmosphere is mostly composed of hydrogen and helium, with a small amount of methane (giving it a blue-green colour) and traces of water and ammonia. Uranus has twenty-seven known moons, named after characters from the works of Shakespeare and Pope. The planet is named after the Greek god of the sky.

## NEPTUNE

Neptune, discovered by Johann Galle in 1846, was the first planet located through mathematical predictions rather than regular observations of the sky. Neptune orbits the Sun once every 165 years and spins once in about 16 hours and 7 minutes. Its magnetic field is twenty-seven times more powerful than the Earth's. Neptune has thirteen known moons of which Triton, the largest, orbits the planet in the opposite direction compared with rest of the moons. It has six known rings, which are relatively new and short-lived. Neptune is named after the Roman god of the sea.

## DID YOU KNOW?

- Mercury, Venus, Mars, Jupiter, and Saturn are visible to the naked eye and have been known since prehistoric times.
- Uranus and Neptune were discovered only after the invention of the telescope.
- In 2006, Pluto was reassigned to a new class known as the dwarf planets.
- Mercury and Venus do not have any moons.
- Jupiter, Saturn, Uranus, and Neptune all have rings.
- Messenger was the first spacecraft to orbit Mercury in 2011.
- The Egyptians named Mars as *Her Desher*, meaning 'the red one'.
- Ceres was the first asteroid, discovered in 1891. It has since been reclassified as a dwarf planet because it is more like a planet than its neighbours in the main asteroid belt.
- Ganymede, Jupiter's moon, is the largest in the solar system. It is larger than the planet Mercury.
- In 1610, Galileo Galilei was the first to gaze at Saturn through a telescope.
- Titan, Saturn's moon, is the second largest moon in the solar system.
- Uranus is the only giant planet whose equator is nearly at right angles to its orbit.

## OTHER HEAVENLY BODIES

### ASTERIODS

An asteroid is a small, metallic, rocky body that orbits the Sun but does not have an atmosphere and is too small to be classified as a planet. An asteroid is also known as a minor planet. There are tens of thousands of asteroids in the so-called main asteroid belt: a large, doughnut-shaped ring located between the orbits of Jupiter and Mars. They can be classified into three broad categories: C-type (carbonaceous), S-type (silicaceous), M-type (metallic). Their compositional differences are related to how far from the Sun they are formed. Gaspra and Ida are the main belt asteroids.

### COMETS

Comets are part of a class of small celestial objects composed of ice, dust, and rocky debris carried from the early formation of the solar system, about 4.5 billion years ago. They orbit the Sun and develop diffused gaseous envelopes and often long luminous tails when near the Sun. The short-period comets take less than 200 years to complete one orbit around the Sun while many of the long-period comets take as long as 30 million years to complete one orbit. The word comet comes from the Greek *kometes*, meaning 'hairy one'. One of the most important comets is Halley's comet, which appears every seventy-five or seventy-six years.

## CONSTELLATION

A constellation is a group of stars forming a conspicuous pattern that is traditionally named after its shape or identified with a figure from mythology.

Forty-eight of the eighty-eight recognized constellations were recorded in the seventh and eighth books of Ptolemy's *Almagest*. Between the 16th and 17th centuries AD, new constellations were discovered mainly by the European explorers like German astronomer Johannes Hevelius, three Dutch cartographers Frederick de Houtman, Pieter Dirksz Keyser and Gerard Mercator, French astronomer Nicolas Louis de Lacaille, and Italian navigator Amerigo Vespucci. In 1930, Eugène Delporte listed eighty-eight constellations with official set of celestial boundaries on behalf of the International Astronomical Union. Hydra is the largest known constellation in terms of its area.

## METEORS

Little chunks of small, stony or metallic natural objects from space are called meteoroids. They become meteors (shooting stars) when they fall through a planet's atmosphere, leaving a bright trail as they are heated to incandescence by the friction. Pieces that survive the journey and hit the ground are called meteorites. It is believed that 1,000–10,000 tonnes of meteoritic material fall on Earth each day. The largest individual meteorite found was the Hoba in south-west Africa.

## MOON

The moon is the Earth's only natural satellite. It has no light of its own, but merely reflects the rays of the Sun. It is believed that 4.5 billion years ago a Mars-sized body collided with the Earth and the resulting debris accumulated to form the moon. The surface of the moon, nearly all of it, is covered by lunar regolith, consisting of gray, powdery dust and rocky debris. It takes 27 days, 7 hours and 43 minutes to complete one lunar revolution. From Earth, we always see the same face of the moon because it rotates once on its own axis in the same time that it travels once around Earth. Neil Armstrong and Edwin Aldrin were the first men to set foot on the Moon on 20 July 1969.

## DID YOU KNOW?

- ◇ The Hubble Space Telescope, named after American astronomer Edwin Hubble, was launched in 1990 and orbits the Earth every 97 minutes at 8 km per second.
- ◇ The Hubble Telescope is at an altitude of 569 km from the Earth.
- ◇ More than 6,000 scientific articles have been published based on the Hubble data.
- ◇ The Spitzer Space Telescope, named after astrophysicist Lyman Spitzer Jr, was launched on 25 August 2003 to study the universe at near-to-far infrared wavelengths.
- ◇ The Moon is simply called the Moon because the existence of other moons was not known until Galileo Galilei discovered four moons orbiting Jupiter in 1610.
- ◇ Aryabhatta Research Institute of Observational Sciences is installing India's largest telescope at a place called Devasthal, near Nainital. The telescope will be operational by 2012.

## SATELLITES

A satellite is a natural object (moon) or spacecraft (artificial satellite) that orbits a larger celestial body. Most known natural satellites orbit planets. Ganymede, Jupiter's largest satellite, is also the biggest in the solar system. All the planets except Mercury and Venus have natural satellites. Our Earth has only one satellite.

## STARS

A star is a huge sphere of hot, glowing gas or plasma held together by gravity. Stars produce their own light and energy by a process called nuclear fusion. Fusion happens when lighter elements are forced to become heavier elements. When this happens, a tremendous amount of energy is created, causing the star to heat up and shine. Stars come in a variety of sizes and colours. The Sun is also a star.

## THE SUN

The Sun, a hot ball of glowing gases, is a star around which objects in the solar system revolve. Its gravitational force holds the planets and the other heavenly bodies of the solar system in their respective places. It is the closest star to Earth and the distance between the two is known as an astronomical unit. The Sun has six distinct regions—the core, the radiative zone, the convective zone in the interior, the visible surface (the photosphere), the chromosphere, and the outermost region—the corona. The energy produced in the core, having a temperature of about 27 million °F, is the source of all heat and light on Earth. The Sun supports life on Earth and interactions between the Sun and Earth determine the seasons, ocean currents, weather and climate. The ancient Greeks called it *helios* and the ancient Romans called it *sol*.

## URSA MAJOR

One of the most famous constellations, Ursa Major, also known as the Great Bear, is the third largest constellation. It contains a group of stars commonly called the Big Dipper, which is often the first group of stars learned by people in the northern hemisphere. The handle of the Dipper is the Great Bear's tail and the Dipper's cup is the Bear's flank.

## URSA MINOR

Also called the Little Bear, it is a constellation of the northern sky, seven of whose stars outline the Little Dipper. It lies at about 15 hours right ascension and 80° north declination.

# THE EARTH

**Axis of the Earth:** A line joining the North and South Poles and around which the earth rotates every twenty-four hours is called the axis of the Earth.

**Equator:** The Equator, at 0° latitude, is a great circle around the earth that is everywhere equidistant from the poles. It lies in a plane perpendicular to the Earth's axis. This geographic, or terrestrial, Equator divides the Earth into the northern and southern hemispheres.

**Hemisphere:** A hemisphere refers to half of the Earth, usually thought to result from the division of the globe into two equal parts: north and south or east and west.

**Latitude:** Parallels of latitude are imaginary circles drawn round the earth, parallel to the Equator. The parallels are numbered according to the angle formed between a line from the line of latitude to the centre of the earth and a line from the centre of the earth to the Equator.

**Longitude:** Longitude is a measurement of location east or west of the prime meridian at Greenwich, the designated imaginary north–south line that passes through both geographic poles and Greenwich, London. It is measured in degrees, minutes, and seconds.

**Lunar Eclipse:** A lunar eclipse occurs when the Earth's shadow blocks most of the sunlight from directly illuminating all—or a portion—of the moon's surface.

**North Pole:** The northernmost point of the Earth's axis is called the North Pole. It lies diametrically opposite to the South Pole.

**Orbit:** The elliptical or circular path taken by a planet as it moves around the sun or by a satellite, natural or man-made, around the planet is called its orbit.

**Prime Meridian:** The 0° meridian, passing through Greenwich, London, from which all other longitudes are determined is called the prime meridian.

**Revolution of the Earth:** The orbital movement of the Earth around the Sun is referred to as the revolution of the Earth. Earth takes around 365¼ days to complete one revolution.

**Rotation of the Earth:** Rotation is the daily motion of the earth around its own axis from west to east once in twenty-four hours causing the occurrence of day and night. It approximately takes 23 hours 56 minutes and 41 seconds to complete one spin about its axis. Deflections of winds and ocean currents are also effects of rotation.

**Solar Eclipse:** A solar eclipse occurs when the moon passes in a direct line between the Earth and the sun. The moon's shadow travels over the Earth's surface and blocks out the sun's light, as seen from Earth.

**South Pole:** The southernmost tip of the Earth's axis is called the South Pole. It lies diametrically opposite the North Pole.

**Tropic of Cancer:** The Tropic of Cancer lies approximately along latitude 23°30" N. Around 21–22 June, the Sun's rays are perpendicular to the ground along this line and the Sun exerts its maximum strength in the northern hermisphere.

**Tropic of Capricorn:** The Tropic of Capricorn is a latitude approximately 23°30" S of the terrestrial Equator. The Sun is overhead at the approximate latitude of 23°30" S on 22–23 December, when the Sun's heat is at its maximum in the southern hemisphere.

## TIME ZONES

**Greenwich Mean Time:** Greenwich Mean Time (GMT) is the basis for world time zones, set by the local time at Greenwich near London. This is located on the Greenwich Meridian, longitude 0° from which other time zones are calculated.

**Indian Standard Time:** Indian Standard Time (IST) is calculated on the basis of the 82.5°E longitude, which is close to the town of Mirzapur near

Allahabad. Though the official timekeeping devices are with the Delhi-based National Physical Laboratory, local time is calculated from a clock tower at the Allahabad Observatory.

**International Date Line:** The International Date Line (IDL) is an imaginary line which runs from the North Pole to the South Pole and is 180° away from the Greenwich Meridian. Twenty-five time zones were established to the east and west of Greenwich, with the IDL lying along the 180° line of longitude. On crossing it from east to west, a day is added; on crossing it from west to east, a day is subtracted.

**Standard Time:** It is the uniform time fixed in a country with reference to the mean time of a certain meridian of the given time zone.

**Seasons:** A season is any of the four divisions of the year marked by consistent and distinct annual changes in the weather. In the northern hemisphere, winter begins on the winter solstice (22 or 23 December), spring on the vernal equinox (20 or 21 March), summer on the summer solstice (21 or 22 June) and autumn on the autumnal equinox (22 or 23 September).

**Equinox:** It refers to either of the two moments in the year when the sun is exactly above the Equator and day and night are of equal length. It is also either of the two points in the sky where the ecliptic (the sun's annual pathway) and the celestial equator intersect.

**Solstice:** It is either of the two moments in the year when the sun's apparent path is farthest north or south from the Equator. In the northern hemisphere, the summer solstice occurs on 20 or 21 June and the winter solstice on 21 or 22 December. The situation is exactly the opposite in the southern hemisphere, where the seasons are reversed.

## EARTH AND ITS SPHERES

**Biosphere:** The biosphere is the realm of the living organisms on earth that extends over the Earth's surface in a thin layer—from a few kilometres into the atmosphere, to the deep-sea openings on the ocean beds. It is a life-supporting global ecosystem, where each living thing depends on another and the environment. The ecosystem includes all living organisms (biotic) and nonliving (abiotic) environment on which they depend for their energy.

**Hydrosphere:** The hydrosphere consists of water covering a greater part of the Earth's surface. A major part is contained in the oceans and inland seas, while the remaining is covered by rivers, freshwater lakes, ice caps, glaciers, and underground water. The deepest point of the hydrosphere is Challenger Deep, a part of the Mariana Trench in the Pacific Ocean.

**Lithosphere:** The lithosphere is the rigid outer portion of the Earth including the crust and the outermost mantle. This layer is thickest in the continental regions and thinnest in the oceans. It constitutes about one per cent of the total earth's volume and 0.4 per cent of its mass. The lithosphere that forms 30 per cent of the total Earth surface comprises soil sand, and rocks.

## THE ATMOSPHERE AND ITS STRUCTURE

The atmosphere is a gaseous layer that envelopes a planet. As the gravitational pull of the planet is greatest near the surface, the density of the atmosphere decreases outward. While the atmospheres of some planets, such as Mercury, are almost nonexistent, the atmosphere of our planet has been able to contain water in its three phases (solid, liquid, and gas), making life possible on earth.

**Troposphere:** The troposphere is the nearest layer to the earth's surface that extends from sea level to a height of about 15 km. This is the densest of all atmospheric layers and is composed of water vapour, moisture and dust. In this region, the temperature decreases with the increase in height. The tropopause separates the troposphere from the stratosphere.

**Stratosphere:** This layer extends from an altitude of about 15 km to 50 km above the Earth. This is a region of uniform temperature, free from water vapour, clouds, and dust.

**Ozone Layer:** The ozone layer lies at an altitude of 20–30 km within the stratosphere. It also houses over 90 per cent of the earth's ozone, formed by interactions between oxygen molecules and UV light. It absorbs 97–99 per cent of the Sun's high frequency UV light, preventing it from penetrating the earth's surface. Every 1 per cent decrease in the Earth's ozone shield is projected to increase the amount of UV light exposure to the lower atmosphere by 2 per cent. Thus the ozone layer is essential to life on Earth.

**Mesosphere:** The mesosphere (literally 'middle sphere') is the third highest layer in our atmosphere, occupying the region 50–80 km above the surface of the Earth, in the region above the troposphere and stratosphere, and below the thermosphere. It is separated from the stratosphere by the stratopause and from the thermosphere by the mesopause. The mesosphere is the coldest of the atmospheric layers, with the temperature dropping to −100°F with increasing altitude. The mesosphere is also the layer in which meteors often burn up while entering the Earth's atmosphere.

**Ionosphere:** The ionosphere is a layer of ionized air that lies immediately above the mesosphere extending from about 80–600 km above the Earth's surface. In this region, the Sun's energy is so strong that it breaks apart molecules and atoms of air, leaving ions and free-floating electrons. The ionosphere influences radio transmission to distant parts of the Earth.

**Thermosphere:** The thermosphere is the outer layer of the atmosphere, separated from the mesosphere by the mesopause. The temperatures rise steeply in this region. The lower part of the thermosphere, from 80–550 km above the Earth's surface, contains the ionosphere.

**Exosphere:** The exosphere is the uppermost region that makes up the outer limits of the atmosphere. The gravity of the Earth is very weak in this region. The atmosphere here merges into space as the air atoms and molecules constantly escape into space from the exosphere. In this region of the atmosphere, the prime components are hydrogen and helium, present in extremely low densities.

## MAJOR LANDFORMS OF THE EARTH

**Continent:** The term 'continent' is used for any of the large continuous masses of land, namely, Asia, Africa, North America, South America, Antarctica, Europe, and Australia, listed in order of size. The continents differ sharply in size and physical features and are not distributed evenly over the surface of the globe. More than two-thirds of the Earth's land surface lies north of the Equator, and all the continents except Antarctica are wedge-shaped, wider in the north than they are in the south.

**Island:** An island is any area of land smaller than a continent and entirely surrounded by water. It may occur in oceans, seas, lakes, or rivers. A group of islands is an archipelago.

**Isthmus:** An isthmus is a narrow strip of land connecting two large land areas otherwise separated by the sea. The two most famous are the Isthmus of Panama, connecting North and South America, and the Isthmus of Suez, connecting Africa and Asia.

**Lake:** A lake is any relatively large body of slowly moving or standing water that occupies an inland basin of appreciable size. Over 98 per cent of the important surface waters available for use are contained in freshwater lakes.

**Mountains:** Mountains are landforms that rise abruptly above their surrounding area, have steep slopes, a summit (which is its highest point), and considerable local relief. They rarely occur individually, and are found in elongated ranges such as the Himalayas.

**Ocean:** The term ocean is used for a continuous body of salt water which are held in large basins on the surface of the Earth.

**Plain:** A plain is any relatively level area of the Earth's surface with gentle slopes and small local relief. They vary widely in size, some occupying only a few hectares, while the largest cover hundreds of thousands of kilometres, for example, the Great Plains of North America. They occupy slightly more than one-third of the terrestrial surface. They occur north of the Arctic circle, in the tropics, and in the middle latitudes.

**Plateau:** A plateau is a flat, elevated area with low relative relief. It it is usually bound by an escarpment on all sides, in some cases, it is enclosed by mountains. Although plateaus stand at higher elevation than their surrounding areas, they differ from mountain ranges in that they are flat. The Colorado Plateau and the Deccan Plateau are examples.

**Peninsula:** A peninsula is defined as a piece of land almost surrounded by water or projecting out into a body of water. The Arabian Peninsula is the largest in the world.

**Sea:** A sea is the expanse of salt water that covers most of the Earth's surface and surrounds its landmasses.

**Strait:** A strait is a narrow passage of water connecting two seas or two other large areas of water. The word English word strait originated from shortening the French word *estreit* meaning 'tight, narrow', and from Latin *strictus* or 'drawn tight'.

## DID YOU KNOW?

Asia is more than five times as large as Australia.

Indonesia, with 17,508 islands, is the largest archipelago in the world.

North America, Africa, and Asia make up about 70 per cent of the total lake water.

The Himalayas include the highest mountains in the world, with over 110 peaks rising to elevations of 7315.2 metres or more above sea level. One of these peaks is Mount Everest.

The Pacific Ocean has double the area and more than double the water volume of the Atlantic Ocean.

Plains are found on all continents except Antarctica.

Plateaus and enclosed basins cover about 45 per cent of the Earth's land surface.

The word peninsula is derived from mid-16th century Latin *paeninsula*, from *paene* which means 'almost' and *insula* meaning 'island'.

The Dead Sea, the lowest body of water on the surface of the Earth, is actually a salt lake.

The Palk Strait in the Bay of Bengal separates India from Sri Lanka.

# ROCKS

The hard material that makes up the earth's crust is called a rock. It is a mixture of minerals, which may be classified as igneous, sedimentary, and metamorphic.

## IGNEOUS ROCKS

Igneous rocks are any of various crystalline or glassy rocks formed when molten earth material cools and solidifies. They are formed from the solidification of magma, which is a hot (600°C to 1,300° C or 1,100°F to 2,400° F) molten or partially molten rock material.

## METAMORPHIC ROCKS

Metamorphic rocks are any of a class of rocks that result from the alteration of pre-existing rocks in response to changing environmental conditions, such as variations in temperature, pressure, and mechanical stress, and the addition or subtraction of chemical components.

## SEDIMENTARY ROCKS

Over millions of years, little pieces of Earth have been eroded by wind and water. These little bits are washed downstream, where they settle at the bottom of rivers, lakes, and oceans. Layer upon layer is deposited. These layers are pressed down more and more through time, until the bottom layers slowly turn into rock. Sedimentary rocks are the most common rocks exposed on the Earth's surface.

# WINDS

Air in motion is called wind. This movement of air cannot be seen but its motion can be measured by the force that it applies on objects. All winds, from gentle breezes to raging hurricanes, are caused by differences in the temperature of the atmosphere, due to the rotation of the Earth, and by unequal heating of the continents and the oceans. A weathervane measures the wind direction and an anemometer measures the wind speed.

## PLANETARY WINDS/PERMANENT WINDS

Air movements can occur on a global scale in response to worldwide variations in temperature. These vast movements are called planetary winds. They are driven by the circulation of air in atmospheric units called cells. The northern and southern hemispheres each have three mirrored cells based on latitude (1) between the Equator (0°) and 30°; (2) between 30° and 60°; and

(3) between 60° and 90°. The planetary winds are of three broad types: (1) trade winds, (2) westerlies, (3) Polar easterlies.

## DOLDRUMS

They are light, variable winds blowing over the east Pacific, the east Atlantic, and from the Indian Ocean to West Pacific.They are bound on the north and south by the trade winds and their extent varies greatly with seasons.

## POLAR EASTERLIES

Winds that occur at 60° latitude in both hemispheres are called the Polar Easterlies. They are formed when the air over the poles cools and sinks, flowing away from the Earth's poles toward the west.

# TRADE WINDS

The flow of air from 30°N and 30°S towards the Equator constitutes the trade winds. They do not blow directly towards the Equator but are deflected by the Earth's rotation because of the Coriolis effect. They are sometimes called the easterlies because they move from east to west. At the borders of the trades are belts of calm, dry air known as the horse latitudes.

## WESTERLIES

Some of the air that settles in the horse latitudes goes back immediately into the trade winds. The rest flows toward the poles and circulates there for a time before edging back towards the Equator. The latter portion becomes deflected toward the east. These winds are the westerlies, or the prevailing westerlies, of the middle latitudes (the area between 30° and 60°, also known as the temperate zone, in each hemisphere). At sea, the westerlies blow strongly enough to give the 40° parallel the name Roaring Forties. The Furious Fifties is a name given to winds found in the latitudes between 50°S and 60°S (just north of the Southern Ocean close to Antarctica) and the Shrieking or Screaming Sixties are winds found in the latitudes below 60°S (close to Antarctica).

## PERIODIC WINDS

Land and sea breezes and monsoon winds are winds of a periodic type. Both are caused by the unequal heating of land and sea. Land and sea breezes occur daily, whereas the occurrence of monsoon winds is seasonal.

## LAND BREEZE

During the night, the land cools quickly, so that it is colder than the sea. A low pressure area is caused over the sea and the cooler, heavier land air begins to flow towards the sea. The general effect of the contrast in heating between land and sea is to produce cooler winters and warmer summers in the centres of continents than along the coasts.

## SEA BREEZE

During the day, the greater heating of the land causes the air to ascend, creating low pressure over land and the cool heavy air from the sea moves in to take its place. The strength of the sea breeze depends on the topography of the coast and the regions.

## MONSOON WIND

These are seasonal winds. For six months they blow from land to sea, and for the other six months, from sea to land. Thus, they may be regarded as land and sea breezes on a large-scale in which the period is a year instead of a day.

## VARIABLE WINDS

**Anticyclone:** A large-scale circulation of winds around a central region of high atmospheric pressure, clockwise in the northern hemisphere but counterclockwise in the southern hemisphere, is called an anticyclone.

**Cyclone:** An area of low atmospheric pressure with winds moving in a spiral about the central low is referred to as a cyclone. This spiral movement is anticlockwise in the Nothern hemisphere and clockwise in the Southern hemisphere.

**Local Winds:** These are small-scale convective winds of local origin caused by temperature differences. Some examples are the Chinook which blows in the eastern slopes of the Rocky Mountains, the Loo which blows over Pakistan and North India and the Misstral which blows across southern France.

# CLOUDS

A visible dense mass of water droplets and/or ice crystals suspended in the air is called a cloud.

## TYPES OF CLOUDS

**Altocumulus Clouds:** These are middle-level clouds made of water droplets that appear as grey, puffy masses, sometimes rolled out in parallel waves or bands. Their appearance on a warm, humid summer morning often means that thunderstorms will occur by late afternoon.

**Cirrus Clouds:** These are thin, wispy clouds blown by high winds into long streamers. They are considered high clouds forming above 6000 m

(20,000 ft). Cirrus clouds usually move across the sky from west to east. They generally indicate fair to pleasant weather.

**Cumulus Clouds:** They are puffy clouds that may look like pieces of floating cotton. The base is often flat and may be only 1,000 m (330 ft) above the ground. The top of the cloud has rounded towers. When the top of the cumulus resembles the head of a cauliflower, it is called cumulus congestus or towering cumulus. These clouds grow upward, and can develop into a giant cumulonimbus, which is a thunderstorm cloud.

**Stratus Clouds:** Uniform greyish clouds that often cover the entire sky, they resemble fog that does not reach the ground. Usually no precipitation falls from them, but it may drizzle.

## FORMS OF CONDENSATION

**Dew:** The waterdrops that deposit on surfaces of objects freely exposed to the sky at night by the condensation of water vapour is called dew.

**Fog:** A cloud that occurs at ground level, resulting in low visibility, is called fog. It forms when two air masses with differing temperature and moisture content mix together.

**Frost:** A deposit of small white ice crystals formed on the ground or other surfaces when the temperature falls below freezing point is called frost.

## FORMS OF PRECIPITATION

**Hail:** A precipitation of balls or pieces of ice with diameters of 5 mm to 10 cm (0.2–4 inches), hail is generally associated with rapidly rising convection currents in low latitudes or the passage of a cold front in temperate latitudes.

**Rain:** A form of precipitation, in which water droplets reach the ground in liquid state, is called rain. When water droplets are small, rain may be called drizzle.

**Sleet:** A form of precipitation found in near-freezing surface air is called sleet. In Great Britain and parts of the US, a mixture of rain and snow is called sleet. The term has sometimes been used for the clear ice on objects, more correctly known as glaze.

**Snow:** A type of solid precipitation which forms at temperatures below the freezing point of water is referred to as snow.

The Puffin Factfinder

## MEASURING DEVICES

| INSTRUMENTS | TO MEASURE |
|---|---|
| Altimeter | Altitude |
| Anemometer | Wind speed |
| Atmometer | Rate of evaporation |
| Barometer | Air pressure |
| Heliometer | Variation of the Sun's diameter |
| Hygrometer | Relative humidity |
| Rain gauge | Amount of liquid precipitation |
| Seismometer | Seismic waves (earthquakes) |
| Snowboard | Snow accumulation |
| Thermometer | Temperature |

## GEOGRAPHICAL SUPERLATIVES

- Largest continent in terms of area: Asia
- Largest country in terms of area: Russia
- Largest country in terms of population: China
- Highest mountain range: The Himalayas
- Highest point on earth: Mount Everest
- Longest river: Nile river
- Largest ocean: Pacific Ocean
- Largest inland body of water: Caspian Sea
- Largest island: Greenland
- Largest hot desert: Sahara, North Africa
- Deepest cave: Jean Bernard, France
- Highest waterfall: Angel Falls, Venezeula
- Largest drainage system in the world: Amazon river
- World's highest continuously active volcano: Cotopaxi, Eucador
- Deepest continental body of water: Lake Baikal, Russia
- Smallest continent on Earth in terms of area: Australia
- Smallest island: Nauru
- Lowest body of water on the surface: Dead Sea

# CONTINENTS AND OCEANS

## AFRICA

Africa is the second largest and the second-most populous continent after Asia. The continent is bound on the west by the Atlantic Ocean, on the north by the Mediterranean Sea, on the east by the Red Sea and the Indian Ocean, and on the south by the Atlantic and Indian oceans. The continent is cut almost equally in two by the Equator. The Prime Meridian passes through this continent. Most of Africa lies within the tropical region, bound on the north by the Tropic of Cancer and on the south by the Tropic of Capricorn. Mount Kilimanjaro in Tanzania is the highest point on the continent.

## ANTARCTICA

The southernmost continent, Antarctica, is also fifth in size among the world's continents. It has a permanent ice cap and the ice sheet that covers it is 4776.21 metres at its thickest point. Antarctica, with an average elevation of about 2,200 metres above sea level, is the world's highest continent. Its highest point is Vinson Massif in the Sentinel Range. The world's lowest recorded temperature (−128.6°F) was recorded at Vostok in Antarctica. Scottish cartographer John George Bartholomew is credited with first using 'Antarctica' as a formal name for the continent in the 1890s.

## ASIA

Asia is the largest and most populous continent in the world. It is located mostly in the eastern and northern hemispheres. It is bordered by the Arctic Ocean to the north, the Pacific Ocean to the east, the Indian Ocean to the south, the Mediterranean and the Black Sea to the south-west, and Europe to the west. The highest peak in the world, Mount Everest (8,850 m), and the lowest place on the Earth's land surface, the Dead Sea (400 m below sea level) are located in Asia. China, Japan, India, Saudi Arabia, and Korea are some of the important countries on this continent.

## AUSTRALIA

The smallest continent of the world, Australia, located between the Indian and Pacific oceans, is the only continent occupied entirely by a single country. Located in the southern hemisphere, this island continent is sometimes called 'the land down under'. The highest point on the Australian mainland is Mount Kosciusko, New South Wales. Nearly 20 per cent of Australia's landmass is classified as desert. The Murray and Darling are the two longest river systems in Australia.

## EUROPE

Europe is the second smallest continent of the world in terms of area, stretching from the Atlantic Ocean in the west to the Ural Mountains in the east. It is the third most populous continent after Asia and Africa. It is bordered on the north by the Arctic Ocean, on the west by the Atlantic Ocean, and on the south by the Mediterranean Sea, the Black Sea, and the Caspian Sea. Mount Elbrus in the Caucasus is Europe's highest peak with Caspian Sea marking its lowest point. The UK, Italy, Germany, France, Spain, Greece are some of the countries of Europe.

## NORTH AMERICA

North America is the third largest continent in terms of area and the fourth largest in the world, in terms of its population. It is almost completely surrounded by water, with the Arctic Ocean on the north, the North Atlantic Ocean on the east, Caribbean Sea on the south-east and the North Pacific Ocean on the west. Alaska, Greenland Canada, the US, Mexico, the Bahamas Islands are all part of North America. The continent, along with South America, is named after the explorer Amerigo Vespucci. The Isthmus of Panama connects North America with South America. The highest point in North America is Mt McKinley and the Death Valley is the lowest point. The US, Mexico, and Canada are some of its major countries.

## SOUTH AMERICA

South America is the fourth largest continent on Earth. It is bordered on the east by the Atlantic Ocean, on the west by the Pacific Ocean, and on the north by the Caribbean Sea. It is connected to North America by the Isthmus of Panama. The Andes is the longest mountain range of the continent, stretching from the southern tip of the continent all the way to Panama, the northernmost part. The highest point is Mt Aconcagua (Argentina). The Amazon Basin is covered by the world's largest tropical rainforest on the banks of the Amazon river. Angel Falls, the world's highest waterfall, is located in the Guiana Highlands. The numerous volcanoes in the Andes are part of the Circum–Pacific volcanic chain called the Ring of Fire. Argentina, Brazil, Chile, Ecuador, Peru, and Venezuela are some of the most important countries in the continent.

# OCEANS

## ANTARCTIC OCEAN

The Antarctic Ocean comprises the southern portions of the Atlantic, Pacific, and Indian oceans and their tributary seas surrounding Antarctica. The deepest point of the ocean (–7,235 m) is at the southern end of the South Sandwich Trench. Two major ports of the ocean are McMurdo and Palmer.

## ARCTIC OCEAN

The Arctic Ocean is the smallest of the five oceans of the world. It is not navigable, as it is completely frozen in winter and covered with drifting ice for the rest of the year. The deepest point of the ocean is at Fram Basin (–4,665 m). The major ports of the ocean are Churchill (Canada), Murmansk (Russia), and Prudhoe Bay (US).

## ATLANTIC OCEAN

The Atlantic Ocean is the second largest of the world's five oceans. Milwaukee Deep in the Puerto Rico Trench (–8,605 m) is the lowest point of the ocean. The Atlantic Ocean provides some of the world's most heavily-trafficked sea routes, between and within the Eastern and Western hemispheres. Some of its major ports are Alexandria (Egypt), Algiers (Algeria), Antwerp (Belgium), Barcelona (Spain), Buenos Aires (Argentina), Casablanca (Morocco), Colon (Panama), Copenhagen (Denmark), London (UK), Montreal (Canada), New York (US), and Rio de Janeiro (Brazil).

## INDIAN OCEAN

The Indian ocean is a body of salt water which covers about one-fifth of the total ocean area of the world. It stretches for more than 9977.93 km between the southern tips of Africa and Australia and, without its marginal seas, has an area of about 73,452,062.80 sq. km. The Indian Ocean is bound by Iran, Pakistan, India, and Bangladesh to the north; the Malay Peninsula, the Sunda Islands of Indonesia, and Australia to the east; Antarctica to the south; and Africa and the Arabian Peninsula to the west. Its average depth is 3889.24 m. and its deepest point, in the Sunda Deep of the Java Trench off the southern coast of Java, is at –7449.92 m feet. Major ports of the Indian Ocean include Durban (South Africa), Karachi, Mumbai, Chennai, and Kolkata on the Indian subcontinent, and Melbourne in Australia.

## PACIFIC OCEAN

The Pacific Ocean is the largest and the oldest of the world's five oceans. The navigator Ferdinand Magellan named it *El Mar Pacifico*, 'the peaceful sea'. It covers 28 per cent of the global surface, almost equal to the total land area of the world. The lowest point (–10,924 m) of the ocean is in Challenger Deep in Mariana Trench. It has the greatest conglomeration of islands grouped as Micronesia, Melanesia, and Polynesia. Major ports of the ocean include Bangkok (Thailand), Hong Kong (China), Los Angeles (US),

Manila (The Philippines), San Francisco (US), Shanghai (China), Singapore, Sydney (Australia), Vladivostok (Russia), Wellington (NZ), and Yokohama (Japan).

# MAJOR RIVERS OF THE WORLD

## AMAZON

The Amazon, with the largest drainage basin in the world, is often called the greatest river of South America. The river begins from the Ucayali–Apurímac river system in the Andes mountains of southern Peru. Covering the vast basin that includes the greater part of Brazil and Peru, significant parts of Colombia, Ecuador, and Bolivia, and a small area of Venezuela, Amazon flows into the Atlantic Ocean, on the north-eastern coast of Brazil. The first European to explore the Amazon, in 1541, was the Spanish soldier Francisco de Orellana, who gave the river its name after reporting pitched battles with tribes of female warriors, whom he likened to the Amazons of Greek mythology.

## AMUR

The Amur is the longest river of the Russian Far East. It rises at the confluence of Argun and Shilka rivers and then flows generally east and south-east, forming much of the border between China and south-eastern Siberia. At the Russian city of Khabarovsk, it turns north-eastward and flows across the Russian territory to the Tatar Strait. The most important tributaries include the Zeya, Bureya, and Amgun. Its Chinese name, Heilong Jiang, means 'Black Dragon River' and its Mongol name, Kharamuren, means 'Black River'.

## CONGO

The Congo or Zaire river, second longest in Africa, rises in the highlands of north-eastern Zambia between Tanganyika and Nyasa (Malawi) lakes as the Chambeshi river and drains into the Atlantic Ocean. Its drainage basin, covering 2,148,474.24 sq km, covers the Republic of the Congo, the Central African Republic, eastern Zambia, northern Angola and parts of Cameroon and Tanzania. Some of its principal tributaries are the Ubangi, Sangha, and Kwa.

## DANUBE

The Danube is the second longest river of Europe. It rises in the Black Forest mountains of western Germany and flows for 2848.53 km to its mouth on the Black Sea. Along its course, it passes through nine countries: Germany, Austria, Slovakia, Hungary, Croatia, Serbia, Bulgaria, Romania, and Ukraine.

Major tributaries of the Danube include Inn, Iller, Lech, Isar, Traun, Enns, and Morava rivers.

## HWANG HO

Hwang Ho is the second longest river of China, with a length of 5463.72 km and its drainage basin is the third largest in China with an area of 7,51,096.55 sq km. The river rises in Qinghai province on the Tibetan plateau. In its lower reaches it becomes a silt-laden stream and floods the North China Plain. For this reason, it has been given such names as 'China's Sorrow' and 'The Ungovernable'. The word *huang* (yellow) is a reference to the fine loess sediments that the river carries to the sea. Fen and Wei are its longest tributaries.

## MEKONG

Mekong river is the longest river in south-east Asia and the seventh longest in Asia (4345.22 km). Rising in south-eastern Qinghai province of China, it flows through the eastern part of Tibet and then forms part of the international border between Myanmar (Burma) and Laos, as well as between Laos and Thailand. The Mun-Chi river system forms one of Mekong's most important tributaries.

## MISSISSIPPI

It is one of the largest rivers of North America. It lies entirely in the US. Rising in Lake Itasca in Minnesota, it flows almost due south across the continental interior, collecting the waters of Missouri river (to the west) and Ohio river (to the east), along its journey to the Gulf of Mexico, a total distance of 3781.95 km from its source.

## MURRAY–DARLING

The Murray–Darling basin is a geographical area in the interior of south-eastern Australia. The name is derived from its two major rivers, Murray and Darling. The system stretches over 3701.49 km and forms the Murray–Darling Basin. Occupying about one-seventh of Australia's area, it is of immense economic significance to the country.

## NILE

The Nile (6649.80 km) is the longest river in Africa as well as the world. Known in Arabic as *Al-Bahr* or *Bahr en-Nil*, it rises just south of the Equator in eastern Africa and flows in a generally northward direction to drain into the Mediterranean Sea. Its basin includes parts of Tanzania, Burundi, Rwanda, Congo (Kinshasa), Kenya, Uganda, and Ethiopia, most of the Sudan, and the cultivated part of Egypt. The Nile is formed by three principal streams: the Blue Nile, the Atbara, and the White Nile.

## RHINE

The Rhine is one of the most important rivers of Europe both culturally and economically, where it plays a vital role in industrial transportation. It flows 1392.08 km from two small headways in the Alps of east-central Switzerland north and west to the North Sea, into which it drains through The Netherlands. The main tributaries of the Rhine include Ill, Dreisam, and Kinzig.

## VOLGA

The Volga is the longest river of Europe and the principal waterway of western Russia. Its basin, sprawling across about two-fifths of the European part of Russia, contains almost half of the entire population of the Russian Republic. Its river system, comprising 151,000 rivers and permanent and intermittent streams, has a total length of about 5,74,535.80 km. Among its many tributaries are the Kama, Oka, Veltuga, and Kerzhenets.

## YANGTZE KIANG

The longest river of Asia is the Yangtze Kiang, which travels a distance of about 6300.58 km. It is also the third longest river in the world, after the Nile and the Amazon. The Yangtze rises in the Kunlun Mountains of Tibet in western China and flows into the East China Sea near Shanghai in east-central China. The eight major tributaries are Yalong, Min, Jialing, Han, Wu, Yuan, Xiang, and Gan. The Yangtze basin produces half of China's total crops and the river is used for fishing, transporting, mining and producing hydroelectric energy.

# DESERTS

## ATACAMA

This cool, arid region in northern Chile is about 1,000–1,100 km long from north to south. Temperatures here are relatively low compared with those in similar latitudes elsewhere. The average summer temperature at Iquique is only 66°F (19°C) and at Antofagasta 65°F (18°C). The desert consists mainly of salt pans at the foot of the coastal mountains on the west and of alluvial fans sloping from the Andean foothills to the east; some of the fans are covered with dunes, but extensive pebble accumulations are more common. It is often referred to as the driest place on Earth. Parts of the desert haven't seen a drop of rain since recordkeeping began.

## GOBI

It is a huge desert and semi-desert region of Central Asia. The Gobi (from Mongolian *gobi*, meaning 'waterless place') stretches across huge portions of both Mongolia and China. The Gobi consists of the Ka-shun, Dzungarian, and Trans-Altai Gobi in the west, the Eastern or Mongolian Gobi in the centre and east, and the Ala Shan Desert in the south. The annual temperature range is considerable, with average lows in January reaching −40°F (−40°C) and average highs in July climbing to 113°F (45°C). Though vegetation in the region is sparse and rare, animal life is varied, with such large mammals as the wild camel, and the *dzeren* (an antelope).

## KALAHARI

The Kalahari is a large semi-arid to arid region in southern Africa, mainly in Botswana, South Africa, and Namibia. Its area is about 3,10,798.57 sq. km. Annual rainfall in the region varies from 500 mm annually in the north-east to no rain in the south-east. Daytime temperatures often reach more than 100°F (38°C) in the summer. The vegetation in the area consists mostly of grasses and acacia thornbush. Animals such as gemsbok, wildebeest, and lions wander much of the Kalahari. A small number of San (bushmen), nomadic hunters and gatherers inhabit the area. The first Europeans to cross the Kalahari were the British explorers David Livingstone and William C. Oswell, in 1849.

## SAHARA

The Sahara, with an area of 8,598,760.52 sq. km, is the largest hot desert in the world. It occupies nearly all of northern Africa. Sand sheets and dunes cover approximately 25 per cent of the Sahara's surface. The Sahara is dominated by two climatic regimes: a dry subtropical climate in the north and a dry tropical climate in the south.The highest temperature ever recorded there was 136°F (58°C) at Al-Azīzīyah, Libya, on the northern margin of the Sahara. Saharan vegetation is generally sparse, with scattered concentrations of grasses, shrubs, and trees in the highlands. Many animals including the gerbil, jerboa, Cape Hare, and desert hedgehog are found in the desert.

## TAKLA MAKAN

It is a great desert of Central Asia and one of the largest sandy deserts in the world. The Takla Makan occupies the central part of the Tarim Basin in the Uygur Autonomous Region of Xinjiang, north-western China. Its climate is moderately warm and markedly continental, with a maximum annual temperature range of 70°F (21°C). Precipitation is extremely low, ranging from 1.5 inches (38 mm) per year in the west to 0.4 inch (10 mm) annually in the east. Vegetation is extremely sparse in the Takla Makan; almost the entire region is devoid of plant cover.

## THAR

The Thar is a desert located partly in India (Rajasthan) and partly in Pakistan. Covering 199429.08 sq. km it is bordered by the irrigated Indus plain to the west, the Aravalli Range to the south-east, the Rann of Kutch to the south, and the Punjab plain to the north and north-east. The desert results from the dryness of the prevailing monsoon winds, which do not bring sufficient rain to keep the region moist. The name Thar is derived from *t'hul*, the general term for the region's sand ridges.

# COUNTRIES AND REGIONS OF THE WORLD

**Name:** Afghanistan

**Map Reference:** Asia

**Capital:** Kabul

**Population:** 30,419,928

**Area (in sq. km):** 6,52,230

**Currency:** Afghani

**Languages Spoken:** Afghan Persian or Dari (official), Pashto (official), Turkic languages (primarily Uzbek and Turkmen)

**Internet Code:** .af

**Name:** Albania

**Map Reference:** Europe

**Capital:** Tirana

**Population:** 32,15,988

**Area (in sq. km):** 28,748

**Currency:** Leke

**Languages Spoken:** Albanian (official), Greek, Vlach, Romani, Slavic dialects

**Internet Code:** .al

All population figures are according to July 2012 estimate

**Name:** Algeria
**Map Reference:** Africa
**Capital:** Algiers
**Population:** 37,100,000
**Area (in sq. km):** 23,81,741
**Currency:** Algerian dinar
**Languages Spoken:** Arabic (official), French, Berber dialects
**Internet Code:** .dz

**Name:** Andorra
**Map Reference:** Europe
**Capital:** Andorra la Vella
**Population:** 85,082
**Area (in sq. km):** 468
**Currency:** Euros
**Languages Spoken:** Catalan (official), French, Spanish, Portuguese
**Internet Code:** .ad

**Name:** Angola
**Map Reference:** Africa
**Capital:** Luanda
**Population:** 1,80,56,072
**Area (in sq. km):** 12,46,700
**Currency:** Kwanza
**Languages Spoken:** Portuguese (official), Bantu, and other African languages
**Internet Code:** .ao

**Name:** Antigua and Barbuda
**Map Reference:** Central America and the Caribbean
**Capital:** Saint John's
**Population:** 89,018
**Area (in sq. km):** 442.6
**Currency:** East Caribbean dollar

**Languages Spoken:** English (official), Antiguan Creole
**Internet Code:** .ag

**Name:** Argentina
**Map Reference:** South America
**Capital:** Buenos Aires
**Population:** 4,21,92,494
**Area (in sq. km):** 27,80,400
**Currency:** Peso
**Languages Spoken:** Spanish (official), Italian, English, German, French
**Internet Code:** .ar

**Name:** Armenia
**Map Reference:** Asia
**Capital:** Yerevan
**Population:** 29,70,495
**Area (in sq. km):** 29,743
**Currency:** Dram
**Languages Spoken**: Armenian, Yezidi, Russian
**Internet Code:** .am

**Name:** Australia
**Map Reference:** Oceania
**Capital:** Canberra
**Population:** 2,20,15,576
**Area (in sq. km):** 76,92,029
**Currency:** Australian dollar
**Languages Spoken:** English, Chinese, Italian, Greek, Arabic, Vietnamese
**Internet Code:** .au

**Name:** Austria
**Map Reference:** Europe
**Capital:** Vienna

**Population:** 82,19,743
**Area (in sq. km):** 83,871
**Currency:** Euro
**Languages Spoken:** German (official), Turkish, Serbian, Croatian (official in Burgenland), Slovene, Hungarian
**Internet Code:** .at

**Name:** Azerbaijan
**Map Reference:** Asia
**Capital:** Baku
**Population:** 94,93,600
**Area (in sq. km):** 86,600
**Currency:** Manat
**Languages Spoken:** Azerbaijani (Azeri), Lezgi, Russian, Armenian
**Internet Code:** .az

**Name:** Bahrain
**Map Reference:** Middle East
**Capital:** Manama
**Population:** 12,48,348
**Area (in sq. km):** 760
**Currency:** Bahraini dinar
**Languages Spoken:** Arabic, English, Farsi, Urdu
**Internet Code:** .bh

**Name:** Bangladesh
**Map Reference:** Asia
**Capital:** Dhaka
**Population:** 16,10,83,804
**Area (in sq. km):** 143998
**Currency:** Taka
**Languages Spoken:** Bangla (official, also known as Bengali), English
**Internet Code:** .bd

**Name:** Barbados
**Map Reference:** Central America and the Caribbean
**Capital:** Bridgetown
**Population:** 2,87,733
**Area (in sq. km):** 430
**Currency:** Barbadian dollar
**Languages Spoken:** English, Bajan
**Internet Code:** .bb

**Name:** Belarus
**Map Reference:** Europe
**Capital:** Minsk
**Population:** 95,42,883
**Area (in sq. km):** 2,07,600
**Currency:** Belarusian rubles
**Languages Spoken:** Belarusian (official), Russian (official)
**Internet Code:** .by

**Name:** Belgium
**Map Reference:** Europe
**Capital:** Brussels
**Population:** 1,04,38,353
**Area (in sq. km):** 30,528
**Currency:** Euro
**Languages Spoken:** Dutch (official), French (official), German (official)
**Internet Code:** .be

**Name:** Belize
**Map Reference:** Central America and the Caribbean
**Capital:** Belmopan
**Population:** 3,27,719
**Area (in sq. km):** 22,966
**Currency:** Belizean dollar

**Languages Spoken:** English (official), Spanish, Creole, Mayan dialects Garifuna, German
**Internet Code:** .bz

**Name:** Benin
**Map Reference:** Africa
**Capital:** Porto-Novo
**Population:** 95,98,787
**Area (in sq. km):** 1,12,622
**Currency:** West African CFA (Communauté Financière Africaine) francs
**Languages Spoken:** French (official), Fon and Yoruba (most common vernaculars in south), tribal languages
**Internet Code:** .bj

**Name:** Bhutan
**Map Reference:** Asia
**Capital:** Thimphu
**Population:** 7,16,896
**Area (in sq. km):** 38,394
**Currency:** Bhutanese ngultrum
**Languages Spoken:** Sharchhopka, Dzongkha (official), Lhotshamkha
**Internet Code:** .bt

**Name:** Bolivia
**Map Reference:** South America
**Capital:** Sucre
**Population:** 1,02,90,003
**Area (in sq. km):** 10,98,581
**Currency:** Boliviano
**Languages Spoken:** Spanish, Quechua, Aymara
**Internet Code:** .bo

**Name:** Bosnia and Herzegovina
**Map Reference:** Europe

**Capital:** Sarajevo
**Population:** 46,22,292
**Area (in sq. km):** 51,197
**Currency:** Konvertibilna markas
**Languages Spoken:** Bosnian, Croatian, Serbian
**Internet Code:** .ba

**Name:** Botswana
**Map Reference:** Africa
**Capital:** Gaborone
**Population:** 20,98,018
**Area (in sq. km):** 5,81,730
**Currency:** Pula
**Languages Spoken:** Setswana (official), English (official), Kalanga, Sekgalagadi, others
**Internet Code:** .bw

**Name:** Brazil
**Map Reference:** South America
**Capital:** Brasilia
**Population:** 20,57,16,890
**Area (in sq. km):** 85,14,877
**Currency:** Real
**Languages Spoken:** Portuguese (official), Spanish, German, Italian, Japanese, English
**Internet Code:** .br

**Name:** Brunei
**Map Reference:** Asia
**Capital:** Bandar Seri Begawan
**Population:** 4,08,786
**Area (in sq. km):** 5,765
**Currency:** Brunei dollar

**Languages Spoken:** Bahasa Melayu (official), English, Chinese
**Internet Code:** .bn

**Name:** Bulgaria
**Map Reference:** Europe
**Capital:** Sofia
**Population:** 70,37,935
**Area (in sq. km):** 1,10,879
**Currency:** Lev
**Languages Spoken:** Bulgarian, Turkish, Roma
**Internet Code:** .bg

**Name:** Burkina Faso
**Map Reference:** Africa
**Capital:** Ouagadougou
**Population:** 1,72,75,115
**Area (in sq. km):** 2,74,200
**Currency:** Communauté Financière Africaine franc
**Languages Spoken:** French (official), native African languages
**Internet Code:** .bf

**Name:** Burundi
**Map Reference:** Africa
**Capital:** Bujumbura
**Population:** 1,05,57,259
**Area (in sq. km):** 27,830
**Currency:** Burundi franc
**Languages Spoken:** Kirundi (official), French (official), Swahili
**Internet Code:** .bi

**Name:** Cambodia
**Map Reference:** Asia
**Capital:** Phnom Penh

**Population:** 1,49,52,665
**Area (in sq. km):** 1,81,035
**Currency:** Riel
**Languages Spoken:** Khmer (official), French, English
**Internet Code:** .kh

**Name:** Cameroon
**Map Reference:** Africa
**Capital:** Yaounde
**Population:** 2,01,29,878
**Area (in sq. km):** 4,75,440
**Currency:** Cooperation Financiere en Afrique Centrale franc
**Languages Spoken:** 24 major African language groups, English (official), French (official)
**Internet Code:** .cm

**Name:** Canada
**Map Reference:** North America
**Capital:** Ottawa
**Population:** 3,43,00,083
**Area (in sq. km):** 99,84,670
**Currency:** Canadian dollar
**Languages Spoken:** English, French (official)
**Internet Code:** .ca

**Name:** Cape Verde
**Map Reference:** Africa
**Capital:** Praia
**Population:** 5,23,568
**Area (in sq. km):** 4,033
**Currency:** Cape Verdean escudo
**Languages Spoken:** Portuguese, Crioulo (a blend of Portuguese and West African words)
**Internet Code:** .cv

**Name:** Central African Republic
**Map Reference:** Africa
**Capital:** Bangui
**Population:** 50,57,208
**Area (in sq. km):** 6,22,984
**Currency:** Cooperation Financiere en Afrique Centrale francs
**Languages Spoken:** French (official), Sangho (lingua franca and national language), tribal languages
**Internet Code:** .cf

**Name:** Chad
**Map Reference:** Africa
**Capital:** N'Djamena
**Population:** 1,09,75,648
**Area (in sq. km):** 1,284,000
**Currency:** Cooperation Financiere en Afrique Centrale francs
**Languages Spoken:** French (official), Arabic (official), Sara (in south) and other dialects
**Internet Code:** .td

**Name:** Chile
**Map Reference:** South America
**Capital:** Santiago
**Population:** 1,70,67,369
**Area (in sq. km):** 7,56,102
**Currency:** Chilean peso
**Languages Spoken:** Spanish (official), Mapudungun, German, English
**Internet Code:** .cl

**Name:** China
**Map Reference:** Asia
**Capital:** Beijing
**Population:** 1,34,32,39,923
**Area (in sq. km):** 95,96,961

**Currency:** Renminbi (yuan)

**Languages Spoken:** Standard Chinese or Mandarin (Putonghua, based on the Beijing dialect), Yue (Cantonese), Wu (Shanghainese), Minbei (Fuzhou), Minnan (Hokkien-Taiwanese), Xiang, Gan, Hakka dialects

**Internet Code:** .cn

**Name:** Colombia

**Map Reference:** South America

**Capital:** Bogota

**Population:** 4,52,39,079

**Area (in sq. km):** 11,38,910

**Currency:** Colombian peso

**Languages Spoken:** Spanish

**Internet Code:** .co

**Name:** Comoros

**Map Reference:** Africa

**Capital:** Moroni

**Population:** 737,284

**Area (in sq. km):** 2,235

**Currency:** Comoran franc

**Languages Spoken:** Arabic (official), French (official), Shikomor (a blend of Swahili and Arabic)

**Internet Code:** .km

**Name:** Democratic Republic of the Congo

**Map Reference:** Africa

**Capital:** Kinshasa

**Population:** 7,35,99,190

**Area (in sq. km):** 23,44,858

**Currency:** Congolese franc

**Languages Spoken:** French (official), Lingala (a lingua franca trade language), Kingwana (a dialect of Kiswahili or Swahili), Kikongo, Tshiluba

**Internet Code:** .cd

**Name:** Republic of the Congo
**Map Reference:** Africa
**Capital:** Brazzaville
**Population:** 43,66,266
**Area (in sq. km):** 3,42,000
**Currency:** Central African CFA franc
**Languages Spoken:** French (official), Lingala and Monokutuba (lingua franca trade languages), many local languages and dialects
**Internet Code:** .cg

**Name:** Costa Rica
**Map Reference:** Central America and the Caribbean
**Capital:** San Jose
**Population:** 46,36,348
**Area (in sq. km):** 51,100
**Currency:** Costa Rican colon
**Languages Spoken:** Spanish (official), English
**Internet Code:** .cr

**Name:** Cote d'Ivoire (Ivory Coast)
**Map Reference:** Africa
**Capital:** Yamoussoukro
**Population:** 2,19,52,093
**Area (in sq. km):** 3,22,463
**Currency:** Communaute Financiere Africaine franc (XOF)
**Languages Spoken:** French (official), sixty native dialects of which Dioula is the most widely spoken
**Internet Code:** .ci

**Name:** Croatia
**Map Reference:** Europe
**Capital:** Zagreb
**Population:** 44,80,043

**Area (in sq. km):** 56,594
**Currency:** Kuna
**Languages Spoken:** Croatian (official), Serbian, Italian, Hungarian, Czech, Slovak, German
**Internet Code:** .hr

**Name:** Cuba
**Map Reference:** Central America and the Caribbean
**Capital:** Havana
**Population:** 1,10,75,244
**Area (in sq. km):** 1,10,860
**Currency:** Cuban peso
**Languages Spoken:** Spanish (official)
**Internet Code:** .cu

**Name:** Cyprus
**Map Reference:** Europe
**Capital:** Nicosia (Lefkoia)
**Population:** 11,38,071
**Area (in sq. km):** 9,251
**Currency:** Euro
**Languages Spoken:** Greek, Turkish, English
**Internet Code:** .cy

**Name:** Czech Republic
**Map Reference:** Europe
**Capital:** Prague
**Population:** 1,01,77,300
**Area (in sq. km):** 78,867
**Currency:** Koruna (Kc)
**Languages Spoken:** Czech, Slovak
**Internet Code:** .cz

**Name:** Denmark
**Map Reference:** Europe
**Capital:** Copenhagen
**Population:** 55,43,453
**Area (in sq. km):** 43,094
**Currency:** Danish krone
**Languages Spoken:** Danish, Faroese, Greenlandic, German
**Internet Code:** .dk

**Name:** Djibouti
**Map Reference:** Africa
**Capital:** Djibouti
**Population:** 7,74,389
**Area (in sq. km):** 23,200
**Currency:** Djiboutian franc
**Languages Spoken:** French (official), Arabic (official), Somali, Afar
**Highest Point:** Moussa Ali 2,028 m
**Lowest Point:** Lac Assal −155 m
**Internet Code:** .dj

**Name:** Dominica
**Map Reference:** Central America and the Caribbean
**Capital:** Roseau
**Population:** 73,126
**Area (in sq. km):** 751
**Currency:** East Caribbean dollar
**Languages Spoken:** English (official), French patois
**Internet Code:** .dm

**Name:** Dominican Republic
**Map Reference:** Central America and the Caribbean
**Capital:** Santo Domingo
**Population:** 1,00,88,598

**Area (in sq. km):** 48,670
**Currency:** Dominican peso
**Languages Spoken:** Spanish
**Internet Code:** .do

**Name:** Ecuador
**Map Reference:** South America
**Capital:** Quito
**Population:** 1,52,23,680
**Area (in sq. km):** 2,83,561
**Currency:** US dollar
**Languages Spoken:** Spanish (official), Amerindian languages (especially Quechua
**Internet Code:** .ec

**Name:** Egypt
**Map Reference:** Africa
**Capital:** Cairo
**Population:** 8,36,88,164
**Area (in sq. km):** 10,01,450
**Currency:** Egyptian pound
**Languages Spoken:** Arabic (official), English, French
**Internet Code:** .eg

**Name:** El Salvador
**Map Reference:** Central America and the Caribbean
**Capital:** San Salvador
**Population:** 60,90,646
**Area (in sq. km):** 21,041
**Currency:** US dollar
**Languages Spoken:** Casitilian (official), Spanish, Nahua
**Internet Code:** .sv

**Name:** Equatorial Guinea
**Map Reference:** Africa
**Capital:** Malabo
**Population:** 6,85,991
**Area (in sq. km):** 28,051
**Currency:** CFA (Communaute Financiere Africaine) franc
**Languages Spoken:** Spanish (official), other (includes French (official), Fang, Bubi)
**Internet Code:** .gq

**Name:** Eritrea
**Map Reference:** Africa
**Capital:** Asmara
**Population:** 60,86,495
**Area (in sq. km):** 1,17,600
**Currency:** Nakfa
**Languages Spoken:** Tigrinya (official), English (official), Afar, Arabic, Tigre and Kunama, other Cushitic languages
**Internet Code:** .er

**Name:** Estonia
**Map Reference:** Europe
**Capital:** Tallinn
**Population:** 12,74,709
**Area (in sq. km):** 45,228
**Currency:** Euro
**Languages Spoken:** Estonian (official), Russian
**Internet Code:** .ee

**Name:** Ethiopia
**Map Reference:** Africa
**Capital:** Addis Ababa
**Population:** 9,38,15,992

**Area (in sq. km):** 11,04,300
**Currency:** Birr
**Languages Spoken:** Amhoric (official), Oromigna, Tigrigna, Somaligna, Guaragigna, Sidamigna, Hadiyigna, English
**Internet Code:** .et

**Name:** Fiji
**Map Reference:** Oceania
**Capital:** Suva (on Viti Levu)
**Population:** 8,90,057
**Area (in sq. km):** 18,274
**Currency:** Fijian dollar
**Languages Spoken:** English (official), Fijian (official), Hindustani
**Internet Code:** .fj

**Name:** Finland
**Map Reference:** Europe
**Capital:** Helsinki
**Population:** 52,62,930
**Area (in sq. km):** 3,38,145
**Currency:** Euro
**Languages Spoken:** Finnish (official), Swedish (official)
**Internet Code:** .fi; (note – Aland Islands assigned .ax)

**Name:** France
**Map Reference:** Europe
**Capital:** Paris
**Population:** 6,56,30,692
**Area (in sq. km):** 6,79,893
**Currency:** Euro
**Languages Spoken:** French, Provencal, Breton, Alsatian, Corsican, Catalan, Basque, Flemish
**Internet Code:** Metropolitan France .fr; French Guiana .gf; Guadeloupe .gp; Martinique .mq; Reunion .re

**Name:** Gabon
**Map Reference:** Africa
**Capital:** Libreville
**Population:** 16,08,321
**Area (in sq. km):** 2,67,667
**Currency:** CFA (Communaute Financiere Africaine) franc
**Languages Spoken:** French (official), Fang, Myene, Nzebi
**Internet Code:** .ga

**Name:** The Gambia
**Map Reference:** Africa
**Capital:** Banjul
**Population:** 18,40,454
**Area (in sq. km):** 11,295
**Currency:** Dalasi
**Languages Spoken:** English (official), Mandinka, Wolof, Fula, other indigenous languages
**Internet Code:** .gm

**Name:** Georgia
**Map Reference:** Eurasia
**Capital:** Tbilisi
**Population:** 45,70,934
**Area (in sq. km):** 69,700
**Currency:** Lari
**Languages Spoken:** Georgian (official), Russian, Armenian, Azeri
**Internet Code:** .ge

**Name:** Germany
**Map Reference:** Europe
**Capital:** Berlin
**Population:** 8,13,05,856
**Area (in sq. km):** 3,57,022
**Currency:** Euro

**Languages Spoken:** German
**Internet Code:** .de

**Name:** Ghana
**Map Reference:** Africa
**Capital:** Accra
**Population:** 2,52,41,998
**Area (in sq. km):** 2,38,533
**Currency:** Cedis
**Languages Spoken:** Asante, Ewe, Fante, Boron (Brong), Dagomba, Dangme, Akyem, Ga, Akuapem, others
**Internet Code:** .gh

**Name:** Greece
**Map Reference:** Europe
**Capital:** Athens
**Population:** 10,767,827
**Area (in sq. km):** 1,31,957
**Currency:** Euro
**Languages Spoken:** Greek
**Internet Code:** .gr

**Name:** Greenland
**Map Reference:** North America
**Capital:** Nuuk
**Population:** 57,695
**Area (in sq. km):** 21,66,086
**Currency:** Danish kroner
**Languages Spoken:** Kalaallisut (official), Danish, English
**Internet Code:** .gl

**Name:** Grenada
**Map Reference:** Central America and the Caribbean
**Capital:** Saint George's

**Population:** 1,09,011
**Area (in sq. km):** 344
**Currency:** East Caribbean dollar
**Languages Spoken:** English (official), Grenadian Creole
**Internet Code:** .gd

**Name:** Guatemala
**Map Reference:** Central America and the Caribbean
**Capital:** Guatemala City
**Population:** 1,40,99,032
**Area (in sq. km):** 1,08,889
**Currency:** Guatemalan quetzal
**Languages Spoken:** Spanish, Amerindian languages
**Internet Code:** .gt

**Name:** Guinea
**Map Reference:** Africa
**Capital:** Conakry
**Population:** 1,08,84,958
**Area (in sq. km):** 2,45,857
**Currency:** Guinean franc
**Languages Spoken:** French (official)
**Internet Code:** .gn

**Name:** Guinea-Bissau
**Map Reference:** Africa
**Capital:** Bissau
**Population:** 16,28,603
**Area (in sq. km):** 36,125
**Currency:** CFA (Communaute Financiere Africaine) franc
**Languages Spoken:** Portuguese (official), Crioulo, African languages
**Internet Code:** .gw

The Puffin Factfinder

**Name:** Guyana
**Map Reference:** South America
**Capital:** Georgetown
**Population:** 7,41,908
**Area (in sq. km):** 2,14,969
**Currency:** Guyanese dollar
**Languages Spoken:** English, Amerindian dialects, Creole, Caribbean Hindustani (a dialect of Hindi), Urdu
**Internet Code:** .gy

**Name:** Haiti
**Map Reference:** Central America and the Caribbean
**Capital:** Port-au-Prince
**Population:** 98,01,664
**Area (in sq. km):** 27,750
**Currency:** Gourde
**Languages Spoken:** French (official), Haitian Creole (official)
**Internet Code:** .ht

**Name:** Honduras
**Map Reference:** Central America and the Caribbean
**Capital:** Tegucigalpa
**Population:** 82,96,693
**Area (in sq. km):** 1,12,090
**Currency:** Lempira
**Languages Spoken:** Spanish, Amerindian dialects
**Internet Code:** .hn

**Name:** Hungary
**Map Reference:** Europe
**Capital:** Budapest
**Population:** 99,58,453
**Area (in sq. km):** 93,028

**Currency:** Forint
**Languages Spoken:** Hungarian (official), German
**Internet Code:** .hu

**Name:** Iceland
**Map Reference:** Europe
**Capital:** Reykjavik
**Population:** 3,13,183
**Area (in sq. km):** 1,03,000
**Currency:** Icelandic Króna
**Languages Spoken:** Icelandic, English, Nordic languages, German
**Internet Code:** .is

**Name:** India
**Map Reference:** Asia
**Capital:** New Delhi
**Population:** 1,20,50,73,612
**Area (in sq. km):** 32,87,263
**Currency:** Indian rupees
**Languages Spoken:** Hindi (official), English (official), Bengali, Telugu, Marathi, Tamil, Urdu, Gujarati, Kannada, Malayalam, Oriya, Punjabi, Assamese, Maithili
**Internet Code:** .in

**Name:** Indonesia
**Map Reference:** South-east Asia
**Capital:** Jakarta
**Population:** 24,82,16,193
**Area (in sq. km):** 19,04,569
**Currency:** Indonesian rupiahs
**Languages Spoken:** Bahasa Indonesia (official, modified form of Malay), English, Dutch, local dialects
**Internet Code:** .id

**Name:** Iran
**Map Reference:** Middle East
**Capital:** Tehran
**Population:** 7,88,68,711
**Area (in sq. km):** 16,48,195
**Currency:** Rial
**Languages Spoken:** Persian (official), Turkic and Turkic dialects, Kurdish, Luri, Balochi, Arabic, Turkish
**Internet Code:** .ir

**Name:** Iraq
**Map Reference:** Middle East
**Capital:** Baghdad
**Population:** 3,11,29,225
**Area (in sq. km):** 4,38,317
**Currency:** Iraqi dinar
**Languages Spoken:** Arabic, Kurdish (official in Kurdish regions), Turkoman (Turkish dialect), Assyrian (Neo-Aramaic), Armenian
**Internet Code:** .iq

**Name:** Ireland
**Map Reference:** Europe
**Capital:** Dublin
**Population:** 47,22,028
**Area (in sq. km):** 70,273
**Currency:** Euro
**Languages Spoken:** English (official) is the language generally used, Irish (Gaelic or Gaeilge) (official) spoken mainly in areas along the western coast
**Internet Code:** .ie

**Name:** Israel
**Map Reference:** Middle East
**Capital:** Jerusalem

**Population:** 75,90,758
**Area (in sq. km):** 20,770
**Currency:** New Israeli shekels
**Languages Spoken:** Hebrew (official), Arabic used officially for Arab minority, English is the most commonly used foreign language
**Internet Code:** .il

**Name:** Italy
**Map Reference:** Europe
**Capital:** Rome
**Population:** 6,12,61,254
**Area (in sq. km):** 3,01,340
**Currency:** Euro
**Languages Spoken:** Italian (official), German, French, Slovene
**Internet Code:** .it

**Name:** Jamaica
**Map Reference:** Central America and the Caribbean
**Capital:** Kingston
**Population:** 28,89,187
**Area (in sq. km):** 10,991
**Currency:** Jamaican dollar
**Languages Spoken:** English (official), Patois
**Internet Code:** .jm

**Name:** Japan
**Map Reference:** Asia
**Capital:** Tokyo
**Population:** 12,73,68,088
**Area (in sq. km):** 3,77,915
**Currency:** Yen
**Languages Spoken:** Japanese
**Internet Code:** .jp

**Name:** Jordan
**Map Reference:** Middle East
**Capital:** Amman
**Population:** 62,69,285
**Area (in sq. km):** 89,342
**Currency:** Jordanian dinar
**Languages Spoken:** Arabic, English (official)
**Internet Code:** .jo

**Name:** Kazakhstan
**Map Reference:** Asia
**Capital:** Astana
**Population:** 1,75,22,012
**Area (in sq. km):** 27,24,900
**Currency:** Tenge
**Languages Spoken:** Kazakh (Qazaq, state language), Russian (official, used in everyday business, designated the 'language of interethnic communication')
**Internet Code:** .kz

**Name:** Kenya
**Map Reference:** Africa
**Capital:** Nairobi
**Population:** 4,30,13,341
**Area (in sq. km):** 5,80,367
**Currency:** Kenyan shilling
**Languages Spoken:** English (official), Kiswahili (official), numerous indigenous languages
**Internet Code:** .ke

**Name:** Kiribati
**Map Reference:** Oceania
**Capital:** Tarawa

**Population:** 11,01,998
**Area (in sq. km):** 811
**Currency:** Australian dollar
**Languages Spoken:** I-Kiribati, English (official)
**Highest Point:** Unnamed elevation on Banaba 81 m
**Lowest Point:** Pacific Ocean 0 m
**Internet Code:** .ki

**Name:** Kosovo
**Map Reference:** Europe
**Capital:** Pristina
**Population:** 18,36,529
**Area (in sq. km):** 10,887
**Currency:** Euro, Serbian dinar
**Languages Spoken:** Albanian (official), Serbian (official), Bosnian, Turkish, Roma
**Internet Code:** Nil

**Name:** Kuwait
**Map Reference:** Middle-East
**Capital:** Kuwait City
**Population:** 26,46,314 (includes 12,91,354 non-nationals)
**Area (in sq. km):** 17,818
**Currency:** Kuwaiti dinar
**Languages Spoken:** Arabic (official), English
**Internet Code:** .kw

**Name:** Kyrgyzstan
**Map Reference:** Asia
**Capital:** Bishkek
**Population:** 54,96,737
**Area (in sq. km):** 1,99,951
**Currency:** Soms

**Languages Spoken:** Kyrgyz (official), Uzbek, Russian (official), Dungun
**Internet Code:** .kg

**Name:** Laos
**Map Reference:** Asia
**Capital:** Vientiane
**Population:** 65,86,266
**Area (in sq. km):** 2,36,800
**Currency:** Laos kip
**Languages Spoken:** Lao (official), French, English, other ethnic languages
**Internet Code:** .la

**Name:** Latvia
**Map Reference:** Europe
**Capital:** Riga
**Population:** 21,91,580
**Area (in sq. km):** 64,589
**Currency:** Lats
**Languages Spoken:** Latvian (official), Russian, Lithuanian.
**Internet Code:** .lv

**Name:** Lebanon
**Map Reference:** Middle-East
**Capital:** Beirut
**Population:** 41,40,289
**Area (in sq. km):** 10,400
**Currency:** Lebanese pound
**Languages Spoken:** Arabic (official), French, English, Armenian
**Internet Code:** .lb

**Name:** Lesotho
**Map Reference:** Africa
**Capital:** Maseru

**Population:** 19,30,493
**Area (in sq. km):** 30,355
**Currency:** Lesotho loti
**Languages Spoken:** Sesotho (southern Sotho), English (official), Zulu, Xhosa
**Internet Code:** .ls

**Name:** Liberia
**Map Reference:** Africa
**Capital:** Monrovia
**Population:** 38,87,886
**Area (in sq. km):** 1,11,369
**Currency:** Liberian dollar
**Languages Spoken:** English (official), some 20 ethnic group languages
**Internet Code:** .lr

**Name:** Libya
**Map Reference:** Africa
**Capital:** Tripoli
**Population:** 67,33,620
**Area (in sq. km):** 17,59,540
**Currency:** Dinar
**Languages Spoken:** Arabic, Italian, English
**Internet Code:** .ly

**Name:** Liechtenstein
**Map Reference:** Europe
**Capital:** Vaduz
**Population:** 36,713
**Area (in sq. km):** 160
**Currency:** Swiss franc
**Languages Spoken:** German (official), Alemannic dialect
**Internet Code:** .li

**Name:** Lithuania
**Map Reference:** Europe
**Capital:** Vilnius
**Population:** 35,25,761
**Area (in sq. km):** 65,300
**Currency:** litai
**Languages Spoken:** Lithuanian (official), Russian, Polish
**Internet Code:** .lt

**Name:** Luxembourg
**Map Reference:** Europe
**Capital:** Luxembourg
**Population:** 5,09,074
**Area (in sq. km):** 2,586
**Currency:** Euro
**Languages Spoken:** Luxembourgish (national language), German (administrative language), French (administrative language)
**Internet Code:** .lu

**Name:** Macedonia
**Map Reference:** Europe
**Capital:** Skopje
**Population:** 20,82,370
**Area (in sq. km):** 25,713
**Currency:** Macedonian denar
**Languages Spoken:** Macedonian, Albanian, Turkish, Roma, Serbian
**Internet Code:** .mk

**Name:** Madagascar
**Map Reference:** Africa
**Capital:** Antananarivo
**Population:** 2,25,85,517
**Area (in sq. km):** 5,87,041

**Currency:** Malagasy ariary
**Languages Spoken:** English (official), French (official), Malagasy (official)
**Internet Code:** .mg

**Name:** Malawi
**Map Reference:** Africa
**Capital:** Lilongwe
**Population:** 1,63,23,044
**Area (in sq. km):** 1,18,484
**Currency:** Malawian kwachas
**Languages Spoken:** Chichewa (official), Chinyanja, Chiyao, Chitumbuka, Chisena, Chilomwe, Chitonga
**Internet Code:** .mw

**Name:** Malaysia
**Map Reference:** Asia
**Capital:** Kuala Lumpur
**Population:** 2,91,79,952
**Area (in sq. km):** 3,29,847
**Currency:** Ringgit
**Languages Spoken:** Bahasa Malaysia (official), English, Chinese (Cantonese, Mandarin, Hokkien, Hakka, Hainan, Foochow), Tamil, Telugu, Malayalam, Punjabi, Thai
**Internet Code:** .my

**Name:** Maldives
**Map Reference:** Asia
**Capital:** Malé
**Population:** 3,94,451
**Area (in sq. km):** 298
**Currency:** Maldivian rufiyaa
**Languages Spoken:** Dhivehi, English
**Internet Code:** .mv

**Name:** Mali
**Map Reference:** Africa
**Capital:** Bamako
**Population:** 1,45,33,511
**Area (in sq. km):** 12,40,192
**Currency:** XOF (Communaute Financiere Africaine) franc
**Languages Spoken:** French (official), Bambara, many African languages
**Internet Code:** .ml

**Name:** Malta
**Map Reference:** Europe
**Capital:** Valletta
**Population:** 4,09,836
**Area (in sq. km):** 316
**Currency:** Euro
**Languages Spoken:** Maltese (official), English (official)
**Internet Code:** .mt

**Name:** Marshall Islands
**Map Reference:** Oceania
**Capital:** Majuro
**Population:** 68,480
**Area (in sq. km):** 181
**Currency:** US dollar
**Languages Spoken:** Marshallese (official), English (official)
**Internet Code:** .mh

**Name:** Mauritania
**Map Reference:** Africa
**Capital:** Nouakchott
**Population:** 33,59,185
**Area (in sq. km):** 10,30,700
**Currency:** Ouguiya

**Languages Spoken:** Arabic (official), Pulaar, Soninke, Wolof (all national languages), French, Hassaniya
**Internet Code:** .mr

**Name:** Mauritius
**Map Reference:** Africa
**Capital:** Port Louis
**Population:** 13,13,095
**Area (in sq. km):** 2040
**Currency:** Mauritian rupees
**Languages Spoken:** English (official), Creole, Bhojpuri, French, others
**Internet Code:** .mu

**Name:** Mexico
**Map Reference:** North America
**Capital:** Mexico City
**Population:** 11,49,75,406
**Area (in sq. km):** 19,64,375
**Currency:** Peso
**Languages Spoken:** Spanish, Indigenous languages like Mayan, Nahuatl
**Internet Code:** .mx

**Name:** Federated States of Micronesia
**Map Reference:** Oceania
**Capital:** Palikir
**Population:** 1,06,487
**Area (in sq. km):** 702
**Currency:** US dollar
**Languages Spoken:** English (official and common language), Chuukese, Kosrean, Pohnpeian, Yapese, Ulithian, Woleaian, Nukuoro, Kapingamarangi
**Internet Code:** .fm

**Name:** Moldova
**Map Reference:** Europe
**Capital:** Chisinau
**Population:** 36,56,843
**Area (in sq. km):** 33,851
**Currency:** Moldovan lei
**Languages Spoken:** Moldovan (official), Russian, Gagauz (a Turkish dialect)
**Internet Code:** .md

**Name:** Monaco
**Map Reference:** Europe
**Capital:** Monaco
**Population:** 30,510
**Area (in sq. km):** 2
**Currency:** Euro
**Languages Spoken:** French (official), English, Italian, Monegasque
**Internet Code:** .mc

**Name:** Mongolia
**Map Reference:** Asia
**Capital:** Ulan Bator
**Population:** 31,79,997
**Area (in sq. km):** 15,64,116
**Currency:** Togrog
**Languages Spoken:** Mongolian (official), Turkic, Russian.
**Internet Code:** .mn

**Name:** Montenegro
**Map Reference:** Europe
**Capital:** Podgorica
**Population:** 6,57,394
**Area (in sq. km):** 13,812

**Currency:** Euro
**Languages Spoken:** Montenegrin (official), Serbian, Bosnian, Albanian
**Internet Code:** .me

**Name:** Morocco
**Map Reference:** Africa
**Capital:** Rabat
**Population:** 3,23,09,239
**Area (in sq. km):** 4,46,550
**Currency:** Moroccan dirham
**Languages Spoken:** Arabic (official), Berber dialects, French (often the language of business, government and diplomacy)
**Internet Code:** .ma

**Name:** Mozambique
**Map Reference:** Africa
**Capital:** Maputo
**Population:** 2,35,15,934
**Area (in sq. km):** 7,99,380
**Currency:** Mozambican metical
**Languages Spoken:** Portuguese (official), Emakhuwa, Xichangana, Elomwe, Cisena, Echuwabo, other Mozambican languages
**Internet Code:** .mz

**Name:** Myanmar
**Map Reference:** Asia
**Capital:** Rangoon (Yangon): Naypyidaw is the administrative capital
**Population:** 5,45,84,650
**Area (in sq. km):** 6,76,578
**Currency:** Kyat
**Languages Spoken:** Burmese (official), Shan, Kayah
**Internet Code:** .mm

**Name:** Namibia
**Map Reference:** Africa
**Capital:** Windhoek
**Population:** 21,65,828
**Area (in sq. km):** 8,24,292
**Currency:** Namibian dollar
**Languages Spoken:** English (official), Afrikaans, German, indigenous languages
**Internet Code:** .na

**Name:** Nauru
**Map Reference:** Oceania
**Capital:** No official capital
**Population:** 9,378
**Area (in sq. km):** 21
**Currency:** Australian dollar
**Languages Spoken:** Nauruan (official), English
**Internet Code:** .nr

**Name:** Nepal
**Map Reference:** Asia
**Capital:** Kathmandu
**Population:** 2,98,90,686
**Area (in sq. km):** 1,47,181
**Currency:** Nepalese rupees
**Languages Spoken:** Nepali, Maithali, Bhojpuri, Tharu (Dagaura/Rana), Tamang, Newar, Magar, Awadhi
**Internet Code:** .np

**Name:** The Netherlands
**Map Reference:** Europe
**Capital:** Amsterdam
**Population:** 1,67,30,632

**Area (in sq. km):** 41,543
**Currency:** Euro
**Languages Spoken:** Dutch (official), Frisian (official)
**Internet Code:** .nl

**Name:** New Zealand
**Map Reference:** Oceania
**Capital:** Wellington
**Population:** 43,27,944
**Area (in sq. km):** 2,67,710
**Currency:** New Zealand dollar
**Languages Spoken:** English (official), Maori (official), Sign language (official)
**Internet Code:** .nz

**Name:** Nicaragua
**Map Reference:** Central America and the Caribbean
**Capital:** Managua
**Population:** 57,27,707
**Area (in sq. km):** 1,30,370
**Currency:** cordobas
**Languages Spoken:** Spanish (official), Miskito
**Internet Code:** .ni

**Name:** Niger
**Map Reference:** Africa
**Capital:** Niamey
**Population:** 1,70,78,839
**Area (in sq. km):** 1.267
**Currency:** CFA (Communauté Financière Africaine) franc
**Languages Spoken:** French (official), Hausa, Djerma
**Internet Code:** .ne

**Name:** Nigeria
**Map Reference:** Africa
**Capital:** Abuja
**Population:** 17,01,23,740
**Area (in sq. km):** 9,23,768
**Currency:** Nairas
**Languages Spoken:** English (official), Hausa, Yoruba, Igbo (Ibo), Fulani
**Internet Code:** .ng

**Name:** North Korea
**Map Reference:** Asia
**Capital:** Pyongyang
**Population:** 2,45,89,122
**Area (in sq. km):** 1,20,538
**Currency:** North Korean won
**Languages Spoken:** Korean
**Internet Code:** .kp

**Name:** Norway
**Map Reference:** Europe
**Capital:** Oslo
**Population:** 47,07,270
**Area (in sq. km):** 3,23,802
**Currency:** Norwegian krone
**Languages Spoken:** Bokmal Norwegian (official), Nynorsk Norwegian (official)
**Internet Code:** .no

**Name:** Oman
**Map Reference:** Middle-East
**Capital:** Muscat
**Population:** 30,90,150 (includes 5,77,293 non-nationals )
**Area (in sq. km):** 3,09,500

**Currency:** Rial

**Languages Spoken:** Arabic (official), English, Baluchi, Urdu, Indian dialects

**Internet Code:** .om

**Name:** Pakistan

**Map Reference:** Asia

**Capital:** Islamabad

**Population:** 19,02,91,129

**Area (in sq. km):** 7,96,095

**Currency:** Pakistani rupee

**Languages Spoken:** Urdu (official), English (official), Punjabi, Sindhi, Siraiki (a Punjabi variant), Pashtu, Balochi, Hindko, Brahui

**Internet Code:** .pk

**Name:** Palau

**Map Reference:** Oceania

**Capital:** Melekeok

**Population:** 21,032

**Area (in sq. km):** 459

**Currency:** US dollar

**Languages Spoken:** English (official), Palauan (official), Tobi, Angaur, Filipino, English, Chinese, Carolinian, Japanese, other Asian languages

**Internet Code:** .pw

**Name:** Panama

**Map Reference:** Central America and the Caribbean

**Capital:** Panama City

**Population:** 35,10,045

**Area (in sq. km):** 75,420

**Currency:** Balboa, US dollar

**Languages Spoken:** Spanish (official), English

**Internet Code:** .pa

**Name:** Papua New Guinea
**Map Reference:** Oceania
**Capital:** Port Moresby
**Population:** 63,10,129
**Area (in sq. km):** 4,62,840
**Currency:** Kina
**Languages Spoken:** Tok Pisin, English, and Hiri Motu are official languages; many indigenous languages spoken
**Internet Code:** .pg

**Name:** Paraguay
**Map Reference:** South America
**Capital:** Asuncion
**Population:** 65,41,591
**Area (in sq. km):** 4,06,752
**Currency:** Guarani
**Languages Spoken:** Spanish (official), Guarani (official)
**Internet Code:** .py

**Name:** Peru
**Map Reference:** South America
**Capital:** Lima
**Population:** 2,95,49,517
**Area (in sq. km):** 12,85,216
**Currency:** Nuevo Sol
**Languages Spoken:** Spanish (official), Quechua (official), Aymara, various minor Amazonian languages
**Internet Code:** .pe

**Name:** The Philippines
**Map Reference:** Asia
**Capital:** Manila
**Population:** 10,37,75,002

**Area (in sq. km):** 3,00,000

**Currency:** Peso

**Languages Spoken:** Filipino (official; based on Tagalog) and English (official); eight major dialects: Tagalog, Cebuano, Ilocano, Hiligaynon or Ilonggo, Bicol, Waray, Pampango, and Pangasinan

**Internet Code:** .ph

**Name:** Poland

**Map Reference:** Europe

**Capital:** Warsaw

**Population:** 3,84,15,284

**Area (in sq. km):** 3,12,685

**Currency:** Zloty

**Languages Spoken:** Polish (official)

**Internet Code:** .pl

**Name:** Portugal

**Map Reference:** Europe

**Capital:** Lisbon

**Population:** 1,07,81,459

**Area (in sq. km):** 92,090

**Currency:** Euro

**Languages Spoken:** Portuguese (official), Mirandese (official but locally used)

**Internet Code:** .pt

**Name:** Qatar

**Map Reference:** Middle-East

**Capital:** Doha

**Population:** 19,51,591

**Area (in sq. km):** 11,586

**Currency:** Riyal

**Languages Spoken:** Arabic (official), English

**Internet Code:** qa

**Name:** Romania
**Map Reference:** Europe
**Capital:** Bucharest
**Population:** 2,18,48,504
**Area (in sq. km):** 2,38,391
**Currency:** Lei
**Languages Spoken:** Romanian (official), Hungarian, Romany
**Internet Code:** .ro

**Name:** Russia
**Map Reference:** Asia
**Capital:** Moscow
**Population:** 13,80,82,178
**Area (in sq. km):** 1,70,98,242
**Currency:** Ruble
**Languages Spoken:** Russian (official), many minority languages
**Internet Code:** .ru; note: Russia also has responsibility for a legacy domain '.su' that was allocated to the Soviet Union and is being phased out

**Name:** Rwanda
**Map Reference:** Africa
**Capital:** Kigali
**Population:** 1,16,89,696
**Area (in sq. km):** 26,338
**Currency:** Rwandan franc
**Languages Spoken:** Kinyarwanda (official), Bantu (vernacular), French (official), English (official), Kiswahili (Swahili)
**Internet Code:** .rw

**Name:** Saint Kitts and Nevis
**Map Reference:** Central America and the Caribbean
**Capital:** Basseterre
**Population:** 50,726
**Area (in sq. km):** 261

**Currency:** East Caribbean dollar
**Languages Spoken:** English
**Internet Code:** .kn

**Name:** Saint Lucia
**Map Reference:** Central America and the Caribbean
**Capital:** Castries
**Population:** 1,62,178
**Area (in sq. km):** 616
**Currency:** East Caribbean dollar
**Languages Spoken:** English (official), French patois
**Internet Code:** .lc

**Name:** Saint Vincent and the Grenadines
**Map Reference:** Central America and the Caribbean
**Capital:** Kingstown
**Population:** 1,03,537
**Area (in sq. km):** 389
**Currency:** East Caribbean dollar
**Languages Spoken:** English, French patois
**Internet Code:** .vc

**Name:** Samoa
**Map Reference:** Oceania
**Capital:** Apia
**Population:** 1,94,320
**Area (in sq. km):** 2831
**Currency:** Tala
**Languages Spoken:** Samoan (Polynesian), English
**Internet Code:** .ws

**Name:** San Marino
**Map Reference:** Europe

**Capital:** San Marino
**Population:** 32,140
**Area (in sq. km):** 61
**Currency:** Euro
**Languages Spoken:** Italian (official), German, French, Slovene
**Internet Code:** .sm

**Name:** Sao Tome and Principe
**Map Reference:** Africa
**Capital:** Sao Tome
**Population:** 1,83,176
**Area (in sq. km):** 964
**Currency:** Dobra
**Languages Spoken:** Portuguese (official)
**Internet Code:** .st

**Name:** Saudi Arabia
**Map Reference:** Middle-East
**Capital:** Riyadh
**Population:** 2,65,34,504 (includes 55,76,076 non-nationals)
**Area (in sq. km):** 21,49,690
**Currency:** Saudi riyal
**Languages Spoken:** Arabic (official)
**Internet Code:** .sa

**Name:** Senegal
**Map Reference:** Africa
**Capital:** Dakar
**Population:** 1,29,69,606
**Area (in sq. km):** 1,96,722
**Currency:** CFA (Communaute Financiere Africaine) franc
**Languages Spoken:** French (official), Wolof, Pulaar, Jola, Mandinka
**Internet Code:** .sn

**Name:** Serbia
**Map Reference:** Europe
**Capital:** Belgrade
**Population:** 72,76,604
**Area (in sq. km):** 77,474
**Currency:** Serbian dinar
**Languages Spoken:** Serbian (official), Hungarian, Bosniak, Romany (Gypsy)
**Internet Code:** .rs

**Name:** Seychelles
**Map Reference:** Africa
**Capital:** Victoria
**Population:** 90,024
**Area (in sq. km):** 455
**Currency:** Seychelles rupee
**Languages Spoken:** English (official), Creole, others
**Internet Code:** .sc

**Name:** Sierra Leone
**Map Reference:** Africa
**Capital:** Freetown
**Population:** 54,85,998
**Area (in sq. km):** 71,740
**Currency:** Leone
**Languages Spoken:** English (official), Mende (principal vernacular in the south), Temne (principal vernacular in the north), Krio (English-based Creole)
**Internet Code:** .sl

**Name:** Singapore
**Map Reference:** Asia
**Capital:** Singapore
**Population:** 53,53,494

**Area (in sq. km):** 697
**Currency:** Singapore dollar
**Languages Spoken:** English (official), Malay (official), Chinese (official), Tamil (official)
**Internet Code:** .sg


**Name:** Slovakia
**Map Reference:** Europe
**Capital:** Bratislava
**Population:** 54,83,088
**Area (in sq. km):** 49,035
**Currency:** Euro
**Languages Spoken:** Slovak (official), Hungarian, Roma, Ukrainian.
**Internet Code:** .sk


**Name:** Slovenia
**Map Reference:** Europe
**Capital:** Ljubljana
**Population:** 19,96,617
**Area (in sq. km):** 20,273
**Currency:** Euro
**Languages Spoken:** Slovene (official), Serbo-Croatian
**Internet Code:** .si


**Name:** Solomon Islands
**Map Reference:** Oceania
**Capital:** Honiara
**Population:** 5,84,578
**Area (in sq. km):** 28,896
**Currency:** Solomon Island dollar
**Languages Spoken:** Melanesian pidgin is lingua franca; English (official but spoken by only 1%–2% of the population); 120 indigenous languages
**Internet Code:** .sb

**Name:** Somalia
**Map Reference:** Africa
**Capital:** Mogadishu
**Population:** 1,00,85,638
**Area (in sq. km):** 6,37,657
**Currency:** Somali shilling
**Languages Spoken:** Somali (official), Arabic, Italian, English
**Highest Point:** Shimbiris 2,416 m
**Lowest Point:** Indian Ocean 0 m
**Internet Code:** .so

**Name:** South Africa
**Map Reference:** Africa
**Capital:** Pretoria, Cape Town, Bloomfontain
**Population:** 4,88,10,427
**Area (in sq. km):** 12,19,090
**Currency:** South African Rand
**Languages Spoken:** Basque, English, Afrikaans, Swazi, Tsonga, Tswana, Venda, Xhosa, Zulu, Northern Ndebele, Southern Ndebele (all official)
**Internet Code:** .za

**Name:** South Sudan
**Map Reference:** Africa
**Capital:** Juba
**Population:** 1,06,25,176
**Area (in sq. km):** 6,44,329
**Currency:** South Sudanese pound
**Languages Spoken:** English (official), Arabic (official), Dinka, Nuer, Bari, Zande, Shilluk
**Internet Code:** .ss

**Name:** South Korea
**Map Reference:** Asia
**Capital:** Seoul

**Population:** 4,88,60,500
**Area (in sq. km):** 99,720
**Currency:** South Korean won
**Languages Spoken:** Korean (official), English
**Internet Code:** .kr


**Name:** Spain
**Map Reference:** Europe
**Capital:** Madrid
**Population:** 4,70,42,984
**Area (in sq. km):** 5,05,370
**Currency:** Euro
**Languages Spoken:** Catalan, Galician, Basque, Occitan (all official)
**Internet Code:** .es


**Name:** Sri Lanka
**Map Reference:** Asia
**Capital:** Colombo
**Population:** 2,14,81,334
**Area (in sq. km):** 65,610
**Currency:** Sri Lankan rupee
**Languages Spoken:** Sinhala (official and national language), Tamil (national language)
**Internet Code:** .lk


**Name:** Sudan
**Map Reference:** Africa
**Capital:** Khartoum
**Population:** 3,42,06,710
**Area (in sq. km):** 18,61,484
**Currency:** Sudanese pound
**Languages Spoken:** Arabic (official), English (official), Nubian, Ta Bedawie, Fur
**Internet Code:** .sd

**Name:** Suriname
**Map Reference:** South America
**Capital:** Paramaribo
**Population:** 5,60,157
**Area (in sq. km):** 1,63,820
**Currency:** Surinamese dollar
**Languages Spoken:** Dutch (official), English, Sranang Tongo, Caribbean Hindustani, Javanese
**Internet Code:** .sr

**Name:** Swaziland
**Map Reference:** Africa
**Capital:** Mbabane
**Population:** 13,86,914
**Area (in sq. km):** 17,364
**Currency:** Emalangeni
**Languages Spoken:** English (official, government business conducted in English), SiSwati, also called Swazi (official)
**Internet Code:** .sz

**Name:** Sweden
**Map Reference:** Europe
**Capital:** Stockholm
**Population:** 91,03,788
**Area (in sq. km):** 4,50,295
**Currency:** Swedish kroner
**Languages Spoken:** Swedish
**Internet Code:** .se

**Name:** Switzerland
**Map Reference:** Europe
**Capital:** Bern
**Population:** 76,55,628
**Area (in sq. km):** 41,277

**Currency:** Swiss franc

**Languages Spoken:** German (official), French (official), Italian (official), Romansch (official), Serbo-Croatian, Albanian, Portuguese, Spanish, English

**Internet Code:** .ch


**Name:** Syria

**Map Reference:** Middle East

**Capital:** Damascus

**Population:** 2,25,30,746

**Area (in sq. km):** 1,85,180

**Currency:** Syrian pound

**Languages Spoken:** Arabic (official), Kurdish, Armenian, Aramaic, Circassian (widely understood), French

**Internet Code:** .sy


**Name:** Taiwan

**Map Reference:** Asia

**Capital:** Taipei

**Population:** 2,31,13,901

**Area (in sq. km):** 35,980

**Currency:** New Taiwan dollar

**Languages Spoken:** Mandarin Chinese (official), Taiwanese (Min), Hakka dialects

**Internet Code:** .tw


**Name:** Tajikistan

**Map Reference:** Asia

**Capital:** Dushanbe

**Population:** 77,68,385

**Area (in sq. km):** 1,43,100

**Currency:** Tajikistani somoni

**Languages Spoken:** Tajik (official), Russian widely used in government and business

**Internet Code:** .tj

**Name:** Tanzania
**Map Reference:** Africa
**Capital:** Dar es Salaam
**Population:** 43601796
**Area (in sq. km):** 947300
**Currency:** Tanzanian shilling
**Languages Spoken:** Kiswahili or Swahili (official), English (official), Arabic
**Internet Code:** .tz

**Name:** Thailand
**Map Reference:** Asia
**Capital:** Bangkok
**Population:** 6,70,91,089
**Area (in sq. km):** 5,13,120
**Currency:** Baht
**Languages Spoken:** Thai (official), English (secondary language of the elite)
**Internet Code:** .th

**Name:** The Bahamas
**Map Reference:** Central America and the Caribbean
**Capital:** Nassau
**Population:** : 3,16,182
**Area (in sq. km):** 13,880
**Currency:** Bahamian dollar
**Languages Spoken:** English (official), Creole (among Haitian immigrants)
**Internet Code:** .bs

**Name:** Togo
**Map Reference:** Africa
**Capital:** Lome
**Population:** 69,61,049
**Area (in sq. km):** 56,785

**Currency:** CFA (Communauté Financière Africaine) franc

**Languages Spoken:** French (official and the language of commerce), Ewe and Mina, Kabye, Dagomba

**Internet Code:** .tg

**Name:** Tonga

**Map Reference:** Ocenia

**Capital:** Nuku'alofa

**Population:** 1,06,146

**Area (in sq. km):** 747

**Currency:** Pa'anga

**Languages Spoken:** Tongan (official), English (official)

**Internet Code:** .to

**Name:** Trinidad and Tobago

**Map Reference:** Central America and the Caribbean

**Capital:** Port of Spain

**Population:** 12,26,383

**Area (in sq. km):** 5,128

**Currency:** Trinidad and Tobago dollar

**Languages Spoken:** English (official), Caribbean Hindustani (a dialect of Hindi), French, Spanish, Chinese

**Internet Code:** .tt

**Name:** Tunisia

**Map Reference:** Africa

**Capital:** Tunis

**Population:** 1,07,32,900

**Area (in sq. km):** 1,63,610

**Currency:** Tunisian dinar

**Languages Spoken:** Arabic (official and one of the languages of commerce), French (commerce)

**Internet Code:** .tn

**Name:** Turkey
**Map Reference:** Middle-East
**Capital:** Ankara
**Population:** 7,97,49,461
**Area (in sq. km):** 7,83,562
**Currency:** Turkish lira
**Languages Spoken:** Turkish (official), Kurdish, other minority languages
**Internet Code:** .tr

**Name:** Turkmenistan
**Map Reference:** Asia
**Capital:** Ashgabat
**Population:** 50,54,828
**Area (in sq. km):** 4,88,100
**Currency:** Turkmen manat
**Languages Spoken:** Turkmen (official), Russian, Uzbek
**Internet Code:** .tm

**Name:** Tuvalu
**Map Reference:** Oceania
**Capital:** Funafuti
**Population:** 10,619
**Area (in sq. km):** 26
**Currency:** Tuvaluan dollar
**Languages Spoken:** Tuvaluan, English, Samoan, Kiribati (on the island of Nui)
**Internet Code:** .tv

**Name:** Uganda
**Map Reference:** Africa
**Capital:** Kampala
**Population:** 3,58,73,253
**Area (in sq. km):** 2,41,038

**Currency:** Ugandan shilling

**Languages Spoken:** English (official national language), Ganda or Luganda (most widely used of the Niger-Congo languages), other Niger-Congo languages, Nilo-Saharan languages, Swahili, Arabic

**Internet Code:** .ug


**Name:** Ukraine

**Map Reference:** Asia, Europe

**Capital:** Kyiv

**Population:** 4,48,54,065

**Area (in sq. km):** 6,03,550

**Currency:** Hryvnia

**Languages Spoken:** Ukrainian (official), Russian

**Internet Code:** .ua


**Name:** United Arab Emirates

**Map Reference:** Middle-East

**Capital:** Abu Dhabi

**Population:** 53,14,317

**Area (in sq. km):** 83,600

**Currency:** Emirati dirham

**Languages Spoken:** Arabic (official), Persian, English, Hindi, Urdu

**Internet Code:** .ae


**Name:** United Kingdom

**Map Reference:** Europe

**Capital:** London

**Population:** 6,30,47,162

**Area (in sq. km):** 2,43,610

**Currency:** British pound

**Languages Spoken:** English, Welsh, Scottish form of Gaelic, Irish, Cornish

**Internet Code:** .uk

**Name:** United States of America
**Map Reference:** North America
**Capital:** Washington, D.C.
**Population:** 31,38,47,465
**Area (in sq. km):** 98,26,675
**Currency:** US dollar
**Languages Spoken:** English (National)
**Internet Code:** .us

**Name:** Uruguay
**Map Reference:** South America
**Capital:** Montevideo
**Population:** 33,16,328
**Area (in sq. km):** 1,76,215
**Currency:** Uruguayan peso
**Languages Spoken:** Spanish, Portunol, Brazilero (Portuguese–Spanish mix)
**Internet Code:** .uy

**Name:** Uzbekistan
**Map Reference:** Asia
**Capital:** Tashkent
**Population:** 2,83,94,180
**Area (in sq. km):** 4,47,400
**Currency:** Uzbekistani soum
**Languages Spoken:** Uzbek, Russian, Tajik
**Internet Code:** .uz

**Name:** Vanuatu
**Map Reference:** Oceania
**Capital:** Port-Vila
**Population:** 2,27,574
**Area (in sq. km):** 12,189

**Currency:** Vatu

**Languages Spoken:** Local languages (more than 100), Pidgin (known as Bislama or Bichelama), English, French

**Internet Code:** .vu

**Name:** Vatican City

**Map Reference:** Europe

**Capital:** Vatican City

**Population:** 836

**Area (in sq. km):** 0.44

**Currency:** Euro

**Languages Spoken:** Italian, Latin, French and other languages

**Internet Code:** .va

**Name:** Venezuela

**Map Reference:** South America

**Capital:** Caracas

**Population:** 2,80,47,938

**Area (in sq. km):** 9,12,050

**Currency:** Bolivar

**Languages Spoken:** Spanish (official), numerous indigenous dialects

**Internet Code:** .ve

**Name:** Vietnam

**Map Reference:** Asia

**Capital:** Hanoi

**Population:** 9,15,19,289

**Area (in sq. km):** 3,31,210

**Currency:** Dong

**Languages Spoken:** Vietnamese (official), English (increasingly favoured as a second language), some French, Chinese, and Khmer; mountain area languages (Mon-Khmer and Malayo-Polynesian)

**Internet Code:** .vn

**Name:** Yemen
**Map Reference:** Middle East
**Capital:** Sanaa
**Population:** 2,47,71,809
**Area (in sq. km):** 5,27,968
**Currency:** Yemeni rial
**Languages Spoken:** Arabic
**Internet Code:** .ye

**Name:** Zambia
**Map Reference:** Africa
**Capital:** Lusaka
**Population:** 1,43,09,466
**Area (in sq. km):** 7,52,618
**Currency:** Zambian kwacha
**Languages Spoken:** Bemba (official), Nyanja (official), Tonga (official),Lozi (official), Chewa, Nsenga, Tumbuka, Lunda (official), Kaonde (official), Lala, Luvale (official), English (official)
**Internet Code:** .zm

**Name:** Zimbabwe
**Map Reference:** Africa
**Capital:** Harare
**Population:** 1,26,19,600
**Area (in sq. km):** 3,90,757
**Currency:** Zimbabwean dollar
**Languages Spoken:** English (official), Shona, Sindebele (the language of the Ndebele, sometimes called Ndebele)
**Internet Code:** .zw

## MAJOR MOUNTAIN RANGES AND PEAKS

### ARAVALLI RANGE

The Aravalli Range runs north-easterly through Rajasthan. It is divided into two sections: the Sambar–Sirohi range and the Sambhar-Khetri range. The former contains Guru Shikhar at Mount Abu, the highest peak of the Aravallis. The rich natural and mineral resources of the range check the spread of the Thar desert in eastern Rajasthan. Several rivers, like the Banas, Luni, Sakhi and Sabarmati, flow amidst the hills.

### EASTERN GHATS

The Eastern Ghats are a series of rugged, hilly, discontinuous ranges running almost parallel to the eastern coast of India. They spread across the four states of Odisha, Andhra Pradesh, Tamil Nadu and Karnataka. Some of the major rivers of India flow through the Eastern Ghats: Mahanadi, Godavari, Krishna and Kaveri. The highest point is Mahendragiri in Tamil Nadu. Among the mountain ranges in the Eastern Ghats are the Nallamala Range, Palkonda Hills, Javadi Hills, and Shevaroy Hills.

### GARO, KHASI AND JAINTIA HILLS

Located in Meghalaya, the Garo, Khasi and Jaintia Hills are named for the major tribes inhabiting the three ranges. The Garo Hills form the western part, the Khasi the central part, and the Jaintia the eastern part. The Garo Hills, running deep into the Bramhaputra Valley in the north and the plains of Bangladesh in the south, are comparatively lower than the other two. The Khasi and Jaintia Hills are plateaus with rolling grasslands, hills and river valleys.

## KANCHENJUNGA

Located in the Himalayan range in Sikkim, it is the world's third highest mountain peak. In Tibetan, 'Kanchenjunga' means 'five treasuries of the great snow'. The mountain holds an important place in local mythological tales and religious rituals of local inhabitants.

## KARAKORAM

Extending from Afghanistan to Kashmir, this is one of the largest mountain systems in the world. K2 is the highest peak of this range. It is also the second highest (8,611 m) in the world. Karakoram is heavily glaciated, with two of the world's longest glaciers, Siachen and Biafo, located there.

## NANDA DEVI

Nanda Devi is a part of the Shivalik range in the Himalayas. It lies in Uttarakhand. At 7,434 m, it is one of the highest peaks in the world.

## NANGA PARBAT

Situated in the western Himalayas, at 8,126 m, this is also one of the world's highest peaks, and is rather difficult to climb. Attempts have been made to scale it since 1895. It was not until 1953 that the Austrian Hermann Buhl successfully climbed the peak.

## PIR PANJAL

This mountain range is part of the western Himalayas, lying in north-western India and northern Pakistan. It extends from the Kishanganga river to the upper Beas river.

## SATPURA RANGE

Part of the Deccan plateau in western India, this mountain range stretches for 900 km across the widest part of peninsular India, through Maharashtra and Madhya Pradesh. The literary meaning of its name is 'seven folds'. This largely forested range forms the watershed between the Narmada and Tapti rivers.

## VINDHYA RANGE

This is a broken range of hills, extending for about 1,086 km across Gujarat, Madhya Pradesh and Uttar Pradesh. It forms the southern edge of the Malwa Plateau. This mountain range gives rise to the main southern tributaries of the Ganga–Yamuna system, including the Chambal, Betwa, Ken and Tons.

## WESTERN GHATS

The Western Ghats, or Sahyadri, run for 1,600 km along the western border of peninsular India, from Tapti river down to Kanyakumari. Anai Mudi is the highest peak, and the source of three ranges: Anaimalai Hills to the north, Palni Hills to the north-east, and Cardamom Hills to the south. The second highest peak, Doda Betta, is located in the Nilgiris. Among the popular hill stations in the Western Ghats are Mahabaleshwar, Kodaikanal and Ooty (Udhagamandalam). The Nilgiris are famous for tea and coffee plantations. The Cardamom Hills derive their name from the cardamom widely grown there.

## ZANSKAR (OR ZASKAR) RANGE

This range is located in Jammu and Kashmir, and separates Ladakh from the rest of the state. It extends for 640 km from Karcha river to the upper Karnali river. Kamet Peak is the highest point. The important passes are Shipki, Lipu Lekh (Lipulieke), and Mana.

# MAJOR PASSES

### BANIHAL PASS

It is located in the Pir Panjal range in Jammu and Kashmir. At an altitude of 2,832 m in Doda district, it forms the main gateway to the Kashmir valley from the Indian plains. The important Jammu–Srinagar road enters the pass through the Jawahar Tunnel.

### KHARDUNG LA

At 5,359 m, Khardung La has the world's highest motorable road. It is around 39 km from Leh. It is historically important as it was located on the major caravan route from Leh to Kashgar in Chinese Central Asia.

### NATHU LA

Nathu La, meaning 'the whistling pass', is of strategic importance on the Indo–China border connecting the state of Sikkim with Tibet. It is a frequently used trading route between India and China, and was reopened for trade in 2006.

### ROHTANG PASS

Rohtang Pass is located on the eastern part of the Pir Panjal range in the Himalayas. Around 50 km from Manali, it connects Kullu valley with the Lahaul and Spiti valleys of Himachal Pradesh. An attractive sight, it is visited by several tourists every year.

## ZOJI LA

This is located across the Himalayas in Jammu and Kashmir. Situated at an elevation of 3,529 m, this corridor carries the only road leading from the Kashmir valley eastwards to Leh. Running across the Srinagar–Leh National Highway, it is mostly closed during the winter.

# DAMS

### BHAKRA NANGAL

The Bhakra Nangal project is located on the Sutlej river in Himachal Pradesh. Consisting of the Bhakra and Nangal dams, it is associated with four states (Punjab, Haryana, Himachal Pradesh, Rajasthan). Situated about 10 km from Nangal, it is one of the highest gravity concrete dams in the world. It forms the beautiful Gobind Sagar Lake, named after the Sikh Guru, Gobind Singh.

### DAMODAR VALLEY DAMS

The Damodar Valley Corporation (DVC) was incorporated on 7 July 1948. This project is the joint venture of Bihar and West Bengal. Earlier, floods in the Damodar river used to devastate lives and property. To control this, the DVC built a series of dams across the Damodar river—at Maithon, Panchet, Tilaiya and Konar—as well as the Durgapur Barrage. DVC supplies hydel power to major industries and water for irrigation, to both Bihar and West Bengal.

### HIRAKUD

The Hirakud dam, constructed across the Mahanadi in Odisha, is one of the longest dams in India. This was the first major multipurpose river valley project in independent India. It is a composite, concrete masonry, earthen structure, 4.8 km long, spreading between the hills Lamdungri on the left and Chandili Dunguri on the right. Its reservoir also forms the biggest artificial lake in Asia.

### NAGARJUNA SAGAR

The Nagarjuna Sagar is a major irrigation dam on the Krishna river. It is located at a distance of 150 km from Hyderabad. Today, it is the world's tallest masonry dam.

### TUNGABHADRA

Tungabhadra dam is situated across the Tungabhadra river, a tributary of the Krishna. It is beneficial in generating electricity, irrigating land, and controlling floods.

# RIVERS

## BRAHMAPUTRA

The Brahmaputra is one of the major rivers of South Asia. It flows about 2,900 km from southern Tibet into the Bay of Bengal. Along its course, it passes through the states of Arunachal Pradesh and Assam, and then into Bangladesh. For most of its length, the river serves as an important inland waterway. The Tista and Meghna are some of its tributaries. Brahmaputra is known as Yarlung Zangbo Jiang in Chinese, Tsangpo in Tibetan.

## GANGA

The Ganga, or Ganges, is regarded by Hindus as the most sacred river of India. It originates in the Gangotri glacier in the Himalayas as the Bhagirathi and is later joined by other rivers such as the Alaknanda, Yamuna, Son, Gomti, Kosi and Ghagra. The Gangetic plain is one of the most fertile and densely-populated areas of the world. Key religious ceremonies are held on the banks of the river. The Ganga widens out into a delta in the Sunderbans swamp of Bangladesh, before it ends its journey by emptying into the Bay of Bengal. It is India's national river.

## GODAVARI

The Godavari is a sacred river of central India. Rising in the Western Ghats and flowing eastwards across the Deccan plateau, along the Maharashtra–Andhra Pradesh border, it reaches the Bay of Bengal, where it empties via its two mouths: the Gautami Godavari and the Vasishta Godavari. Its total length is about 1,465 km and it has a drainage basin of 3,13,000 sq. km. Major tributaries are Darna, Purna, Manjra, Pranhita and Indravati.

## INDUS

The Indus is one of the longest rivers in the world, having a length of 2,900 km. It has a total drainage area of about 11,65,500 sq. km, of which 4,53,247.91 sq. km lie in the Himalayas and the rest in the semi-arid plains of Pakistan. The river rises in south-west Tibet at an altitude of about 5,500 m. The most notable tributaries are from the eastern Punjab plain. These five rivers—Jhelum, Chenab, Ravi, Beas, Sutlej—give the state Punjab its name. The word Punjab is a compound of two Persian words, *panj* ('five') and *ab* ('water').

## KAVERI

The Kaveri is one of the sacred rivers of southern India. It rises from Brahmagiri hill of the Western Ghats in Karnataka, flows through Karnataka and Tamil Nadu, and drains into the Bay of Bengal near Cuddalore, Tamil Nadu. Kabbani, Amaravati, Noyil and Bhavani rivers are its main tributaries.

## KRISHNA

The Krishna is one of the most important rivers of southern India, rising in Maharashtra in the Western Ghats range near Mahabaleshwar. It flows through Karnataka and into Andhra Pradesh. It flows to its delta head at Vijayawada, and from there into the Bay of Bengal after a course of about 1,290 km. The Bhima and the Tungabhadra are two of its largest tributaries.

## MAHANADI

This is one of the important rivers of central India, rising in the hills of south-east Madhya Pradesh. The Mahanadi ('Great River') follows a course of 900 km and has an estimated drainage area of 1,32,100 sq. km. Its tributaries include Seonath, Jonk, Hasdeo, and Mand. It drains into the Bay of Bengal at False Point.

## NARMADA

An important river of central India, the Narmada rises in the Maikala Range in Madhya Pradesh and flows across Madhya Pradesh and Gujarat, before entering the Gulf of Khambhat through an estuary, just below Bharuch. Draining the northern slopes of the Satpura range along its 1,300-km course, it flows through the gorges at Mandhata and Murakta. The river has numerous waterfalls and tributaries.

## YAMUNA

The Yamuna is a major river of northern India, flowing through Uttarakhand and Uttar Pradesh. It rises on the slopes of the Banderpunch massif in the Great Himalayas near Yamnotri, and passes through the Himalayan foothills on to the Indo-Gangetic Plain. It has a number of southern tributaries, the largest of which are Chambal, Sindh, Betwa and Ken. Near Allahabad, after a course of 1,376 km, the Yamuna joins the Ganga; their confluence is a very sacred place for Hindus.

# NATIONAL SYMBOLS

## NATIONAL ANIMAL

The tiger or *Panthera tigris*, a powerful big cat, is the national animal of India. This agile and graceful animal, with a thick amber coat of fur with black stripes, replaced the Asiatic Lion as the national animal in 1972.

## NATIONAL ANTHEM

The national anthem, *Jana Gana Mana*, was written by 'Viswa Kavi' Rabindranath Tagore. Originally composed in Bengali, its Hindi version was adopted by the Constituent Assembly as the national anthem of India on 24 January 1950. It was first sung on 27 December 1911 at the Calcutta Session of the Indian National Congress. At Madanapalle campus in present-day Andhra Pradesh, Rabindranath Tagore translated the anthem into English and called it 'the morning song of India'.

## NATIONAL AQUATIC ANIMAL

The Gangetic river dolphin is India's national aquatic animal. As it can survive only in pure and fresh water, it represents the purity of the Ganga. Locally nown as *susu* (and in some places, *susuk*), because of the noise it makes while breathing, it lives in parts of the Ganga, Meghna and Brahmaputra in India, Nepal, Bhutan and Bangladesh, and the Karnaphuli river in Bangladesh.

## NATIONAL BIRD

The peacock is the national bird of India. It is a large, colourful bird known for its tail with 'eye' markings in blue, gold, red and other hues that appear to change when viewed from different angles. These tail feathers, which spread out in a prominent train, form more than 60 per cent of the bird's total body length. The peacock enjoys an important place in Indian mythology and tradition.

## NATIONAL CALENDAR

The national calendar, with Chaitra as its first month, is based on the Saka era which is believed to have been started by King Kanishka. It was adopted officially from 22 March 1957 (along with the Gregorian calendar) for official purposes. In the national calendar, 1 Chaitra corresponds with 22 March normally, and 21 March in a leap year.

## NATIONAL EMBLEM

The state emblem of India is an adaptation from the Lion Capital of Ashoka in Sarnath. It has four lions, three visible and one hidden. The wheel appears in relief in the centre of the abacus with a bull on the right and a horse on the left. The words *Satyameva Jayate* from the Mundaka Upanishad, meaning 'truth alone triumphs', are inscribed below in Devanagari script.

## NATIONAL FLAG

The national flag, also referred to as the tricolour, has deep saffron on top, white in the middle, and dark green at the bottom, in equal proportions, with a navy blue wheel or *chakra* in the centre of the white portion. Saffron stands for courage, sacrifice and the spirit of renunciation; white signifies purity and truth; and green represents faith and fertility. The *chakra* with twenty-four spokes depicts the wheel of life in movement and death in stagnation. It is taken from the Dharma Chakra, or 'wheel of law', of the Lion Capital. The design was adopted by the Constituent Assembly on 22 July 1947.

## NATIONAL FLOWER

Lotus is the national flower, depicted in various aspects in religion and culture in India. Various Indian rites and customs are incomplete without the lotus.

## NATIONAL FRUIT

Mango is the national fruit. There are over 100 varieties of mangoes grown in India, which vary in size, shape and colour. Praise for the mango has been sung in ancient times by the poet Kalidas as well as the Chinese pilgrim Hiuen Tsang. Mughal emperor Akbar planted 1,00,000 mango trees in Darbhanga, Bihar, at a place now known as Lakhi Bagh.

## NATIONAL GAME

Hockey is India's national game. India has an excellent record in the sport in the Olympics, with eight gold medals. The winning streak started in Amsterdam in 1928. India achieved two hat-tricks of gold medals, in 1928 (Amsterdam), 1932 (Los Angeles), 1936 (Berlin), and again in 1948 (London), 1952 (Helsinki), 1956 (Melbourne). The eighth gold came in 1980 at Moscow.

## NATIONAL HERITAGE ANIMAL

In 2010, the Indian government, with the aim of improving measures for its protection, declared the elephant as the national heritage animal. The elephant occupies a unique status in our heritage and cultural tradition. Latest figures indicate that India has about 35,000 elephants in the wild. They are generally seen in Kerala, Karnataka, Tamil Nadu, West Bengal, Odisha, and the north-eastern states.

## NATIONAL RIVER

The Ganga is the national river. The Gangetic basin is one of the most fertile areas of the world covering 10,00,000 sq. km. The Ganga has major religious significance in India, with the holy cities of Varanasi, Haridwar and Allahabad situated on its banks.

## NATIONAL SONG

The national song of India is *Vande mataram*, composed in Sanskrit by Bankim Chandra Chattopadhyay. It first appeared in the novel *Anandamath*. It was a source of inspiration to Indians in their struggle for freedom. It was first sung at the 1896 Calcutta session of the Indian National Congress.

## NATIONAL TREE

The Indian fig tree, *Ficus bengalensis*, commonly known as the banyan, is the national tree. The tree is special in that its branches can root themselves like new trees over a large area and give rise to more trunks and branches. This characteristic, along with its long life, has given rise to the belief that this tree is immortal. It is a vital part of the myths and legends of India.

## NATIONAL CURRENCY

The Indian rupee sign is a blend of Indian and Roman letters—capital 'R' and Devanagri 'Ra'—with two parallel horizontal stripes running at the top, representing the national flag and also the 'equal to' sign. The Indian rupee sign was designed by D. Udaya Kumar and adopted by the Government of India on 15 July 2010.

# CLASSICAL DANCES OF INDIA

**Bharatanatyam:** Bharatanatyam is one of the classical dances of India. It originated in Tamil Nadu and is considered to be over 2,000 years old. This dance form is known to be *ekaharya*, where one dancer takes on many roles in a single performance. The accompanying orchestra consists of a vocalist (*nattuvanar*), a mridangam player, a violinist or a veena player, a flautist, and a cymbals player. Noted practitioners are Rukmini Devi Arundale, Mrinalini Sarabhai, Yamini Krishnamurthy, and T. Balasaraswati.

**Kathak:** Kathak is a classical dance form born as a result of Mughal influence on Indian culture. It originated in northern India. The name is derived from the word *katha* (story). Some of the important *gharanas* include Jaipur and Lucknow. Among the noted performers are Birju Maharaj and Lachchhu Maharaj.

**Kathakali:** Kathakali is a classical dance style of Kerala. The characters in a Kathakali performance are broadly divided into *satvika*, *rajasika* and *tamasika*, depending on the characters they portray. They put on elaborate costumes, wear masks and use colour codes. Well-known Kathakali dancers are Guru Gopinath and Kalamandalam Ramankutty Nair.

**Kuchipudi:** Kuchipudi is indigenous to Andhra Pradesh. In fact, Kuchipudi is the name of the village where the dance originated. It began in the 17th century with the creation of this dance by Sidhyendra Yogi of the dance drama *Bhama Kalapam*, a story of Satyabhama, the wife of Lord Krishna. Some famous performers are Raja and Radha Reddy.

**Manipuri:** The Manipuri dance form is indigenous to Manipur and characterized by a variety of forms linked to folk tradition and ritual. Themes are generally taken from episodes in the life of Krishna. A flowing sway of the body and a liquid movement of the arms and hands characterize the women's style; stronger and more forceful movements are used by men. The Jhaveri sisters are exponents of this art form.

**Mohiniattam:** Mohiniattam, one of the youngest classical dances of India, originated in Kerala. Its name comes from the words *mohini* ('beautiful woman') and *attam* ('dance'). The theme of the dance is generally *shringara* or love. It is essentially a solo dance and performed by women with tender and graceful body movements belonging to the *lasya* style. Hand gestures play an important part as a medium of communication. Some of the leading exponents were: Sri Swathi Thirunal Rama Varma, Sri Vallathol Narayana Menon and Smt. Kalamandalam Kalyanikutty Amma.

**Odissi:** Odissi is a dance mode prevalent in Odisha. It is a highly stylized dance and closely follows the tenets laid down in the *Natya Shastra*. Facial expressions, hand gestures and body movements are used to suggest a certain feeling, an emotion or one of the nine *rasas*. Kelucharan Mohapatra and Sanjukta Panigrahi are some of the famous performers of Odissi.

## FAIRS AND FESTIVALS OF INDIA

### CHRISTMAS

Christmas commemorates the birth of Jesus Christ on 25 December. Common tradition includes decorating a Christmas tree with fairy lights and ornaments. It is also believed that Santa Claus gives gifts on Christmas. Christmas is often abbreviated to 'Xmas', 'X' being the first letter of the Greek word *Christos*, meaning Christ.

### DIWALI

Diwali, the Hindu festival of lights, is held in October or November, and commemorates the return of Lord Rama to his kingdom, Ayodhya, after fourteen years of exile. Goddess Lakshmi, who symbolizes wealth and luck, is worshipped. The word Deepavali (of which Diwali is a shortened version) literally means rows of *diyas* or lamps. Homes are decorated with earthen lamps and candles, and people burn crackers in this festival.

## DURGA PUJA

Durga Puja is an annual festival held in honour of goddess Durga. It proclaims the victory of good over evil. The four most important days are referred to as Shaptami, Ashtami, Navami and Dashami. It usually takes place in October or November, and is celebrated with much fanfare in West Bengal.

## DUSSEHRA

In the months of October or November, Hindus observe a ten-day ceremony of fasting, rituals, celebrations and feasts to honour the Mother Goddess and the triumph of Lord Rama over Ravana. Dussehra also symbolizes the triumph of warrior goddess Durga over the buffalo demon Mahishasura. In Himachal Pradesh, a week-long fair in the hill town of Kullu is a part of the Dussehra celebrations. In south India, the Mysore palace is illuminated for a whole month during Dussehra and caparisoned elephants lead a colourful procession through gaily decorated streets.

## EID-UL-FITR

Eid-ul-Fitr (Festival of Breaking Fast) occurs as soon as the new moon is sighted after a month of fasting during Ramadan, the ninth month of the Islamic calendar. The word 'fitr' is derived from *fatar*, meaning 'to break', referring to the breaking of the fast. Devotees gather together to pray, after which they exchange greetings.

## GANESH CHATURTHI

Lord Ganesha is one of the most widely worshipped deities of Hinduism. Ganesh Chaturthi is most popular in Maharashtra but it is now also celebrated in other parts of the country. During the ten-day festival, large idols of Ganesha are worshipped.

## HOLI

Holi, the festival of colours, is celebrated in March. The story of Prahlad is seen to symbolize good overcoming evil and that is why traditionally bonfires are lit on Holi. Holi is also known as Dhuli Vandana in Sanskrit, and as Dhulheti, Dhulandi or Dhulendi in various other languages. People celebrate by throwing coloured powder and water at each other.

## JANMASHTAMI

Janmashtami is celebrated on the eighth day of the month of Sravana, to commemorate the birth anniversary of Lord Krishna, the human incarnation of Lord Vishnu. In many places, 'Raslila' is performed to recreate incidents from the life of Krishna. This festival is also known as Krishnashtami or Gokulashtami.

## KUMBH MELA

According to Hindu astrologers, the Kumbh Mela takes place when the planet Jupiter enters Aquarius and the sun enters Aries. A sacred Hindu pilgrimage, it celebrates the victory of the gods over the demons for the *kumbh* (pot) of *amrit* (nectar of immortality). The normal Kumbh Mela takes place every three years alternatively at Prayag (Allahabad), Haridwar, Ujjain and Nasik, places where the *kumbh* was kept during the clashes between the gods and demons. The Ardh Kumbh is held every six years, the Purna Kumbh every twelve years, and the Maha Kumbh after every twelve Purna Kumbhs, or after 144 years.

## PUSHKAR FAIR

The Pushkar Fair in Rajasthan is one of the largest fairs in India. In this week-long fair, a staggering number of camels, horses, cows and sheep are traded. For the first five days, the animals are sold and purchased. On the last day, pilgrims converge for a holy dip in the lake and to pay obeisance at the Brahma temple.

## RATH YATRA

Ratha Yatra, the Festival of Chariots of Lord Jagannatha, is celebrated every year at Puri in Odisha. The presiding deities of the main temple—Lord Jagannatha, Lord Balabhadra, and Goddess Subhadra—are taken out from the temple precincts in an elaborate ritual procession in their respective chariots. The huge, brightly decorated chariots are drawn by hundreds and thousands of devotees to the Gundicha temple. After a stay for seven days, the deities return to their abode in Srimandira.

## SHIV RATRI

Shiv Ratri is a Hindu festival celebrated all over the country to honour Lord Shiva. Devotees observe a strict fast on this day. On this day, the *shivalingam* is worshipped with *bael* leaves and flowers, and bathed with honey, milk, yoghurt, and sandalwood.

## SONEPUR CATTLE FAIR

One of Asia's largest cattle fairs, it is held at Sonepur in Bihar on the banks of the Ganga on the full moon day of the Hindu month of Kartik. Sonepur is situated at the confluence of the Ganga and the Gandak. A bath at the confluence and a visit to the Hariharnath Temple is the aim for thousands of devotees on this auspicious day. Sonepur Fair is the only one of its kind where a large number of elephants are sold. Apart from elephants, a large number of cattle and horses are also brought to the fair for sale.

## SURAJKUND CRAFTS FAIR

The tourism department of Haryana has been organizing the handloom and handicrafts fair, Surajkund Crafts Fair, every February since 1987. The fair is popular with artists and craftsmen displaying and selling their work, including paintings, textiles, woodcraft, ivory work, pottery, terracotta, stonework, lac work and cane and grass work.

## TARNETAR MELA

A unique three-day fair is held at Tarnetar in Gujarat every year, to celebrate the wedding of Arjuna with Draupadi in the Mahabharata. It is held in the first week of the Hindu calendar month of Bhadra. There is a *kund* (reservoir) there called Papanshu, where taking a dip is considered as holy as taking a dip in the Ganga. The fair coincides with the festival at the Trineteshwar temple. Tribes from adjoining areas also come to the fair.

# ART AND CULTURE

### APPLIQUE EMBROIDERY

Applique, a French term, describes a technique by which the decorative effect is brought about by putting patches of coloured fabrics on a basic fabric and stitching the edges. Though the form is also practised in other parts of India, it is in Odisha, especially Pipli, that the craft has a living and active tradition.

### BIDRIWORK

Bidri is identified as a decorative metal object, ornamented with a type of inlay work made of tin, copper, lead and zinc. It is named after the Bidar district of Karnataka.This traditional craft was introduced by the Persians, Syrians and Iranians 4,000 years ago, and its craftsmen were patronized in the Mughal courts.

### CHIKANKARI EMBROIDERY

Lucknow is famous for its unique craft involving delicate and artistic hand embroidery called chikankari. It is done on a variety of textile fabrics like muslin, silk, chiffon, organza, and organdy. There are thirty-six types of stitches used in chikankari, of which *murri*, *bakhia*, *jali*, *tepchi*, *tappa*, *dhum*, and *katao* are widely used. Some of the famous artisans of chikankari were Ustad Faiyaaz Khan and Hasan Mirza Saheb.

## KALAMEZHUTHU

Kalamezhuthu is a unique form of art native to Kerala. It is the tradition of drawing representations of deities like Kali and Lord Ayyappa on the floor, at the entrances of homes and temples. It is similar to a *rangoli*.

## KANTHA EMBROIDERY

Kantha stitching is an age-old traditional craft, which has its origin in rural Bengal. The embroidery utilizes waste material. Pieces of cloth are sewn with simple running stitches, which run in several directions to form various motifs.

## KASUTI EMBROIDERY

Kasuti is a form of embroidery in Karnataka. It dates back to the Chalukya period (6th to 10th century AD) and is mainly concentrated in Dharwad, Belgaum, Hubli and Mangalore. Its uniqueness lies in its precise geometric designs. The embroidery appears the same on both sides of the cloth. Since it is done by counting threads of the warp and the weft, even a minor error can spoil the pattern.

## MADHUBANI PAINTING

Madhubani, also called Mithila art (as it flourishes in Mithila, Bihar), is a style of painting characterized by line drawings filled in with bright colours prepared from natural pigments. This style of painting has been traditionally done by the women of the region, though today, men are also involved in order to meet the demand.

## PATTACHITRA PAINTING

The pattachitra style of painting is one of the oldest and most popular art forms of Odisha. The name has evolved from the Sanskrit words *patta*, meaning 'canvas' and *chitra*, meaning 'picture'. Translated thus, it means a painting done on canvas. They are colourful, have creative motifs and designs, and portray simple themes, mostly mythological. The paintings are made using natural dyes and pigments, such as lamp soot and powdered conch shells.

## PHULKARI EMBROIDERY

Phulkari, meaning 'flower work', is a style of embroidery famous in Punjab, Haryana and Rajasthan. It is considered auspicious and is thus a part of most celebrations. The work is extremely intricate and so it is difficult to distinguish between the left and the right, or the upward and the downward side.

## TANJORE ART

Tanjore painting ranks among the greatest traditional art forms of Tamil Nadu. It originated in Thanjavur and reached great heights during the reign of the Chola kings. Its most common themes are mythological in nature. The characteristics of Tanjore paintings include striking colour schemes, decorative jewellery with stones and cut glasses, and brilliant gold-leaf work.

## TIE AND DYE

It is a method in which parts of a silk or cotton cloth are tied tightly with wax thread before the whole cloth is dipped in a vat of dye. The threads are untied afterwards, the parts so protected being left uncoloured. The technique is used in many parts of India, but the ones produced in Gujarat and Rajasthan are still noted for the finest work.

## WARLI FOLK PAINTING

Warli is a style of folk painting from Maharashtra. Named after one of the largest tribes around Mumbai, it was originally done on the walls of houses to transmit folklore to the masses. These paintings are usually made by women and generally depict social life. They are painted on a mud base using only white, with occasional dots in red and yellow. The colour white is obtained by grinding rice into a white powder.

# MAJOR INSTITUTIONS AND ORGANIZATIONS

## ALL INDIA INSTITUTE OF MEDICAL SCIENCES (AIIMS)

AIIMS, located in New Delhi, was established in 1956 as an institution of national importance by an Act of Parliament to establish a standard of teaching in all branches of undergraduate and postgraduate medical education.

## ALL INDIA RADIO (AIR)

Also known as Akashvani, AIR is a national service planned, developed and operated by the Prasar Bharati Broadcasting Corporation of India. It was started in 1936 as a government organization to inform, educate and entertain the masses. It is headquartered in New Delhi. Today, AIR has a network of 237 broadcasting centres, covering 91.85 per cent of India and serving 99.18 per cent of the population.

## BORDER SECURITY FORCE (BSF)

The BSF, established in 1965, is headquartered in New Delhi. BSF deals with the security of the border of India and matters connected therewith. Its ethos is 'any task, any time, any where'.

## BHABHA ATOMIC RESEARCH CENTRE (BARC)

Established in 1954 as the Atomic Energy Establishment (AEET), BARC provides a broad spectrum of scientific and technological activities in nuclear power generation and related areas. It is headquartered in Mumbai.

## CENTRAL BUREAU OF INVESTIGATION (CBI)

Established in 1963 as the Delhi Special Police Establishment, the CBI initially investigated offences related only to corruption by central government employees. With time all government employees, including those working in public sector units and nationalized banks, came within its ambit. It is headquartered in New Delhi.

## DOORDARSHAN

Doordarshan is the public service broadcaster of India. It was started in New Delhi on 15 September 1959 to transmit educational and development programmes. The range of the transmitter was only 40 km around Delhi. Soon, the frequency and duration of the programmes were increased. Entertainment and information programmes were introduced from August 1965, along with social education programmes. *Krishi Darshan*, a programme for farmers, began in 1967 and became a huge hit. From 1 January 1976, commercials came to be telecast at all the centres. Another significant development in the same year was the splitting up of Doordarshan from AIR. Today, Doordarshan operates thirty channels in twenty-two languages and has one of the largest terrestrial networks in the world.

## FILM AND TELEVISION INSTITUTE OF INDIA (FTII)

The FTII was established in 1960 to impart training in film-making and TV production. It is located in Pune. Over the years, the alumni of FTII have excelled in various fields of film and TV production. It is now a premier institute of India.

## INDIA POST

India Post is the government-operated postal system of India, established way back in 1764. Headquartered in New Delhi, it is the largest postal network in the world, with one post office serving 7,160 people and covering an area of 21.2 sq. km. The first postage stamp valid across the country, fixed by weight and not by distance, was issued on 1 October 1854. Besides postal services, it provides a diverse range of services through its vast network, including postal life insurance and banking.

## IMPORTANT TERMS ASSOCIATED WITH THE POSTAL SERVICE

**Inland letter:** An Inland letter is a sheet of paper with prescribed size and folding, for communication. Inland letter is used for transmission within India only.

**Meghdoot postcard:** Introduced on 2 September 2002, Meghdoot is priced at 25 paisa (half the cost of a regular postcard). The writing space available on the address side of a regular postcard is made available for advertising in multicolour in the case of Meghdoot.

**Money order:** A money order is an order issued by a post office for the payment of a sum of money to the person in whose name the money order is sent, through the agency of the post office. A 'payee' is the person named in a money order to whom the money is to be paid. The advantage of sending money to someone through money order is that the money is delivered at the person's place of stay.

**Pin code:** Postal Index Number (PIN) is a six-digit code. There are eight PIN regions in India. The first digit indicates one of the regions. The first two digits together indicate the subregion or one of the postal circles. The first three digits together indicate a sorting/revenue district. The last three digits refer to the delivery post office.

## INDIAN INSTITUTE OF MANAGEMENT (IIM)

The IIMs— at Ahmedabad, Kolkata, Bangalore, Lucknow, Indore, Kozhikode and Shillong—are institutions of excellence, set up with the objectives of imparting high quality management education and training, conducting research, and providing consultancy services in the field of management to various sectors of the Indian economy. IIM Calcutta and IIM Ahmedabad were established in 1961.

## INDIAN INSTITUTE OF TECHNOLOGY (IIT)

The IITs are a group of fifteen autonomous engineering and technology-oriented institutes. They were created to train scientists and engineers so that they could contribute to the development of the country after 1947. They have been declared as institutes of national importance by the Parliament. The IITs are located in Kharagpur, Mumbai, Chennai, Kanpur, Delhi, Guwahati, Roorkee, Ropar, Bhubaneswar, Hyderabad, Gandhinagar, Patna, Jodhpur, Mandi and Indore. The first IIT was set up in 1950 in Kharagpur, West Bengal.

## INDIAN MILITARY ACADEMY (IMA)

The IMA was established as the Military Academy in 1932 in Dehradun, Uttarakhand, as a premier officer training school for the Indian Army, in line with the famed Sandhurst Military Academy in England. The institute was later renamed IMA.

# INDIAN RAILWAYS

The Indian Railways, established in 1853 and headquartered in New Delhi, provide the principal mode of transportation for freight and passengers in the country. The first historic journey took place in 1853 between Bori Bunder and Thane. On that day, fourteen railway carriages were hauled by three locomotives (Sultan, Sindh, Sahib), over a distance of 34 km. The journey took fifty-seven minutes. Today, Indian Railways has grown into a vast network of over 6,853 stations spread over a route length of 63,028 km with a fleet of 7,566 locomotives, 37,840 coaching vehicles, and 2,22,147 freight wagons.

## SOME TERMS ASSOCIATED WITH THE INDIAN RAILWAYS

**Berth:** A sleeping bunk in a compartment.

**Bogie:** In colloquial Indian English, the term is often used to refer to a passenger compartment in a coach or to the coach itself, if it is subdivided into compartments.

**Gauge**: The width of the railway track measured as the distance between the rails.

**PNR:** Abbreviation of Passenger Name Record. It is a travel record of a single person or group of persons that is stored in the computerized reservation system.

**Return journey**: A return journey ticket is the ticket for the second half of a round trip, or the final section of a circular journey.

**Tier**: The number of berths that are provided one above the other determines the number of tiers. A two-tier coach has one upper bunk and a lower one (which forms the seats for daytime travel), a three-tier one has two bunks above the lowest. Three-tier coaches usually have a combination of three-tier arrangements crosswise and two-tier arrangements lengthwise along one side of the coach.

## IMPORTANT TRAINS

The **Rajdhani Express** is a passenger train service for providing high-speed connections between New Delhi and other important destinations, especially state capitals. The first Rajdhani Express was introduced in 1969, running from New Delhi to Howrah, a distance of 1,445 km, in 17 hours 20 minutes.

The word *shatabdi* means 'centenary' in Sanskrit, Hindi and several Indian languages. The first **Shatabdi Express** was started in 1988 to commemorate the birth centenary of Pandit Jawaharlal Nehru.

The **Palace on Wheels** was conceived in 1981–1982, when Rajasthan Tourism Development Corporation and Indian Railways decided to launch a special heritage tourist train for providing an unforgettable experience to tourists visiting Rajasthan. Powered by a steam engine, the train made its inaugural trip on 26 January 1982.

The **Deccan Odyssey**, is a special luxury train that was modelled on the Palace on Wheels to provide fillip to tourism on the Konkan route. The route starts in Mumbai (Bombay) and travels to Ratnagiri, Sindhudurg, Goa, Belgaum, Kolhapur, Pune, Nashik, Aurangabad, Ajanta-Ellora, and then back to Mumbai.

The **Jan Shatabdi Express** (literally 'People's Shatabdi') is the more affordable variety of the Shatabdi Express. It has both air conditioned and regular accommodation.

# INDIAN SPACE RESEARCH ORGANIZATION (ISRO)

The Indian Space Research Organization (ISRO), established in 1969, is headquartered in Bangalore. The objective of ISRO is to develop space technology and apply it to various national tasks. ISRO has created two major satellite systems, the INSAT, for communication, TV broadcasting and meteorological services, and the IRS, for resources monitoring and management. ISRO has also developed two satellite launch vehicles, PSLV and GSLV, to place INSAT and IRS satellites in orbit.

# NATIONAL DEFENCE ACADEMY (NDA)

The NDA was inaugurated on 16 January 1955, for providing training to cadets of the three wings (Army, Navy, Air Force) of the armed forces before they are sent for their pre-commission training to their respective academies. NDA is located in Khadakwasla, Pune.

# NATIONAL INSTITUTE OF DESIGN (NID)

Located at Ahmedabad in Gujarat, the NID was established in 1961. It is an autonomous national institute of excellence under the aegis of the commerce and industry ministry. It offers education, applied research and service and advanced training in industrial, communication, textile, and IT-integrated design. NID offers a wide spectrum of design domains while encouraging transdisciplinary design projects.

# NATIONAL INSTITUTE OF FASHION TECHNOLOGY (NIFT)

NIFT was set up in 1986 under the aegis of the textile ministry as a premier institute for developing professionals for the fashion industry. It has a network of twelve institutes in New Delhi, Bangalore, Chennai, Gandhinagar, Hyderabad, Kolkata, Mumbai, Rae Bareli, Bhopal, Kannur, Patna and Shillong. NIFT has also opened an international centre in Mauritius.

# NATIONAL SCHOOL OF DRAMA (NSD)

Established in 1959 in New Delhi, the NSD is one of the foremost theatre training institutions in the world and the only one of its kind in India. It was set up by the Sangeet Natak Akademi as one of its constituent units, and later became an autonomous institution financed by the culture ministry.

# NATIONAL CADET CORPS (NCC)

The NCC was established in 1948 as a tri-services organization comprising the Army, the Navy and the Air Force. It engaged itself with grooming the youth into disciplined and patriotic citizens. It is headquartered in New Delhi. It also has a girls' division. The NCC has approximately thirteen lakh cadets in its fold.

# AWARDS IN INDIA

## ASHOK CHAKRA

The Ashok Chakra was instituted on 4 January 1952 to recognize the most prominent bravery or pre-eminent act of valour or self-sacrifice, other than in the face of the enemy. While a replica of Ashoka's Chakra (surrounded by a lotus wreath) is embossed on the obverse side, the reverse side has the words 'Ashok Chakra' embossed in both Hindi and English.

## BHARAT RATNA

The Bharat Ratna is the highest civilian honour, given for exceptional service towards the advancement of art, literature and science, and in recognition of public service of the highest order. It was introduced in 1954. The first ever Indian to receive this award was the famous scientist, C.V. Raman. There is no written provision that the Bharat Ratna should be awarded to Indian citizens only. It has been awarded to a naturalized Indian citizen, Mother Teresa (1980), and to two non-Indians, Khan Abdul Ghaffar Khan (1987) and Nelson Mandela (1990). It is also not mandatory that Bharat Ratna be awarded every year.

## LIST OF BHARAT RATNA AWARDEES

| | | | |
|---|---|---|---|
| Dr Sarvepalli Radhakrishnan | 1954 | Public affairs | Tamil Nadu |
| Dr Chandrasekhara Venkata Raman | 1954 | Science and engineering | Tamil Nadu |
| Chakravarti Rajagopalachari | 1954 | Public affairs | Tamil Nadu |
| Dr M. Vishweshwariah | 1955 | Civil service | Karnataka |
| Jawaharlal Nehru | 1955 | Public affairs | Uttar Pradesh |
| Dr Bhagwan Das | 1955 | Literature and education | Uttar Pradesh |
| Pt Govind Ballabh Pant | 1957 | Public affairs | Uttar Pradesh |
| Dr Dhondo Keshav Karve | 1958 | Social work | Maharashtra |
| Purushottam Das Tandon | 1961 | Public affairs | Uttar Pradesh |
| Dr Bidhan Chandra Roy | 1961 | Public affairs | West Bengal |
| Dr Rajendra Prasad | 1962 | Public affairs | Bihar |
| Dr Zakir Hussain | 1963 | Public affairs | Andhra Pradesh |
| Dr Pandurang Vaman Kane | 1963 | Social work | Maharashtra |

| | | | |
|---|---|---|---|
| Lal Bahadur Shastri | 1966 | Public affairs | Uttar Pradesh |
| Indira Gandhi | 1971 | Public affairs | Uttar Pradesh |
| V.V. Giri | 1975 | Public affairs | Odisha |
| Kumaraswamy Kamraj | 1976 | Public affairs | Tamil Nadu |
| Mother Teresa | 1980 | Social work | West Bengal |
| Acharya Vinoba Bhave | 1983 | Social work | Maharashtra |
| Khan Abdul Ghaffar Khan | 1987 | Social work | Pakistan |
| Marudur Gopalan Ramachandran | 1988 | Public affairs | Tamil Nadu |
| Dr Nelson Rolihlahla Mandela | 1990 | Public affairs | South Africa |
| Dr Bhimrao Ramji Ambedkar | 1990 | Public affairs | Maharashtra |
| Sardar Vallabhbhai Patel | 1991 | Public affairs | Gujarat |
| Rajiv Gandhi | 1991 | Public affairs | Delhi |
| Morarji Ranchhodji Desai | 1991 | Public affairs | Gujarat |
| Satyajit Ray | 1992 | Arts | West Bengal |
| Maulana Abul Kalam Azad | 1992 | Public affairs | West Bengal |
| Jehangir Ratanji Dadabhai Tata | 1992 | Trade and industry | Maharashtra |
| Gulzari Lal Nanda | 1997 | Public affairs | Gujarat |
| Aruna Asaf Ali | 1997 | Public affairs | Delhi |
| Dr A.P.J. Abdul Kalam | 1997 | Science and engineering | Delhi |
| M.S. Subbulakshmi | 1998 | Arts | Tamil Nadu |
| Chidambaram Subramaniam | 1998 | Public affairs | Tamil Nadu |
| Pt Ravi Shankar | 1999 | Arts | US |
| Loknayak Jayprakash Narayan | 1999 | Public affairs | Bihar |
| Lokpriya Gopinath Bordoloi | 1999 | Public affairs | Assam |
| Prof. Amartya Sen | 1999 | Literature and education | UK |

| Ustad Bismillah Khan | 2001 | Arts | Uttar Pradesh |
| Kumari Lata Dinanath Mangeshkar | 2001 | Arts | Maharashtra |
| Pt Bhimsen Gururaj Joshi | 2008 | Arts | Karnataka |

## DADASAHEB PHALKE AWARD

In 1969, to commemorate the centenary of the father of Indian cinema, Dadasaheb Phalke, an award was instituted to honour distinguished film personalities for outstanding contributions to Indian cinema. The award initially consisted of 11,000 rupees, a plaque, and a shawl. The first award was presented to Devika Rani, the renowned actress and pioneer of the studio system in India.

## GANDHI PEACE PRIZE

The Government of India launched the International Gandhi Peace Prize in 1995 on the occasion of the 125th birth anniversary of Mahatma Gandhi. It is a very prestigious award and carries an amount of one crore rupees, a citation, and a plaque. Every year the award is selected by a jury under the chairmanship of the prime minister. This is an annual award given to individuals and institutions for their outstanding contributions towards social, economic and political transformation through non-violence, and other Gandhian methods, amelioration of human sufferings, particularly of the less privileged sections of the society, and social justice and harmony. The award is open to all persons regardless of nationality, race, creed, or sex.

## JNANPITH AWARD

The Jnanpith Award is the highest literary award in India, instituted in 1965. The very first Jnanpith Award went to Malayalam poet G. Sankara Kurup, who heralded the modernist phase in Malayalam poetry. Some other awardees are Mahashweta Devi, Girish Karnad, M.T. Vasudevan Nair and Amrita Pritam.

## MAHA VIR CHAKRA

The Maha Vir Chakra is the second most important award for bravery in India, given to an individual for extraordinary gallantry in the face of the enemy. The award was instituted on 26 January 1950. This is a silver medal with a five-pointed star, with the national emblem embossed at the centre.

## NATIONAL FILM AWARD

The National Film Awards, popularly called the National Awards, are given by the government to promote aesthetic and technical standards of Indian films. It was started in 1954 on the recommendation of the Film Enquiry Committee. Initially, only three awards were instituted: President's Gold Medal for Best Feature Film and Best Documentary, and Prime Minister's Silver Medal for Best Children's Film. The need to promote cinema encouraged the government to introduce awards in various Indian languages and dialects in 1955. Separate awards for artistes and film technicians were initiated in 1968.

## PADMA AWARDS

The Padma Awards consist of the Padma Vibhushan, the highest one, the Padma Bhushan, and the Padma Shri. These are given for exceptional service in any field, including service rendered by government servants. The awards are cast in bronze. The recommendations are received from state governments/UT administrations, central ministries/departments, institutions of excellence, and so on, and then considered by an awards committee. The Padma awards are announced on the eve of the Republic Day. Most recipients are first awarded the Padma Shri, and then for further meritorious works, the Padma Bhushan and, ultimately, the Padma Vibhushan.

## PARAM VIR CHAKRA

The Param Vir Chakra, the highest decoration for valour in India, was instituted on 26 January 1950 to recognize the most striking act of bravery or self-sacrifice in the presence of the enemy. The award consists of a circular bronze medal with four replicas of Lord Indra's *vajra* and the state emblem embossed in the centre. On its reverse are the words 'Param Vir Chakra', in Hindi and English. It may be awarded posthumously. Some of the winners are Flying Officer Nirmal Jiit Singh Sekhon and Captain Vikram Batra.

## SAHITYA AKADEMI AWARD

The Sahitya Akademi annually confers awards on the most outstanding books of literary merit published in any of the major Indian languages, recognized by the Akademi. It was first awarded in 1955. Some of the winners are R.K. Narayan, Amitav Ghosh and Anita Desai.

# ARMED FORCES OF INDIA

The Indian government is responsible for ensuring the defence of the country. The president is the Supreme Commander of the Indian Armed Forces. The responsibility for national defence rests with the cabinet. This is discharged through the defence ministry, which provides the policy framework and resources to the armed forces to discharge their responsibilities. The forces comprise three major divisions: Indian Army, Indian Navy, and Indian Air Force.

## INDIAN AIR FORCE

The Indian Air Force is the air arm of the Indian armed forces, officially established on 8 October 1932. The motto of the force is the Sanskrit term *Nabhah Sparsham Diptam* which means 'touch the sky with glory'.

## INDIAN ARMY

The land-based branch of the Indian Armed Forces, the Indian Army, as we know it today, became operational after India became independent. Its headquarters are located in New Delhi and it functions under the Chief of Army Staff (COAS), responsible for the command, control and administration. The general motto is 'one for all and all for one'. The tradition is never to question, but to do or die for the three Ns: *naam* of the unit/army/nation, *namak* (salt) or loyalty to the nation, and *nishan* or the insignia/flag of one's unit/regiment/army/nation.

## INDIAN NAVY

The foundation of the modern Indian Navy was laid in the 17th century when the East India Company had established a maritime force, thereby graduating in time to the establishment of the Royal Indian Navy in 1934. Headquartered in New Delhi, the Indian Navy is under the command of the Chief of the Naval Staff. The motto is *Shano Varuna*, meaning 'May the lord of the oceans be auspicious unto us'.

# PAINTERS OF INDIA

### BOSE, NANDALAL (1882–1966)

Nandalal Bose was a well-known painter of the Bengal school. His classic works include paintings of scenes from Indian mythology, as well as of women and village life.

### HUSSAIN, M.F. (1915–2011)

M.F. Hussain was an Indian painter, film-maker and Padma awardee. Some of his distinguished paintings are *Gaja Gamini*, *Gandhari*, *Ganesh*, *Holi*, *Horses*, *Maya*, *Battle of Ganga and Jamuna* and *Mahabharata 12*. He has also made films like *Through the Eyes of a Painter*, *Gaja Gamini* and *Meenaxi: A Tale of Three Cities*.

## MENON, ANJOLIE ELA (b. 1940)

Anjolie Ela Menon is one of the leading contemporary artists of India. She is also a Padma Shri awardee. Some of her celebrated paintings are *Goat Herd, Window,* and *Ram, Rahim: Two Faces of India*. In 2010, she released her biography, *Anjolie Ela Menon: Through the Patina*.

## ROY, JAMINI (1887–1972)

Jamini Roy was mostly influenced by Kalighat Pat. Some of his acclaimed paintings include *Bride and Two Companions, Dual Cats with One Crayfish, Cats Sharing a Prawn, Krishna and Radha* and *Virgin and Child*.

## SHER-GIL, AMRITA (1913–1941)

Amrita Sher-Gil was an important painter of 20th-century India. She mostly painted the everyday life of common people. Some of her popular paintings are *Young Girls, Camel, Three Girls, Hill Women, Tribal Women,* and *Bride's Toilet*.

## TAGORE, ABANINDRANATH (1871–1951)

Abanindranath Tagore was a prominent artist and one of the founders of the Bengal school of art. He was one of the early painters to include *swadeshi* values in Indian art. He was also a noted author. His celebrated works for children include *Kshirer Putul, Buro Angla, Raj Kahini,* and *Shakuntala*.

## VARMA, RAJA RAVI (1848–1906)

Raja Ravi Varma was an Indian painter from the princely state of Travancore who achieved recognition for his depiction of scenes from the epics, the Mahabharata and the Ramayana. Some of his well-known paintings are *Lakshmi, Murugun, Saraswati, Shakuntala,* and *Draupadi*.

# STATES OF INDIA

**Name:** Andhra Pradesh

**Capital:** Hyderabad

**Population:** 8,46,65,533

**Area:** 2,75,000 sq. km

**Principal Languages:** Telugu, Urdu, English

**Places to See:** Charminar, Salarjung Museum, Golconda Fort, Lord Venkateswara Temple (Tirupati), Nagarjuna Sagar, Araku Valley

All population figures are according to July 2012 estimate

**Name:** Arunachal Pradesh

**Capital:** Itanagar

**Population:** 13,82,611

**Area:** 83,743 sq. km

**Principal Languages:** Monpa, Miji, Aka, Sherdukpen, Nyishi, Apatani, Tagin, Hill Miri, Adi, Digaru-Mismi, Idu-Mishmi, Khamti, Miju-Mishmi

**Places to See:** Tawang Monastery, Malinithan, Parashuram Kund, Ziro, Sela Pass, Bomdila, Tipi, Dirang

**Name:** Assam

**Capital:** Dispur

**Population:** 3,11,69,272

**Area:** 78,438 sq. km

**Principal Languages:** Assamese, Bodo, Karbi, Bengali

**Places to See:** Sualkuchi, Majuli, Sibsagar, Bhalukpung, Haflong, Kaziranga National Park, Manas National Park, Kamakhya Temple

**Name:** Bihar

**Capital:** Patna

**Population:** 10,38,04,637

**Area:** 94,163 sq. km

**Principal Languages:** Hindi, Maithili, Bhojpuri, Magahi, Angika

**Places to See:** Bodh Gaya, Rajgir, Nalanda, Vaishali, Pawapuri, Vikramshila, Sasaram, Madhubani

**Name:** Chhattisgarh

**Capital:** Raipur

**Population:** 2,55,40,196

**Area:** 1,36,034 sq. km

**Principal Languages:** Hindi, Chattisgarhi

**Places to See:** Chitrakoot Waterfalls, Tirathgarh Falls, Kutumbsar and Kailash caves, Bambleshwari Devi temple, Bastar, Kangherghati National Park

**Name:** Goa
**Capital**: Panaji
**Population:** 14,57,723
**Area:** 3,702 sq. km
**Principal Languages:** Marathi and Konkani
**Places to See:** Calangute Beach, Colva Beach, Anjuna Beach, Basilica of Bom Jesus, Se Cathedral, Dudhsagar and Harvalem Waterfalls, Aguada Fort

**Name:** Gujarat
**Capital:** Gandhinagar
**Population:** 6,03,83,628
**Area:** 1,96,024 sq. km
**Principal Languages:** Gujarati, Hindi
**Places to See:** Saputara, Gir Forest, Modhera, Porbander, Dandi, Sabarmati Ashram, Dwarka, Somnath, Ahmedpur-Mandvi and Chorwad beaches

**Name:** Haryana
**Capital:** Chandigarh
**Population:** 2,53,53,081
**Area:** 44,212 sq. km
**Principal Languages:** Hindi, Haryanvi
**Places to See:** Surajkund, Damdama, Morni Hills, Sultanpur Bird Sanctuary, Kurukshetra, Panipat

**Name:** Himachal Pradesh
**Capital:** Simla
**Population:** 68,56,509
**Area:** 55,673 sq. km
**Principal Languages:** Hindi, Pahari
**Places to See:** Shimla, Manali, Chamba, Kullu, Dharamsala, Lahaul Valley, Dalhousie, Kangra, Paonta Sahib, Manikaran

**Name:** Jammu and Kashmir
**Capital:** Srinagar (summer), Jammu (winter)

**Population:** 1,25,48,926

**Area:** 2,22,236 sq. km (includes 78,114 sq. km considered under illegal occupation of Pakistan, 5,180 sq. km handed over by Pakistan to China, and 37,555 sq. km under occupation of China)

**Principal Languages:** Urdu, Dogri, Kashmiri, Pahari, Punjabi, Ladakhi, Balti, Gojri, Dadri

**Places to See:** Chashmashahi springs, Shalimar Bagh, Dal Lake, Dachigam, Gulmarg, Pahalgam, Sonmarg and Amarnath shrine, Vaishnodevi shrine, Ladakh

**Name:** Jharkhand

**Capital:** Ranchi

**Population:** 3,29,66,238

**Area:** 79,714 sq. km

**Principal Languages:** Hindi, Bhojpuri, Angika, Maithili

**Places to See:** Ichagarh and Udhava bird sanctuaries, Hundru Falls, Hazaribagh National Park, Baidyanath Temple, Dalma Wildlife Sanctuary, Tilaya Dam

**Name:** Karnataka

**Capital:** Bengaluru

**Population:** 6,11,30,704

**Area:** 1,91,791 sq. km

**Principal Languages:** Kannada, Konkani, Kodava, Tulu, Hindi

**Places to See:** Coorg, Mysore, Hampi, Srirangapatna, Chikmagalur, Gokarna, Agumbe, Jog Falls, Bandipur National Park, Chitradurga

**Name:** Kerala

**Capital:** Thiruvananthapuram

**Population:** 3,33,87,677

**Area:** 38,863 sq. km

**Principal Languages:** Malayalam, English

**Places to See:** Alappuzha, Neyyar Dam, Varkala, Kottayam, Chinnar Wildlife Sanctuary, Ernakulam, Wellington Islands, Palakkad

**Name:** Madhya Pradesh
**Capital:** Bhopal
**Population:** 7,25,97,565
**Area:** 3,08,000 sq. km
**Principal Languages:** Hindi
**Places to See:** Kanha National Park, Bandhavgarh National Park, Khajuraho, Amarkantak, Marble Rocks at Bedaghat, Bhimbetka, Chanderi, Chitrakoot, Sanchi

**Name:** Maharashtra
**Capital:** Mumbai
**Population:** 11,23,72,972
**Area:** 3,07,713 sq. km
**Principal Language:** Marathi
**Places to See:** Mahabaleswar, Lonavla, Elephanta Caves, Gateway of India, Alibaug, Raigad Fort, Sinhadurg Fort, Panchgani, Ajanta and Ellora Caves, Juhu Beach

**Name:** Manipur
**Capital:** Imphal
**Population:** 27,21,756
**Area:** 22,327 sq. km
**Principal Languages:** Manipuri
**Places to See:** Shri Govindajee Temple, Saheed Minar, War Cemetery, Manipur Zoological Garden, Singda, Langthabal, Red Hill (Maibam Lokpa Ching), Bishnupur, Loukoipat, Phubala, Moirang, Loktak Lake, Kaibul Lamjao National Park, Kaina, Khongjom, Andro, Churachandpur

**Name:** Meghalaya
**Capital:** Shillong
**Population:** 29,64,007
**Area:** 22,429 sq. km
**Principal Languages:** Khasi, Garo, English
**Places to See:** Wards Lake, Lady Hydari Park, Elephant Falls, Shillong Peak, Bara Pani, Beadon-Bishop Falls, Cherrapunji

**Name:** Mizoram
**Capital:** Aizawl
**Population:** 10,91,014
**Area:** 21,087 sq. km
**Principal Languages:** Mizo and English
**Places to See:** Aizawl, Champhai, Tam Dil, Vantawng Falls

**Name:** Nagaland
**Capital:** Kohima
**Population:** 19,80,602
**Area:** 16,527 sq. km
**Principal Languages:** English, Nagamese
**Places to See:** Rangapahar Reserve forest, Longkhum Village, Mount Pauna, Mt Tiyi, Glory Peak

**Name:** Odisha
**Capital:** Bhubaneswar
**Population:** 4,19,47,358
**Area:** 1,55,707 sq. km
**Principal Languages:** Oriya
**Places to See:** Bhitarknika National Park, Simlipal National Park, Lingaraj Temple, Mukteswar Temple, Rajarani Temple, Shanti Stupa, Jagannath Temple, Sun Temple, Barabati Fort, Chilka Lake, Puri Beach, Udaigiri-Khandagiri Caves, Gahirmatha

**Name:** Punjab
**Capital:** Chandigarh
**Population:** 2,77,04,236
**Area:** 50,362 sq. km
**Principal Languages:** Punjabi
**Places to See:** Golden Temple, Summer Palace of Maharaja Ranjit Singh, Jallianwala Bagh, Wagah Border, Qila Mubarak

**Name:** Rajasthan
**Capital:** Jaipur
**Population:** 6,86,21,012
**Area:** 342,239 sq. km
**Principal Languages:** Hindi and Rajasthani
**Places to See:** Jantar Mantar, Dilwara Temples, Hawa Mahal, Chittorgarh Fort, Lake Palace, Dargah of Khwaja Moinuddin Chisti, Mehrangarh Fort, Udaipur, Mount Abu, Sariska Tiger Sanctuary, Ranthambhore National Park

**Name:** Sikkim
**Capital:** Gangtok
**Population:** 6,07,688
**Area:** 7,096 sq. km
**Principal Languages:** Lepcha, Bhutia, Limbu, and Nepali
**Places to See:** Yumthang, Namtse, Changu Lake, Rumtek Monastery, Dharma Chakra Centre, Pemayantshe Monastery, Pelling

**Name:** Tamil Nadu
**Capital:** Chennai
**Population:** 7,21,38,958
**Area:** 1,30,058 sq. km
**Principal Languages:** Tamil
**Places to See:** Ooty, Kodaikanal, Nilgiri Hills, Cardamom Hills, Meenakshi Temple, Brihadishwara Temple, Marina Beach, Mahabalipuram

**Name:** Tripura
**Capital:** Agartala
**Population:** 36,71,032
**Area:** 10,491.69 sq. km
**Principal Languages:** Bengali, Kokborok
**Places to See:** Sepahijala Wildlife Sanctuary, Trishna Wildlife Sanctuary, Gumti Wildlife Sanctuary, Rowa Wildlife Sanctuary, Rudra Sagar (Neer Mahal), Kamala Sagar, Brahmakund, Udaipur, Deotamura, Dumbur, Pilak, Jampui Hills, Unakoti, Tripura Sundari Temple, Ujjayanta Palace

**Name:** Uttarakhand

**Capital:** Dehradun

**Population:** 1,01,16,752

**Area:** 53,483 sq. km

**Principal Languages:** Hindi, Garhwali, Kumaoni

**Places to See:** Gangotri, Yamnotri, Badrinath, Kedarnath, Haridwar, Rishikesh, Mussoorie, Nainital, Dehradun, Corbett National Park, Nanda Devi National Park

**Name:** Uttar Pradesh

**Capital:** Lucknow

**Population:** 19,95,81,477

**Area:** 2,36,286 sq. km

**Principal Languages:** Hindi and Urdu

**Places to See:** Taj Mahal, Agra Fort, Chitrakoot, Ayodhya, Jhansi, Mathura, Kapilavastu, Varanasi, Sarnath, Fathepur Sikri, Vrindavan, Agra

**Name:** West Bengal

**Capital:** Kolkata

**Population:** 9,13,47,736

**Area:** 88,752 sq. km

**Principal Language:** Bengali

**Places to See:** Kolkata, Victoria Memorial, Indian Museum, Kalighat Temple, Dakhineswar Kali Temple, Belur Math, Birla Planetarium, Shahid Minar, Howrah Bridge, Vidyasagar Setu, Science City, Botanical Gardens

## UNION TERRITORIES OF INDIA

**Name:** Andaman and Nicobar Islands

**Capital:** Port Blair

**Population:** 3,79,944

**Area:** 8,249 sq. km

**Principal Languages:** Hindi, Nicobarese, Bengali, Tamil, Malayalam, Telugu

**Places to See:** Cellular Jail, Ross Island, Havelock Island, Gandhi Park, Corbyn's Cove Beach, Viper Island and Chidiyatapu

**Name:** Chandigarh
**Capital:** Chandigarh
**Population:** 10,54,686
**Area:** 114 sq. km
**Principal Languages:** Hindi, Punjabi, English
**Places to See:** Government Museum and Art Gallery, Museum of Evolution of Life, International Dolls Museum, Punjab Kala Kendra, Rock Garden, Sukhna Lake, Rose Garden, Leisure Valley

**Name:** Dadra and Nagar Haveli
**Capital:** Silvassa
**Population:** 3,42,853
**Area:** 491 sq. km
**Principal Languages:** Gujarati, Hindi
**Places to See:** Tadekeshwar Shiva Mandir, Bindrabin, Deer Park at Khanvel, Vanganga Lake and Island Garden, Vanvihar Udhyan Mini Zoo, Bal Udyan, Tribal Museum, Hirvavan Garden at Silvassa

**Name:** Daman and Diu
**Capital:** Daman
**Population:** 2,42,911
**Area:** 112 sq. km
**Principal Language:** Gujarati
**Places to See:** Bom Jesus Church, Our Lady of Sea Church; Our Lady of Remedios Church, Forts of Moti Daman and Nani Daman, Jampore and Devka Beaches; Public Garden and Moti Daman Jetty, Pargola Garden, Moti Daman, Amusement Park

**Name:** Lakshadweep
**Capital:** Kavaratti
**Population:** 64,429
**Area:** 32 sq. km
**Principal Languages:** Malayalam, Jeseri (Dweep Bhasha) and Mahi
**Places to See:** Agatti, Bangaram, Kalpeni, Kadmat, Kavaratti and Minicoy

**Name:** Puducherry

**Capital:** Puducherry

**Population:** 12,44,464

**Area:** 479 sq. km

**Principal Languages:** Tamil, Telugu, Malayalam, English, French

**Places to See:** Auroville, Shri Aurobindo Ashram, Puducherry Museum, Sacred Heart Church, Manakula Vinayagar Koil Temple, Sacred Heart of Jesus Church

**Name:** The Government of NCT of Delhi

**Capital:** Delhi

**Population:** 1,67,53,235

**Area**: 1,483 sq. km

**Principal Languages:** Hindi, Punjabi, Urdu and English

**Places to See:** Red Fort, Purana Qila, Qutab Minar, India Gate, Bahai's House of Worship, Rashtrapati Bhavan, Rajghat, Humayun's Tomb, Parliament House, Jama Masjid, Jantar Mantar

### FOLK DANCES

| DANCE FORM | STATE |
|---|---|
| Bhangra | Punjab |
| Bhavai | Rajasthan, Gujarat |
| Bhortal Nritya | Assam |
| Bihu | Assam |
| Cheraw | Mizoram |
| Chhau | Seraikela (Bihar), Purulia (West Bengal), Mayurbhanj (Odisha) |
| Dandiya | Gujarat |
| Garba | Gujarat |
| Jatra | West Bengal, Odisha |
| Kummi | Tamil Nadu |
| Poikkal Kudirai Attam | Tamil Nadu |
| Thabal Chongba | Manipur |
| Yakshagana | Karnataka |

## FIRSTS IN INDIA

**Bharat Ratna awardees:** Dr Sarvepalli Radhakrishnan, C. Rajagopalachari, Dr C.V. Raman (1954)

**Cosmonaut**: Squadron Leader Rakesh Sharma (1984)

**Chief Justice of India:** H.J. Kania (1947–1951)

**Dadasaheb Phalke award winner :** Devika Rani (1969)

**Governor-general of independent India:** Louis Mountbatten, Ist Earl Mountbatten (1947)

**Field Marshal:** Sam Manekshaw (1973)

**Governor-General of independent India:** C. Rajagopalachari (1948)

**Indian ICS officer:** Satyendranath Tagore (1863)

**Man to scale Mount Everest**: Capt. (later Lt Col.) Avtar Singh Cheema

**Miss universe:** Sushmita Sen (1994)

**Miss world:** Reita Faria (1965)

**Olympics, individual gold medal:** Abhinav Bindra for 10 m air rifle (2008 Summer Olympics, Beijing)

**Olympics, individual medal (and individual bronze)**: K.D. Jadhav for wrestling (1952 Summer Olympics, Helsinki)

**Olympics, individual medal by a woman**: Karnam Malleswari for weightlifting 54 kg class (2000 Summer Olympics, Sydney)

**Olympics, individual silver medal:** Rajyavardhan Singh Rathore for men's double trap (2004 Summer Olympics, Athens)

**Oscar for Lifetime Achievement:** Satyajit Ray (1992)

**Oscar winner:** Bhanu Athaiyya for Best Costume Design for *Gandhi* (1982)

**President:** Rajendra Prasad (tenure: 1950–1962)

**Prime minister:** Jawaharlal Nehru (tenure: 1947–1964)

**Satellite**: *Aryabhata*, launched on 19 April 1975

**Silent film:** *Raja Harishchandra,* directed by Dada Saheb Phalke (1913)

**Sound film:** *Alam Ara,* directed by Ardeshir Irani (1931)

**Speaker of Lok Sabha:** G.V. Mavlankar (1952–1956)

**Swimmer to cross the English Channel**: Mihir Sen (1958)

**Vice-president**: S. Radhakrishnan ( 1952–1962)

**Woman cabinet minister in independent India**: Rajkumari Amrit Kaur (1947–1957)

**Woman chief minister**: Sucheta Kriplani ( 1963–1967)

**Woman IPS officer:** Kiran Bedi (1972)

**First woman governor of a state:** Sarojini Naidu (1947–1949)

**Woman president**: Pratibha Patil (2007–2012 )

**Woman prime minister:** Indira Gandhi (1966)

**Woman speaker of the Lok Sabha:** Meira Kumar (2009)

**Woman to scale Mount Everest:** Bachendri Pal (23 May 1984)

**Woman to swim across the English Channel:** Arati Saha (1959)

**3-D film**: *My Dear Kuttichathan*, Malayalam (1984), dubbed in Hindi as *Chhota Chetan*

## MONUMENTS IN INDIA

### AGRA FORT

Agra Fort, a UNESCO world heritage site in India, is also known as the Red Fort of Agra. Its construction was started in 1565 during Akbar's reign but was eventually completed by Shah Jahan. Some of the exquisite buildings here are Moti Masjid, a white marble mosque akin to a perfect pearl; Diwan-e-Aam, Diwan-e-Khaas, Jahangir's Palace, Khaas Mahal, and Sheesh Mahal.

### AJANTA CAVES

About 100 km from the city of Aurangabad in Maharastra, the Ajanta rock caves are among the finest examples of early Buddhist architecture, cave painting and sculpture. These caves are carved in a horseshoe-shaped bend of rock surface nearly 76 m in height overlooking a narrow stream called Waghora. In all thirty excavations were hewn out of rock, and there is also an unfinished one. Of these, five (cave numbers 9, 10, 19, 26, 29) are *chaityagrihas* and the rest are *viharas*. Among the most interesting paintings are those based on the Jataka tales, illustrating diverse stories relating to the various incarnations of Buddha.

### BAHA'I TEMPLE

The lotus-shaped popular temple is a Bahai house of worship and important tourist spot in New Delhi. Designed by Fariborz Sahba, it gives the impression of a half-open lotus flower, afloat on nine ponds. Each component of the temple is repeated nine times.

## BASILICA OF BOM JESUS

The Basilica of Bom Jesus is one of the most popular churches in Goa. Bom Jesus means 'infant Jesus'. The layout follows Renaissance norms, while the detailing and decoration are related to the style of European architechture. It is an opulent structure incorporating white marble and beautifully gilded altars decorated with frescoes and inlay work.

## CHARMINAR

The Charminar is one of the landmarks of the city of Hyderabad, built by Mohammed Quli Qutab Shah in 1591 to commemorate the end of plague outbreak in the city. The monument is a magnificent square edifice of granite, built upon four grand arches. These arches support two floors of rooms and gallery of archways. At each corner of the square structure is a minaret. The building is nearly 56 m tall. It is these four (*char*) minarets (*minar*) that give the building its name.

## CHHATRAPATI SHIVAJI TERMINUS

Mumbai's Chhatrapati Shivaji Terminus, formerly Victoria Terminus, is a fine example of Victorian Gothic revival architecture in India, with a blend of themes derived from Indian traditional architecture. The building, designed by British architect F.W. Stevens, was built between 1878 and 1888. It has become an inseparable part of the people of Mumbai as the station operates both suburban and long distance trains. This magnificent terminus serves as the headquarters of the Central Railways in India and is one of the busiest stations of India.

## ELLORA CAVES

The Ellora caves are located 30 km from Aurangabad. This is one of the largest rock-hewn monastic temple complexes in the entire world. Ellora is also renowned for the largest single monolithic excavation in the world, the great Kailasa. The cave excavations at Ellora represent three different religious creeds: Buddhism, Brahminism and Jainism.

## FATEHPUR SIKRI

The royal city at Fatehpur Sikri, 41.84 km from Agra, was built under the orders of Mughal Emperor Akbar in honour of Shaikh Salim Chisti in the 1570s. The Jami Mosque was perhaps among the first buildings to come up. The Buland Darwaza was added some five years later. Among other important buildings are the *taksal* (mint), *karkhanas* (royal workshop), *khazana* (treasury), *hakim*'s quarters, Diwan-i-Aam (hall of public audience),

House of Maryam or Sunahra Makan (Golden House), Palace of Jodha Bai, and Birbal's house.

## GATEWAY OF INDIA

The Gateway of India, designed by British architect George Wittet, is one of the most distinguished monuments of Mumbai. It was built as a triumphal arch to commemorate the visit of King George V and Queen Mary to Mumbai. The archway, facing the Arabian Sea, is 26 m high and joined by four turrets and intricate latticework carved on stones. The arch alone was built at a cost of Rs 21 lakhs.

## GOL GUMBAZ

The Gol Gumbaz, located at Bijapur in Karnataka, is the mausoleum of Mohammed Adil Shah (AD 1626– AD 1656) of the Adil Shahi dynasty of Indian sultans. It is a remarkable testimonial to Indo-Islamic architecture, known for its amazing size and unique acoustic features. The construction was completed in AD1034. It is the largest dome in India and the second largest in the world. It has a 'Whispering Gallery', where even the lowest whisper is audible and a single loud clap is distinctly echoed more than ten times.

## GOLCONDA FORT

The Golconda Fort, located near Hyderabad, is the fortresses in the Deccan plateau. It is built on a 400-ft high hill with a circumference of 7 km of the fort wall containing eight gates and 87 bastions, each 15-18 m high. The fort has a remarkable signalling device. The numerous edifices transmit sound to faraway points. If one claps standing at the centre of the entrance portal, the sound is deflected by the opposite building, which is constructed at an angle to the entrance. Similarly if a clapping sound is made from the opposite building, that sound will carry to the hilltop, although at other close points it may not be heard at all. The Golconda Fort contains a vault where the famous Kohinoor and Hope diamonds were stored.

## GOLDEN TEMPLE

Sri Harmandir Sahib, also known as Sri Darbar Sahib or Golden Temple (on account of its golden coating), situated in Amritsar, Punjab, is the most sacred temple of the Sikhs. Construction of this temple began in 1570s and was completed by September 1604. Guru Arjan Sahib installed the then newly created Guru Granth Sahib, the holy book of the Sikhs, in Harmandir Sahib and appointed Baba Budha ji as its first *granthi* (reader).

## MONUMENTS AT HAMPI

Hampi, the 14th-century capital of the Vijayanagar empire, lies in the Deccan heartland in Karnataka. The monuments of the Vijayanagar city, also known as Vidyasagar in honour of the sage Vidyaranya, were built between 1336 and 1570. They are noted for their large dimensions, elaborate ornamentation, bold and delicate carvings, stately pillars and magnificent pavilions. The monuments contain a great wealth of iconographic and traditional depictions, including subjects from the Ramayana and the Mahabharata.

## GWALIOR FORT

Gwalior Fort in the city of Gwalior is one of the most invincible forts of India. It was built on a hill of sandstone and towers 100 m from the plain. The outer wall is almost 3.2 km long and the width varies from 200 m to 1 km. It was here that Tantia Tope and the Rani of Jhansi fought during the First War of Indian Independence. The Rani of Jhansi laid down her life in an assault by the British to capture this fort.

## MONUMENTS AT MAHABALIPURAM

Mahabalipuram is a temple town situated along the shores of the Bay of Bengal, about 60 km from Chennai. The Shore Temple at Mahabalipuram, a coastal village 50 km south of Madras, was built in the 7th century, during the reign of Pallava king Rajasimha. The temple, with its beautiful polygonal dome, enshrines Lord Vishnu and Shiva. The magnificent *ratha* cave temples of Mahabalipuram were built by Pallava king Narsimha in the 7th and 8th centuries. It is famous for its *rathas* (temples in the form of chariots), *mandapas* (cave sanctuaries), and giant open-air reliefs such as the famous 'Descent of the Ganges'.

## HAWA MAHAL

The signature building of Jaipur, the Hawa Mahal, a multilayered palace, was built by Sawai Pratap Singh in 1799. The Hawa Mahal is an interplay of red and pink sandstone, carefully outlined with white borders and motifs, having pink semi-octagonal and delicately honeycombed sandstone windows. It was originally built to allow royal ladies to observe everyday life in the street below without being seen themselves.

## INDIA GATE

India Gate, a major tourist attraction in Delhi, is a memorial built to commemorate the sacrifice of over 80,000 Indian soldiers in World War I and the Third Anglo-Afghan War. An imposing 42 m high arch, it was designed by the famous architect Edwin Lutyens and initially named All India War Memorial. The building is made of red and pale sandstone and granite. 'INDIA' is written on both sides on the top of arch. It is also the site of the Indian Army's Tomb of the Unknown Soldier. Here burns the Amar Jawan Jyoti (the flame of the immortal soldier).

## JAMA MASJID

The Jama Masjid of Delhi, built in 1656, is the country's largest mosque. It was built by Mughal Emperor Shah Jahan. It has a courtyard capable of holding 25,000 devotees. It is also known as Masjid-i-Jahanuma or 'mosque commanding a view of the world'. It was built with red sandstone and white marble.

## JANTAR MANTAR

Sawai Jai Singh II of Jaipur, a keen astronomer and a noble in the Mughal court, built the Jantar Mantar, an observatory with large masonry instruments to correct the errors of brass and metal astronomical instruments. Some of the devices in the observatory are the Samrat Yantra, a simple equal hour sundial; the Ram Yantra for reading altitudinal angles; Jai Prakash for ascertaining the position of the Sun and other celestial bodies; and the Misra Yantra, which is a combination of four scientific gadgets.

## KAMAKHYA TEMPLE

The Kamakhya Temple, situated aloft Neelachal Parbat in Guwahati, was built in honour of Goddess Kamakhya or Sati, an incarnation of Goddess Durga or Shakti. King Nara Narayana of Cooch Behar rebuilt it in 1665 after it was destroyed by foreign invaders.

## HUMAYUN'S TOMB

Built in 1570, the famous Humayun's tomb in Delhi is a fine specimen of Mughal architecture. This historic monument was erected by Humayun's queen Hamida Banu Begam at a huge cost. High rubble walls enclose a square garden separated into four large squares by causeways and water channels. Each square is again divided into smaller squares by pathways, forming a typical Mughal garden in the *charbagh* style. The last Mughal emperor, Bahadur Shah Zafar II, had taken refuge in this tomb during the First War of Indian Independence in 1857.

## KHAJURAHO MONUMENTS

Khajuraho, the ancient Kharjjuravahaka, is located in Madhya Pradesh and was the principal seat of authority of Chandella rulers. Yasovarman (AD 954) built the temple of Vishnu, now famous as Lakshmana temple, while the others are Visvanatha, Parsvanatha and Jagadambi. The largest and grandest temple of Khajuraho is the immortal Kandariya Mahadeva, attributed to King Ganda (AD 1017– AD 1029).

## MEENAKSHI TEMPLE

The ancient city of Madurai was built by Pandyan king Kulashekarar in the 6th century BC. One of the most beautiful buildings in the city is the Meenakshi Temple, dedicated to Meenakshi, the consort of Lord Shiva. There are 985 richly carved pillars adorned with exquisite murals that celebrate the ethereal beauty of Meenakshi and scenes of her wedding with Shiva.

## MYSORE PALACE

The Mysore Palace, built in Indo-Saracenic style with domes, turrets, arches, and colonnades in Mysore, Karnataka, has often been compared with the Buckingham Palace. The palace was built by the twenty-fourth Wodeyar Raja in 1912 and has been converted into a museum, holding souvenirs, paintings, jewellery and royal costumes once possessed by the Wodeyars. The Golden Royal Elephant Throne, the Durbar Hall, and the Kalyan Mandap (wedding hall) are the main attractions.

## NALANDA

Nalanda, founded in the 5th century AD, is famous as the ancient seat of Buddhist learning. Hiuen Tsang stayed here in the 7th century AD and recorded a detailed description of the excellence of the education system and purity of monastic life practised here. Around 2,000 teachers and 10,000 monks-students across the Buddhist world lived and studied here at one time. Emperor Ashoka and Harshavardhana were some of its most celebrated patrons. They built temples, monasteries, and *viharas* here.

## PURANA QUILA

Purana Quila in Delhi has been built on a small hill standing on the banks of the Yamuna river, with its massive rubble wall and imposing gateway. The structure houses a mosque, which has a double-storeyed octagonal tower. The construction was carried out by the Afghan ruler Sher Shah Suri between 1538 and 1545.

## QUTB MINAR AND ITS MONUMENTS

The Qutb Minar, built in the 13th century, is the highest tower in India at 72.5 m. It has a diameter of 14.32 m at the base and 2.75 m at the top. The complex has many other important monuments such as the Alai Darwaza, Quwwat-ul-Islam mosque, the tomb of Iltumish, and the Alai Minar.

## RED FORT

The Red Fort is so called because of the red stone with which it is built. Mughal emperor Shah Jahan laid the foundation stone of the Red Fort in 1618. With a circumference of 2.41 km, the fort is an irregular octagon and has two entrances, the Lahore and Delhi Gates. Built on the banks of the Yamuna, it served as the capital of the Mughals till 857. The Red Fort was declared a UNESCO world heritage site in 2007.

## SUN TEMPLE, KONARK

The Sun Temple in Konark, located in Odisha near the sacred city of Puri, is dedicated to Surya, the sun god. It is built in the shape of an enormous chariot. Its twenty-four wheels are decorated with symbolic designs and it is led by a team of six horses. The temple, declared a world heritage site by UNESCO, was built in AD 1250 during the reign of the Eastern Ganga king, Narasimhadeva. Sailors once called it the Black Pagoda because it was supposed to draw ships into the shore and cause shipwrecks.

## TAJ MAHAL

Mughal emperor Shah Jahan built the Taj Mahal on the bank of the Yamuna river in Agra, in memory of his beloved wife Mumtaz Mahal. Begun in 1631, it took seventeen years in its making. In all, twenty-eight kinds of rare, semi-precious, and precious stones were used for inlay work. The chief building material—white marble—was brought from the quarries of Makrana, in Rajasthan.

# FOOD IN INDIA

## SOME INTERESTING FACTS

**Dal churma bati** is an iconic Rajasthani dish, in which *dal* (lentils) is accompanied by *bati* (ball-shaped bread) cooked with wheat and cereal powders and *churma* (sweet dish).

**Junglee maas** or **lal maas (red meat)** is a non-vegetarian dish that evolved for the maharajas. Due to scarcity of exotic ingredients in camp kitchens, the game brought in from the hunt was simply cooked in pure ghee, salt and plenty of red chillies. The chillies gave a bright red colour to the dish.

**Wazwan** is a thirty-six-course wedding banquet from Jammu and Kashmir. It ends with qahwa, a green tea used to wash down a meal.

Asaf Jah, the first Nizam of Hyderabad, chose the *kulcha* as the official emblem of the Asaf Jahi dynasty.

Hyderabad **haleem** is a popular dish eaten during Ramadan. It is a stew made of pounded wheat and goat meat, cooked in *ghee* over firewood for twelve hours.

**Sadya** is the traditional vegetarian feast of Kerala. Usually served as lunch, it consists of parboiled pink rice, side dishes, savouries, pickles, and desserts spread out on a plantain leaf. Tradition insists that the tapering end of the leaf points to the left of the seated guest. Rice is served on the lower half of the leaf.

Asaf-ud-Daulah's aim in building the Bara Imambara in Lucknow was to provide employment for people in the region who were devastated by persistent famines.

According to a story, the 12th-century Hoysala king, Veera Ballala II, lost his way on a hunting spree. The hungry king was treated by an old woman to *benda kalu* (Kannada, for boiled beans). The grateful king remembered this place as Bendakaluru, which over time became Bengaluru.

The fabulous *kakori kebab* is named after a sleepy town near Lucknow. Legend has it that the extremely soft kebabs were developed for the dining pleasure of one of the local nawabs, who had lost his teeth but not his appetite. Other scholars speculate that the soft kebabs were meant for aged pilgrims who visited Sufi saint Bhikan Shah's tomb.

## DID YOU KNOW?

- There are 9 PIN regions in the country. The first 8 are geographical regions and the digit 9 is reserved for the APO- Army Post office or FPO- Field Post Office.

- Chaturanga, a Sanskrit name for a battle formation mentioned in the Indian epic Mahabharata, is often regarded as the earliest precursor to modern chess.

- The common styles of kalamkari originated in the state of Andhra Pradesh and are named as 'Srikalahasti' and 'Machalipatnam'

- The tandoor is a clay oven. Used originally in northern India and Pakistan, its name is derived from Arabic tannur meaning 'oven'.

- The name 'Banyan' comes from a Gujarati word meaning 'man of the trading caste'. Though it originally denoted a Hindu merchant, the term came to be applied by Europeans to a tree under which such traders worked.

- The Kaziranga National Park in Assam contains about fifteen species of the threatened mammals in India. It has the world's largest population of Indian rhinoceros and a huge population of elephants.

- The Red panda is the state animal of Sikkim.
- The Great Indian Bustard was one of the names to be proposed when the national bird of India was under consideration.

## CALENDAR OF EVENTS

### NATIONAL AND INTERNATIONAL DAYS

| JANUARY | |
|---|---|
| 12 | NATIONAL YOUTH DAY |
| 15 | ARMY DAY |
| 15–21 | PIN CODE WEEK |
| 23 | NETAJI SUBHAS BOSE'S BIRTHDAY ANN./ NATIONAL DAY OF PATRIOTISM / DESH PREM DIVAS |
| 25 | INDIA TOURISM DAY |
| 26 | REPUBLIC DAY |
| 30 | MARTYRS' DAY |
| 30 | NATIONAL CLEANLINESS DAY |
| FEBRUARY | |
| 24 | EXCISE DAY |
| MARCH | |
| 8 | INTERNATIONAL WOMEN'S DAY |
| 15 | CONSUMERS DAY |
| 16 | IMMUNIZATION DAY |
| 21 | WORLD FORESTRY DAY |
| 21 | INTERNATIONAL DAY FOR THE ELIMINATION OF RACIAL DISCRIMINATION |
| 22 | WORLD DAY FOR WATER |
| 23 | WORLD METEOROLOGICAL DAY |
| 24 | WORLD TB DAY |

| APRIL | |
|---|---|
| 7 | WORLD HEALTH DAY |
| 13 | JALLIANWALA BAGH MASSACRE / BAISAKHI |
| 14 | CUSTOMS DAY |
| 22 | WORLD EARTH DAY |
| 23 | WORLD BOOK DAY |

| MAY | |
|---|---|
| 1 | INTERNATIONAL LABOUR DAY / MAY DAY |
| 5 | NATIONAL LABOUR DAY |
| 8 | WORLD RED CROSS DAY |
| 17 | WORLD TELECOMMUNICATIONS DAY |
| 31 | NO TOBACCO DAY |

| JUNE | |
|---|---|
| 5 | WORLD ENVIRONMENT DAY |
| 26 | INTERNATIONAL DAY AGAINST DRUG ABUSE AND ILLICIT TRAFFICKING |

| JULY | |
|---|---|
| 11 | WORLD POPULATION DAY |

| AUGUST | |
|---|---|
| 1–7 | WORLD BREASTFEEDING WEEK |
| 15 | INDEPENDENCE DAY |
| 23–6 | NATIONAL FORTNIGHT ON EYE DONATION |

| SEPTEMBER | |
|---|---|
| 5 | TEACHERS' DAY |
| 8 | INTERNATIONAL LITERACY DAY |
| 14 | HINDI DIVAS |
| 23 | WORLD DEAF DAY |
| 27 | WORLD TOURISM DAY |

| OCTOBER | |
|---|---|
| 1 | NATIONAL VOLUNTARY BLOOD DONATION DAY |
| 1 | INTERNATIONAL DAY FOR ELDERLY PEOPLE |
| 2 | MAHATMA GANDHI'S BIRTHDAY |
| 2 | ANTI-LEPROSY DAY |
| 2–8 | ANTI-UNTOUCHABILITY WEEK |
| 8 | AIR FORCE DAY |
| 9 | WORLD POST DAY |
| 10 | NATIONAL POST DAY |
| 13 | INTERNATIONAL DAY FOR NATURAL DISASTER REDUCTION (IDNDR) |
| 16 | WORLD FOOD DAY |
| 24 | UN DAY |
| 28 | WORLD THRIFT DAY |
| 31 | INDIRA GANDHI'S DEATH ANNIVERSARY (ANTI-TERRORISM DAY) |

| NOVEMBER | |
|---|---|
| 2 | ALL SAINTS' DAY |
| 9 | LEGAL SERVICES DAY |
| 14 | NEHRU'S BIRTHDAY/CHILDREN'S DAY |
| 16 | INTERNATIONAL DAY FOR TOLERANCE AND PEACE |
| 19 | NATIONAL INTEGRATION DAY (INDIRA GANDHI'S BIRTHDAY) |
| 20 | CHILD RIGHTS DAY |

## DECEMBER

| | |
|---|---|
| 1 | WORLD AIDS DAY |
| 2 | NATIONAL POLLUTION CONTROL DAY |
| 3 | INTERNATIONAL DAY OF DISABLED PERSONS |
| 3 | BHOPAL GAS TRAGEDY DAY |
| 4 | NAVAL DAY |
| 10 | HUMAN RIGHTS DAY |
| 14 | NATIONAL ENERGY CONSERVATION DAY |

# LANGUAGE AND LITERATURE

## GLOSSARY OF LITERARY TERMS

**Adventure novel:** The adventure novel is a literary genre of fiction that deals primarily with exciting incidents. It involves physical action, risk and danger, and is characterized by a fast-paced plot. Examples: *Treasure Island* by Robert Louis Stevenson; *The Swiss Family Robinson* by Johann David Wyss.

**Allegory:** Allegory is the use of a story, poem or picture to convey a meaning other than the literal one. Symbolic actions or representations are used to reveal a hidden meaning, typically moral or political. Examples: *The Lord of the Rings* by J.R.R. Tolkien; *The Wonderful Wizard of Oz* by Frank Baum.

**Antagonist:** An antagonist is a character or an institution that opposes the main character, or the main characters in a literary work. Examples: Iago in William Shakespeare's *Othello, the Moor of Venice;* The Queen of Hearts in *Alice's Adventures in Wonderland* by Lewis Carroll.

**Autobiography:** An autobiography is a book about the life of a person, written by that person. Examples: *My Experiments with Truth* by Mohandas Karamchand Gandhi; *The Story of My Life* by Helen Keller.

**Ballad:** A ballad is a form of verse, often a narrative set to music. Examples: *The Rime of the Ancient Mariner* by Samuel Taylor Coleridge; *Ballad of Reading Gaol* by Oscar Wilde.

**Biography:** A biography is a description or account of someone's life and times. Examples: *Oscar Wilde* by Richard Ellman; *Steve Jobs: The Exclusive Biography* by Walter Issacson.

**Couplet:** A pair of successive lines in a verse, which typically rhyme and have the same metre is a couplet. However, not all couplets necessarily rhyme, and a poem may use white space to mark out couplets that do not rhyme. Example: 'True wit is nature to advantage dress'd / What oft was thought, but ne'er so well express'd '—Alexander Pope, *An Essay on Criticism*, Part II.

**Detective Fiction:** Detective fiction is a branch of crime fiction in which one or more detectives, either professional or amateur, investigate a crime, often murder. Examples: *Sherlock Holmes* series by Arthur Conan Doyle; *Nancy Drew* series by Carolyn Keene.

**Dialogue:** It is basically a conversation between two or more people which forms a part of a book, play or film, and leads to the exploration of a subject or resolution of a conflict. Its origins can be found in classical Greek and Indian literature. Example: The dialogue between Krishna and Arjuna in the Mahabharata which forms the basis of the Bhagavad Gita.

**Drama:** A play for theatre, radio, film or television. It is also defined as a composition which in prose or verse is intended to portray life in general, or to portray a particular character. It is characterized by conflicting and contrasting emotions, and is generally of a serious nature. Examples: *Hamlet, Prince of Denmark* by Shakespeare; *Oedipus the King* by Sophocles.

**Elegy:** In literature, an elegy is a mournful or plaintive poem, especially a funeral song or a lament for the dead. Examples: *Easter 1916* by W.B. Yeats; *Elegy Written in a Country Churchyard* by Thomas Grey.

**Epic:** An epic is a lengthy narrative poem, containing details of heroic deeds and events significant to a culture or nation. Examples: *Odyssey* by Homer; Ramayana by Valmiki.

**Fiction:** Fiction is any form of narrative which deals, in part or in whole, with events that are not factual, but rather imaginary and invented by its author. Examples: *Harry Potter* series by J.K. Rowling; *The Count of Monte Cristo* by Alexandre Dumas

**Genre:** Genre is a style or category of art or literature. Some of the different genres of literature are adventure, romance, fiction, suspense, and thriller.

**Gothic Novel:** Gothic fiction (also Gothic horror) is a genre of literature that combines elements of both horror and romance. Examples: *Frankenstein* by Mary Shelley; *Strange Case of Dr Jekyll and Mr Hyde* by Robert Louis Stevenson.

**Lyric:** Lyric is usually a form of poetry with rhyme schemes that express personal and emotional feelings. Example: Shakespeare's sonnets.

**Monologue:** In a monologue, the character may be speaking his or her thoughts aloud, directly addressing another character, or speaking to the audience. Monologues are common across the range of dramatic media. Examples: 'To be or not to be' in Shakespeare's *Hamlet*.

**Narrator:** A narrator is, within any story (literary work, movie, play, verbal account), the person who conveys the story to the audience. When the narrator is also a character within the story, he or she is sometimes known as the viewpoint character. Example: Ishmael in *Moby Dick* by Herman Melville.

**Non-fiction:** Non-fiction or is an account, narrative or representation of a subject based on facts. Examples: *The Second World War* by Winston Churchill; *The Art of Happiness* by Dalai Lama.

**Novel:** A novel is a long narrative in prose. Examples: *Oliver Twist* by Charles Dickens; *The Great Gatsby* by F. Scott Fitzgerald.

**Ode:** An ode is typically a lyrical verse written in praise of, or dedicated to, something or someone which captures the poet's interest or serves as an inspiration for the ode. Examples: *Ode to the West Wind* by P.B. Shelley; *Ode to Autumn* by John Keats.

**Prologue:** A prologue is an opening to a story that establishes the setting and gives background details, often some earlier story that tie into the main one, and other miscellaneous information. Example: Prologue to *The Canterbury Tales* by Geoffrey Chaucer.

**Prose:** Prose is the common written or spoken language, without a defined metrical structure. It has been adopted for the majority of spoken dialogue, factual discourse as well as in topical and fictional writings due to its loosely defined structure. Examples: *Collected Prose* by Charles Olson, *Short Stories* by O. Henry.

**Protagonist:** A protagonist is the main character of a literary, theatrical, cinematic, video game, or musical narrative, around whom the events of the plot revolve and with whom the audience is supposed to share the most empathy. Examples: Jim Hawkins in *Treasure Island* by R.L. Stevenson; Phileas Fogg in *Around the World in Eighty Days* by Jules Verne.

**Rhyme:** A rhyme is a repetition of similar sounds in two or more words and is most often used in poetry and songs. The word 'rhyme' may also refer to a short poem, such as a rhyming couplet or other brief rhyming poems such as nursery rhymes. Example: *The Dyer's Hand* by W.H. Auden.

**Short Story:** A short story is a work of fiction that is usually written in prose. Since the short story format includes a wide range of genres and styles, the actual length is determined by the individual author's preference. Examples: *Aesop's Fables* by Aesop; *A Quiver Full of Arrows* by Jeffrey Archer.

**Sonnet:** The sonnet is one of several forms of lyric poetry originating in Europe. It has come to signify a poem of fourteen lines that follows a strict rhyme scheme and specific structure. Examples: *Shall I Compare Thee to a Summer's Day* by Shakespeare; *On His Blindness* by John Milton.

**Theme:** A theme is the main idea, or message, of an essay, paragraph, or a book. The message may be about life, society, or human nature. Themes often explore ageless and universal ideas and may be implied rather than stated explicitly.

**Verse:** A verse is a single line in metrical composition. However, the word has come to represent any division or grouping of words in such a composition, traditionally called a stanza. Example: 'Whirl up, sea / Whirl your pointed pines / Splash your great pines / On our rocks / Hurl your green over us / Cover us with your pools of fir.' Taken from the poem 'Oread' by Hilda Doolittle.

# SOME ENGLISH WORDS WITH INDIAN ORIGINS

**Avatar:** incarnation, from Sanskrit word *avataar*

**Bandanna:** headscarf, from the Hindi word *bandhana*

**Bungalow:** from Hindi *bangla* 'belonging to Bengal', from a type of cottage built for early European settlers in Bengal

**Chit:** a letter or note, from the Hindi word *chitthi*

**Cot:** portable bed, from the Hindi word *khat*

**Yoga:** Hindu spiritual and ascetic discipline, from the Sanskrit word *yog*.

**Dacoit:** a member of a class of criminals who engage in organized robbery and murder, from the Hindi word *dakait*

**Jungle:** another word for wilderness or forest, from the Hindi word *jangal*

**Ayurveda:** knowledge of life, from the Sanskrit word *ayurveda*

**Candy:** piece of sugar, from the Sanskrit word *khanda*

**Dinghy:** tiny boat, from the Hindi word *dingi*

**Catamaran:** tied-up wood, from the Tamil word *kattu maram*

**Coir:** rope or thread to be twisted, from the Malayalam word *kayaru*

**Mango:** a fruit, from the Tamil word *manga*

**Bangle:** a type of bracelet, from the Hindi word *baangli*

# AUTHORS OF INDIA

## ANAND, MULK RAJ (1905-2004)

Mulk Raj Anand was an Indian author of novels, short stories, and essays on criticism in English, known for his realistic and sympathetic portrayal of the poor in India. He was one of the first Indian novelists to write in English, using Hindi and Punjabi phrases to enrich the language. His classic novels are the *Untouchable* and *Coolie*.

## BHARATHIAR, SUBRAMANIA (1882-1921)

Tamil poet Subramania Bharathiar is often regarded as the father of modern Tamil. He was one of the earliest to envision a united India. In his poems and prose writings, he implored Indians to bury regional differences and foster a strong bonding. Later, his powerful lyrics appeared in the collections *Swadesa Gitangal* (1908) and *Janma Bhoomi* (1909).

## CHANAKYA (350 BC–383 BC)

Chanakya, also known as Kautilya and Vishnugupta, was a statesman and philosopher who wrote a classic treatise on polity, *Arthashastra*. He was an advisor to the first Mauryan emperor Chandragupta and helped him overthrow the powerful Nanda dynasty at Pataliputra, Magadha. *Arthashastra* discusses monetary and fiscal policies, welfare, international relations and war strategies in detail. *Nitishastra* is a treatise on the ideal way of life, and demonstrates Chanakya's in-depth study of the Indian way of life.

## CHATTERJEE, BANKIM CHANDRA (1838–1894)

Bankim Chandra Chatterjee's novels established prose as a literary form in Bengali. He was born in a Brahmin family, and served as a deputy magistrate in the Indian Civil Service from 1858, until his retirement in 1891. His first novel *Durgeshnondini* is also the first ever novel in Bengali. Some of his other notable works are *Rajmohan's Wife, Kapalkundala, Mrinalini, Bisabrksa, Indira, Yugalanguriya Radharani, Chandrasekhar, Rajani, Debi Chaudhurani*, and *Anandamath*. He also composed India's national song, *Vande mataram*.

## CHATTOPADHYAY, SARATCHANDRA (1876–1938)

Saratchandra Chattopadhyay was one of the most popular Bengali novelists of the early 20th century. Born in Devanandapur, Bengal, his childhood was spent in poverty. The two stories written in his youth that have survived are 'Korel' and 'Kashinath'. Saratchandra came of age at a time when the national movement was gaining momentum. He chose the novel as an apt medium for depicting the social turmoil, and in his hands it became a powerful weapon of socio-political reform. Some of his best known novels are *Palli Samaj* (1916), *Charitraheen* (1917), *Devdas* (1917), *Nishkriti* (1917), *Srikanta* in four parts (1917, 1918, 1927, 1933), *Griha Daha* (1920), *Sesh Prasna* (1929), and *Sesher Parichay* (published posthumously, 1939). His works have been translated into all the major Indian languages and adapted into film and for the stage.

## CHAUDHURI, NIRAD C. (1897–1999)

Nirad C. Chaudhuri was an Indian-born author, scholar and cultural commentator. Born in 1897 in a small town of Bangladesh, he moved to the

UK in the 1970s. He wrote his first work *The Autobiography of an Unknown Indian* when he was in his early fifties. Some of his other remarkable works include *A Passage to England* and *Clive of India*. He was awarded the Sahitya Akademi Award for *Scholar Extraordinary*, his biography of Max Muller.

## DESAI, ANITA (b. 1937)

Anita Desai is an Indian novelist, short story writer, children's author and Emeritus John E. Burchard Professor of Humanities at the Massachusetts Institute of Technology. She was born in Mussoorie and published her first story at the age of nine. As a novelist, she made her debut in 1963 with *The Peacock*. Her other novels include *Voices of the City, Fire on the Mountain, Clear Light of Day, In Custody*, and *Fasting, Feasting*. Her book *The Village by the Sea* (1982) won the Guardian Children's Fiction Award.

## DESAI, KIRAN (b. 1971)

Born in 1971, Kiran Desai received her education in India, England, and the US. While her first book, *Hullabaloo in the Guava Orchard*, won the Betty Trask Award, her second novel, *The Inheritance of Loss*, received the 2006 Man Booker Prize and the National Book Critics Circle Fiction Award. She is the daughter of noted author Anita Desai.

## DEVI, MAHASHWETA (b. 1926)

Mahashweta Devi is a social activist and writer. Her first book, *Jhansir Rani (The Queen of Jhansi)*, was published in 1956. This work also marked the beginning of a prolific literary career. In the last forty years, she has published twenty collections of short stories and close to 100 novels, primarily in Bengali. Some of her works are *Amrita Sanchay, Andhanmalik, Hajar Churashir Ma* (Mother of 1084*)* and *Aranyer Adhikar* (Rights of the Forest). For her contribution to literature, she was awarded the Jnanpith Award in 1996 and the Magsaysay Award in 1997.

## GHALIB, MIRZA (1797-1869)

Mirza Asadullah Baig Khan was an all-time great classical Urdu and Persian poet of the Indian subcontinent. He wrote several ghazals, which have been interpreted and sung in many different ways by various artistes. He became famous in 1850 when he was appointed poet laureate to the last Mughal emperor Bahadur Shah II or Bahadur Shah Zafar, himself an accomplished poet. Ghalib is considered to be one of the most influential poets to have composed ghazals.

## GHOSH, AMITAV (b. 1956)

Amitav Ghosh is one of the best-known contemporary Indian authors, writing in English. Born in Calcutta, he studied at Dehradun, New Delhi, Alexandria, and Oxford. His first job was at the *Indian Express* newspaper in New Delhi. His books include *The Circle of Reason*, *The Shadow Lines*, *In an Antique Land*, *The Calcutta Chromosome*, *The Glass Palace*, *The Hungry Tide*, and *River of Smoke*. He was awarded the Padma Shri in 2007, Grand Prize for Fiction, Frankfurt eBook Award (2001) for *The Glass Palace* and Sahitya Akademi Award (1990) for *The Shadow Lines*.

## KABIR (1440–1518)

Kabir was an Indian mystic poet and saint, who greatly influenced the Bhakti movement through his writings. He is famous for his *dohas* (two-line verses) that he recited in vernacular Hindi. His greatest work is *Bijak* ('The Seedling'), a collection of poems based on spirituality. He tried to unite Hindus and Muslims by preaching unity of all religions. He was also the forerunner of Sikhism, later established as a religion by Guru Nanak.

## KALIDASA (AD 5TH CENTURY)

Kalidasa was India's greatest Sanskrit poet and dramatist. Tradition mentions Kalidasa as a contemporary and court poet of King Chandragupta Vikramaditya of the Gupta dynasty. He is said to be the most brilliant of the 'nine gems' at the king's court. History records that about forty-one works are attributed to Kalidasa but the following seven are undoubtedly his best: two lyric poems, *Ritusamhara* and *Meghaduta*; two mahakavyas *Kumarasambhavam* and *Raghuvamsham*; and three plays, *Malavikagnimitram*, *Vikramorvashiyam* and *Abhijnanashakuntalam*. However, apart from his works nothing is known with certainty about his life.

## KAMBAN (AD 9TH CENTURY)

Kamban was a renowned poet and a scholar of Tamil and Sanskrit. He is the writer of *Ramavataram*, the Tamil version of Valmiki's Ramayana. Kamban's Ramayana, as it is also known, is not a translation of the Sanskrit epic by Valmiki, but an original retelling of the story of Rama as the incarnation of Lord Tirumal (Mahavishnu). It earned him the title Kavichakravarti ('emperor among poets'). Kamban's version of Ramayana is a landmark in the history of Tamil literature.

## KHUSRAU, AMIR (1253–1325)

Amir Khusrau Dehlavi, a Persian poet associated with the royal courts of more than seven rulers of the Delhi Sultanate, is also popular in much of north India and Pakistan because of the playful riddles, songs and legends attributed to him. He was the son of a Turkish officer in the service of Iltutmish, sultan of Delhi. Sometimes known as the 'parrot of India', he wrote numerous works, among them five *divans*. His *Khamsah* deals with general themes famous in Islamic literature. In addition to his poetry, he is known for a number of prose works, and two historical poems such as *Nuh Sipihr* ('The Nine Heavens') and *Tughluq-namah* ('The Book of Tughluq'). He also made a notable contribution to Sufi music.

## BHARATA MUNI

Bharata Muni was an ancient Indian sage who authored *Natya-Shastra*, a detailed treatise and handbook on dramatic art, that deals with all aspects of the classical Sanskrit theatre, music, and dance. He lived around 400 BC. According to legend, Lord Shiva sent his disciple Tandu to teach Bharata Muni the authentic principles of dance. Bharata included these principles in the chapter entitled 'Tandava Lakshana' in *Natya-Shastra*. Bharata Muni then went on to evolve ten basic postures of the body, nine of the neck, thirty-six of the hand, and thirteen of the head—postures that require the disciplined use of the entire body and all of its expressions.

## NARAYAN, R.K. (1906–2001)

R.K. Narayan was one of India's best-known authors writing in English. Born Rasipuram Krishnaswami Ayyar Narayanswami in Madras in 1906, he graduated from the University of Mysore in 1930. Narayan worked as a teacher and, in 1935, published his first novel, *Swami and Friends*. The novel related stories of a group of boys in the fictional southern Indian town of Malgudi that went on to become the setting for much more of Narayan's fiction. His novels include *The English Teacher*, *Waiting for the Mahatma* and *The Guide*. He was bestowed with the Sahitya Akademi award in 1958 for *The Guide*. He died on 13 May 2001, in Chennai.

## LAHIRI, JHUMPA (b. 1967)

Jhumpa Lahiri is an Indian American author who became famous when her debut short story collection *The Interpreter of Maladies* won the 2000 Pulitzer Prize for Fiction. Her first novel *The Namesake* was adapted into a film. Born in London, the daughter of Bengali Indian immigrants, she grew up in Rhode Island and now lives in New York. Her second and latest collection of short stories, *Unaccustomed Earth*, was published in 2008.

## PANINI (5TH CENTURY BC)

Panini was a Sanskrit grammarian who developed a comprehensive and scientific theory of phonetics, phonology and morphology. Sanskrit was the classical literary language of the Indian Hindus and Panini is considered a major exponent of the language and literature. A treatise called *Astadhyayi* (or *Astaka*) is Panini's seminal work.

## PREMCHAND, MUNSHI (1880-1936)

Born Dhanpat Rai Srivastava, Premchand was one of the most prominent authors in Hindi. Born near Varanasi, his early education was in a *madarasa*, where he learnt Urdu and later became a schoolteacher. He initially wrote as a freelancer in Urdu. In his early short stories, he depicted the nationalist sentiment that was sweeping India in the first decade of the 20th century. *Soz-e-Watan*, a collection of such stories published by Premchand in 1907, attracted the attention of the British government and was banned. Premchand shifted to writing in Hindi after he had already developed his reputation as an Urdu writer. Premchand was the first Hindi author to introduce realism in his writings and to address social problems. Some of his most famous works are *Sevasadan, Rangamanch, Ghaban, Nirmala* and *Godan*.

## PRITAM, AMRITA (1919-2005)

Amrita Pritam was a famous Punjabi author of the 20th century. Born in 1919 in Gujranwala (now in Pakistan), she wrote more than 100 books. Her poems express the deep anguish of the carnage of the Partition of India that she witnessed in 1947. Some of her works include *Khamoshi Se Pehle, Rang Ka Patta* and *Pinjar*. She received the Jnanpith Award in 1981 for *Kagaj Te Canvas*. Loved across the borders of India and Pakistan, Amrita Pritam died on 31 October 2005.

## RAO, RAJA (1908-2006)

Raja Rao was a writer of novels and short stories. Born in 1908 in Mysore, he was educated at Aligarh Muslim University and later in France. He generally wrote in English, and some of his most famous works are *The Serpent and the Rope, Kanthapura* and *Great Indian Way: A Life of Mahatma Gandhi*. From 1965 to 1983, Rao lectured on Indian philosophy at the University of Texas, Austin. He died of heart failure on 8 July 2006 in Austin.

## ROY, ARUNDHATI (b. 1959)

Arundhati Roy is an Indian author writing in English. She became the first Indian to win the Booker Prize for her debut novel *The God of Small Things*

(1997). She is also an activist who focuses on issues related to social justice. Born in 1959 in Shillong, she spent her childhood in Kerala and went on to study architecture in Delhi. Following the success of her debut novel, she concentrated her writing on political issues. Some of her works include *The Greater Common Good*, *The End of Imagination* and *The Cost of Living*. In January 2006, she was awarded the Sahitya Akademi Award for her collection of essays, *The Algebra of Infinite Justice*, but she declined it.

## RUSHDIE, SALMAN (b. 1947)

Salman Rushdie is a British-Indian novelist and essayist. He gained worldwide recognition after his second novel, *Midnight's Children*, won the Booker Prize in 1981. Born in 1947 in Bombay, Rushdie was educated at Rugby School and the University of Cambridge in England. He worked in London as an advertising copywriter and published his first novel *Grimus* in 1975. His next novel was *Midnight's Children* (1981), an allegory about modern India. The *Satanic Verses* was his most controversial work. Some of his other remarkable works include *The Moor's Last Sigh*, *The Ground Beneath Her Feet*, *Fury*, and *Shalimar the Clown*.

## SETH, VIKRAM (b. 1952)

Vikram Seth is a famous poet, author, travel writer and biographer. He is chiefly known for the novel *A Suitable Boy*, considered to be one of the longest novels ever published in a single volume in the English language. Born in Kolkata, he studied at Oxford University and later persued classical Chinese poetry at Nanking University in China. His first novel, *The Golden Gate* (1986), a novel written in verse, impressed readers with its uniqueness of form. His award-winning travelogue *From Heaven Lake* (1983) is based on his experiences of a hitchhiking trip from China through Nepal to India.

## SHARMA, VISHNU

The scholar Vishnu Sharma is credited with the composition of the ancient book of children's fables called *Panchatantra*. The stories were created to teach the three dull-witted sons of King Amrashakti the five secrets of good administration, kingship, and worldly affairs. The five *tantras* have been expounded with the help of animal fables.

## TAGORE, RABINDRANATH (1861–1941)

Rabindranath Tagore was a Bengali poet, novelist, musician, painter, and playwright who reshaped Bengali literature and music. In 1913, he became the first Indian to win the Nobel Prize for Literature. Born in 1861 in a wealthy family of Calcutta, he received his initial education at home.

In 1874, his first poem *Abhilaash* ('Desire') was published anonymously in a magazine called *Tattobodhini*. Some of his celebrated poems include *Manasi* ('The Ideal One'), *Sonar Tari* ('The Golden Boat'), *Gitimalya* ('Wreath of Songs'), and *Balaka* ('The Flight of Cranes'). He wrote *Sahaj Path* to help children learn Bengali in a lucid way. Tagore's most acclaimed rendering of his own poems in English is the 103 translated poems of *Gitanjali* ('Song Offerings') published in 1912 on his second tour to London. Tagore's major plays are *Raja* ('The King of the Dark Chamber'), *Dakghar* ('The Post Office'), *Muktadhara* ('The Waterfall'), and *Raktakaravi* ('Red Oleanders'). His famous novels are *Gora* (1910), *Ghare-Baire* (*The Home and the World*, 1916), and *Yogayog* (Crosscurrents, 1929). Besides these, he wrote musical dramas, dance dramas, short stories, essays, travel diaries, and two autobiographies. He was knighted by the British government in 1915. However, a few years later he relinquished the honour as a protest against British policies in India. Tagore died on 7 August 1941.

## TULSIDAS (1543–1623)

Tulsidas is considered one of the greatest poets in the history of medieval Hindi literature. He was probably born at Rajapur in 1543 and lived most of his life in Varanasi. He wrote *Ramcharitmanas* ('Sacred Lake of the Acts of Rama') in Awadhi, an eastern Hindi dialect. Eleven other works are attributed with some certainty to him. These include *Krishna Gitavali*, a series of sixty-one songs in honour of Krishna; *Vinay Pattrika*, a series of 279 verse passages addressed to Hindu sacred places and deities (chiefly Rama and Sita); and *Kavitavali*, telling incidents from the story of Rama.

## VARMA, MAHADEVI (1907–1987)

Mahadevi Varma was one of the most famous modern Hindi poets belonging to the Chhayavaad generation, a period of romanticism in modern Hindi poetry. She was awarded the Sahitya Akademi Fellowship, and the Jnanpith Award followed by both the Padma Bhushan and the Padma Vibhushan. She is renowned for her book of memoirs, *Atit Ke Chalchitra* ('Moving Frames of the Past'), and *Smriti Ki Rekhayen* ('Lines of Memory'), and *Deepshikha* ('Flame of an Earthen Lamp'), a book of fifty-one lyrics. Some of her other famous publications are *Nihar, Rashmi, Neerja,* and *Sandhya Geet.*

# AUTHORS OF THE WORLD

## AUSTEN, JANE (1775–1817)

Jane Austen was a reputed English novelist who depicted in her writings the English upper and middle class society and the lives of early 19th-century women. She was educated primarily by her father, who was a clergyman. Her literary masterpieces are *Sense and Sensibility, Pride and Prejudice, Mansfield Park*, and *Emma*. She died on 18 July 1817. Virginia Woolf called Austen 'the most perfect artist among women'.

## BLAKE, WILLIAM (1757-1827)

William Blake was an acclaimed English poet and painter. His works are rich in religious references. William went to school only long enough to learn to read and write, and then he worked in his father's shop. His parents together brought out an edition of Blake's poems and drawings, called *Songs of Innocence*. A later volume, *Songs of Experience*, tells of a mature person's realization of pain and terror in the universe. Blake died on 12 August 1827 in utter poverty.

## BLYTON, ENID (1897-1968)

Enid Mary Blyton, also known as Mary Pollock, was one of 20th century's most successful children's story writers in English. Her first poem appeared in a children's magazine when she was only fourteen and her first book of poems, *Child Whispers*, was published in 1922, when Blyton was working as a teacher and a governess. She wrote several series of adventure novels, such as *The Famous Five* and *The Secret Seven*, which are popular with children to this day. Blyton is the fourth most translated author worldwide, according to UNESCO'S Index Translationum.

## BROWNING, ROBERT (1812-1889)

Robert Browning was considered one of the greatest English poets of his time. Browning received most of his education at home. His writings popularized the use of colloquial English. His most celebrated poems include *Paracelsus, My Last Duchess, Pied Piper of Hamelin, Cavalier Tunes, Pauline, Bells and Pomegranates, How They Brought the Good News from Ghent to Aix, The Boy and the Angel, Pippa Passes* and others. One of his greatest works, *The Ring and the Book* tells the story of a murder from several points of view. As a playwright, he wrote *A Blot in the 'Scutcheon* and the historical play *Strafford: A Tragedy*. He died in 1889 in Venice, Italy.

## BYRON, LORD (1788-1824)

George Gordon or Lord Byron was an English poet and a leading figure in Romanticism. Born with a defect in his foot, he tried very hard to overcome his physical drawback and became a good swimmer, rider, boxer, and marksman. Some of his most acclaimed works are *She Walks in Beauty, When We Two Parted*, in addition to the narrative poems, *Childe Harold's*

*Pilgrimage* and *Don Juan*. His verse play *Manfred* is considered a classic. He died of fever at Mesolongion in Greece.

## CARROLL, LEWIS (1832–1898)

British author Charles Lutwidge Dodgson, better known as Lewis Carroll, is famous for his delightful limericks and children's books. After completing school, Charles entered Christ Church College, Oxford University, where he studied, worked, and lived for the rest of his life. He taught mathematics and took interest in photography. He is most remembered for his works *Alice's Adventures in Wonderland*, *Through the Looking Glass* and *The Hunting of the Snark*. He died on 14 January 1898.

## CHAUCER, GEOFFREY (1343–1400)

Geoffrey Chaucer is known to be the first notable poet writing in English. In 1386, he was elected Member of Parliament for Kent. He also served as a justice of peace. He held a number of other posts at court, serving both Edward III and his successor Richard II. Chaucer's most celebrated works are *The Canterbury Tales*, *The Legend of Good Women*, and *Troilus and Criseyde*. Chaucer disappears from historical records in around 1400, and is believed to have died soon after.

## CHEKHOV, ANTON (1860–1904)

Anton Pavlovich Chekhov wrote remarkable stories and plays, which provide deep insights into contemporary Russian society. Born in Tagonrog, he moved to Moscow, studied medicine, and started writing short, humorous pieces for journals. Some of his finest short stories were 'The Steppe', 'Ward Number Six', 'Neighbors', 'The Black Monk', 'Murder', 'Ariadne', 'My Life', and 'The Man in a Case'. His masterpieces in drama are *Uncle Vanya*, *The Seagull*, *Three Sisters*, and *The Cherry Orchard*. Chekov suffered a severe attack of tuberculosis and died on 15 July 1904 in Germany.

## COLERIDGE, SAMUEL TAYLOR (1772–1834)

Samuel Coleridge was a pioneer of 19th-century English lyrical poetry. His first book, *Poems on Various Subjects*, was published in 1796. The following year along with William Wordsworth, he published *The Lyrical Ballads*, the manifesto of English romanticism. The most remarkable feature of Coleridge's poetry is his imaginative power. There is a remarkably intense use of the supernatural noted in *The Rime of the Ancient Mariner*, *Christabel*, and *Kubla Khan*. *Biographia Literaria* is his most valuable prose work. Coleridge died in England in 1834.

## DAHL, ROALD (1916-1990)

Roald Dahl was a British author famed for his books for children filled with memorable, magical, often bizarre characters. His early life was troubled by the sudden death of his father and elder sister. Later, his career in the British Royal Air Force ended after he suffered a serious injury. His stories about the military were published in popular magazines and in the book *Over to You*. His other famous works are *The Gremlins, James and the Giant Peach, Charlie and the Chocolate Factory* and *Matilda*. Some of these have been adapted into movies. Dahl also wrote scripts for movies like *Chitty Chitty Bang Bang* and *You Only Live Twice*. His autobiographies are *Boy: Tales of Childhood* and *Going Solo*. Roald Dahl died in Oxford, England, in November 1990.

## DEFOE, DANIEL (1660-1731)

Daniel Defoe was a famous English writer, journalist and pamphleteer. He was fluent in several languages including Greek, Latin, French, Italian, and Spanish. Though he started his career as a businessman, he went on to write about society calling for reforms in religious practices, economy, social welfare, and politics using satire as a tool. In 1719, he shot into fame with *Robinson Crusoe* followed by *Moll Flanders, A Journal of the Plague Year* and *Roxana*. He died in London on 24 April 1731.

## DICKENS, CHARLES (1812-1870)

Charles John Huffam Dickens was one of the most popular authors of the 19th century, who realistically depicted in his writings the daily life of contemporary society. Severe poverty forced Charles to leave school and work in a factory. He wrote about the harsh conditions of the working class in many of his works. Some of his most celebrated works are *The Pickwick Papers, David Copperfield, Oliver Twist, A Christmas Carol, The Old Curiosity Shop, Hard Times, A Tale of Two Cities*, and *Great Expectations*. Dickens died on 9 June 1870, leaving his last novel, *The Mystery of Edwin Drood*, unfinished.

## DOYLE, ARTHUR CONAN (1859-1930)

Arthur Conan Doyle was a notable British writer, journalist, and cricketer. He studied medicine and worked as a surgeon on a whaling boat and also as a medical officer. He is best known for creating the character Sherlock Holmes who first appeared in *A Study of Scarlet*. Doyle also wrote *The Lost World* and various non-fictional works. A cricketer, Doyle played ten first-class matches for Marylebone Cricket Club. He died of a heart attack on 7 July 1930.

## DUMAS, ALEXANDRE, (1802–1870)

Alexandre Dumas was a famous French author known for the use of wit and colourful historical backgrounds in his novels. One of his most successful works is the Renaissance drama *Henry III and His Court*. Some of his famous historical novels are *The Three Musketeers*, *Twenty Years After*, *Ten Years Later*, *The Count of Monte Cristo* and *The Black Tulip*. He died in December 1870 in France. In 2002, his remains were placed in the Panthéon, in Paris, alongside those of France's greatest citizens.

## GRIMM BROTHERS

[Jacob Carl Grimm (1785–1863) and Wilhelm Carl Grimm (1786–1859)]

German-born Jacob and Wilhelm Grimm brothers are credited with collecting almost all of the Western world's fairy tales known today. This collection of over 200 tales is commonly called *Grimms' Fairy Tales*. The first volume, *Children's and Household Tales*, was published in 1812. They popularized the now-favourite characters like Snow White, Rapunzel, Cinderella, Little Red Riding Hood, and Rumpelstiltskin. They also held various positions in the government and worked as professors and librarians.

## HARDY, THOMAS (1840–1928)

Thomas Hardy was an accomplished British novelist and poet of the Victorian era. Born in Dorset, Hardy trained as an architect and moved to London where he worked while writing verse and essays. His homeland forms the setting of most of his writings, under its old name of Wessex. His remarkable works are *Far from the Madding Crowd*, *Under the Greenwood Tree*, *The Return of the Native*, *Tess of the D'Urbervilles* and *Jude the Obscure*. He died in Dorchester on 11 January 1928.

## HENRY, O. (1862–1910)

O. Henry, born William Sydney Porter, was an American writer famous for his striking short stories. He worked at Texas on a friend's ranch where he started writing stories and jokes for a newspaper. For a year, he edited a humorous weekly called *The Rolling Stone*. In 1904, he brought out his first collection of stories, *Cabbages and Kings*. Some of his most popular short stories are 'The Gift of the Magi' and 'The Ransom of Red Chief'. O. Henry died in New York City on 5 June 1910.

## JOYCE, JAMES (1882–1941)

Irish-born James Joyce is considered to be one of the most influential writers of the modernist movement of the early 20th century. After graduating from University College, he went to Paris to study medicine. In 1914, with the assistance of Ezra Pound, James Joyce's first novel, *A Portrait of the Artist as a Young Man*, began to appear in serial form. His major works include *Dubliners*, *Ulysses* and *Finnegan's Wake*. In 1940, Joyce was forced to flee to France ahead of the Nazi invasion. He died at the age of fifty-nine, on 13 January 1941 in Zurich, where he and his family had been given asylum.

## KEATS, JOHN (1795–1821)

John Keats was one of the key figures among the English Romantic poets. Initially an apprentice to a surgeon, he turned to writing poetry at a young age. His earliest attempt at verse was *Imitation of Spenser*, published in 1817 in *Poems*, his first volume of verse. Some of his celebrated poems are *Endymion, Isabella, On a Summer's Day, Ode to a Nightingale, Ode to Autumn* and *Hyperion*. Among his famous sonnets are *On First Looking into Chapman's Homer* and *When I Have Fears That I May Cease to Be*. Keats' personal life was scarred with misery and he died of tuberculosis in Rome on 23 February 1821.

## MAUPASSANT, GUY DE (1850–1893)

Henri René Albert Guy de Maupassant, born in the French province of Normandy, was a master of short stories with dramatic plots. While in Paris as a government clerk, he visited literary gatherings at the house of the famous novelist Gustave Flaubert and these inspired his works. His stories revolve around the city, familiar people and real events of life. His most significant collection of short stories include *La Maison Tellier* and *Mademoiselle Fifi*. He also wrote full-length novels like *Une Vie, Bel Ami* and *Mont Oriol*. Maupassant's last few years were tragic as he was confined to a mental asylum where he died on 6 July 1893.

## MILTON, JOHN (1608–1674)

John Milton was an English poet, pamphleteer and historian, and considered one of the most significant English authors after Shakespeare. In most of his prose work, Milton wrote about public affairs and attacked the corrupt practices of the state and the church. In *Areopagitica* (1644) he demanded the liberty of the press. He became completely blind in 1652. Milton's magnificent epic poem, *Paradise Lost,* published seven years after the Restoration of monarchy, had an immense influence on English thought.

Some of his other important works are *L'Allegro, Il Penseroso, Comus, Lycidas, Paradise Regained*, and *Samson Agonistes*. He passed away on 8 November 1674.

## ORWELL, GEORGE (1903–1950)

George Orwell, a famous English author and journalist, was born Eric Arthur Blair in present-day Bihar. After studying at Eton College, he joined the office of the Indian Imperial Police but resigned later and spent several years among the poor and outcast of Europe. These experiences surface in his works *Down and Out in Paris and London* and *The Road to Wigan Pier*. He is remembered for his works like *Animal Farm* and *Nineteen Eighty-four*. Orwell died in 1950 in London.

## SCOTT, SIR WALTER (1771–1832)

Sir Walter Scott was a Scottish novelist, poet, historian, and biographer, considered both the inventor and the greatest practitioner of the historical novel. His major literary works are *Minstrels of the Scottish Border, The Lay of the Last Minstrel, Marmion* and *Ivanhoe*. He also wrote poetry, drama and biography. In 1820, King George IV conferred on him the title of baronet.

## SHAKESPEARE, WILLIAM (1564–1616)

William Shakespeare, born in Stratford-upon-Avon, England, is one of the greatest playwrights in the history of English literature. He began a successful career in London as an actor, writer, and part-owner of a theatrical company called Lord Chamberlain's Men. His early plays were mainly comedies and histories, followed by tragedies. His celebrated tragedies were *Othello, King Lear, Macbeth, Hamlet* and *Romeo and Juliet*. Some of his important comedies were *As You Like it, A Midsummer's Night's Dream, The Two Gentlemen of Verona, Love's Labour Lost* and *The Tempest. Anthony and Cleopatra, Richard I, Julius Caesar, Henry V,* and *King John* are some of his noted historical plays. He also wrote sonnets and two long narrative poems, *Venus and Adonis* and *The Rape of Lucrece*. Shakespeare retired from the theatre in about 1610 and died in his home town on 23 April 1616.

## SHAW, GEORGE BERNARD (1856–1950)

George Bernard Shaw, born in Dublin in 1856, was one of the greatest playwrights of all time. He was also a literary critic and a socialist propagandist. He began his literary career by writing music, drama criticism, and novels. His early works were called *Plays Pleasant and Unpleasant* and his masterpieces include *Saint Joan, Caesar and Cleopatra, Major Barbara*, and *Pygmalion*. He was the first person to have been awarded both a Nobel Prize for Literature (1925) and an Academy Award (1939) for his work on *Pygmalion*.

## SHELLEY, PERCY BYSSHE (1792-1822)

P.B. Shelley is regarded as one of the finest English lyric poets. Some of the works that mark his greatest achievements are *Queen Mab* , *The Cenci, Prometheus Unbound, Adonais, Alastor, The Revolt of Islam, Epipsychidion, Hellas, Hymn to Intellectual Beauty* and *The Indian Serenade*. On 8 July 1822, Shelley drowned while sailing with a friend off Livorno in Tuscany.

## STEVENSON, ROBERT LOUIS (1850-1894)

R.L. Stevenson was a gifted Scottish poet, storyteller and essayist. Since childhood illness deprived him of many pleasures, he created a beautiful romantic world of his own. He could not attend regular school but visited lighthouses and harbours with his father. The experiences of his travel found expression in his works. His best works include *An Inland Voyage, Treasure Island, Kidnapped* and *Strange Case of Dr Jekyll and Mr Hyde*. His last work, the unfinished novel, *Weir of Hermiston*, was published posthumously in 1896.

## SWIFT, JONATHAN (1667-1745)

Jonathan Swift was a famous Irish satirist, pamphleteer, and poet, chiefly remembered for the novel *Gulliver's Travels*, which recounts the story of Lemuel Gulliver, a practical-minded Englishman trained as a surgeon, who takes to the seas when his business fails. Some of his other works are *A Modest Proposal, A Journal to Stella* and *Drapier's Letters*. Swift originally published his works under pseudonyms including Lemuel Gulliver, Isaac Bickerstaff, and M.B. Drapier. He died on 19 October 1745.

## THE BRONTE SISTERS (1816-1855)

Charlotte Bronte (1816–1855) and her sisters Emily (1818–1848) and Anne (1820–1849) have produced classics that have charmed readers from the Victorian Age to the present. Charlotte's famous works include *Jane Eyre* and *Villette*, while Anne wrote *Agnes Grey* and *The Tenant of Wildfell Hall*. Emily Bronte published only one novel in her lifetime, the enduring tragic romance called *Wuthering Heights*.

## TOLSTOY, LEO (1828-1910)

Leo Tolstoy or Count Lyev Nikolayevich Tolstoy, born in 1828 into an aristocratic family in the Tula province of the Russian empire, was a renowned novelist who created timeless masterpieces. He was orphaned at an early age and his work *Childhood, Boyhood and Youth* is a vivid fictional record of his real-life experiences. After the Crimean War, Tolstoy returned from the army and opened a school for peasant children on his estate. Tolstoy's literary masterpieces are *War and Peace*, *Anna Karenina*, *Resurrection* and *The Death of Ivan Ilyich*. His ideas on non-violent resistance, expressed in such works as *The Kingdom of God is Within You*, had a great impact on later thinkers. In 1910, he died of a heart attack at the train station of Astapovo.

### TWAIN, MARK (1835–1910)

Mark Twain, born Samuel Langhorne Clemens, is considered one of the greatest American authors. After school, he worked as a delivery boy, grocery clerk, and blacksmith's assistant, and grew up to be a Mississippi river-boat pilot. The river becomes a central character in most of his writings as in *Life on the Mississippi*. He is best known for *The Adventures of Huckleberry Finn*, *The Adventures of Tom Sawyer*, *The Innocents Abroad*, *Roughing It*, *A Tramp Abroad* and *The Prince and the Pauper*. Twain interwove a serious view of life with a crisp humour in his works. Twain died on 21 April 1910.

### VERNE, JULES (1828–1905)

French author Jules Verne is known as one of the first science fiction writers. He undertook an in-depth study of science in order to make his stories more realistic, and many of his imaginative ideas led to radical developments that actually took place in science, years later. Verne's most famous adventure works are *Five Weeks in a Balloon*, *Twenty Thousand Leagues Under the Sea*, *Around the World in Eighty Days*, *From the Earth to the Moon* and *The Mysterious Island*. Verne died in Amiens, France, on 24 March 1905.

### WILDE, OSCAR (1854–1900)

Oscar Fingal O'Flahertie Wills Wilde, born in Dublin, was a prominent writer, poet, and London's most popular playwright of his time. He established himself as a poet by winning the coveted Newdigate Prize in 1878 with a long poem, *Ravenna*. His most celebrated works include *The Importance of Being Earnest*, *Lady Windermere's Fan*, *The Picture of Dorian Gray* and *A Woman of No Importance*. He died in Paris on 30 November 1900.

### WORDSWORTH, WILLIAM (1770–1850)

William Wordsworth was one of the greatest poets, who ushered in the Romantic movement in English Literature. In 1798, Wordsworth and

Coleridge published their famous collection of *Lyrical Ballads* that launched. His best-remembered works are *The Prelude, Ode: Intimations of Immortality, An Evening Walk,* and *Descriptive Sketches, Tintern Abbey, Daffodils, The Solitary Reaper, Westminster Bridge, To Milton* and the *Lucy* poems. He was made poet laureate in 1843. He died at Rydal Mount on 23 April 1850.

## YEATS, WILLIAM BUTLER (1865–1939)

W.B. Yeats, one of the greatest English-language poets of the 20th century, was an Irish poet, dramatist and prose writer. He attended Metropolitan School of Art. Some of his remarkable works include *Easter 1916, The Ballad of Moll Magee Down, The Stolen Child* and *The Lake Isle of Innisfree.* He also established Dublin's Abbey theatre. Some of his outstanding works for the theatre are *The Countess Cathleen* (1892), *The Land of Heart's Desire* (1894), and *The King's Threshold* (1904). He received the Nobel Prize for Literature in 1923.

# MAJOR AWARDS IN LITERATURE

## MAN BOOKER PRIZE

The Man Booker Prize is an esteemed British award given annually to a full-length novel by English language writers from the UK, the Commonwealth countries, and the Republic of Ireland. Booker McConnell, a multinational company, established the award in 1968. The winner is usually announced in London's Guildhall in early October, where the winners receive 50,000 pounds. Eminent recipients of the prize include V.S. Naipaul, Nadine Gordimer, Ruth Prawer Jhabvala, Iris Murdoch, J.M. Coetzee, A.S. Byatt, Kingsley Amis, Michael Ondaatje, Ian McEwan, Peter Carey, and Kiran Desai.

## PULITZER PRIZE

The Pulitzer Prize is a series of annual prizes awarded by Columbia University, New York City, for outstanding public service and achievement in American journalism and letters. These prizes were first awarded in 1917 from the gift of 500,000 dollars made by newspaper magnate Joseph Pulitzer. The awards are decided by Columbia University on the recommendation of The Pulitzer Prize Board, composed of judges appointed by the university. Siddhartha Mukherjee received the 2011 Pulitzer Prize for his book *The Emperor of All Maladies: A Biography of Cancer.*

## DID YOU KNOW?

- Charles Dickens originally wanted to be an actor. In the 1830s, he was scheduled for an audition at Covent Garden, but missed his appointment due to a bad cold.

- Mulk Raj Anand, the famous author, has written a cookbook titled Curries and Other Indian Dishes.

- The word 'Quark', used to signify the fundamental constituents of matter, was taken from James Joyce's novel Finnegan's Wake.

- In Indian Railways, the Mumbai-Gorakhpur Godan Express is named after Premchand's famous novel Godan.

- In 1909, Swedish author Selma Lagerlöf became the first woman to be awarded the Nobel Prize in Literature.

- When Wilfred Owen died in 1918, a paper with verses of Rabindranath Tagore's Gitanjali written on it was found in his pocket.

- Sigmund Freud was nominated for twelve years for the Nobel Prize in Medicine. Romain Rolland, a Nobel laureate himself, and an acquaintance of Freud, nominated him for the Nobel Prize in Literature in 1936.

- J.M. Barrie gave all the rights to Peter Pan to Great Ormond Street Hospital in 1929.

- In his will, Shakespeare left his wife the 'second-best bed'.

# MUSIC & ENTERTAINMENT

## ARTISTS OF INDIA

### AKHTAR, BEGUM (1914-1974)

Akhtari Bai Faizabadi, popularly known as Begum Akhtar, was a legendary vocalist of the thumri, ghazal, and dadra forms of Indian classical music of the Patiala gharana. Her refined rendition earned her the title of Mallika-e-Ghazal or 'empress of ghazals'. She received several awards including the Sangeet Natak Akademi Award (1972) and the Padma Bhushan (1975, posthumously).

### AMONKAR, KISHORI (b. 1931)

Kishori Amonkar is one of the foremost singers in the Hindustani classical tradition and a leading exponent of the Jaipur gharana. Daughter of the famous vocalist Moghubai Kurdikar, she is known for her renderings of traditional ragas, namely Jaunpuri, Patta Bihag, Ahir, and Bhairav. She also sings bhajans, thumris, and khayals.

### BALAMURALIKRISHNA, M. (b. 1930)

M. Balamuralikrishna is a Carnatic vocalist, poet, and music composer. He was born in Andhra Pradesh and trained under Sri Parupalli Ramakrishna Pantulu, the direct descendant of the *sisya parampara* of Sant Thyagaraja. He has many interesting collaborations to his credit, which includes being featured as a soloist in an award-winning British choir, singing in French. He has won several National Film Awards and been awarded the Chevalier des Arts et Letters by the French government.

## CHAURASIA, HARIPRASAD (b. 1938)

Hariprasad Chaurasia is a classical instrumentalist, renowned for playing the flute. He belongs to the Maihar gharana of Hindustani classical music. He and Pt Shiv Kumar Sharma composed music for films in collaboration as Shiv–Hari. He was awarded the Padma Vibhushan in 2000. Chaurasia heads the World Music Department at the Rotterdam Music Conservatory.

## DEVI, GIRIJA (b. 1929)

Girija Devi is an Indian classical singer of the Benaras *gharana*. Trained in khayal and tappa by the reputed vocalist and sarangi player Sarju Prasad Mishra, she evolved as one of the finest *thumri* singers of her time. She is well known for her performances and has received awards like the Sangeet Natak Akademi Award (1977) and the Padma Bhushan (1989).

## GANDHARV, KUMAR (1924–1992)

Sirivaputra Sidhram Komkali, also known as Kumar Gandharv, was an Indian classical singer of the Gwalior *gharana*. His important compositions—*Geet Hemant, Geet Varsha, Geet Shishir*, and *Triveni* (bhajans of the three great saints Kabir, Surdas, and Meera)—proved sensational hits. He was awarded the Padma Vibhushan in 1990.

## HUSSAIN, USTAD ZAKIR (b. 1951)

Zakir Hussain is a famous tabla player of global renown. Son of Ustad Allah Rakha, another renowned *tabaliya*, Zakir's has contributed immensely to world music with much historic collaboration, including Shakti, a group he co-founded with John McLaughlin, an English guitarist, and composer and L Shankar, an Indian-born American violinist, singer and composer. Hussain won a Grammy Award in 2009 for *Global Drum Project*.

## JASRAJ, PANDIT (b. 1930)

Pandit Jasraj is a renowned vocalist and the foremost exponent of the Mewati gharana of Hindustani classical music. He has done extensive research into *haveli sangeet* under Baba Shyam Manohar Goswami Maharaj and created many melodious *bandishein* (compositions). He has also evolved a style of jugalbandi called the *jasrangi jugalbandi*. He received the Padma Vibhushan in 2000. The University of Toronto has instituted a scholarship in his name.

## JOSHI, BHIMSEN (1922–2011)

A wizard of Indian classical music, Pandit Bhimsen Joshi was one of the greatest Hindustani vocalists of the Kirana *gharana*. He was known for the

khayal form of singing as well as his rendition of bhajans. He received the
Bharat Ratna in 2008. He received a National Film Award for Best Male
Playback Singer in 1984 for *Ankahee*.

## KHAN, ALI AKBAR (1922–2009)

Ali Akbar Khan, a classical musician and a sarod player, is credited with
popularizing Indian classical music in the West. Son of Ustad Allauddin
Khan, he was the first to record a long-playing album of Indian classical
music in the US and to give a sarod recital on American TV. He was also
the first Indian musician to receive the MacArthur Foundation Fellowship
in 1991 and was nominated for Grammy Awards five times. He composed
music for *The Householder* (1963), the first Merchant Ivory production. He
was honoured with the Padma Vibhushan in 1989.

## KHAN, AMJAD ALI (b. 1945)

Amjad Ali Khan is an Indian classical musician famous for playing the sarod.
He was born into the famous Bangash lineage rooted in the Senia Bangash
School. Taught by his father and guru, Haafiz Ali Khan of Gwalior, he has
received numerous awards including the Padma Vibhusan (2001) and the
Crystal Award by the World Economic Forum.

## KHAN, BADE GHULAM ALI (1902–1968)

Bade Ghulam Ali Khan was a Hindustani classical singer and the greatest
interpreter of the Patiala *gharana*. He composed several *bandishein* under
the pen name Sabarang. He is still remembered for his renditions of *Hari Om
Tatsat* and *Aaye Na Balam*. He received the Padma Bhushan in 1962.

## KHAN, BISMILLAH (1916–2006)

Ustad Bismillah Khan was a famous instrumentalist, known for playing the
shehnai. He received his training under his uncle, the late Ali Baksh 'Vilayatu',
a musician attached to the Vishwanath Temple in Varanasi. Bismillah Khan
had the rare honour of performing at the Red Fort in Delhi on the eve of
India's independence in 1947, and again on the eve of the country's first
Republic Day ceremony in 1950. He is one of the few people to have received
all the three Padma awards and also the Bharat Ratna (2001).

## PALUSKAR, VISHNU DIGAMBAR (1921–1955)

Vishnu Digambar Paluskar was a famous Hindustani classical vocalist. Trained
by Pandit Chintamanrao Paluskar and Pandit Mirashi Buwa, he inherited
the Gwalior *gharana* and the Gandharva Mahavidyalaya, but advocated the

intermingling of gharanas and styles. Besides pure classical music, he was also a great bhajan singer. He is also famous for an unforgettable duet with Ustad Amir Khan in the film *Baiju Bawra*.

## SUBBULAKSHMI, M.S. (1916–2004)

M.S. Subbulakshmi, popularly known as MS, was a distinguished Carnatic vocalist. She was trained in classical music by her mother and S.S. Iyer, a doyen of Carnatic music. She recorded her first album in 1926 and made her film debut with *Sevasadanam* in 1938. The success of the film *Meera* (1945) made her a household name. She has sung bhajans and shlokas in various languages. Some of her most popular recordings are *Shree Venkatesha Surabhatam* and *Hanuman Chalisa*. In 1998, she became the first musician ever to be awarded the Bharat Ratna, India's highest civilian award.

## SHANKAR, RAVI (b. 1920)

Ravi Shankar is a famous sitar player, composer, and founder of the National Orchestra of India. A disciple of Baba Allauddin Khan, he composed music for Satyajit Ray's *Apu Trilogy*, *Gandhi* and many other notable films. He has authored compositions for violinist Yehudi Menuhin, flute virtuoso Jean-Pierre Rampal, and shakuhachi player Hozan Yamamoto. Former Beatles member, George Harrison, called him 'Godfather of World Music'. In 1967, he became the first Indian musician to bag a Grammy for his performance in *West Meets East* with violinist Yehudi Menuhin in the Best Chamber Music Performance category. He has received many awards including the Bharat Ratna (1999), and the Magsaysay Award (1992).

## SHANKAR, UDAY (1900–1977)

Uday Shankar was a dancer and choreographer who adapted Western theatrical techniques to traditional dances and popularized the ancient art forms of India in Europe and the US. During the 1920s he performed with the ballerina Anna Pavlova and created two of his most famous compositions: *Hindu Wedding* and the duet *Radha and Krishna*. In 1938, he founded the Uday Shankar India Culture Centre in Almora, Uttar Pradesh. Together with his brother, the sitarist Ravi Shankar, he explored classical and folk dances and created dance dramas that included social commentary.

## SHARMA, SHIV KUMAR (b. 1938)

Shiv Kumar Sharma is a santoor maestro. Trained by his father, Pandit Uma Dutt Sharma, he has elevated the status of this folk instrument from Kashmir. In 1967, he teamed up with flute maestro Pandit Hariprasad Chaurasia and slide guitarist Pandit Brij Bhushan Kabra to produce the album, *The Call of the Valley*, one of the greatest hits in Indian classical music. He has received the Padma Vibhushan and the International Cultural Ambassador Award by the World Bank among other prestigious awards.

## TANSEN, MIYAN (1506–1589)

Acclaimed as one of the greatest composers and practitioners of Hindustani classical music, he was born Ramtanu Pandey. While in the court of Raja Man Singh Tomar, he developed the Gwalior *gharana*. He joined the court of Emperor Akbar and was included among the *navaratnas* or 'nine jewels'. There are numerous popular accounts of Tansen's musical genius. It is said that he could charm the beasts of the forest with his singing. He was instrumental in creating several *ragas*, including Miyan Ki Todi and Miyan Ki Malhar, both of which carry his sobriquet 'Miyan'.

# MUSICAL INSTRUMENTS

**Percussion Instrument:** An instrument that produces sound upon being struck, rubbed, shaken, plucked and scraped.

**Stringed Instrument:** An instrument is one that produces sound by the vibration of stretched strings, which may be made of vegetable fibre, metal, animal gut, silk, or artificial materials such as plastic or nylon.

**Wind Instrument:** An instrument that uses air as the primary vibrating medium for the production of sound.

## INDIAN MUSICAL INSTRUMENTS

| STRINGED INSTRUMENT | WIND INSTRUMENT | PERCUSSION INSTRUMENT |
| --- | --- | --- |
| Ektara | Conch Shell | Tabla |
| Santoor | Flute | Damru |
| Sarod | Shehnai | Dholak |
| Sitar | Khung | Mridangam |
| Veena | Srnga (Horn) | Pakhawaj |
| Mohan Veena | Pungi | Ghatam |
| Vichitra | Veena | Maddal |
| Sarangi | Kombu | Kanjira |
| Tanpura | Tribal Mohori | Jalatarang (waves of water) |

# MAJOR FILM PERSONALITIES OF INDIA

### ANAND, DEV (1923–2011)

Dev Anand was an Indian film actor, director and producer. Born in Pakistan in 1923, he moved to Mumbai to pursue a career in acting. He made his debut with *Hum Ek Hain* in 1946. Some of his major hits are *Ziddi*, *CID*, *Funtoosh*, *Taxi Driver*, *Nau Do Gyarah*, *Kala Pani*, *Jewel Thief*, and *Johnny Mera Naam*. In 1949, he launched Navketan Films. He turned to direction with *Prem Pujari* in 1970. He won two Filmfare Awards for *Kala Pani* and *Guide*. He received the Padma Bhushan in 2001 and the Dadasaheb Phalke Award in 2002.

### BACHCHAN, AMITABH (b. 1942)

Amitabh Bachchan is a legendary film actor. Born in Allahabad in 1942 to poet Harivansh Rai Bachchan, he made his debut in 1969 as a protagonist in *Saat Hindustani*. In the 1970s, he became extremely popular when he donned the image of the 'angry young man' in *Zanjeer*. Some of his major box office hits are *Abhimaan*, *Namak Haram*, *Majboor*, *Deewar*, *Sholay*, *Kabhi Kabhie*, *Amar Akbar Anthony*, *Akhri Raasta*, *Black*, and *Cheeni Kum*. Bachchan has won numerous National Film Awards and Filmfare Awards, as well as the highest civilian honour of France, the Legion of Honour. He was named 'Actor of the Millennium' in a BBC News Poll, ahead of such luminaries as Charlie Chaplin, Sir Lawrence Olivier, and Marlon Brando.

### BHONSLE, ASHA (b. 1933)

Asha Bhonsle is considered to be one of the most versatile singers of India. Her repertoire includes film music, pop, ghazals, bhajans, traditional Indian classical music, folk songs, and qawwalis. She has sung in over eighteen languages. She has also collaborated with many international artistes and even sung a song with Australian cricketer Brett Lee. The Government of India honoured her with the Dadasaheb Phalke Award in 2000 and the Padma Vibhushan in 2008. According to the *Guinness Book of World Records*, she has sung the most studio recordings (singles) as an artiste.

### DUTT, GURU (1925–1964)

Guru Dutt was a pioneering actor, director, and producer of Hindi films. Born Vasanth Kumar Shivashankar Padukone in Bangalore on 9 July 1925, he started working as a choreographer with Prabhat Film Company in 1944. He made his directorial debut with *Baazi,* under the banner of Dev Anand's Navketan Films. He first appeared on screen in *Baaz*. Some of his successful films as actor and director were *Aar Paar, Mr & Mrs 55, CID, Pyaasa, Kaagaz Ke Phool, Chaudhvin Ka Chand*, and *Sahib Bibi Aur Ghulam*.

## KAPOOR, RAJ (1924–1988)

Raj Kapoor was a legendary Hindi film actor, producer, and director. Born Ranbir Raj Kapoor to Rama and Prithviraj Kapoor, he was attracted towards cinema from an early age. He worked as an assistant on the sets of Dilip Kumar's first film, *Jwar Bhata*. After a few inconsequential roles, he got his break as a hero in 1947, in Kidar Sharma's *Neel Kamal* opposite Madhubala. The next year, he formed R.K. Films and made his directorial debut with *Aag*. Some of his iconic films as director include *Awara, Shri 420, Barsaat, Jis Desh Mein Ganga Behti Hai, Bobby and Jagte Raho*. He was awarded the Padma Bhushan in 1971 and the Dadasaheb Phalke Award in 1987.

## KHAN, AAMIR (b. 1965)

An iconic figure in the contemporary Hindi film industry, Aamir Khan the son of film-maker Tahir Hussain, Aamir took an interest in acting from childhood. He was involved in theatre and worked as a child artiste in *Yaadon Ki Baraat*. He shot to fame with his debut film in the lead role in *Qayamat Se Qayamat Tak* followed by hits like *Jo Jeeta Wohi Sikander, Andaaz Apna Apna, Hum Hain Rahi Pyaar Ke, Akele Hum Akele Tum, Rangeela, Ghulam, Sarfarosh, Lagaan: Once Upon a Time in India, Dil Chahta Hai, Rang De Basanti, Ghajini, 3 Idiots*, and others. He ventured into direction with the hit *Taare Zameen Par*, for which he won the Filmfare Award for Best Director.

## KHAN, SHAH RUKH (b. 1965)

Shah Rukh Khan is a prominent Hindi film actor, producer, and TV host. Born in 1965, he made his mark in the tele serial *Fauji* and went on to act in films. His first few movies were *Deewana, Dil Aashna Hai*, and *Chamatkar*. Since then, he has acted in numerous successful productions including *Baazigar, Darr, Dilwale Dulhaniya Le Jayenge, Kuch Kuch Hota Hai, Kal Ho Naa Ho, Devdas, Om Shanti Om, My Name is Khan, Chak De India!*, and *Ra.One*. He has won several Filmfare Awards, has been honoured with the Padma Shri in 2005, and has a wax statue at Madame Tussauds in London. In 2008, he was conferred the title of 'Datuk' by the Malaysian government.

## KHANNA, RAJESH (1942–2012)

Rajesh Khanna was a megastar of the late 1960s and early 1970s. Born Jatin Khanna in 1942 in Amritsar, his first appearance as an actor was in *Aakhri Khat* (1966). His performances in *Aradhana, Kati Patang, Anand, Safar, Khamoshi, Amar Prem, Bawarchi*, and *Namak Haram* earned him the status of a superstar. Later, he turned to politics and served a five-year tenure as Member of Parliament from 1991 to 1996. He has won numerous awards, including three Filmfare Awards for Best Actor.

## KUMAR, DILIP (b. 1922)

A legendary actor of the Indian film industry, Dilip Kumar was born Yusuf Khan in Peshawar and moved to Maharashtra as a fruit merchant. He was recruited by Bombay Talkies and renamed by novelist Bhagwati Charan Varma. He shot into fame with *Andaaz* in 1961. He gave outstanding performances in several roles including the drama *Devdas, Azaad,* and the historical romance *Mughal-E-Azam.* He was the first to receive the Filmfare Best Actor Award in 1954. He also directed a few films, including *Ganga Jamuna, Dil Diya Dard Liya,* and *Kalinga.* His hits include *Jwar Bhata, Shaheed, Babul, Daag, Footpath, Musafir, Ram Aur Shyam,* and *Saudagar.* He received the Padma Bhushan in 1991 and the Dadasaheb Phalke Award in 1994.

## KUMAR, KISHORE (1929–1987)

Kishore Kumar was a popular playback singer, actor, and director of many films. He made his acting debut with the 1946 film *Shikari.* His most famous films include *Half Ticket, Chalti Ka Naam Gaadi* and *Jhumroo.* As a playback singer, he lent his voice to some of the most famous actors of his time, including Dev Anand in *Nau Do Gyarah, Jewel Thief, Hare Rama Hare Krishna;* Rajesh Khanna in *Aradhana, Kati Patang, Roti, Amar Prem;* and Amitabh Bachchan in *Don, Sholay, Satte Pe Satta, Abhimaan.* Kishore Kumar also directed films such as *Door Gagan Ki Chhaon Mein* and *Door Ka Rahi.*

## KUMARI, MEENA (1933–1972)

Born Mahajabeen Baksh in 1933 in Mumbai, Meena Kumari was the daughter of a Parsi theatre actor, singer, and music teacher, Ali Baksh. As a child actor, she made her debut with *Leatherface.* Later, she received a big break in Vijay Bhatt's *Baiju Bawra* (1952) and became the first actress to win a Filmfare Award. She gave some of her most memorable performances in *Miss Mary, Parineeta, Do Bigha Zameen, Yehudi, Sahib Bibi Aur Ghulam,* and *Pakeezah.*

## MADHUBALA (1933–1969)

Begum Mumtaz Jehan, popularly known as Madhubala, was one of the most popular actresses of the Hindi film industry. Born on 14 February 1933, her first major hit was Kidar Sharma's *Neel Kamal,* opposite Raj Kapoor.

Some of her important films are *Lal Dupatta, Mahal, Mughal-e-Azam, Mr and Mrs 55, Chalti Ka Naam Gaadi, Howrah Bridge, Kala Pani, Jhumroo*, and *Half Ticket*. She was married to Kishore Kumar and had started directing *Farz Aur Ishq* just before she died in 1969.

## MANGESHKAR, LATA (b. 1929)

Lata Mangeshkar is an iconic Indian artiste and one of the finest female playback singers of the Indian film industry. Daughter of Deenanath Mangeshkar, an eminent classical singer, her career spans over sixty years. She has recorded more than 30,000 songs in almost twenty Indian languages. She first did playback for the Marathi film *Kiti Hasaal* at the age of thirteen. She received the Maharashtra government's Best Music Director Award for *Sadhi Manase* in 1965. Among many prestigious awards, she has won the Bharat Ratna, the Padma Vibhushan, the Dadasaheb Phalke Award (1989), Padma Vibhushan (1999), and the Bharat Ratna (2001).

## NARGIS (1929–1981)

Nargis, born Fatima Rashid, was a leading actress of Hindi cinema. Born to film-maker Jaddanbai in 1929, she made her acting debut as a child in *Talash-e-Haq*. She appeared in various successful films, many of which were opposite Raj Kapoor. These include *Barsaat, Andaz, Awara, Shri 420, Chori Chori, Jagte Raho* and *Pardesi*. The pinnacle of her career was *Mother India*, a film nominated for the Academy Award in the Best Film in Foreign Language category. She died of cancer in 1981.

## PHALKE, DADASAHEB (1870–1944)

Dhudiraj Govind Phalke, a pioneering Indian director, producer, and screenwriter, popularly known as Dadasaheb Phalke, was born in 1870 in Nasik. Starting with the famous film *Raja Harishchandra* in 1913, he made ninety-five movies and twenty-six short films in the span of nineteen years, till 1932. Some of his famous films include *Lanka Dahan, Shrikrishna Janma, Kaliya Mardanam*, and *Bhakta Prahlad*. The Dadasaheb Phalke Award, one of the most prestigious awards in Indian cinema, given for lifetime contribution to cinema, was instituted in his honour by the Government of India in 1969.

## RAFI, MOHAMMAD (1924–1980)

One of the finest playback singers of our country, Rafi has recorded over 25,000 songs. Born in Kotla Sultan Singh village, now in Pakistan, he trained under Ustad Abdul Waheed Khan and Ghulam Ali Khan. He made his debut with the Punjabi film *Gul Baloch* (1944). After moving to Mumbai, he was given an opportunity by Naushad in *Pehle Aap* (1944). Since then his contribution to Indian playback music remains uncontested. He has sung not only in Hindi but in several regional languages as well. Apart from numerous film awards, he was conferred the Padma Shri in 1967. In 2000, two decades after his death, he was awarded the Best Singer of the Millennium Award.

## RAHMAN, A.R. (b. 1966)

A.R. Rahman, born Dileep Kumar, is an Indian music composer who has gained worldwide recognition. He was born in Chennai and worked for a decade as a keyboardist in the troupe of Ilaiyaraja. He has composed music for several films including *Roja, Bombay, Dil Se,* and *Slumdog Millionaire*. He has won several Filmfare Awards, National Film Awards, two Academy Awards, two Grammy Awards, a BAFTA Award, and a Golden Globe. He composed the theme song of the 2010 Commonwealth Games.

## RAY, SATYAJIT (1921–1992)

Ray is regarded as one of India's greatest film directors. He began his career as a commercial artiste and made his first film *Pather Panchali,* in 1955, following it up with *Aparajito* and *Apur Sansar*. The Apu trilogy, especially *Pather Panchali,* is a landmark in the history of Indian cinema. His other films include *Goopy Gyne Bagha Byne, Hirak Rajar Deshe, Jalsaghar, Kanchenjunga, Charulata, Pratidwandi, Seemabaddha, Jana Aranya, Ganashatru* and *Agantuk*. He was also an acclaimed fiction writer and adapted two of his popular stories from the Feluda series, *Sonar Kella* and *Joy Baba Felunath,* into films. Ray received many major awards, including thirty-two National Film Awards, many awards at international film festivals, and an Honorary Academy Award in 1992.

# MAJOR AWARDS OF THE WORLD

## ACADEMY AWARDS

The Academy Awards, popularly known as the 'Oscars', are presented annually by the Academy of Motion Pictures Arts and Sciences honouring professionals from the film industry. The award, the statuette of a knight standing on a film reel and holding a sword, is bestowed upon winners in up to twenty-five categories. The academy also presents scientific and technical awards, special achievement awards, honorary awards, the Jean Hersholt Humanitarian Award, the Irving G. Thalberg Memorial Award (for excellence in production), and the Gordon E. Sawyer Award (for technological contributions), although these are not necessarily awarded annually. The Awards were first presented on 16 May 1929, in a ceremony at the Hollywood Roosevelt Hotel.

## GRAMMY AWARDS

The Grammy Awards are a series of awards presented annually in the US by the National Academy of Recording Arts & Sciences to recognize achievements in the music industry. There are a total of seventy-eight categories of nomination. The winners receive a golden statuette of a gramophone. The Grammy Awards were first presented in 1959, when twenty-eight prizes were given away. Indian winners include Ravi Shankar, Zakir Hussain and A.R. Rahman.

# SP🏐RT

## SPORTING TOURNAMENTS OF THE WORLD

### ASIAN GAMES

The Asian Games is a multi-sport event held every four years in an Asian city, where athletes from all over Asia participate. In terms of the number of participants, it is the second largest such event after the Olympics. It is organized and regulated by the Olympic Council of Asia under the supervision of the International Olympic Committee. The brainchild of the then secretary-general of the Indian Olympic Association, Professor Guru Dutt Sondhi, the first Asiad was held in 1951 in New Delhi. The motto of the Games is 'Ever Onward'.

### COMMONWEALTH GAMES

First held in 1930 in Hamilton, Canada, the Commonwealth Games is a popular international event held every four years where only countries, which were once part of the British empire, take part. The event was first held in 1930. Initially called the British Empire Games, after a couple of name changes, it finally adopted its present moniker at the 1978 Edmonton Games. The 2014 Games will take place in Glasgow.

### DAVIS CUP

The Davis Cup is a premier competition in tennis. Teams are selected from various countries. It began in 1900 as a competition between just two countries—the US and Great Britain. France became the third nation to join. Now, over 130 countries play in the tournament. The countries are divided into various groups, and progress from regional groups to the world group, and then to the semi-finals and final. The record for winning the most number of singles matches for India is held by Ramanathan Krishnan.

## FIFA WORLD CUP

The FIFA World Cup is the world's premier football tournament. FIFA, or Federation Internationale de Football Association, is the governing body of world football. A group of visionary French football administrators, led by the then FIFA President, Jules Rimet, is credited with the idea of bringing the world's strongest national football teams together to compete for this title. The original gold trophy bore Rimet's name. The current trophy was lifted for the first time at the 1974 World Cup in Germany. The first World Cup took place in 1930 in Uruguay, when Uruguay defeated Argentina to claim the cup for the first time. The 2010 edition was held in South Africa and was won by Spain, a first-time champion. The other champions are Brazil (five times), Italy (four times), Germany (three times), Argentina (two times), Uruguay (two times), France (once), and England (once).

## GRAND SLAMS

The four Grand Slam tournaments–Australian Open, French Open, Wimbledon, US Open—are the important tennis tournaments of the world. The oldest, Wimbledon, started in London in 1877. The tournaments were open initially only to amateurs. In 1968, they were opened up to professionals also and thus the word 'Open' was added to their names. Their present venues are Melbourne Park (Melbourne), Roland Garros (Paris), Wimbledon (London), and Flushing Meadows (New York City). A player or team winning all Grand Slams in a single calendar year achieves a 'Grand Slam', and if they win all four in a year, along with an Olympic gold, the honour is termed a 'Golden Slam'. In 1938, Don Budge was the first person to complete a Grand Slam. In 1988, Steffi Graf became the first player in history to win a Golden Grand Slam.

## ICC CRICKET WORLD CUP

The first attempt to hold a world championship in cricket happened in 1912, when a three-team series was arranged between the then Test-playing nations: Australia, England, and South Africa. It was revived in 1975 when, following the success of domestic One-Day competitions, the then six Test-playing nations—England, Australia, New Zealand, West Indies, India, Pakistan—along with Sri Lanka and East Africa, played in the first World Cup in England, which the West Indies won. It was then held every four years. India, led by the inimitable Kapil Dev, won the 1983 edition. In 2011, Mahendra Singh Dhoni led India to its second World Cup victory.

## OLYMPIC GAMES (SUMMER, WINTER)

The Olympic Games is a multi-sport event held every four years. It traces its origin to the Games with similar name held in ancient Greece. In 1896, Baron Pierre de Coubertin revived the Olympic Games in its present form. The Winter Olympics began in 1924 in Chamonix, France. Besides these two, there are the Paralympic Games for physically disabled athletes, and the Youth Olympic Games for teenage athletes. Integral to the Olympic Games are the torch relay (carrying the Olympic flame from Greece, where it is lit, to the host city), lighting of the flame at the Olympic stadium, and the hoisting of the Olympic flag.

## 2012 LONDON OLYMPICS: SOME HIGHLIGHTS

- The 2012 Olympic Games took place in London. By hosting the games, London became the first city to host the Summer Olympic Games thrice.

- In the 2012 Olympic Games at London, Usain Bolt became the first man in history to win the 100 m, 200 m and 4×100 m relay sprints twice in succession. In the 100 m final, he set an Olympic record time and in the 4×100 m relay he anchored the Jamaican team to a record-breaking performance.

- Before appearing in the 2012 Olympic Games, Michael Phelps had already won 14 Gold medals in previous Olympics. In 2012, he continued his golden run winning four more in 100 m butterfly, 200 m individual medley, 4×200 m freestyle relay and 4×100 m medley relay. With a total of 22 medals (18 Golds, 2 Silvers and 2 Bronze from three Olympics) he became the most decorated Olympian of all time.

- A British middle and long distance runner of Somalian descent, Mohamed Mo Farah completed a rare double in the 2012 Olympic Games when he won the 10,000 m and also the 5,000 m race.

- In the 2012 Olympic Games, Serena Williams won double Gold medals in Women's singles and doubles (with her sister Venus) and became the first person, to complete a career Golden Slam (winning all the Grand Slams and a gold at the Olympic Games in one's career) in both singles and doubles.

- India won six medals in the 2012 Olympic Games, which was by far its best medal haul in any Olympics so far. Vijay Kumar in 25 m rapid fire pistol and Sushil Kumar in 66 kg freestyle wrestling won silver medals. Gagan Narang (10m air rifle), Saina Nehwal (women's singles-badminton), M.C. Mary Kom (women's flyweight-boxing) and Yogeshwar Dutt (60 kg freestyle-wrestling) won individual bronze medals. Sushil Kumar became the first Indian to win two individual Olympic medals, as he had won a bronze medal in the earlier 2008 Olympic Games.

❧ The 2012 Olympic Games saw many champions and world records, but table tennis player Natalia Partyka of Poland and 400 m sprinter Oscar Pistorius of South Africa deserve special mention. Partyka was born without a right hand and forearm, and Pistorius has both his legs amputated. However they competed at the Games with able bodied players and stunned audiences with their performance.

## SOME CUPS AND TROPHIES IN INDIA

**Hockey:** Beighton Cup, Dhyan Chand Trophy

**Cricket:** Duleep Trophy, Ranji Trophy, Indian Premier League

**Football:** Durand Cup, Federation Cup, IFA Shield, I-League, Santosh Trophy

**Rowing:** Wellington Trophy

**Badminton:** Narang Cup

**Polo:** Radha Mohan Cup, Prithvi Singh Cup

## FAMOUS SPORTSPERSONS

### ADVANI, PANKAJ (b. 1985)

Pankaj Advani is the winner of three world titles in billiards and snooker. He became the first player to complete a grand double by winning both the points format as well as the time format titles in the IBSF World Billiards Championship in 2005. He became a professional in 2007. He has been conferred the Arjuna Award in 2004, the Rajiv Gandhi Khel Ratna in 2005, and the Padma Shri in 2009.

### ANAND, VISHWANATHAN (b. 1969)

Vishwanathan Anand is an Indian chess Grandmaster. In 1987, Vishy, as he is known to his fans, became the first Asian to win the World Junior Championship. He also earned the coveted Grandmaster title. Anand won the FIDE World Chess Championship in 2000. He became the undisputed world chess champion in 2007 and defended his title against Vladimir Kramnik in 2008. He also became the first player in chess history to have won the world championship in three different formats: knockout, tournament, and match. He was awarded the Arjuna Award in 1985, the Padma Shri in 1987, the Padma Bhushan in 2000, and the Padma Vibhushan in 2008. In 1991, he became the first recipient of the Rajiv Gandhi Khel Ratna. He has received the Chess Oscar, given to the Best Chess Player of the Year in 1997,

1998, 2003, 2004, and 2007. In 2012, he defeated Boris Gelfand to defend his World Chess Championship title

## BECKENBAUER, FRANZ (b. 1945)

Franz Beckenbauer is a former West German footballer and national team manager. Nicknamed 'Der Kaiser', Beckenbauer is the first person to have captained as well as coached World Cup winning sides. In an international career that stretched from 1965 to 1977, he earned 103 caps and scored fourteen goals. He was twice selected as the European Footballer of the Year. The peak of achievement for Beckenbauer was captaining his country to World Cup victory in 1974. In 1990, the German team, with him as coach, defeated Argentina in the final to win the World Cup.

## BECKHAM, DAVID (b. 1975)

David Beckham is a footballer representing England. Beckham is the only Englishman to score in three different World Cups, and is only the fifth player in World Cup history to score twice from direct free kicks. He was captain of the English national team from November 2000 to July 2006. He was made an Officer of the Order of the British Empire by Queen Elizabeth II in 2003 and became a UNICEF Goodwill Ambassador in 2005.

## BHUPATHI, MAHESH (b. 1974)

Mahesh Bhupathi is one of the best professional tennis players to have emerged from India. He turned professional in 1995. In 1999, he won three doubles titles with Leander Paes, including the French Open and the Wimbledon. Leander and he became the first doubles team to reach the finals of all four Grand Slams in the same year since 1952. On 26 April 1999, they became the number 1 doubles team in the world in the ATP rankings.

## BHUTIA, BAICHUNG (b. 1976)

Bhaichung Bhutia is a famous football player who has played more than 100 international matches for India. Nicknamed 'Sikkimese Sniper', Bhutia first played for India in the 1995 Nehru Cup in Chennai, where he scored against Uzbekistan, becoming India's youngest-ever international goal scorer at nineteen. He was the 1996 Indian Player of the Year. He made his professional club debut in 1993 for East Bengal. Significantly, he was the first Indian footballer to play professionally in Europe, when he played for English club Bury FC from 1999 to 2002. During his time, India won two Nehru Cups, four SAFF Championships, and the 2008 AFC Challenge Cup, thus qualifying for the 2011 Asian Cup. The Indian team played against Bayern Munich in his farewell match in January, 2012.

## BINDRA, ABHINAV (b. 1982)

Abhinav Bindra created history when he became India's first gold medallist in an individual sport in the Olympic Games. He won the 10 m air rifle event at the 2008 Beijing Olympics. This was India's first gold in twenty-eight years, since the men's field hockey team won gold at the 1980 Moscow Olympics. In 2001, he became the youngest recipient of the Rajiv Gandhi Khel Ratna Award, at the age of eighteen.

## BORDER, ALLAN (b. 1955)

Australian Allan Border is one of the most successful cricket captains of all times. At his retirement, he had featured in most Tests, most consecutive Tests, and most Tests as captain. He had also taken more catches than any other player. He also had a batting average of 50 runs. From the World Cup win in 1987 and regaining the Ashes two years later, Australia cruised under Border until 1993, when they came within one ball of conquering the world by beating West Indies. After retirement Border served the game as coach and selector. His contribution is recognized annually when the Australian Player of the Year receives the Allan Border Medal.

## BOYCOTT, GEOFF (b. 1940)

Geoffrey Boycott is a former Yorkshire and England cricketer. In a prolific cricketing career from 1964 to 1982, he established himself as one of England's most successful opening batsmen. After 108 Test match appearances for England, Boycott ended his international career in 1982 with over 8,000 Test runs. Since retiring, Boycott has been a respected TV commentator, analyst, and columnist.

## BRADMAN, DON (1908-2001)

Sir Donald Bradman, often referred to as The Don, was an Australian cricketer, widely acknowledged as the greatest batsman of all time. His career Test batting average of 99.94 is claimed to be statistically the greatest achievement in any major sport. He played fifty-two Tests during his twenty-year career (1928–48). In 1930, he scored 974 runs in a series in England, 309 of them in one amazing day at Headingley. During his stint, Australia lost the Ashes only once, in 1932–33, when England devised a controversial system of bowling called Bodyline. Bradman scored a total of twenty-nine Test centuries.

## CHOWDHURY, BULA (b. 1970)

Bula Chowdhury is a former national women's swimming champion, who splashed across the national aquatic scene in the 1980s. Chowdhury took up long distance swimming in 1989 and crossed the English Channel. In August 2004, she became the first woman in the world to cross the seven seas when she swam across the Palk Straits from Talaimannar (Sri Lanka) to Dhanushkodi (Tamil Nadu). Other waterbodies she has crossed are the English Channel, Strait of Gibraltar, Tyrrhenian Sea (Italy), Toroneus Gulf (Greece) and Cook Strait (New Zealand). She was awarded the Padma Shri in 2008.

## CRUYFF, JOHANN (b. 1947)

Former Dutch footballer, Johann Cruyff debuted for the Dutch national side against Hungary in September 1966 and went on to make forty-eight appearances for the 'Oranje' before retiring in October 1977. At club level, Cruyff won the European Cup three times in a row with Ajax. In 1973, he moved to Spain to join Barcelona, collecting the league title in his first season. He was the European Footballer of the Year in 1971, 1973, and 1974. He has been inducted in the FIFA 100 list of the greatest footballers.

## DEV, KAPIL (b. 1959)

Kapil Dev is a former Indian cricketer and captain who was India's greatest fast bowling all-rounder of all time, the only player in the world to have taken more than 400 wickets and scored more than 5,000 runs in Tests. He was voted India's Cricketer of the Century by *Wisden* magazine in 2002. He led India to victory in the 1983 World Cup as captain, and took over the world record aggregate of Test wickets from Richard Hadlee, a record he retired with in 1994.

## DHONI, MAHENDRA SINGH (b. 1981)

Mahendra Singh Dhoni is the captain and wicketkeeper of the Indian cricket team. He was appointed captain of the Twenty20 squad for the World Championship in 2007, and soon after made the ODI captain. In 2011, Dhoni led India to a World Cup win defeating Sri Lanka in the final match. He also plays for the Chennai Super Kings IPL team.

## DOSANJIH SR, BALBIR SINGH (b. 1924)

Balbir Singh has a glorious record in Indian hockey, having helped India claim multiple gold medals in the Olympics and Asiads. He is a triple Olympic gold medallist, in 1948 in London, in 1952 in Helsinki, and in 1956 in Melbourne (the last one as captain). Besides, he also helped India win a silver at the 1958 Tokyo Asian Games. As a coach and manager, he helped India win the 1971 Barcelona World Cup silver and 1975 Kuala Lumpur World Cup gold. He was the first hockey player to win the Padma Shri in 1957.

## GANGULY, SOURAV (b. 1972)

Sourav Ganguly is a former captain of the Indian cricket team, and one of its most successful, winning twenty-one out of forty-nine matches. He made his Test debut on the tour of England in 1996, scoring 131 runs in the first Test. When he became captain, India started winning Tests on foreign soil, and the team put together a splendid streak that took it all the way to the World Cup final in 2003. After being dropped, he made a fairy tale comeback in 2006 by putting up brilliant performances in both Tests and ODIs. The left-handed Ganguly is a prolific ODI batsman, with over 11,000 runs to his credit.

## GAVASKAR, SUNIL (b. 1949)

Sunil Gavaskar is a former Indian cricket captain and skilled batsman. His opening style was built around a near perfect technique and enormous powers of concentration. He held the world record for the highest number of Test centuries for a long time, till he was overtaken by Sachin Tendulkar. Gavaskar was widely admired for his technique against fast bowling, with a particularly high average of 65.45 against the West Indies, which possessed a four-pronged fast bowling attack regarded as the most vicious in Test history. Since retiring, Gavaskar has been a respected TV commentator, analyst and columnist, and has served various responsibilities with the BCCI Board of Control for Cricket in India) and the ICC (International Cricket Council).

## GEORGE, ANJU BOBBY (b. 1977)

Anju Bobby George is an Indian long jumper who made history when she won a bronze at the 2003 World Athletics Championships in Paris, with a jump of 6.70 m, thus becoming the first Indian athlete to win a medal at these championships. She went on to win a silver at the IAAF World Athletics Final in 2005, a performance she considers her best. She was awarded the Rajiv Gandhi Khel Ratna Award in 2003.

## GOPICHAND, PULLELA (b. 1973)

Pullela Gopichand is a former badminton player. He won the All England Championship in 2001, the second Indian to do so after Prakash Padukone in 1980. Gopichand was awarded the Rajiv Gandhi Khel Ratna in 2001. He won his first national championship title in 1996, carrying on for five times in a row, till 2000. He also received the Dronacharya Award in 2009 for his contribution to Indian badminton as a coach.

## HADLEE, RICHARD (b. 1951)

Sir Richard Hadlee was a former captain and fast bowler of the New Zealand cricket team. By the time he retired from international cricket in 1990, Hadlee had cemented his position as one of the greatest fast bowlers of all time. In December 2002, he was chosen by *Wisden* magazine as the second greatest Test bowler of all time. He was the first player to take 400 Test wickets, in just eighty matches.

## KHAN, IMRAN (b. 1952)

Imran Khan is a former cricketer and captain of the Pakistan cricket team. He led his team to win the 1992 ICC World Cup trophy. With his lithe bounding run, his leap and his reverse-swinging yorker, he inspired thousands to take up fast bowling. He made himself into an all-rounder acclaimed for his batting as well. His averages in Test matches (thirty-seven with the bat, twenty-two with the ball) put him at the top of the quartet of all-rounders who dominated Test cricket in the 1980s.

## KUMAR, SUSHIL (b. 1983)

Sushil Kumar Solanki, hailing from Baprola village in Delhi, is a champion wrestler who won the gold medal in the 66 kg freestyle competition at the 2010 World Wrestling Championships and the bronze medal in the 66 kg freestyle wrestling event at the 2008 Beijing Olympics. Sushil Kumar also won gold at the 2010 Commonwealth Games in Delhi. He received the Arjuna Award in 2005. In 2009, he was conferred the country's highest sporting honour, the Rajiv Gandhi Khel Ratna Award. Sushil Kumar led the Indian contingent at the 2012 London Olympics and carried the flag. He also won the silver medal for 66 kg freestyle wrestling.

## KUMBLE, ANIL (b. 1970)

Anil Kumble is a former Indian cricketer and captain of the Test team. A right-arm leg-spin bowler, he is currently the leading wicket-taker for India in both Test and One-Day International matches. He is also the second bowler in the history of cricket to have taken all ten wickets in a Test innings, which he achieved against Pakistan in Delhi in 1999. After playing for eighteen years, he retired in November 2008, after playing his last Test against Australia at Feroz Shah Kotla in Delhi.

## LILLEE, DENNIS (b. 1949)

Dennis Lillee is a former Australian cricketer, was rated one of the most outstanding fast bowlers of his generation. When Lillee came on to the international scene, his pace impressed all. He went on to claim thirty-one Test wickets at a rate of 17.67 during the 1972 Ashes tour. Throughout his career, Lillee had a superb partnership with wicketkeeper Rod Marsh. The dismissal 'caught Marsh, bowled Lillee' appears ninety-five times on Test cards, a record pairing that is yet to be challenged.

### LLOYD, CLIVE (b. 1944)

Clive Lloyd is a former West Indian cricketer and one of the most successful captains of all time. He captained the West Indies from 1974 to 1985, during which period the team had a run of twenty-seven undefeated matches (wins and draws), including eleven wins in succession, and reached three World Cup finals (1975, 1979, 1983), winning twice. He was the first West Indian to play 100 Test matches. His twenty years in Test cricket produced more than 7,000 runs. His side changed the way Test cricket was played, as other nations initiated their formula of fast bowling and intimidation.

### MARADONA, DIEGO (b. 1960)

Diego Maradona is a former Argentine national team footballer and one of the greatest sportsmen ever. He was the manager of the Argentine national team. He won the Youth World Championship in Japan in 1979. He made his international debut in 1977 against Hungary. He was the World Cup champion in Mexico (1986) and runner-up in Italy (1990), with twenty-one matches in four World Cups. He received the Golden Ball for being the best player at the1986 World Cup in Mexico. In 2000, he was considered to be one of the FIFA Players of the Century. In 2002, his second goal against England in the 1986 World Cup was honoured as the FIFA Goal of the Century.

### MARY KOM, M.C. (b. 1983)

Mangte Chungneijang Mary Kom, who hails from Manipur, is currently one of the world's best women boxers. She began boxing in 2000. She is a five-time world champion, winning the Women's World Amateur Boxing Championships in 2002, 2005, 2006, 2008, and 2010. In 2009, Mary Kom received India's highest sporting honour, the Rajiv Gandhi Khel Ratna Award. She was also honoured with the prestigious Arjuna Award in 2003 and the Padma Shri for 2006. At the 2012 Olympic Games, she won a bronze medal.

### MESSI, LIONEL (b. 1987)

Lionel Messi is an Argentine footballer who currently plays for Spanish club FC Barcelona and the Argentine national team. In October 2004, Messi made his official debut for the first team of FC Barcelona against RCD Espanyol, becoming the third-youngest player to ever play for the club. He scored his first senior goal for the club against Albacete in 2005. In 2005, Messi played for the Argentina U-20 team that won the Youth World Championship, picking up the Golden Ball as the best player of the tournament as well as the Golden Boot as the top scorer. Messi was declared Goodwill Ambassador for UNICEF in 2010.

## MIRZA, SANIA (b. 1986)

Sania Mirza started playing tennis at the age of six at Nizam Club, Hyderabad. She played international tournaments from 1999, first representing India in the World Junior Championship in Jakarta. She won the 2003 Wimbledon girls doubles title. In February 2005, she became the first Indian woman to win a WTA singles title, defeating Alyona Bondarenko of Ukraine in the Hyderabad Open. In 2006, she was awarded a Padma Shri. Mirza is the highest-ranked female tennis player ever from India, with a career-best ranking of 27 in singles. She is the first Indian woman to be seeded in a Grand Slam tournament. In winning the mixed doubles event at the 2009 Australian Open with Mahesh Bhupathi, she became the first Indian woman to win a Grand Slam title. In 2012, she won the French Open mixed doubles title, again with Mahesh Bhupathi.

## MURALITHARAN, MUTTIAH (b. 1972)

Muttiah Muralitharan, often referred to as Murali, is a Sri Lankan cricketer rated the greatest Test match bowler ever by *Wisden Cricketers' Almanack* in 2002. Murali is the highest wicket-taker in both Tests and ODIs. He duly passed Shane Warne's Test record of 708 wickets against England in December 2007, fittingly at his home ground in Kandy. He achieved the grand double of being the highest wicket-taker in ODIs as well when he moved past Wasim Akram's record of 502 wickets in 2009.

## NEHWAL, SAINA (b. 1990)

Saina Nehwal is one of the world's top badminton players. She was the first Indian woman to win the World Junior Badminton Championship. Her highest career ranking is World Number 2. Saina won gold in the women's singles at the 2010 Commonwealth Games in New Delhi. In 2010, she became the youngest recipient of the Rajiv Gandhi Khel Ratna Award. In 2012, Saina Nehwal became the first Indian to win a medal in badminton at the Olympics, when she won the bronze medal at the 2012 London Olympic Games.

## PADUKONE, PRAKASH (b. 1955)

Prakash Padukone is a former badminton player. He was the first Indian to win the prestigious All England Badminton Championship in 1980 and the first Indian to hold the World Number 1 rank in 1980-81. He won the Danish Open and the Swedish Open in 1980. He was the winner of the Badminton World Cup at Kuala Lumpur in 1981 and a gold medallist at the Edmonton Commonwealth Games in 1978. He has won several awards, such as the Arjuna Award in 1972 and the Padma Shri in 1982.

## PAES, LEANDER (b. 1973)

Leander Paes is one of India's best professional tennis players. He won the 1990 singles junior Wimbledon title. He has been a member of the Davis Cup squad since 1990. He has won twenty-two straight Davis Cup doubles matches (with Mahesh Bhupathi). He won the singles bronze at the 1996 Atlanta Olympics. In 1996, Leander Paes was awarded with the Rajiv Gandhi Khel Ratna Award. In 2001, he received the Padma Shri.

## PELE (b. 1940)

Edison Arantes do Nascimento, popular as Pele, is mentioned by FIFA as the 'King of Football'. He joined the Santos club at the age of fifteen. In the 1958 World Cup, his goal for Brazil against Wales made him the youngest scorer in FIFA World Cup history, at the age of seventeen. In warring Nigeria, a ceasefire was declared when Pele played in Lagos in 1969. The port city of Santos declared 19 November as 'Pele Day', to celebrate the anniversary of his 1,000th goal. He was a member of the Brazilian World Cup winning squads of 1958, 1962, and 1970. His individual awards include the Golden Ball at the 1970 World Cup and the Silver Ball at the 1958 World Cup.

## PILLAY, DHANRAJ (b. 1968)

Dhanraj Pillay is a former hockey player and captain of the Indian national team. He is the only Indian to play in four Olympics, four World Cups, four Champions Trophies, four Asian Games, and four Asia Cups. He made his international debut in 1989 at the Asia Cup in New Delhi. He led the national team to gold at the 1998 Asian Games in Bangkok and at the 2003 Asia Cup in Kuala Lumpur. He was the only Indian player to figure in the World Eleven side in the 1994 World Cup at Sydney. He has been awarded the Padma Shri in 2001, the Rajiv Gandhi Khel Ratna in 1999, and the Arjuna Award in 1995.

## RATHORE, RAJYAVARDHAN SINGH (b. 1970)

An officer in the Indian Army, Rajyavardhan Singh Rathore is the first of his countrymen to claim an individual silver for independent India at the Olympic Games. He won the silver in the men's double trap event in shooting in Athens in 2004. He received the Arjuna Award in 2003. He was selected for the country's highest sporting honour, the Rajiv Gandhi Khel Ratna Award, in 2004. He was conferred the Padma Shri in 2005.

## RICHARDS, VIVIAN (b. 1952)

Sir Vivian Richards is a former West Indian batsman, voted one of the five Cricketers of the Century in 2000 by *Wisden* magazine. The International Cricket Council has also ranked him as the number one ODI batsman of all time. Until 2005, he held the credit of being the only man to score a century and take five wickets in the same ODI, against New Zealand at Dunedin in 1986-87. He remains one of only four non-English cricketers to have scored 100 first-class centuries.

## RONALDO, CRISTIANO (b. 1985)

Cristiano Ronaldo is a Portuguese footballer, winger, and forward for Spanish club Real Madrid. Earlier he had a very successful spell at English club Manchester United, whose manager Alex Ferguson signed him on as an eighteen-year-old in 2003. The following season, Ronaldo won his first club honour, the FA Cup, and reached the Euro 2004 final with Portugal, losing to Greece. In the same tournament, he also scored his first international goal. In 2008, he was named the FIFA World Player of the Year, in addition to becoming Manchester United's first Ballon d'Or (European Player of the Year) winner in forty years.

## SEHWAG, VIRENDER (b. 1978)

Virender Sehwag is a batsman and an off-break bowler of the Indian cricket team. He grew up worshipping Tendulkar and, in fact, his first ODI 100 against New Zealand started with him substituting for his injured idol. Sehwag holds the Indian record for the highest score made by an Indian in a Test match (319), as well as in ODIs (219) and is also the only Indian and one of only three cricketers to have surpassed 300 twice in Tests.

## SINGH, DHYAN CHAND (1905–1979)

Dhyan Chand Singh, born on 29 August 1905, was a hockey player considered to be among the all-time greatest players to grace the game of hockey. He worked with the 1st Brahmin Regiment of the British Army and learnt hockey from Bale Tiwari. Dhyan Chand represented the United Provinces in an inter-provincial championship. In 1928, he led the Indian team to the Amsterdam Olympics and won gold. In 1932, his team again won gold at the Los Angeles Olympics. In 1932, India also scored 338 goals in thirty-seven matches, of which 133 were scored by him! In 1936, a hat-trick of gold medals was achieved at the Berlin Olympics where he met Hitler. Impressed by his immense talent, Hitler offered him a post in the German Army, which he refused. Chand's birthday, 29 August, is celebrated as National Sports Day in India.

## SINGH, MILKHA (b. 1935)

Milkha Singh represented India in the 1960 Olympics in Rome and the 1964 Olympics in Tokyo. He was nicknamed the 'Flying Sikh'. In the 1958 Asiad in Tokyo, he won the 400 m and 200 m events. In the 1960 Rome Olympics, he missed the bronze by a whisker in the 400 m. He went on to win gold in 400 m in the 1962 Jakarta Asian Games. In 1959, he was awarded the Padma Shri.

## SINGH, PARGAT (b. 1965)

Pargat Singh is a well-known hockey player. He played as fullback for India and was one of the country's best defenders. He was awarded the Padma Shri in 1998 and the Arjuna Award in 1989. He captained India at the 1992 Barcelona Olympics and the 1996 Atlanta Olympics. He was nicknamed 'Paggo' by his teammates.

## SINGH, VIJENDER (b. 1985)

Boxer Vijender Singh Beniwal hails from Kalwash, India's 'Village of Boxers', in Bhiwani district of Haryana. He became the first Indian boxer to win an Olympic medal when he won bronze in the middleweight category at the 2008 Beijing Olympics. In 2006, he was awarded the Arjuna Award. In 2009 he was honoured with the Rajiv Gandhi Khel Ratna Award. In 2010, he was conferred the Padma Shri.

## SOBERS, GARY (b. 1936)

Sir Garfield Sobers is a former West Indian cricketer. Apart from being an accomplished batsman he was remarkably versatile with the ball too, bowling two styles of spin (left-arm orthodox and wrist spin) as well as pace. He set the Test record for an individual batsman with a mammoth 365 against Pakistan in 1958. His achievements are numerous, including six consecutive sixes off an over. He was also successful as a captain, with the spectacular success in England in 1966 earning him the title 'King of Cricket'. In February 1975 Garfield St Aubrun Sobers was knighted by Queen Elizabeth II at Barbados.

## TENDULKAR, SACHIN (b. 1973)

Sachin Tendulkar is a former captain and a member of the Indian cricket team. He is arguably India's biggest cricket icon. He was only sixteen when he made his Test debut and seventeen when he scored his first Test century. He had sixteen Test tons before he turned twenty-five. In 2008, he passed Brian Lara as the leading Test run-scorer and, in the years after, he achieved the landmark of 13,000 Test runs and 30,000 ODI runs. He currently holds the record for most hundreds in both Tests and ODIs. In February 2010 he scored the first double-century in one-day cricket. In 2011, he won his first World Cup trophy when he proved crucial to his team's success in the premier tournament. In 2012, he became the first player to score 100 international hundreds (Test and ODIs combined).

## USHA, P.T. (b. 1964)

Pilavullakandi Thekkeparambil Usha or P.T. Usha was one of the greatest athletes from India. Nicknamed 'Payyoli Express' after her home town of Payyoli in Kerala, she made her debut in athletics in 1979. She participated in the Los Angles Olympics Games in the 400 metres hurdles and missed the bronze medal by 1/100th of a second. In 1986, she performed brilliantly at the Seoul Asian Games, winning the 200 m, 400 m, 400 m hurdles, and 4×400 m relay events. She was the recipient of both the Arjuna Award and the Padma Shri in 1984. In the Seoul Asiad, she won the Adidas Golden Shoe award for being the best athlete.

## WAUGH, STEVE (b. 1965)

Former Australian cricketer Steve Waugh retired as the most capped Test player in history with 168 appearances. He led the Australian Test team from 1999 to 2004. He succeeded Mark Taylor as Test captain in 1999, and later led Australia to fifteen of their world-record sixteen successive Test victories. He won the Allan Border Medal as Australia's best player of 2001. He finally retired after the 2003–04 series against India.

## WOODS, TIGER (b. 1975)

Eldrick Tont Woods is an American golfer, nicknamed 'Tiger' after a soldier who had befriended his father in Vietnam. Woods began playing golf at the age of two and turned professional in 1996. The following year he reached number one world ranking. In 2001, Tiger became the first ever to hold all four professional major championships at the same time. He has won World Golf Championships sixteen times. He has been awarded PGA Player of the Year for a record ten times and considered the highest earning golfer.

## ZIDANE, ZINEDINE (b. 1972)

Zinedine Yazid Zidane is a former footballer from the French national team, born in Marseilles. In 1998, he won the FIFA World Cup and the Euro 2000 for France. In Juventus, Zidane won the 1996 European Super Cup, the 1996 European/South American Cup, the 1997 League Super Cup, and the 1997 and 1998 Serie A. His individual awards include the European Award, Golden Ball in 1998, and FIFA Player of the Year in 1998 and 2000. In 2004, Zidane was named the best European football player of the past fifty years by the UEFA Golden Jubilee Poll and included in the FIFA 100 as well as Pele's list of the 125 greatest living footballers.

## DID YOU KNOW?

◊ In the 1928 Olympics in Amsterdam, a symbolic fire was lit during the Games for the first time. The fire was placed in a cauldron placed atop a tower in the stadium, designed by celebrated Dutch architect Jan Wils. At the opening ceremony, the team from Greece led the Parade of Nations, with the host Dutch team marching in last. Greece leading the parade and the hosts bringing up the rear has been the Olympic protocol ever since.

◊ Dhyan Chand Singh represented India at three Olympics: Amsterdam (1928), Los Angeles (1932), Berlin (1936). He captained India in the last Olympics he played. His Olympic count would have been more, if World War II had not broken out. Dhyan Chand played till the age of forty-two, and retired from the game in 1948. In 1935, he met the cricket great Don Bradman at Adelaide. After watching him play, Bradman commented: 'He scores goals like we score runs in cricket.'

◊ As per FIFA, in international matches, all items of jewellery (necklaces, rings, bracelets, earrings, leather bands) are strictly forbidden and must be removed. Even using tape to cover jewellery is not acceptable. Referees are also prohibited from wearing ornaments (except for a watch or similar device for timing the match).

◊ Tatenda Taibu (Zimbabwe) and Nawab Mansur Ali Khan Pataudi (India) are the only two cricketers to captain their teams in a Test before they turned twenty-two.

◊ Leander Paes' father Vece Paes was a member of the Indian hockey team, which won the bronze medal in the 1972 Munich Olympics. In 1996, at

Atlanta, Leander himself won the bronze medal in men's singles. He also holds the record of making the most appearances at the Olympics by an Asian athlete.

◇ Before she turned nine, sprinter Wilma Rudolph suffered from double pneumonia, scarlet fever, whooping cough, measles, chicken pox, and also contracted polio. In the 1960 Rome Olympics, Rudolph became 'the fastest woman in the world' and the first American woman to win three golds in one Olympics. She won the 100 m and 200 m races and anchored the US team to victory in the 4x100 m relay, breaking records along the way.

◇ Before the 1975 'Thrilla in Manila' match between Joe Frazier and Muhammad Ali, their rivalry was fuelled by Frazier's feeling that Ali had repeatedly insulted and mocked him. However, Frazier came to Ali's defence when Ali was forced to give up his championship belt after refusing to fight in the Vietnam War. At one point, Frazier even lent money to the down-and-out former champion.

◇ The Calcutta Cup, which is awarded to the champions of the Six Nations Tournament for rugby, came into being when the members of Calcutta Football Club, closed their bank accounts and withdrew the entire balance in silver. The metal was melted down and crafted by the finest Indian workmen in the late 1800s to fashion the cup.

◇ Originally known as water ballet, synchronized swimming was first demonstrated in the 1962 Olympics. It became an official Olympic sport in 1984. It happens to be the only Olympic water sport where just women take part.

◇ In 1994, the National Sports of Canada Act stipulated: 'The game commonly known as ice hockey is hereby recognized and declared to be the national winter sport of Canada and the game commonly known as lacrosse is hereby recognized and declared to be the national summer sport of Canada'. Canada is thus one of the very few countries that recognizes more than one game as their national sport.

# SCI≷NCE

## MAJOR INVENTIONS AND DISCOVERIES

**Willis Carrier:** Air conditioning

**Louis Pasteur, Jules-Francois Joubert:** Antibiotics

**Alexander Fleming:** Discovery of penicillin

**Joseph Lister (surgery):** Antiseptic

**Ernest Rutherford:** Atomic structure (formulated nuclear model of atom, Rutherford model)

**Karl Benz:** Automobile (first with internal combustion engine, 250 rpm)

**Karl D. von Sauerbronn:** Bicycle

**John Napier:** Calculating machine

**George Eastman:** Camera

**Charles Babbage:** Computers (first design of analytical engine)

**William Sturgeon:** Electromagnet

**Galileo Galilei:** Falling Bodies (law)

**Narinder Kapany:** Fibre optics

**Isaac Newton:** Gravitation (law)

**Gregor Mendel:** Hereditary (laws)

**Benjamin Franklin:** Bifocal lens

**George Stephenson:** Locomotive (first practical, due to multiple-fire-tube boiler)

**Zacharias Janssen:** Compound microscope

**Thomas A. Edison:** Motion picture camera

**Michael Faraday:** Electric motor

**Karl Scheele:** Oxygen

**Lewis E. Waterman:** Fountain pen
**Johann Gutenberg:** Printing press
**Samuel Colt:** Revolver
**Walter Hunt:** Safety pin
**Elias Howe:** Sewing machine
**Rene Laennec:** Stethoscope
**Samuel F.B. Morse:** Telegraph
**Alexander Graham Bell:** Telephone
**Galileo Galilei:** Astronomical telescope, open-column thermometer
**John B. Dunlop:** Pneumatic rubber tyre
**William Stanley:** Electric transformer
**Christopher Sholes, Carlos Glidden:** Typewriter
**Tim Berners-Lee:** World Wide Web

# FAMOUS PEOPLE FROM THE FIELD OF SCIENCE

## ARCHIMEDES (287BC–212BC)

Archimedes was the most famous mathematician and inventor of ancient Greece. He is credited with discovering many principles of physics, especially the relation between the surface and volume of a sphere and its circumscribing cylinder. He is also known for formulating a hydrostatic principle (Archimedes' principle) and creating a device for uplifting water (Archimedes' screw). The story that he determined the proportion of gold and silver in a wreath made for Hieron by weighing it in water is probably true, but the version that has him leaping from the bath in which he supposedly got the idea and ran naked through the streets shouting *Eureka!* ('I've found it!') is more legend than fact.

## BHABHA, HOMI JEHANGIR (1909–1966)

Indian scientist Homi Jehangir Bhabha is often considered the chief architect of India's nuclear programme. He has many achievements to his credit. He derived the correct expression for the probability of scattering positrons by electrons, a process now known as 'Bhabha scattering'. In a paper written jointly with W. Heitler, he described how primary cosmic rays from space interact with the upper atmosphere to produce particles observed at the ground level. He established two great research institutions, Tata Institute of Fundamental Research (TIFR) and Atomic Energy Establishment at Trombay, renamed Bhabha Atomic Research Centre (BARC) after his death.

## BOSE, JAGADISH CHANDRA (1858–1937)

Jagadish Chandra Bose was an Indian scientist, botanist, physicist, and author. He was the first to produce millimetre-length radio waves and study their properties. In plant physiology, he deduced that plants can feel pain and understand affection. For his investigations, he invented several novel and highly sensitive instruments including the crescograph, an instrument to measure the growth of a plant.

## BOYLE, ROBERT (1627–1691)

Robert Boyle was a British natural philosopher best known for his works in chemistry. His discoveries regarding air pressure and vacuum appeared in his *New Experiments Physico-Mechanical, Touching the Spring of the Air, and its Effects* in 1660. Boyle discovered several physical characteristics of air, including its role in combustion, respiration, and the transmission of sound. One of his findings, published in 1662 later came to be known as 'Boyle's law'.

## COPERNICUS, NICOLAUS (1473–1543)

Polish astronomer Nicolaus Copernicus studied liberal arts at the University of Cracow (Kraków) but left before completing his degree. He resumed his education at the University of Bologna. He proposed that the planets have the Sun as the fixed point to which their motions are to be referred; that the earth is a planet which, besides orbiting the Sun annually, also turns once daily on its own axis; and that very slow, long-term changes in the direction of this axis account for the precession of the equinoxes. This representation of the heavens is usually called the heliocentric (sun-centred) system. Copernicus theory had important consequences for later thinkers of the scientific revolution, including Galileo, Kepler, Descartes, and Newton.

## CURIE, MARIE (1867–1934)

Polish-born physicist and chemist Marie Curie was one of the most famous scientists of her time. Born in Warsaw, she went to Paris to study physics and mathematics at the Sorbonne where she met physician Pierre Curie. They married in 1895, worked together and discovered two new chemical elements, polonium and radium. For her contribution to science, Marie was awarded the Nobel Prize for Physics in 1903, along with Pierre and Henri Becquerel. She received a second Nobel Prize, for chemistry, in 1911. In 1906, she became the first woman to teach at the Sorbonne. The element curium is named after the Curies.

## DALTON, JOHN (1766–1844)

John Dalton was an well-known meteorologist and chemist. Born in Eaglesfield, England, he started his career as a teacher in Kendal and later moved to Manchester, where he brought out what is thought to be the first publication on colour blindness. His most significant contribution to science, though, was his atomic theory and Dalton's law, which states that the total pressure of a mixture of gases is equal to the sum of the partial pressures of the individual component gases.

## DARWIN, CHARLES (1809–1882)

Charles Darwin was a British scientist who laid the foundations of the theory of evolution and transformed the way we think about the natural world. Darwin initially planned to follow a medical career but later switched to divinity studies. In 1831, he joined a five-year scientific expedition on *HMS Beagle*. The circumnavigation of the globe gave him an opportunity to explore and read extensively. After returning from the voyage, he formulated his theory on evolution in 1837–39, and later published it as *On the Origin of Species* (1859). This book deeply influenced modern Western society and thought.

## EDISON, THOMAS ALVA (1847–1931)

Thomas Alva Edison is one of the greatest scientists and inventors of all time. Born in Ohio, US, he attended school only for five years. His interest in creating objects led him to invent many devices. In his lifetime, he patented 1,093 inventions and created the world's first industrial research laboratory. His most celebrated invention was the incandescent light bulb. Besides the light bulb, Edison developed the phonograph and the 'kinetoscope' (a small box for viewing moving films). He also improved upon the original design of the stock ticker, the telegraph, and Alexander Graham Bell's telephone. He is often referred to as 'The Wizard of Menlo Park'.

## EINSTEIN, ALBERT (1879–1955)

Albert Einstein is often considered the most influential physicist of the 20th century. He is famous for developing the theories of relativity. Born in Germany, he had a great interest in mathematics and science from an early age. He decided to pursue these subjects so he could become a teacher. Failing to find such a job, he joined the patents office. While working there, he wrote papers about his ideas on several topics on physics. In 1908, he begin teaching at the university of Bern while continuing to publish his ideas on physics. He was honoured with the Nobel Prize for Physics in 1921 for his explanation of the photoelectric effect. Einstein was so highly thought of that he was offered the presidency of Israel in 1952. He had to decline the offer because of ill health. Einstein died in 1955 in Princeton, New Jersey.

## FARADAY, MICHAEL (1791–1867)

Michael Faraday was a British chemist and physicist who contributed significantly to the study of electromagnetism and electrochemistry. In 1831, he discovered electromagnetic induction, the principle behind the electric transformer and generator. He also contributed to coining many familiar words including electrode, cathode, and ion. He gave his name to the farad, originally describing a unit of electrical charge but later a unit of electrical capacitance.

## FLEMING, ALEXANDER (1881–1955)

Alexander Fleming was a Scottish bacteriologist, whose discovery of penicillin led the way for the effective practice of antibiotic therapy for infectious diseases. In 1928, while working at St Mary's, where he was professor of bacteriology, he noticed a bacteria-free circle around a mould growth (spores of *Penicillium notatum*) that was contaminating a culture of the staphylococci. During investigation, he found a substance in the mould that prevented growth of the bacteria. He called it penicillin, which was non-toxic but inhibited the growth of many types of disease-causing bacteria. He was awarded the Nobel Prize for Physiology or Medicine in 1945 along with Ernst Boris Chain and Howard Walter Florey.

## FRANKLIN, BENJAMIN (1706–1790)

Benjamin Franklin was a statesman, diplomat, writer, scientist, and inventor. He was also a leading figure in the American struggle for independence. His inventions included the Franklin stove and the lightning rod. With his famous kite experiment he demonstrated that lightning and electricity are identical.

## GALILEI, GALILEO (1564–1642)

Galileo Galilei was an Italian natural philosopher, astronomer, and mathematician who made remarkable contributions to the sciences of motion, astronomy, and strength of materials and to the development of the scientific method. His formulation of (circular) inertia, the law of falling bodies, and parabolic trajectories marked the beginning of a significant change in the study of motion. His discoveries with the telescope revolutionized astronomy and paved the way for acceptance of the Copernican heliocentric system.

## HIPPOCRATES (C. 460 BC–C. 375)

Hippocrates was an ancient Greek physician who lived in the classical period and is regarded as the father of medicine. It is difficult to isolate the facts of Hippocrates' life from the later tales about him. About sixty extant medical writings bear his name, but most of them were not actually written by him. He is revered for his ethical standards in medical practice, mainly for the Hippocratic Oath. Meno, a pupil of Aristotle, specifically stated in his history of medicine the views of Hippocrates on the causation of diseases, namely, the idea that undigested residues that were produced by incorrect diet excreted vapours, which passed into the body generally and produced diseases.

## JENNER, EDWARD (1749–1823)

Edward Jenner was an English doctor, pioneer of smallpox vaccination, and father of immunology. In 1796, he carried out his now-famous experiment on eight-year-old James Phipps. Jenner inserted pus taken from a cowpox pustule into an incision on the boy's arm. Jenner subsequently proved that having been inoculated with cowpox Phipps was immune to smallpox. In 1798, the results were finally published and Jenner coined the word vaccine from the Latin *vacca* for cow.

## KEPLER, JOHANNES (1571–1630)

Johannes Kepler was a German astronomer who discovered three major laws of planetary motion: (1) the planets move in elliptical orbits with the Sun at one focus; (2) the time necessary to traverse any arc of a planetary orbit is proportional to the area of the sector between the central body and that arc (the 'area law'); and (3) there is an exact relationship between the squares of the planets' periodic times and the cubes of the radii of their orbits (the 'harmonic law'). He also provided a new and correct account of how vision occurs.

## LINNAEUS, CARL (1707–1778)

Swedish naturalist and explorer Carl Linnaeus was the first to frame principles to define natural genera and species of organisms and to create a uniform system for naming them (binomial nomenclature). He is known as the father of modern taxonomy.

## MARCONI, GUGLIELMO (1874–1937)

Italian physicist Marconi was the originator of wireless telegraph signals. He created means of overcoming many of the hurdles to the commercialization of the wireless. He was the first to transmit signals across the ocean without cables. He continued to work in improving radio and was eventually able to send messages around the globe. He also performed experiments with the radar and microwave, proving that microwaves could also travel beyond the horizon of the Earth.

## MENDEL, GREGOR (1822–1884)

Gregor Mendel was an Austrian botanist and teacher. He was the first scientist to lay the mathematical foundation of the science of genetics, in what came to be called Mendelism. While working in the garden at a monastery at Brunn he began to take a close interest in garden peas. He noticed that peas had certain characteristics that seemed to have passed from generation to generation. Over seven years, Mendel carried out numerous experiments with these plants, studying characteristics such as height, seed shape, seed colour, and flower colour. Despite knowing nothing about DNA or the biochemistry of inheritance, Mendel developed his two Laws of Heredity, which become the basis of modern genetics.

## NEWTON, SIR ISAAC (1642–1727)

English physicist and mathematician Isaac Newton was the greatest figure of the scientific revolution of the 17th century. Born in Woolsthorpe, England, he was greatly interested in building models of machines, such as clocks and windmills, even as a child. He later went on to make significant discoveries in various fields. In optics, his discovery of the composition of white light integrated the phenomena of colours into the science of light and laid the foundation for modern physical optics. In mechanics, his three laws of motion, the basic principles of modern physics, resulted in the formulation of the law of universal gravitation. In mathematics, he was the original discoverer of the infinitesimal calculus. Newton's *Philosophiae Naturalis Principia Mathematica* ('Mathematical Principles of Natural Philosophy', 1687), is one of the most seminal works in the history of modern science.

## NOBEL, ALFRED (1833–1896)

Alfred Nobel was a Swedish chemist and the inventor of dynamite. He was particularly interested in the safe manufacture and use of nitroglycerine, a highly unstable explosive. Nobel incorporated nitroglycerine into silica, an inert substance, which made it safer and easier to manipulate. He patented this in 1867, under the name 'dynamite'. In 1895, Nobel signed his will stating that much of his wealth would provide the funds for the establishment of the Nobel Prize. This wealth was to be distributed yearly in five equal parts as prizes to either individuals or institutions that had most helped mankind. A prize was to be awarded in each of the five fields: physics, chemistry, physiology or medicine, literature, and peace. Economics was also added as a field in 1968. The awards are presented annually on 10 December, Nobel's death anniversary.

## PASTEUR, LOUIS (1822–1895)

Louis Pasteur was a French chemist and biologist who proved the germ theory of disease and invented the process of pasteurization. He was able to demonstrate that organisms such as bacteria were responsible for souring wine and beer (he later extended his studies to prove that milk was similarly affected), and that bacteria could be removed by boiling and then cooling the liquid. This process is now called pasteurization. He is best known for his work on the development of vaccines for rabies. In 1888, a special institute, Institut Pasteur, was founded in Paris for the treatment of diseases. He explained the causes of many diseases, including anthrax, cholera, tuberculosis, and smallpox, and also their method of prevention by vaccination.

## PLANCK, MAX (1858–1947)

Max Planck was a theoretical physicist whose quantum theory won him the Nobel Prize for physics in 1918. This theory revolutionized our understanding of atomic and subatomic processes. He continued to contribute at a high level to various branches of optics, thermodynamics and statistical mechanics, physical chemistry, and other fields. He was also the first prominent physicist to champion Einstein's special theory of relativity.

## RAMAN, CHANDRASEKHARA VENKATA (1888–1970)

C.V. Raman was the first Indian Nobel Laureate in physics. He was awarded the prize in 1930 for his discovery that when light passes through a transparent material, some of the light that is deflected changes in wavelength. He was awarded the Bharat Ratna in 1954. India celebrates National Science Day on 28 February of every year to commemorate the discovery of the Raman Effect.

## RAY, PRAFULLA CHANDRA (1861–1944)

Chemist and entrepreneur, Prafulla Chandra Ray was the founder of the Indian School of Modern Chemistry. He worked on nitrites and on compounds of gold, platinum, iriduim, etc. He devoted himself to various spheres of human interest: educational reform, scientific development, employment generation, and poverty alleviation. He even invested his own money into forming Bengal Chemical and Pharmaceutical Works.

## SAHA, MEGHNAD (1893–1956)

Meghnad Saha was an Indian astrophysicist, whose theory of thermal ionization, which explained the origin of stellar spectra, was one of India's most important contributions to world science. He had great organizational skills. Among the institutions he set up are National Academy of Sciences (Allahabad), Indian Physical Society (Kolkata), Indian Science News Association (Kolkata), and Saha Institute of Nuclear Physics (Kolkata). He was also an active member of the Planning Commission and chairman of the Indian Calendar Reform Committee. He advocated large-scale industrialization in order to to bring about social development.

## WATT, JAMES (1736–1819)

James Watt was a Scottish inventor and mechanical engineer, renowned for his improvements in steam engine technology. Born in Scotland, he moved to Glasgow at the age of seventeen to learn the art of mathematical instrument making. There, he made improvements on Newcomen's steam engine and took out the famous patent for 'A New Invented Method of Lessening the Consumption of Steam and Fuel in Fire Engines'. He patented several other important inventions including the rotary engine, the double-action engine, and the steam indicator, which records steam pressure inside the engine. In 1785, Watt was elected Fellow of the Royal Society.

## WRIGHT BROTHERS

[(Wilbur Wright (1867–1912), Orville Wright (1871–1948)]

Wilbur and Orville Wright were American inventors and aviation pioneers. Born in Milleville and Dayton, respectively, they did not attend college. Instead, they started a bicycle sales and repair shop. The experience of designing and building lightweight, precision machines of wood, wire, and metal tubing was ideal preparation which helped them to construct flying machines later. They achieved the first powered, sustained, and controlled airplane flight in 1903. They also built and flew the first fully practical airplane in 1905. In 1908, Orville made the world's first flight of over one hour in a demonstration for the US Army. The Wright planes were the world's first military airplanes.

# SOME ACCIDENTAL INVENTIONS

**Saccharine:** In 1879, Dr Constantin Fahlberg, a chemist, was working with coal tar derivatives in the hope of discovering a new food preservative. After he went home, he noticed that the rolls he was eating tasted particularly sweet. He realized the taste must have come from his hands—which he hadn't washed. The next day he went back to the lab and started tasting his work until he found out what had caused the sweetness. That's how saccharine was discovered.

**Vulcanized rubber:** Charles Goodyear spent a decade finding ways to make rubber easier to work with, while being resistant to heat and cold. One day he spilled a mixture of rubber, sulphur and lead on to a hot stove. The heat charred the mixture, but didn't ruin it. When he picked up the accidental produce, he noticed that the mixture had hardened but was still usable. Vulcanized rubber is today used in everything from tyres to shoes to hockey pucks.

**Plastic:** In 1907, shellac was used as insulation in electronics. As it was expensive, chemist Leo Hendrik Baekeland tried to produce an alternative for shellac. Instead, his experiments yielded a mouldable material that could absorb high temperatures without being distorted. Baekeland thought his 'Bakelite' might be used for phonograph records, but it was soon clear that the product had many other uses. Today plastic, which was derived from Bakelite, is used everywhere.

**Radioactivity:** In 1896, Antoine Henri Becquerel ran a series of experiments to see if naturally fluorescent minerals produced X-rays after they had been left out in the Sun. Since it was winter, he left his equipment wrapped up together in a drawer and waited for a sunny day. When he got back to work, Becquerel realized that the uranium rock he had left in the drawer had imprinted itself on a photographic plate without being exposed to sunlight first. There was something very special about that rock. Working with Marie and Pierre Curie, he discovered that the distinctive quality was radioactivity.

**Pacemaker:** When scientist Wilson Greatbatch was building a circuit to help record fast heart sounds, he reached into a box for a resistor to finish the circuit and pulled out a 1-megaohm resistor instead of a 10,000-ohm one. The circuit pulsed for 1.8 milliseconds and then stopped for one second. Then it was repeated. The sound was as old as human life, a perfect heartbeat. It led to the invention of the pacemaker.

**Penicillin:** One day in 1928, Alexander Fleming didn't clean up his workstation before going on vacation. When he returned, Fleming noticed that there was a strange fungus on some of his cultures. Even stranger was that bacteria didn't seem to thrive near those cultures. Penicillin became the first and still is, one of the most widely used antibiotics.

**Microwave oven:** The microwave oven was invented by chance, when Percy Spencer found that a chocolate bar had been melted by an experiment he was running on radar systems. He repeated the experiment with popcorn.

## SOME GREAT SCIENTIFIC EXPERIMENTS

### DARWIN'S FLOWERS

As Darwin studied several orchid species, he realized that intricate orchid shapes were adaptations that allowed the flowers to attract insects which would then pollinate nearby flowers. Each insect was perfectly shaped and designed to pollinate a certain type of orchid. For example, the Star of Bethlehem orchid (*Angraecum sesquipedale*) stores nectar at the bottom of a tube up to 30 cm long. Darwin predicted that a 'matching' animal existed. In 1903, scientists discovered that the hawk moth sported a long proboscis uniquely suited to reach the bottom of the orchid's nectar tube. Darwin used his data on orchids and their insect pollinators to reinforce his theory of natural selection. He argued that cross-pollination produced orchids more equipped for survival than orchids produced by self-pollination, a form of inbreeding that reduces genetic diversity and, ultimately, affects the survival power of a species.

### DECODING DNA

James Watson and Francis Crick unlocked the mystery of DNA, but their discovery was based on the work of Alfred Hershey and Martha Chase who, in 1952, had conducted a famous experiment that identified DNA as the molecule responsible for heredity. Hershey and Chase worked with a type of virus known as a bacteriophage. Then scientists like Rosalind Franklin used a technique called X-ray diffraction to study DNA. Franklin's famous photo of DNA shows an X-shaped pattern that Watson and Crick knew was a signature of a helical (or spiral) molecule. They could also determine the helix's width, which suggested that two strands made up the molecule, leading to the double-helix shape we all know today.

### THE FIRST VACCINATION

In the 18th century, smallpox caused by the variola virus killed every tenth child born in Sweden and France. British physician Edward Jenner noticed that dairymaids who had had cowpox seemed to be protected from smallpox. So in 1796, Jenner infected a young boy by the name of James

Phipps. He made cuts on Phipps' arms and then inserted some fluid from the cowpox sores of a local dairymaid named Sarah Nelmes. Phipps subsequently contracted cowpox and recovered. Forty-eight days later, Jenner exposed the boy to smallpox, only to find that the boy was immune. Cowpox viruses and smallpox viruses are so similar that the body's immune system could not distinguish them. The antibodies created to fight cowpox viruses will attack and kill smallpox viruses as if they were identical.

## SCIENTIFIC PRINCIPLES BEHIND POPULAR ACTIONS

### DOPPLER EFFECT

The pitch of the siren of the police car changes, first becoming higher as it approaches, then lower as it passes. This is due to a shift in the frequency of sound waves around the object, commonly known as the Doppler Effect. It is named after Austrian mathematician and physicist Christian Doppler, who first discovered this principle in the mid-1800s. When something is moving towards us, sound waves bunch up, leading to an increase in pitch due to this compression. When it's moving away from us, the waves expand, leading to a decrease in sound. Most meteorologists rely on the Doppler radar system to provide accurate results on the distance and direction of rain.

### BERNOULLI PRINCIPLE

Daniel Bernoulli, a Swiss physicist and mathematician, discovered this principle of physics in the 1700s. According to the law, the pressure of a fluid decreases as its speed increases. An airplane in flight demonstrates this principle well. The air creates lower pressure above the wing than beneath it. This pressure difference is what allows the wings to push upward and the plane to take flight. The faster the wing moves, the more lift is created, enabling the plane to stay up.

### GRAVITATIONAL PULL

Sir Isaac Newton gave us the Universal Law of Gravitation. Gravity is the force that attracts objects towards Earth, the result being that all objects fall at the same rate, regardless of mass. However gravitational force or pull can vary on other celestial bodies. On Earth, the force is always equal to the weight of the object, as opposed to a location like the moon, where the force of gravity is about 1/6th that of Earth.

## REFRACTION

Isaac Newton showed that after a prism has separated a beam of sunlight into rainbow colours a second prism can bring the different colours together again. Therefore, white light is a combination of all the rainbow colours. The prism separates its colours because the angle by which a beam of light is bent, when it enters glass, differs from one colour to the next. Those colours can be seen more individually every time a rainbow is formed in the sky, and that's where the idea of refraction comes into play. When light passes through transparent material—in this case, raindrops—its velocity slows down, causing the light to bend. The angle of bending varies slightly for each wavelength, which leads to the formation of the rainbow.

## DID YOU KNOW?

◇ Tree crickets are often referred to as the poor man's thermometer because their rate of activity is directly afftected by the temperature. Count the number of chirps a cricket makes in 15 seconds, then add 37 to the number. The result will be close to the outside temperature in Fahrenheit!

◇ A TV screen shows 24 pictures in a second while a fly sees 200 images a second. It would see TV as still pictures with darkness in between!

◇ Thermal expansion makes the Eiffel Tower 15 cm taller in the summer.

◇ Where would you weigh less: North Pole or the Equator? You weigh less if you stand at the equator because the equator is further away from the centre of the earth, so the force of gravity is less.

◇ The energy that exists between the atoms of 1 kg of butter is the same as that in 1 kg of TNT.

◇ Though gold leaf is pure gold, it can cover large areas very cheaply as it is very thin, is less than 0.00008 millimetres thick.

◇ The rate of acceleration of a flea, when it jumps, is about 20 times higher than that of a space shuttle during launch.

◇ Depending on the size of raindrops, the maximum speed at which they can fall at is around 30 km/hr.

◇ Whales often make loud clicking noises to talk to each other. As sound waves travel well underwater, they can hear each other from as far away as 160 km.

◇ 201 decibels – the loudest noise ever. It is believed to have been produced by engineers at NASA. It is so loud that it can make holes in solid materials.

◇ One Venus day is longer than its year. It takes 225 Earth days to revolve around the Sun (a Venusian year) but 243 Earth days to rotate on its axis (a Venusian day).

The Puffin Factfinder

# FACTS ON NOISE

❧ Unwanted sound is often referred to as noise. It is measured in decibels (dB). To an average listener, an increase of 10 decibels will cause the noise to be perceived as sounding twice as loud.

❧ The smallest change in noise level that the human ear can detect is about 3 decibels.

❧ The noise level will decrease by 3 to 4.5 decibels for each doubling of distance from the source.

# FACTS ON SOUND

❧ Sound travels at the speed of 1239.19 km per hour.

❧ When does a sonic boom occur? It occurs when an object breaks the speed of sound. It is caused by the clash of sound waves behind and in front of the object.

❧ At 115 dB, a baby's cry is louder than a car horn.

❧ A dog's sense of hearing is more sensitive than that of human beings. Dogs can hear much higher frequencies, which is why they respond to 'silent' dog whistles.

❧ Acoustics plays a large part in the design of modern concert halls and similar buildings. The walls and ceilings of many such buildings have strange shapes—discs, panels and saucers—to absorb or reflect the sounds.

# FACTS ON HEAT

❧ Though Mercury is the closest planet to the sun, it is not the hottest planet in the solar system. That is Venus. This is because Venus has a dense atmosphere that traps the Sun's heat, giving it an average temperature of 863°F (462°C). Mercury peaks at 801°F (427°C) during the day but drops to −297°F (−183°C) at night.

❧ Dallol in Ethiopia is the hottest inhabited place on the planet, with an average annual temperature of 93°F (34°C).

❧ The peak temperature of lightning is 54,032°F (30,000°C), five times hotter than the surface of the Sun. When a bolt of lightning strikes sand, it instantly melts and turns to glass.

❧ Fulgurites (from the Latin *fulgur* for 'lightning') or material formed of sand or other sediment as a result of lightning are often named after deserts in which they are found (saharite from the Sahara). They are usually found under the surface of the sand and shatter when touched.

- The normal body temperature of a healthy adult male is 98.2°F (36.8°C). Any increase in bodily temperature above 104°F (40°C) is dangerous.

- The average body temperature of most mammals is similar but birds have a slightly higher average temperature [104°F (40°C)–107.6°F (42°C)] because they require a high metabolic rate for flying.

- Bread, at 309°F (154°C), undergoes the Maillard reaction, named for the French chemist who first described it in 1910. This reaction takes place when heat breaks down the structure of proteins and sugars on the bread's surface giving it new flavour and a brown colour.

- Why do our mouths feel cold if we suck on a peppermint? Gums and mints are made up of a substance called menthol, which contains proteins that mimic the action of cold temperatures on our nervous system. They bond with the receptor neurons called TRM8s, which usually open up by temperatures less than 53.6°F (12°C), and send the 'it's cold' signal to the brain.

## FACTS ON SPEED

- If you stand on the Equator, the speed of the Earth's rotation around its own axis is about 1673.71 kmph. As you approach the poles, this decreases and so if you stand on either pole, you barely move at all. Earth is moving around the Sun at 107826.05 kmph

- Speed is a relative measurement and according to Einstein's theory of special relativity, the constant against which the speed of all objects in the universe is measured is the speed of light (299,792,458 metre per second).

- The speed at which an object falls gradually evens out as a result of air resistance. This is known as a body's terminal velocity. For the average raindrop, 28.96 kmph; for a human being, 201.16 kmph. In normal atmospheric pressure, it takes about 1,880 ft (573 m) or 14 seconds to reach this speed; at higher altitudes, a faster fall is possible as the air is less dense.

## FACTS ON LIGHT

- Solar winds are plumes of electrically charged particles spewed out by the sun that occasionally hit Earth. The planet's protective magnetic field pushes these particles to the poles, where they react with oxygen and nitrogen atoms in the atmosphere to produce light. These eerily beautiful curtains of light are the aurora borealis and australis (or Northern and Southern Lights).

- Crystals glow when warmed. This is called thermoluminescence–the property of some materials that have absorbed energy over a long period of time to become luminescent when subjected to high temperatures. It was first discovered by the British chemist Robert Boyle in 1663.

- The giant squid, *Taningia danae*, has the largest light-producing organs of any living creature. The lemon-yellow light organs are called photophores and are found at the tip of the two of the squid's feeding arms.

- Many people respond to bright lights by sneezing. This is called the photic sneeze reflex or ACHOO syndrome (Autosomal-dominant Compelling Helio-Ophthalmic Outburst).

- The first commercially viable incandescent light bulb, patented by Thomas Alva Edison in 1880, used a filament made from burned bamboo.

## MEASUREMENT

The grain was the earliest unit of mass, equal to 0.065 grams. It was defined as the weight of a designated number of dry wheat (or other edible grain) kernels taken from the middle of the ear. It was also used as the original basis for the medieval English inch, which was defined as the length of 3 medium barleycorns placed end to end (about 2.54 cm). The Sumerian shekel equalled the weight of 180 wheat grains; the British silver penny sterling was set at the weight of 32 wheat grains. The metric grain of 50 mg is used to weigh precious stones. Anthropomorphic units are derived directly from the dimensions of the human body (form).

### DIGIT

*Digit* is a Latin word meaning 'finger'. As a unit of length, the digit is currently standardized to be a sixteenth of a foot.

### PALM AND HAND

Palm and hand, or handbreadth, have both historically been used in English to refer to specific lengths. The hand or handbreadth is currently standardized to be 4 inches, whereas the palm is standardized to be 3 inches. Horse heights are measured in hands.

### SPAN

A span is the width of a human hand, from the tip of the thumb to the tip of the pinky finger. The span, from ancient times, has been considered to be 1/2 cubit. The span is currently standardized to 9 inches. The standardized English foot is 12 inches.

## CUBIT

The cubit is the length of the forearm (from the elbow to the fingertips). The cubit is a very old unit of measurement used in many ancient cultures with different length values. The modern cubit is standardized to be 45.72 cm or 18 inches.

## FATHOM

The fathom is a unit of length derived from an old English word meaning 'outstretched arms'. It is currently standardized to be 182.88 cm or 72 inches.

## FURLONG

The furlong is a unit of length derived from the Old English words *furh* (furrow) and *lang* (long). It was originally defined as the length a plough team was to be driven without resting. It was later standardized as 40 rods or 220 yards.

## ACRE

An acre was the amount of land tillable by one man behind one ox in one day. Traditional acres were long and narrow due to the difficulty in turning the plough.

## MILE

The current definition of a mile as 5,280 feet dates to the 13th century. The mile is a modern derivation of the Ancient Roman *mille passus*, literally 'a thousand paces'.

## DID YOU KNOW?

- ◇ Long bones are hollow, and their cross-sectional shape is a circle. Engineers will confirm that this structure is difficult to bend or twist. Under load—walking, running and lifting—our bones do flex a little, but their basic shape helps to prevent them from grossly deforming or collapsing.

- ◇ The lens is made of layers and layers of transparent cells laid over one another like the skins of an onion. These are added throughout life, so it never stops growing.

- ◇ The most common solid tissue transplanted in the world is the cornea.

# The Puffin Factfinder

- Seven microlitres (seven one-thousandths of a millilitre) is the volume of tears on the surface of our eyes while resting.

- If you stretched out your entire DNA from just one cell, it would be 2 metres long.

- Bats make a sound that humans cannot hear. They send out sound waves that hit objects. A fraction of a second later, an echo comes back to their large ears. Bats not only hear the echo but are able to tell how far away an object is, and in which direction. All of this happens so quickly that the bat is able to use the echo to locate the object, even though it may be far away. This is called 'echolocation'.

- Chameleons only change colour when in imminent danger. Their regular skin colour, a light khaki, keeps them hidden from enemies during other times. Nearly half the world's chameleon species live in Madagascar, but they are also found in Africa, the Middle East, and southern Europe and in India.

- Other bears and human poachers are the biggest threats to the polar bear, but by blending into the blindingly white snow of the Arctic with equally white fur coats, some danger can be avoided. Only its nose and foot pads are without fur.

- The shell of turtles camouflage them from large predators like alligators.

- Arctic owls have a coat of snow-white feathers to keep them warm and safe from predators, such as foxes and wolves.

- To hide from their prey, gaboon vipers—among the most venomous snakes on Earth—make the most of their brownish-gray, mottled scales. These big snakes hide in the layer of dead leaves that carpets the African rain forest floors. They also like to snuggle into forest floor peat and sneak up on unsuspecting prey.

- Complete with fake leaf stalk, fake leaf veins, and perfect dead-leaf colouring, leaf butterflies fool birds that pass them by without a second glance since these insects from south-east Asia look more like dead leaves than butterflies.

- Carbon exists in its elemental form in diamonds and graphite as continuous structures. It also exists in a molecule form, the simplest of these being buckminsterfullerene, more commonly known as fullerene, and which has sixty carbon atoms arranged in the shape of a soccer ball.

- The nomadic tribes of the Mediterranean used the stomachs of calves as containers to carry milk. The milk was curdled by rennin produced in the calf's stomach and, with the gentle rocking, thickened to become the first soft cheeses.

# NANOTECHNOLOGY

Nanotechnology is the understanding and control of matter at the nanoscale, at dimensions between approximately 1 and 100 nanometers. A nanometer (nm) is one-billionth of a meter, smaller than the wavelength of visible light and a hundred-thousandth the width of a human hair. Nanotechnology can make materials stronger, lighter, more durable, more reactive, more sieve-like, or better electrical conductors, among many other traits.

## USES OF NANOTECHNOLOGY

Nanoparticles of zinc oxide or titanium oxide are the ingredients of many sunscreens. While the older sunscreen formula used larger particles, the new ones use smaller particles which does not leave a whitish tinge on the skin

There are many ways in which nanotechnology is used in clothing. While some fabrics are coated with zinc oxide nanoparticles to give better protection from UV radiation, many others use nanoparticles in the form of little hair or whiskers to repel liquids and other materials, making the clothing stain-resistant.

Nanoparticles of silver have been used by scientist Robert Burrell to create a process of manufacturing antibacterial bandages.

## STEM CELLS

Many diseases kill cells within organs causing death or impairing the body's ability to carry out normal functions. Stem cell research aims to replace dead cells with fresh cells. A stem cell is the building block of the human body. Stem cells can divide for long periods, and can develop into specialized cells. The earliest stem cells in the human body are found in the embryo, and these eventually give rise to every cell, tissue, and organ in the foetus' body. Unlike a regular cell, which can only replicate to create more of its own kind, a stem cell is pluripotent (can become any type of cell). When it divides, it can make any one of the 220 different cells in the human body. Stem cells also have the capability to renew—they can reproduce themselves many times over. Stem cells may be embryonic stem cells, adult stem cells, or induced pluripotent stem cells.

## CLONING

Any of various techniques used to reproduce genetically identical organisms from an individual organism is called cloning. The organisms so produced are called clones. The term 'cloning' also refers to the technique used in genetic engineering to produce identical segments of DNA and to the asexual reproduction of organisms in nature. Cloning is used commercially to reproduce individual plants and animals that have desirable traits. Plants can be cloned using such techniques as cutting and tissue culture. Animals can be cloned using either embryonic or adult cells. Tissue culture came into commercial use in the 1950s, primarily to reproduce orchids. Frogs were the first animals to be cloned using embryonic cells. In 1996, a sheep called Dolly was the first vertebrate cloned from an adult body cell. The first animal cloned in India was 'Garima', a buffalo calf (2009), and the second was 'Noorie', a pashmina goat (2012).

## CELL PHONE

The cell phone is actually an extremely sophisticated radio. Earlier, people who really needed mobile communications installed radio telephones in their cars. In this system, there was one central antenna tower per city, and perhaps twenty-five channels available. This central antenna meant that the phone in a car needed a powerful transmitter—big enough to transmit over 70 km. The genius of the cellular system is the division of a city into smaller cells. This allows extensive frequency reuse across a city, so that millions of people can use cell phones simultaneously.

## ROBOTICS

A robot has a movable physical structure, a motor, a sensor system, a power supply, and a computer 'brain' that controls all these elements. Essentially, robots are man-made machines that replicate human and animal behaviour. Most roboticists specify that robots have a reprogrammable brain (a computer) that moves a body. Like the bones in your body, the individual segments are connected together with joints. The robot's computer controls everything attached to the circuit. To move the robot, the computer switches on all the necessary motors and valves. Most robots are reprogrammable—to change the robot's behaviour, you simply write a new program to its computer. Robots generally have the sense of movement— ability to monitor their own motion. The term robot comes from the Czech word *robota* or 'forced labour'. This describes the majority of robots fairly well. Most robots in the world are designed for heavy, repetitive manufacturing work. They handle tasks that are difficult, dangerous or tedious to human beings. An industrial robot with six joints closely resembles a human arm—it has the equivalent of a shoulder, an elbow and a wrist. Typically, the shoulder is mounted to a stationary base structure rather than to a movable body. This type of robot has six degrees of freedom, meaning it can pivot in six different ways. A human arm, by comparison, has seven degrees of freedom.

# DISEASES

## AVIAN INFLUENZA (BIRD FLU)

Avian influenza is an infectious disease of birds caused by certain strains of the influenza virus. The infection can cause severe epidemics among birds. The viruses do not normally infect humans. However, there have been cases of respiratory disease in humans, from close contact with infected poultry or with objects contaminated by their faeces. There is concern that the virus could mutate to become easily transmissible between birds and humans, raising the possibility of an influenza pandemic.

## CANCER

Cancer is the uncontrolled growth and spread of cells. It can affect almost any part of the body. The growths often invade surrounding tissues. Many cancers can be prevented by avoiding exposure to common risk factors, such as tobacco smoke. A significant proportion of cancers can be cured by surgery, radiotherapy, or chemotherapy, especially if they are detected early.

## CHICKEN POX

Chicken pox is a highly contagious disease caused by the varicella-zoster virus. It usually affects children, is spread by direct contact or respiratory droplets, and is characterized by the appearance on the skin and mucous membranes of successive crops of vesicular lesions that break and scab easily. Chicken pox is relatively benign in children but may be complicated by pneumonia and encephalitis in adults.

## CHOLERA

Cholera is an acute intestinal infection caused by ingesting food or water contaminated with the bacterium *Vibrio cholerae*. It has a short incubation period, from one to five days, and produces an enterotoxin that causes copious, painless, watery diarrhoea that can quickly lead to severe vomiting, dehydration and even death if treatment is not promptly provided.

## CORONARY HEART DISEASE

Coronary heart disease (CHD) is a condition in which plaque builds up inside the coronary arteries, which supply the heart muscle with oxygen-rich blood. Plaque narrows the arteries and reduces blood flow to the heart muscle, making it more likely for blood clots to form. This can cause a heart attack, whose symptoms include pain in the chest, shoulders, arms, neck, jaw, or back. Without quick treatment, a heart attack can lead to death. CHD is the most common type of heart disease.

## DENGUE

Dengue, also known as breakbone fever, is caused by the bite of an Aedes mosquito infected with any of the four dengue viruses. It occurs in tropical and sub-tropical areas of the world. Symptoms appear three to fourteen days after the infective bite. Dengue is a febrile illness that affects infants, young children, and adults. Symptoms range from a mild fever to incapacitating high fever, with severe headache, pain behind the eyes, muscle and joint pain, and rashes.

## DIARRHOEA

Diarrhoea is the abnormal passage of several loose or liquid stools per day. It is a symptom of gastrointestinal infection, which can be caused by a variety of bacterial, viral, and parasitic organisms. Infection is spread through contaminated food or drinking water, or from person to person as a result of poor hygiene. Severe diarrhoea leads to fluid loss, and may be life-threatening, particularly in children, malnourished people, and those with impaired immunity.

## DIPTHERIA

Diphtheria is an infectious disease which spreads via respiratory droplets produced during coughing and sneezing. It normally breaks out two to five days after infection. Diphtheria affects the tonsils, pharynx, larynx, and the skin. Symptoms range from a moderately sore throat to toxic life-threatening diphtheria of the larynx or of the lower and upper respiratory tracts. The disease can be fatal, and patients can die despite being properly treated.

## ENCEPHALITIS

Viral encephalitis is inflammation of the brain, caused by any one of a number of viruses. Symptoms include high fever, headache, sensitivity to light, stiff neck and back, vomiting, confusion and, in severe cases, seizures, paralysis, and coma. Infants and elderly people are particularly at risk of severe illness. Viruses transmitted through insect bites are among the most common causes of viral encephalitis, and include Japanese encephalitis and tick-borne encephalitis viruses.

## FILARIASIS

Filariasis is a group of infectious diseases caused by a parasitic worm, transmitted by an infected mosquito. It is divided into three groups depending on which parts of the body the worms occupy: lymphatic filariasis, subcutaneous filariasis, and serous cavity filariasis. Lymphatic filariasis, or elephantiasis, puts at risk more than 1 billion people in more than eighty countries. In its most obvious manifestations, lymphatic filariasis causes enlargement of the entire leg or arm, the genitals, vulva, and breasts.

## HEPATITIS

Hepatitis is an inflammation of the liver, commonly caused by a viral infection. There are five main hepatitis viruses, referred to as types A, B, C, D, and E. Hepatitis A and E are typically caused by ingestion of contaminated food or water. Hepatitis B, C, and D usually occur as a result of contact with infected body fluids (such as blood transfusions). Symptoms include jaundice, darkened urine, extreme fatigue, nausea, vomiting, and abdominal pain.

## HIV/AIDS

The human immunodeficiency virus (HIV) is a retrovirus, which infects cells of the immune system, destroying or impairing their function. As the infection progresses, the immune system becomes weaker, and the person becomes more susceptible to infections. The most advanced stage of HIV infection is acquired immunodeficiency syndrome (AIDS). It can take ten to fifteen years for an HIV-infected person to develop AIDS; antiretroviral drugs can slow down the process even further. HIV is transmitted through unprotected sexual intercourse, transfusion of contaminated blood, sharing of contaminated needles, and between a mother and her infant during pregnancy, childbirth, and breastfeeding.

## JAUNDICE

Jaundice is excess accumulation of the bile pigment, bilirubin, in the bloodstream and bodily tissues, causing yellow discolouration of the skin, whites of the eyes, and mucous membranes. Jaundice is often symptomatic of certain diseases such as hepatitis. Jaundice can be caused by too many red blood cells retiring for the liver to handle, the liver being overloaded or damaged or the bilirubin from the liver being unable to move through the biliary tract to the gut.

## LEISHMANIASIS (KALA AZAR)

Leishmaniasis is caused by protozoan parasites belonging to the genus *Leishmania*. The parasites are transmitted by the bite of the tiny phlebotomine sandfly. Not all phlebotomine species transmit leishmaniasis, though. Only the female sandfly transmits the *Leishmania* parasites, after getting infected with them while sucking blood from an infected person or animal. The disease is known as *kala azar* in India, where, along with Bangladesh, Nepal, Sudan, and Brazil, most of the cases in the world occur.

## LEPROSY

Leprosy is a chronic infectious bacterial disease caused by *Mycobacterium leprae*. The disease mainly affects the skin, peripheral nerves, mucosa of the upper respiratory tract, and the eyes. Leprosy has afflicted humanity since time immemorial, and was well recognized in the oldest civilizations of China, Egypt, and India. It is estimated that there are between 1 and 2 million people visibly and irreversibly disabled due to past and present leprosy.

## MALARIA

Malaria is caused by the parasite *Plasmodium*, transmitted via the bites of infected mosquitoes. In the human body, the parasites multiply in the liver, and then infect red blood cells. Symptoms include fever, headache and vomiting, and usually appear between ten and fifteen days after the mosquito bite. If not treated, malaria can quickly become life-threatening by disrupting the blood supply to vital organs. In many parts of the world, the parasites have developed resistance to a number of malaria medicines.

## MEASLES

Measles is a highly contagious viral disease, which affects mostly children. It is transmitted via droplets from the nose, mouth, or throat of infected persons. Initial symptoms include high fever, runny nose, bloodshot eyes, and tiny white spots on the inside of the mouth, with rashes developing a few days later. Most people recover within three weeks. However, in malnourished children and people with low immunity, measles can cause serious complications. It can be prevented by immunization.

## MENINGITIS

Meningitis is a disease that affects the membranes, or meninges, covering the brain and spinal cord, and the cerebrospinal fluid surrounding them. It is most often caused by infection (bacterial, viral, fungal) but can also be produced by chemical irritation, subarachnoid haemorrhage, cancer, and other conditions. Bacterial meningitis is characterized by acute onset of fever, headache, stiff neck and altered consciousness, and is one of the most feared infectious diseases of children.

## MUMPS

Mumps is a viral infection, primarily affecting the salivary glands. The virus is transmitted by direct contact, or via airborne droplets. Initial symptoms usually appear two to three weeks after infection, and include headache, muscle pain, and light fever. Soon after, the characteristic swelling of one or both parotid glands appears. The virus usually causes mild illness in children but in adults can lead to complications such as meningitis and orchitis. Mumps can be prevented by immunization.

## PERTUSSIS (WHOOPING COUGH)

Pertussis is a major cause of infant deaths worldwide and continues to be a public health concern even in countries with high vaccination coverage. Following an incubation period of nine to ten days, patients develop symptoms related to inflammation of the nose and throat, including cough. In the course of one to two weeks, coughing paroxysms ending in the characteristic whoop occur. It can be averted through vaccination.

## PLAGUE

Plague is a bacterial disease caused by *Yersinia pestis*, which primarily affects wild rodents. It is spread among rodents by fleas. Humans bitten by an infected flea usually develop bubonic plague, characterized by swelling of lymph nodes in the groin and armpits. If the bacteria reach the lungs, the patient develops pneumonia, resulting in pneumonic plague, which then becomes transmissible through coughing. Bubonic plague can be successfully treated with antibiotics, However, pneumonic plague can cause death within twenty-four hours of infection.

## PNEUMONIA

Pneumonia is an inflammatory condition of the lungs, characterized also by the filling up of the lungs with fluid. Bacteria are the most common cause of pneumonia, though it can also be caused by viruses and parasites. Typical symptoms include cough, chest pain, fever, and difficulty in breathing. Pneumonia is common, occurring in all age groups, and is a leading cause of death among the young, the old, and the chronically ill.

## POLIOMYELITIS

Poliomyelitis (polio) is a highly infectious viral disease, which mainly affects young children. The virus is transmitted through contaminated food and water, and multiplies in the intestine, from where it can invade the nervous system. Many infected people have no symptoms, but do excrete the virus in their faeces, hence transmitting the infection. Initial symptoms of polio include fever, fatigue, headache, vomiting, stiffness in the neck, and pain in the limbs. In a small proportion of cases, the disease causes paralysis, which is often permanent. Polio can only be prevented by immunization.

## RABIES

Rabies is a viral disease affecting many domestic and wild animals, transmitted to humans mainly through bites or scratches of infected/rabid dogs, through infected saliva. It is known to be prevalent on all continents except Antarctica. Rabies is nearly always fatal if untreated.

## SEVERE ACUTE RESPIRATORY SYNDROME (SARS)

Severe Acute Respiratory Syndrome (SARS) is a respiratory illness caused by a virus. SARS was first reported in Asia in 2003. It spread worldwide over several months before the outbreak ended. SARS can be life-threatening. Its symptoms include high fever, headache, body aches, dry cough and, later on, pneumonia. SARS spreads mainly by infected droplets while coughing or sneezing. There is as yet no treatment for SARS.

## SLEEPING SICKNESS

Human African trypanosomiasis (sleeping sickness) is a parasitic disease. The parasites are protozoa transmitted to humans by the bites of tsetse flies, which have acquired their infection from humans or animals harbouring the parasites. Tsetse flies are found just in sub-Saharan Africa though only certain species transmit the disease. The symptoms include drowsiness during the day but insomnia at night. Sleep becomes uncontrollable as the disease gets worse, and can culminate in a coma.

## SMALLPOX

Smallpox is an acute contagious disease caused by the variola virus. It is transmitted via infected aerosols and nasal droplets. Symptoms appear twelve to fourteen days after infection, and include fever, headache, prostration, severe back pain, and sometimes abdominal pain and vomiting. After two to three days, the body temperature falls and rashes appear on the face, hands, and forearms. Following a global immunization campaign by the World Health Organization, smallpox was declared eradicated in 1980; it no longer occurs naturally.

## TUBERCULOSIS

Tuberculosis (TB) is an infectious bacterial disease caused by *Mycobacterium tuberculosis*, which most commonly affects the lungs. It is transmitted from person to person via droplets from the throat and lungs. In healthy people, infection often causes no symptoms, since the person's immune system acts to 'wall off' the bacteria. The symptoms of active TB of the lungs are coughing (sometimes with sputum or blood), chest pains, weakness, weight loss, fever, and night sweats.

## TYPHOID

Typhoid is a bacterial disease caused by *Salmonella typhi*. It is transmitted by the ingestion of food or drink contaminated by the faeces or urine of infected people. Symptoms usually develop one to three weeks after exposure, and may be mild or severe. They include high fever, uneasiness, headache, constipation or diarrhoea, rose-coloured spots on the chest, and enlarged spleen and liver. After recovering from an acute illness, the healthy often become carriers. Hence, healthy carriers should avoid handling food.

# APEX SCIENTIFIC BODIES

## INDIAN SPACE RESEARCH ORGANIZATION (ISRO)

Space activities in India started during the early 1960s when small sounding rockets were used for scientific investigations of upper atmosphere and ionosphere over the magnetic equator that passes over Thumba near Thiruvananthapuram. ISRO's objective is to develop space technology and its application to various national tasks. It has operationalized two major satellite systems: Indian National Satellites (INSAT) for communication services and Indian Remote Sensing (IRS) satellites for management of natural resources. Satish Dhawan Space Centre at Sriharikota, with two launch pads, is the main launch centre of ISRO.

## BHABHA ATOMIC RESEARCH CENTRE (BARC)

Homi Jehangir Bhabha, who realized the immense potential of nuclear energy as a viable alternative source for electric power generation, launched India's nuclear programme in March 1944. Dr Bhabha initiated nuclear research in India following the discovery of nuclear fission phenomena by Otto Hahn and Fritz Strassman and the feasibility of sustained nuclear chain reactions by Enrico Fermi. BARC provides a broad spectrum of scientific and technological activities extending from bench-scale research to plant-level operations. Its functional domain covers all walks of science and technology.

## NATIONAL AERONAUTICS AND SPACE ADMINISTRATION (NASA)

An executive branch agency of the US government, it is responsible for the US civilian space programme and aeronautics and aerospace research. Established by the National Aeronautics and Space Act on 29 July 1958, it has led many US space exploration efforts, including the Apollo moon landing and the Skylab space station. The Mercury, Gemini, and Apollo programmes helped NASA understand the dynamics of flight in space. This led to the first human landing on the moon in 1969.

## EUROPEAN ORGANIZATION FOR NUCLEAR RESEARCH (CERN)

An international scientific organization that facilitates collaborative research into high-energy particle physics, CERN came into being in 1954 and is headquartered near Geneva. It was one of Europe's first joint ventures and now has twenty member states.

---

### MEN ON THE MOON

◇ So far, twelve astronauts have walked on the moon, between them bringing back 382 kg of rocks, pebbles, sand and dust.

◇ On 20, July 1969 Neil Armstrong became the first man to walk on the moon.

◇ Alan Bean, the fourth person on the moon, is the only painter to have visited another world.

◇ Alan Shepard was the first American to venture into space and the first man to play golf on the moon!

◇ Edgar Mitchell threw the first javelin on the moon. On his way back, he conducted his own research into consciousness and extra-sensory perception.

◇ In December 1972, Eugene Cernan became the last man to stand on the moon.

◇ Harrison Schmitt is the only professional geologist to visit the moon. He took the most reproduced photograph in human history—the 'Blue Marble' picture of Earth—while singing *'When I was strolling on the moon one day'*.

---

## HOW DO ASTRONAUTS EAT IN SPACE?

In a low-gravity environment, food and drinks would simply float away. Therefore, food is carefully contained and drinks are packaged as dehydrated powders. The astronauts add water to beverages through a special tube before drinking. Astronauts eat three meals a day (plus periodic snacks). Meals are organized in the order in which the astronauts will eat them, and stored in locker trays held by a net so they won't float away. Astronauts go into the galley area in the shuttle's middeck. There they add water to freeze-dried foods and dehydrated drinks from a rehydration station that dispenses both hot and cold water. They heat food in a forced-air convection oven. It takes 20–30 minutes to rehydrate and heat an average meal.

## ANIMAL SUPERLATIVES

- Fastest land animal, over short distances : Cheetah
- Fastest water mammal: Dall porpoise
- Fastest land bird: Ostrich
- Fastest sky bird : Peregrine falcon
- Fastest fish: Sailfish
- Loudest animal: Blue whale
- Deadliest animal: Female Anopheles mosquito
- Strongest animal: Rhinoceros beetle
- Most venomous animal: Sea wasp
- Largest animal: Blue whale
- Largest land animal: African elephant
- Largest invertebrate: Giant squid
- Largest land invertebrate: Coconut crab
- Smallest vertebrate: Infantfish
- Smallest bird: Adult bee hummingbird
- Smallest mammal: Adult bumblebee bat

# MAπHEMATICS

## MATHEMATICIANS AND THEIR CONTRIBUTIONS

### ARYABHATA (AD 476–AD 550)

Aryabhata was an Indian astronomer and mathematician of the 5th century AD. He lived and worked in Kusumapura (now in Bihar). He is best known for *Aryabhatiya*, his treatise on mathematics and astronomy in Sanskrit. In *Ganita,* a section of *Aryabhatiya,* he named the first ten decimal places and provided algorithms for arriving at square and cubic roots, utilizing the decimal number system. He treated geometric measurements using π. He was the first Indian astronomer to state that the Earth is spherical and rotates on its axis. India's first unmanned Earth satellite is named after him.

### BHASKARA I (LIVED c. 629)

Bhaskara I was an eminent Indian astronomer and mathematician of the 7th century. Little is known about his life; I is appended to his name to distinguish him from a 12th-century Indian astronomer of the same name. Bhaskara I is famous for disseminating Aryabhata's works through his composition of the three treatises *Mahabhaskariya* ('Great Book of Bhaskara'), *Laghubhaskariya* ('Small Book of Bhaskara'), and *Aryabhatiyabhashya.* Bhaskara's works were particularly popular in south India.

### BHASKARA II (1114–1185)

Bhaskara II, a pioneering astronomer and mathematician of the 12th century, was the first to write a work with detailed and systematic use of the decimal number system. In his mathematical works, particularly *Lilavati* ('The Beautiful') and *Bijaganita* ('Seed Counting'), he used the decimal system and compiled problems from other mathematicians. Bhaskara II used letters to represent unknown quantities, much as in modern algebra, and solved indeterminate equations of the first and second degrees. He reduced quadratic equations to a single type and solved them.

## BRAHMAGUPTA (AD 598- AD 665)

Brahmagupta was one of India's most accomplished astronomers and mathematicians. He laid the foundation of two major fields in Indian mathematics: arithmetic and algebra. His most remarkable contribution to the field of mathematics was his definition of the digit zero. He defined zero as a result of subtracting a number from itself.

## DESCARTES, RENE (1596–1650)

Descartes was an acclaimed French mathematician, scientist and philosopher. He described what is known as the system of Cartesian coordinates or coordinate geometry, which is used to locate a point in space by its relative distance from perpendicular intersecting lines. He also made contributions to analytical geometry that shows equations in two variable quantities to define plane curves.

## EUCLID (c. 300)

Euclid, one of the most prominent mathematicians of Greco-Roman antiquity, is best known for his treatise on geometry, *Elements*. He defined a prime number as a number whose only proper divisor is 1, a composite number as a number that is not prime, and a perfect number as one that equals the sum of its proper divisors. From there, Euclid proved a sequence of theorems that marked the beginning of the number theory. He also proposed the method to find the greatest common divisor of two whole numbers. This fundamental result is now called the Euclidean algorithm in his honour.

## FIBONACCI, LEONARDO (c. 1170–c. 1240)

Leonardo Fibonacci, also known as Leonardo of Pisa, was a talented Italian mathematician of the middle ages. He played a significant role in disseminating the knowledge of Hindu-Arabic numerals. He formulated the Fibonacci sequence that was also proved to occur in nature. This path-breaking work led to a number of great discoveries like that of the Golden Ratio.

## GAUSS, CARL FRIEDRICH (1777–1855)

Carl Friedrich Gauss is regarded as one of the greatest German mathematicians for his contributions to the number theory, geometry, and probability theory. In 1792, his first significant discovery was that a regular polygon of seventeen sides can be constructed by a ruler and compass alone. He also proved the fundamental theorem of algebra.

## JACOBI, CARL (1804–1851)

Carl Jacobi was a renowned German mathematician who. in collaboration with Niels Henrik Abel of Norway, founded the theory of elliptic functions, based on four theta functions. He made a significant contribution to the theory of determinants. Jacobi carried out important research in partial differential equations of the first order. The Hamilton–Jacobi equation now plays a significant role in the presentation of quantum mechanics.

## PASCAL, BLAISE (1623–1662)

Blaise Pascal was a leading French mathematician, physicist and religious philosopher. He laid the foundation for the modern theory of probability and formulated what came to be known as Pascal's law of pressure. Some of his greatest contributions include the invention of the syringe and hydraulic press, an instrument based upon the principle that became known as Pascal's law. He published papers on the problem of the vacuum.

## PTOLEMY (c. 100–170 AD)

Ptolemy was an Egyptian astronomer, mathematician, and geographer of Greek descent. He lived in Alexandria during the 2nd century AD. His writings represent the achievement of Greco-Roman science, particularly his model of the universe, the Ptolemaic system. His first major astronomical work was titled *Almagest*.

## PYTHAGORAS (580 BC–500 BC)

Pythagoras was a distinguished ancient Greek mathematician and philosopher. He is credited with formulation of the theory of the functional significance of numbers in the objective world. His name is generally associated with the Pythagoras theorem, which states that the sum of the square of the base and perpendicular in a right angle triangle is equal to the square of the hypotenuse.

## RAMANUJAN, SRINIVASA (1887–1920)

Ramanujan was an Indian mathematician who significantly contributed to the theory of numbers, including discovery of the properties of partition function. His knowledge of mathematics was phenomenal. He worked out the Riemann series, the elliptic integrals, hypergeometric series, the functional equations of the zeta function, and his own theory of divergent series. He was the first Indian to be elected to the Royal Society of London. His birthday is celebrated as State IT Day in Tamil Nadu every year.

## INTERESTING MATHEMATICAL FACTS

⚘ The equals sign '=' was invented by Robert Recorde in 1557.

⚘ The atmospheric temperature can be calculated by the rate at which a cricket chirps. It is known as Dolbear's Law, as it was proved by Amos Dolbear.

⚘ The Greek letter pi or $\pi$, usually taken as 22/7 or 3.14, is actually an irrational number (it cannot be expressed as a fraction or a ratio), so the digital sequence never ends or repeats itself. Other irrational numbers include the Golden Ratio. Such numbers are called 'surds' or deaf numbers.

⚘ Pascal's triangle is a triangular array of numbers where every digit is a sum of the two digits above it, except for the edges, which are 1. It is named after Blaise Pascal, even though the sequence was already known before him.

⚘ Squaring a number—multiplying a number by itself—is so called because in classical geometry the sides of a square figure are multiplied to get the area.

⚘ The Fibonacci sequence, where each number is the sum of the previous two numbers (1, 1, 2, 3, 5, 8, 13, 21...) is also seen in nature. The petals of a sunflower and the spirals of a pineapple always occur in the Fibonacci sequence.

## MATHEMATICAL CHARTS AND FIGURES

| NAME OF POLYGON | NUMBER OF SIDES | SUM OF INTERNAL ANGLES |
|---|---|---|
| Triangle | 3 | 180° |
| Tetragon | 4 | 360° |
| Pentagon | 5 | 540° |
| Hexagon | 6 | 720° |
| Heptagon | 7 | 900° |
| Octagon | 8 | 1080° |
| Nonagon | 9 | 1260° |
| Decagon | 10 | 1440° |
| Undecagon | 11 | 1620° |
| Dodecagon | 12 | 1800° |

# TOOL BAR

| SYMBOLS | READ AS | EXPLANATION |
|---|---|---|
| = | equal to | If x = y, then x and y represent the same value. |
| ≠ | not equal to | If x ≠ y, then x and y do not represent same value. |
| < | less than | If x < y, then x is less than that of y. |
| > | greater than | If x > y, then the value of x is greater than y. |
| ≤ | less than or equal to | If x ≤ y, then x represents a value less than or equal to y. |
| ≥ | greater than or equal to | If x ≥ y, then x represents a value greater than or equal to y. |
| ± | plus–minus | a ± b means both a + b and a–b. |
| ≅ | is congruent to | $\triangle ABC \cong \triangle DEF$ means the triangles are congruent or identical in form. |
| → | implies | If A → B then if A is true, B is also true; but when A is false then nothing can be said about B. |
| ⊥ | perpendicular | AB ⊥ CD means the line AB is perpendicular to the line CD. |
| ‖ | parallel | If AB ‖ CD, then the lines AB and CD are parallel to each other. |
| √ | square root | $\sqrt{a^2} = a$ |
| ∞ | infinity | It refers to a quantity without bound or end. |
| ∝ | proportionality | If A ∝ B then A= qB, where q is a constant. |
| : | is to | If A : 4 = B : 5 then 5A = 4B. |
| ∴ | therefore, hence | Man is mortal. Ram is a man. ∴ Ram is mortal |
| ∵ | because | 2 is a prime number ∵ it has only two factors, itself and one |
| Σ | summation, sum over | $\sum_{k=1}^{n} a_k$ means $a_1 + a_2 + \ldots + a_n$. |
| Π | product over | $\prod_{k=1}^{n} a_k$ means $a_1 a_2 \cdots a_n$. |

# ᑅNDEX

4X games, 111–112
6600 supercomputer, 108
8-inch floppy diskette, 108

Academy awards, 299
Accidental inventions, 327–328
Acid rain, 121, 122
Acre, 334
AD (Anno Domini), 1
Advani, Pankaj, 304
Adventure novel, 269, 280
Afforestation, 122, 128
Afghanistan, 46, 65–67, 77–79, 165, 222
Agra Fort, 253, 257
Aibak, Qutb-ud-din, 57, 64
Air pollutants, 120
Air pollution, 120
Ajanta Caves, 257
Ajatashatru, 57, 61, 84
Akbar, 57–59, 61, 64, 81, 82, 228, 258, 294
Akhtar, Begum, 290
Albania, 165
Alexander the Great, 9–10, 54, 67, 81
Algae, 122
Algeria, 160, 166
Ali, Aruna Asaf, 43, 242
Ali, Hyder, 58, 71, 79
Ali, Salim Abdul, 130
All India Institute of Medical Sciences (AIIMS), 235
All India Radio (AIR), 235–236
Allegory, 269, 278

Alto workstation, 108
Altocumulus clouds, 155
Amazon, 157, 159, 161, 163
Ambedkar, Bhimrao, 43, 44, 90
American Civil War, 15, 28
American Revolution, 15–16, 34
Amonkar, Kishori, 290
Amte, Baba, 130
Amur, 161
Anand, Dev, 295, 297
Anand, Mulk Raj, 272, 289
Anand, Vishwanathan, 304
Anarchy, 35, 82, 104
Andaman and Nicobar Islands, 52, 253
Andhra Pradesh, 88, 101, 127, 221, 225–227, 229, 241, 246, 264, 290
Andorra, 166
Anglo-Sikh Wars, 80
Angola, 161, 166
Animal superlatives, 346
Antagonist, 269
Antarctic Ocean, 159–160
Antarctica, 138, 151, 152, 154, 158–160, 343
Anticyclone, 155
Antigua and Barbuda, 166
Apple Computer Inc., 109
Apple II, 109
Applique embroidery, 233
Apps on smart phones, 112
Aravalli Range, 165, 221
Archimedes, 319
Arctic Ocean, 158–160

Argentina, 159–160, 167, 302, 305, 311
Aristotle, 9, 54–56, 103, 323
Arkham Asylum, 112
Armed forces of India, 244–245
Armenia, 96, 167
Armstrong, Neil, 145, 345,
Arpanet, 108
Art and culture, 233–235
Artificial intelligence, 113–114, 117
Arunachal Pradesh, 225, 247
Arya Samaj, 51, 85, 87
Aryabhata, 347
Aryabhatta Research Institute of Observational Sciences, 146
ASCII (American Standard Code for Information Interchange), 108
Ashok Chakra, 240–241
Ashoka, 59, 62, 82, 83, 138, 227, 240, 241, 262
Ashrama system, 8
Asian Games, 301, 307, 312, 314, 315
Assam, 225, 242, 247, 255
Asteroid, 144
AT&T designs Dataphone, 108
Atacama Desert, 163
Atari 2600, 109
Atari Video Computer System, 109
Atatürk, Mustafa Kemal, 21
Atharva Veda, 7
Atlantic Ocean, 152, 158–161
Atmosphere and its structure, 150–151
Atmosphere, 123
Atomic Energy Establishment (AEET), 236
Attila the Hun, 10
Aurangzeb, 59–60, 69
Austen, Jane, 279–280
Australia, 14, 36, 97, 105, 151, 152, 157, 158, 160–162, 167, 302, 306, 315
Austria, 12, 20, 41, 161, 167
Autobiography, 47, 100, 269
Avatar, 272
Avian influenza (Bird flu), 338
Awards in India, 240–242
Ayurveda, 272
Azad, Abul Kalam, 44–45, 77, 90, 242

Azad, Chandra Shekhar, 44, 53
Azerbaijan, 168

Babbage, Charles, 116, 117, 318
Babur, 60–61, 64, 66, 81, 82
Bachchan, Amitabh, 295, 297
BackRub, 110, 117
Badminton, 303, 304, 308, 311, 312
Baha'i Temple, 257
Bahrain, 168
Bahugana, Sunderlal, 130
Balamuralikrishna, M., 290
Balban. 62
Ballad, 269
Bandanna, 272
Bandaranai ke, Sirimavo, 22
Banerjee, Rakhaldas, 5
Bangladesh, 50, 98, 105, 160, 168, 221, 225, 227, 273, 340
Bangle, 272
Banihal Pass, 223
Barbados, 169, 315
BASIC (Beginner's All-purpose Symbolic Instruction Code), 108, 109, 115
Basilica of Bom Jesus, 248, 258
Battle of Chausa, 64, 72, 80
Battle of Ghaghra, 60, 81
Battle of Haldighati, 81
Battle of Hydaspes, 10, 81
Battle of Waterloo, 11, 16
Battle of Terrain, 63, 68, 82
Battle of Buxar, 80
Battle of Khanua, 60, 81
Battle of Panipat (First), 60, 66, 81, 82
Battle of Panipat (Second), 57, 82
Battle of Plassey, 70, 71, 81–82
BC (Before Christ), 1
BCE (before the Common Era), 1
Bean, Alan, 345
Beat 'Em Up and Hack-and-Slash, 111
Beckenbauer, Franz, 305
Beckham, David, 305
Belarus, 12, 139, 169
Belgium, 12, 20, 160, 169
Belize, 169
Bell, Alexander Graham, 319, 321
Benin, 170
Benz, Karl, 318

Berner-Lee, Tim, 319
Bernoulli Principle, 329
Besant, Annie, 45, 76, 86
Bhabha Atomic Research Centre (BARC),
   236, 319, 344
Bhabha, Homi Jehangir, 319, 344
Bhakra Nangal dam, 224
Bhangra, 255
Bharat Ratna, 241
   Bharat Ratna awardees, 241–243
Bharata Muni, 276
Bharatanatyam, 229
Bharathiar, Subramania, 272–273
Bhaskara I, 347
Bhaskara II, 347
Bhavai, 255
Bhave, Vinoba, 86, 87, 242
Bhimbetka, 3, 250
Bhonsle, Asha, 295
Bhopal gas tragedy, 138–139, 268
Bhopal Tragedy Day, 119, 268
Bhortal Nritya, 255
Bhupathi, Mahesh, 305, 311, 312
Bhutan, 37, 138, 170, 227
Bhutia, Baichung, 305
Bidri work, 233
Bihar, 8, 9, 57, 60, 70, 72, 74, 75, 80,
   81, 100, 101, 127, 224, 228, 232,
   234, 241, 242, 247, 255, 285, 347
Bihu, 255
Bimbisara, 57, 61, 84
Bindra, Abhinav, 256, 306
Bindusara, 61, 62, 67
Biodegradable, 120, 123
Biography, 47, 63, 100, 131, 246, 269,
   274, 285
Biological diversity, 123
Biomass, 120, 123, 125
Biosphere, 123, 149
Bismarck, Otto von, 22
Bit, 115
Blake, William, 280
Blyton, Enid, 280
Bolivar, Simon, 23
Bolivia, 23, 161, 170
Bombe, 107
Bonaparte, Napoleon, 11, 16, 23
Border Security Force (BSF), 236

Border, Allan, 306
Borlaug, Norman Ernest, 130
Bose, Jagadish Chandra, 320
Bose, Khudiram, 45
Bose, Subhas Chandra, 46, 76, 265
Bose, Nandalal, 91, 245
Bosnia and Herzegovina, 170
Botswana, 164, 171
Boycott, Geoff, 306
Boyle, Robert, 320, 333
Bradman, Don, 306, 316
Brahmagupta, 348
Brahmaputra, 225, 227
Brahmo Samaj, 85, 88
Brazil, 105, 159–161, 171, 302, 312,
   340
British Constitution, 91
Browning, Robert, 280
Brunei, 171
Bucephala, 10
Buddhism, 83
Bug, 115
Bulgaria, 20, 161, 172
Bungalow, 272
Burkina Faso, 172
Burundi, 162, 172
Byron, Lord, 117, 280

C++ programming language, 109
Cache, 116
Caesar, Julius, 23–24, 285
Cama, Madame Bhikaji, 46–47
Cambodia, 172
Cameron, David, 35
Cameroon, 161, 173
Canada, 14, 107, 135, 159, 160, 173,
   301, 317
Cancer, 121, 123, 130, 139, 148, 158,
   288, 298, 338, 341
Candy, 272
Cape Verde, 173
Carbon dioxide (CO2), 121
Carbon monoxide (CO), 120–121
Carbon, 14 Dating, 3
Carrier, Willis, 318
Carroll, Lewis, 269, 281
Carson, Rachel, 131
Castro, Fidel, 24

Catamaran, 272
Catherine the Great, 11–12
CE (Common Era), 1
Cell phone, 111, 337
Central African Republic, 161, 174
Central Bureau of Investigation (CBI), 236
Cernan, Eugene, 345
Chad, 174
Chalcolithic Age, 1, 2
Chamberlain, Neville, 25
Chanakya, 67, 273
Chandigarh, 248, 251, 254
Chandragupta II, 62
Charlemagne, 12–13
Charminar, 246, 258
Chatterjee, Bankim Chandra, 229, 273
Chattopadhyay, Saratchandra, 273
Chaucer, Geoffrey, 271, 281
Chaudhury, Nirad C., 273–274
Chauhan, Prithviraj, 63, 68, 82, 296
Chaurasia, Hariprasad, 291, 293
Chekhov, Anton, 281
Cheraw, 255
Chernobyl nuclear disaster, 139–140
Chhatrapati Shivaji Terminus, 258
Chhattisgarh, 247
Chhau Seraikela, 255
Chicken pox, 317, 338
*Chikankari*, 233
Chile, 159, 163, 174
China, 3, 4, 19, 20, 25, 30, 35, 37, 83, 105, 157, 158, 160–164, 174, 223, 249, 278, 341
Chinese civilization, 3
Chipko Movement, 129, 130, 133
Chit, 272
Chlorofluorocarbons (CFC), 121
Chola I, Rajendra, 63
Cholera, 31, 325, 338
Chowdhury, Bula, 306
Christianity, 54, 55, 83, 85
Christmas, 13, 230
Churchill, Winston, 24–25, 271
Classical dances, 229–230
Climate change, 123, 134, 136
Climate system, 123
Clinton, Hillary Rodham, 36

Cloning, 336–337
Cloud computing, 115
Clouds, 155–156
Clouds, types of, 155–156
Coir, 272
Coleridge, Samuel Taylor, 269, 281, 288
Colombia, 23, 161, 175
Colt, Samuel, 319
Comets, 141, 144–145
Commonwealth Games, 299, 301, 309, 311, 312
Communism, 104
Communist Manifesto, 29
Comoros, 175
Complex Number Calculator (CNC), 107
Computer glossary, 115–116
Confucius, 4, 25
Congo or Zaire, 161, 162, 175, 176, 217
Conservation, 123, 131, 132,133–136, 268
Constellation, 145, 147
Constituent Assembly of India, 90, 91
Constitution of India, 90–91
Constitution of the German Reich, 91
Constitution of the UK, 104–105
Constitution of the United States Of America, 104
Constitutions of the World, 104–105
Continent, 23,151, 157–159, 343
Continents and oceans, 158–159
Cookie, 115
Copernicus, Nicolaus, 40, 320
Coronary heart disease, 338
Costa Rica, 176
Cot, 272
Cote d'Ivoire (Ivory Coast), 176
Countries and regions of the world, 165–168
Couplet, 269, 271
Crick, Francis, 328
Cricket(game), 282, 302, 304, 306–310, 313, 315, 316,
    cricket (animal) 330, 350
Crimean War, 16–17, 31, 287
Croatia, 161, 176
Cromwell, Oliver, 26
Crusades (the Holy Wars), 17, 40
Cruyff, Johann, 307

Cuba, 24, 177
Cubit, 333, 334
Curie, Marie, 320, 327
Curie, Pierre, 320, 327
Cyclone, 155
Cyprus, 177
Czech Republic, 96, 177

Dacoit, 272
Dadasaheb Phalke Award, 243, 256,
  295–298
Dadra and Nagar Haveli, 254
Dahl, Roald, 282
Dal churma bati, 263
Dalton, John, 321
Daman and Diu, 254
Damodar Valley Corporation (DVC), 224
Damodar Valley Dams, 224
Dandiya, 255
Danube, 12, 161, 162
Darwin, Charles (1809–1882), 321, 328
Darwin's flowers, 328
Das Kapital, 29
Davis Cup, 301, 312
Dayanand Saraswati, Swami, 51, 85, 87
DDT, 123
Decagon, 350
Deccan Odyssey, 239
Decoding DNA, 328
Defoe, Daniel, 282
Deforestation, 123, 124, 134, 136
Democracy, 37, 104
Democratic Republic, 90, 104
Democratic Republic of the Congo, 175
Dengue, 339
Denmark, 22, 133, 160, 178, 270
Desai, Kiran, 274, 288
Desai Anita, 244, 274
Descartes, Rene, 320, 348
Desertification, 123
Deserts, 163–165
Desktop Computers, 110
Detective Fiction, 270
Dev, Kapil, 302, 307
Devi, Girija, 291
Devi, Mahashweta, 243, 274
Dew, 156

Dholavira, 6
Dhoni, Mahendra Singh, 302, 307
Dialogue, 270, 271
Diarrhoea, 338, 339, 344
Dickens, Charles, 271, 282
Dictatorship, 103
Digit, 115, 237, 333, 348, 350
Dinghy, 272
Diptheria, 339
Diwali, 230
Djibouti, 178
Dodecagon, 350
Doldrums, 154
Dominica, 178
Dominican Republic, 178
Doordarshan, 236
Doppler Effect, 329
Dosanjih Sr, Balbir Singh, 307
Downing Street, UK, 105
Doyle, Arthur Conan, 270, 282
Drama, 54, 270, 281, 283, 285, 293
Drought, 123, 128–129, 136
Dumas, Alexandre, 270, 283
Dunlope, John B., 319
Durga Puja, 231
Dussehra, 231

Earth, 120–124, 126, 128, 134–136,
  141–143, 145–154, 157–159,
  157–159, 163, 276, 287, 320, 324,
  329–330, 332, 335, 345, 347
  and its spheres, 149–150
  major landforms of, 151–152
Earth Day, 119, 266
Eastern Ghats, 221
Eastman, George, 318
Ecosystem, 111, 121, 123, 124, 128,
  136, 140, 149
Ecuador, 23, 159, 161, 179
Edison, Thomas Alva, 318, 321, 333
Egypt, 3, 5, 6, 10, 14, 23, 55, 73, 112,
  160, 163, 179, 341
Egyptian civilization, 4
Eid-ul-Fitr, 231
Einstein, Albert, 321–322, 325, 332
El Salvador, 179
Election Commission of India, 94

Election in India, 94–95
    facts on, 95–96
Elections of the World, 96–97
Elegy, 270
Elk Cloner, 109
Ellora Caves, 250, 258
Emirate, 104
Emissions, 121, 124, 137
Encephalitis, 338, 339
Endangered species, 124
Energy, 120, 124–126, 128, 131, 132,
    137, 146, 147, 149, 150, 163, 33,
    344, 345
English words with Indian origins, 272
ENIAC (Electronic Numerical Integrator
    and Computer), 107
Enlightenment in Europe, 40–41
Environment calendar, 119
Environmental and industrial disasters,
    138–140
Epic, 63, 264, 270, 275, 284
Equator, 147
Equatorial Guinea, 180
Equinox, 149
ERA 1101, 107
Erasmus, Desiderius, 40, 54
Eritrea, 180
Erosion, 124, 128
Estonia, 180
Ethernet, 108
Ethical hackers, 115
Ethiopia, 162, 180, 331
Euclid, 348
European Environmental Agency (EEA),
    134
European Organization for Nuclear
    Research (CERN), 116, 345
Exosphere, 151
Extinct species, 124
Exxon Valdez oil spill, 139–140

Facebook, 112, 117, 118
Facts on,
    heat, 331–332
    light, 332–333
    noise, 331
    sound, 331
    speed, 332

Fairs and festivals, 230–231
Famous scientists, 319–326
Faraday, Michael, 318, 322
FAT virus, 113
Fatehpur Sikri, 58, 65, 258
Fathom, 334
Federal republic, 104
Fencing, 128
Fibonacci sequence, 348, 350
Fibonacci, Leonardo, 348, 350
Fiction, 114, 269, 270, 271, 274–276, 287
FIFA World Cup, 302, 312, 316
Fiji, 181
Filariasis, 339–340
Film and Television Institute of India
    (FTII), 236
Film personalities of India, 295–299
Finland, 106, 181
First,
    internet browser, 110
    modern analog computer, 107
    person shooter video game, 111
    programmable binary computing
        machine Z1, 107
    web-based e-mail service, 110
    in India, 256–257
Fleming, Alexander, 318, 322, 327
Fodder, 128
Fog, 122, 126, 156
Folk dances, 255
Food in India, 263–264
Football, 302, 304, 305, 312, 316, 317
Forestry, 128
Forms of condensation, 156
Forms of government, 103–104
Forms of precipitation, 156
FORTRAN (FORmula TRANslator), 107
Fossey, Dian, 131
Four RS of waste management,
    127–128
Franco, Franciscol, 19
Franklin, Benjamin, 318, 322,
Franklin, Rosalind, 328
French Revolution, 17, 41, 56
Frost, 156
Fuelwood, 128
Fukushima Daichi Nuclear Disaster, 140
Furlong, 334

Gabon, 182
Galilei, Galileo, 40, 144, 146, 318–320, 322
Gandharv, Kumar, 291
Gandhi Peace Prize, 243
Gandhi, Indira, 97, 98, 102, 129, 130, 242, 257, 267
Gandhi, Mahatma, 47–48
Gandhi, Rajiv, 98, 102, 242
Ganesh Chaturthi, 231
Ganga, 225, 232, 233
Ganguly, Sourav, 308
Garba, 255
Garo, Khasi, and Jaintia Hills, 221
Gateway of India, 259
Gates, Bill, 109, 115–117
Gauss, Carl Friedrich, 348
Gavaskar, Sunil, 308
Genre, 111, 269, 270
Geographical superlatives, 157
George II, 105
George, Anju Bobby, 308
Georgia, 33, 182
Germany, 10, 12, 19–23, 26, 29, 31, 38, 41, 46, 47, 103, 105, 159, 161, 182, 281, 302, 321
Ghalib, Mirza, 274
Ghana, 183
Ghori, Muhammad, 57, 63, 67–68, 82
Ghosh, Aurobindo, 48,
Ghosh, Amitav, 244, 275
Gillard, Julia, 36
Glidden, Carlos, 319
Global warming, 124, 134, 134–137
    fast facts about, 135–137
Goa, 239, 248, 258
Godavari, 221, 225
Gol Gumbaz, 259
Golconda Fort, 246, 259
Golden Temple, 84, 251, 259
Goodall, Dame Jane, 131
Google, 110, 111–112, 117
Gopichand, Pullela, 308
Gore, Albert, Jr, 131, 134
Gothic Novel, 270
Government of India Act, 1935, 91
Grammy awards, 300
Grand Slam, 302, 303, 305. 311

Gravitational pull, 329
Great Wall of China, 4
Greece, 9, 10, 21, 40, 137, 159, 183, 281, 303, 307, 313, 316. 319
Green Consumer Day, 119
Greenhouse effect, 124
Greenhouse gases, 124, 125, 136
Greenland, 157, 159, 183
Greenpeace, 134–135
Greenwich Mean Time, 148
Grenada, 183
Grey Hat Hackers, 114
Grimm Brothers, 283
Groundwater, 121, 122, 124
Guatemala, 184,
Guinea-Bissau, 184
Guinea, 180, 184, 203
Guinness Book of World Records 2008, 96
Gujarat, 47, 51, 78, 87, 102, 128, 132, 133, 222, 226, 233, 235, 240, 242, 248, 255
Gulf of Mexico Oil Spill, 140
Gulf War Oil Spill, 140
Gutenberg, Johann, 40, 319
Guyana, 185
Gwalior Fort, 260

Habitat, 124, 136, 137
Hacking, 114, 115
Hadlee, Richard, 307, 309
Hail, 156
Haiti, 185
Haleem, 264
Hampi, 249, 260
Harappa, 5, 6
Hardware, 116
Hardy, Thomas, 283
Harshavardhana, 63, 262
Haryana, 128, 224, 233, 235, 248, 314
Hawa Mahal, 252, 260
Hazardous waste, 125, 127
Hemisphere, 147
Henry VIII, 13
Henry, O., 271, 283
Hepatitis, 340
Heptagon, 350
Hewlett-Packard, 108

Hexagon, 350
Hillary, Edmund, 131
Himachal Pradesh, 223, 224, 231, 248
Hinduism, 60, 86, 88, 89, 231
Hippocrates, 54–55, 137, 323
Hirakud dam, 224
Hitler, Adolf, 20, 26, 33, 103, 314
HIV/AIDS, 340
Hobes, Thomas, 55
Hockey, 228, 304, 306, 307, 312–314,
     317, 327
Holi, 231
Hollande, Franoise, 36
Honduras, 185
Hopper, Grace, 115
Hotmail, 110
Howe, Elias, 319
HP-2115, 108
HTML (HyperText Markup Language),
     109
Hubble Space Telescope, 146
Humayun's Tomb, 255, 261
Humayun, 57, 61, 64, 72, 80, 82, 255,
     261
Hundred Years' War, 18, 27
Hungary, 10, 20, 161, 185, 307, 310
Hunt, Walter, 319
Hussain, Ustad Zakir, 291, 300
Hussain, M.F., 245
Hwang Ho, 3, 162
Hydrochlorofluorocarbons (HCFCs), 125
Hydroelectricity, 125
Hydrofluorocarbons (HFCs), 125
Hydrosphere, 123, 149
Hypertext Transfer Protocol (HTTP),
     110,116

IBM 650 magnetic drum calculator, 107
IBM PC, 109
ICC Cricket World Cup, 302
Iceland, 186
Igneous Rocks, 153
Iltutmish, 62, 64, 65, 71, 276
Important Trains, 239
India Gate, 255, 260
India Post, 237
Indian Air Force, 245

Indian Army, 238, 245, 261
Indian Institute of Management (IIM),
     237
Indian Institute of Technology (IIT), 238
Indian Military Academy (IMA), 238
Indian musical instruments, 294
Indian Navy, 245
Indian Ocean, 154, 158–160, 210
Indian Railways, 238–239
     some terms associated with,
          238–239
Indian Space Research Organization
     (ISRO), 98, 239, 344
Indian Standard Time, 148
Indonesia, 39, 152, 160, 186
Indus river, 225
Indus Valley civilization, 5–6
Industrial Revolution, 42
Inland Letter, 237
Inorganic, 125
Inspirations from other constitutions, 91
Institutions and organizations, 235–240
Integrated resource planning, 125
Interesting facts on,
     environment, 138
     recycling, 137
     water, 137
Intergovernmental Panel on Climate
     Change (IPCC), 132, 134, 135, 136
International Date Line, 149
International Day for Natural Disaster
     Reduction, 119, 267
Internet World Exposition, 110
Inventions and discoveries, 318–319
Ionosphere, 150, 151, 344
Iran, 64, 84, 105, 112, 160, 187
Iraq, 6, 187
Ireland, 33, 187, 288
Irish Constitution, 91
Iron Age, 1, 2
Islam, 58, 59, 83, 85
Island, 151, 152, 157
Israel, 39, 187, 322
Isthmus, 151, 159
Italy, 10, 12, 19, 20, 21, 30, 38, 40, 55,
     56, 103, 159, 188, 280, 302, 307,
     310

Jacobi, Carl, 349
Jahangir, 58, 65, 69, 257
Jainism, 67, 84, 258
Jamaica, 188, 303
Jammu and Kashmir, 91, 223, 224, 248, 263
Jan Shatabdi Express, 239
*Jana Gana Mana*, 227
*Janapada*, 8–9
Janmashtami, 231
Janssen, Zacharias, 318
Jantar Mantar, 252, 255, 261
Jasraj, Pandit, 291
Jatra, 232, 255
Jaundice, 340
Jenner, Edward, 323, 328, 329
Jharkhand, 249
Jinah, Muhamad Ali, 48, 49
Jintao, Hu, 37
Jnanpith Award, 243
Joan of Arc, 18, 27
Jobs, Steve, 109, 115, 116, 118
Jordan, 189
Joshi, Bhimsen, 243, 291
Joyce, James, 284, 289
Jules-Francois, Joubert, 318
Jungle, 272
Junglee maas or lal maas (red meat), 263
Jupiter, 141–144, 146

Kabir, 275, 291
Kalahari, 164
Kalam, A.P.J. Abdul, 98, 103, 242
*Kalamezhuthu*, 234
Kalibangan, 6
Kalidasa, 62, 275
Kalinga War, 82
Kamakhya temple, 247, 261
Kamban, 275
Kanchenjunga, 222
Kanishka, 65, 227
*Kantha* embroidery, 234
Kapany, Narinder, 318
Kapoor, Raj, 296, 297–298
Karl Scheele, 318
Karnataka, 61, 221, 225, 226, 228, 233, 234, 241, 243, 249, 255, 259, 260, 262

*Kasuti* embroidery, 234
Kathak, 229
Kathakali, 229
Kaveri river, 221, 225–226
Kazakhstan, 189
Keats, John, 271, 284
Kenbak-1, the first personal computer, 108
Kenya, 134, 162, 189
Kepler, Johannes, 320, 323
Kerala, 228–230, 234, 249, 264, 278, 315
Khajuraho monuments, 250, 261, 262
Khalji, Ala-ud-din, 66
Khan, Aamir, 296
Khan, Ali Akbar, 292
Khan, Amjad Ali, 292
Khan, Bade Ghulam Ali, 292
Khan, Bismillah, 243, 292
Khan, Imran, 309
Khan, Shah Rukh, 296
Khanna, Rajesh, 296, 297
Khardung La, 223
Khusrau, Amir, 62, 276
King, Martin Luther, Jr, 27,
Kiribati, 189, 190, 216
Kosovo, 190
Kuchipudi, 229
Kumar, Dilip, 296, 297
Kumar, Kishore, 297–298
Kumar, Sushil, 303, 304, 309
Kumari, Meena, 297
Kumbh Mela, 232
Kumble, Anil, 309
Kummi, 255
Kuwait, 140, 190
Kyi, Aung San Suu, 37
Kyrgyzstan, 190

Laennec, Rene, 319
Lagarde, Christine, 37–38
Lahiri, Jhumpa, 276
Lake, 151
Lakshadweep, 254
Lama, Dalai, 38, 271
Land breeze, 154
Land degradation, 123, 125,
Laptop, 110
Latitude, 147

Latvia, 191
Le, Tim Berners, 109, 115, 116–117
Lead, 121
Lebanon, 191
Leishmaniasis (kala azar), 340
Leprosy, 130, 267, 341
Lesotho, 191, 192
Liberia, 192
Libya, 164, 192
Liechtenstein, 192
Life simulation games, 111
Lillee, Dennis, 309, 310
Lincoln, Abraham, 15. 28, 96
Linnaeus, Carl, 323
Lisa, 109
Lister, Joseph, 318
Lithosphere, 149–150
Lithuania, 12, 139, 191, 193
Lloyd, Clive, 310
Local self-government, 94
Local winds, 155
Lodi, Ibrahim, 60, 66, 82
LOGO, 108
Lok Sabha, 92–94, 97, 99–101, 256, 257
Longitude, 147
Lothal, 6
Lotus 1-2-3, 109
Lovelace, Ada, 117
Lunar Eclipse, 148
Lunyu (Analects), 25
Luxembourg, 193
Lyric, 270, 271

Maathai, Wangari, 132
Macedonia, 9, 33, 54, 67, 81, 193
Macintosh, 109, 118
Madagascar, 193–194, 335
Madhubala, 296, 297
Madhubani painting, 234
Madhya Pradesh, 3, 102, 133, 138,
    222, 226, 250, 261
Maha Vir Chakra, 243
Mahabalipuram, 260
Mahajanapadas, 8–9
Mahanadi, 221, 224, 226
Maharashtra, 52, 76, 100, 130, 133,
    222, 225, 226, 231, 235, 241–243,
    250, 297, 298

Mahmud of Ghazni, 66–67
Mainframe Computers, 110
Major awards, 288, 299–300
Major landforms of the Earth, 151–152
Malaria, 341
Malawi, 161, 194
Malaysia, 194, 296
Maldives, 194
Mali, 195
Malta, 195
Man Booker Prize, 274, 288
Manchester Small Scale Experimental
    Machine (The Baby), 107
Mangeshkar, Lata, 243, 298
Mango, 228, 272
Manipur, 230, 250, 255, 310
Manipuri, 230
Maradona, Diego, 310
Marconi, Guglielmo, 324
Mars, 141, 142, 144
Marshall Islands, 195
Marx, Karl, 29–30
Mary Kom, M.C., 303, 310
Mathematicians and their contributions,
    347–350
Mathematics tool bar, 351
Maupassant, Guy de, 284
Mauritania, 195–196
Mauritius, 196, 240
Maurya, Chandragupta, 61, 62, 67,
    273
McCarthy, John, 113
Measles, 317, 341
Measurement, 11, 147, 332–324, 347
Measuring devices, 157
Meenakshi Temple, 262
Meghalaya, 221, 250
Meghdoot Postcard, 237
Mehrgarh, 3
Mekong river, 162
Melbourne (Lord), 15
Mendel, Gregor, 318, 324
Meningitis, 341, 342
Menon, Anjolie Ela, 246
Men on the moon, 345
Mercury, 141, 142, 144, 146, 150, 331, 344
Merkel, Angela, 38
Mesolithic Period, 1, 2, 3

Mesopotamian civilization, 6
Mesosphere, 150, 151
Messi, Lionel, 310–311
Metamorphic rocks, 153
Meteors, 145, 150
Mexico, 140, 159, 162, 196, 310
Micronesia, 160, 196
Microsoft Corporation, 109
Microsoft Word, 109
Microsoft's MS-DOS, 109
Microwave oven, 328
Mile, 334
Milky Way, 141
Milton, John, 271, 284–285
Minamata Bay mercury poisoning, 139
Minh, Ho Chi, 20, 30
Mirza, Sania, 311
Missionaries of Charity, 33
Mississippi, 16, 162
Mitchell, Edgar, 345
Mizoram, 251, 255
Mohenjo-daro, 5, 6,
Mohiniattam, 230
Moldova, 139, 197
Monaco, 197
Monarchy, 18, 33, 103,105, 104
Money order, 237
Mongolia, 164, 197
Monologue, 270
Monsoon wind, 155
Montenegro, 197
Monti, Mario, 38
Monuments in India, 257–263
Moon, 12, 142, 145, 146, 148, 231, 232, 329, 344, 345
Morocco, 160, 198
Morse, Samuel F.B., 319
Mountains, 131, 151, 152, 155, 159, 161, 163
Mouse potato, 116
Mozambique, 198
Mukherjee, Pranab, 99, 103
Multi-Tool Word, 109
Mumps, 341–342
Muralitharan, Muttiah, 311
Murray–Darling basin, 162
Musical instruments, 294

Mussolini, Benito, 30–31, 103
Myanmar, 37, 162, 198
Mysore Palace, 231, 262

Nagaland, 251
Nagarjuna Sagar, 224
Naidu, Sarojini, 49, 90, 257
Nalanda, 83, 247, 262
Namibia, 164, 199
Nana Sahib, 68
Nanda Devi, 222
Nanga Parbat, 222
Nanotechnology, 336
Naoroji, Dadabhai, 49, 50, 76
Napier, John, 318
Napster, 114
Narayan, R.K., 244, 276
Nargis, 298
Narmada Bachao Andolan, 132
Narmada river, 130, 133, 222, 226
Narrator, 270
Nathu La, 223
National Cadet Corps (NCC), 240
National Defence Academy (NDA), 24
National Institute of Design (NID), 240
National Institute of Fashion Technology (NIFT) 240
National School of Drama (NSD), 240
National & international days, 265–268
National Aeronautics and Space Administration (NASA), 330, 344
National Film Awards, 244
National Symbols, 226–229
Natural resource, 120, 123, 125, 344
Nauru, 157, 199
Nehru, Jawaharlal, 54, 76, 90, 95, 98, 99, 101, 102, 239, 241, 256. 267
Nehwal, Saina, 303, 311
Nelson, Mandela, 28–29, 241, 242
Neolithic Period, 1–3
Nepal, 68, 83, 131, 138, 199, 227, 252, 278, 340
Neptune, 141, 143, 144
Nero, 13–14
Netanyahu, Benjamin, 39
Netscape Communications Corporation, 110

Netscape, 110
New Zealand, 14, 97, 131, 200, 302, 307, 309, 313
Newton, Isaac, 40, 118, 318, 320, 324, 329
NeXT, 109
Nicaragua, 200
Nicholas I (the Czar), 16, 19
Niger, 200, 217
Nigeria, 201, 312
Nightingale, Florence, 17, 31
Nile river, 162, 287
Nitrogen oxides (NOx), 121
Nivedita, Sister, 87
Nobel, Alfred, 324–325
Noise Pollution, 122
Nonagon, 350
Non-fiction, 271, 282
Nonrenewable resources, 120
North America, 15, 151, 152, 159, 162, 173, 183, 196, 218
North Korea, 201
North Pole, 148, 149
Norway, 201, 349
Novel, 43, 56, 229, 269–274, 276–279, 282, 284–286, 288, 289
Nuclear fission, 120, 125, 344
Nuclear fusion, 125, 146

Obama, Barack, 36, 39
Octagon, 350
Ode, 271
Odisha(Orissa), 70, 80, 221, 224, 228, 230, 232–234, 242, 251, 255, 263
Odissi, 230
Oligarchy, 103
Olympic Games (Summer, Winter), 303, 304, 306, 310, 311, 313
Oman, 201
Orbit, 148
Organic compounds, 125
Organic, 125
Organs of the Indian government, 92–94
Orkut, 112
Orwell, George, 285
Osborne I, 109
Overwrite Virus, 113

Ozone (O₃), 121
Ozone Layer, 121, 123, 125, 150

P2P sharing, 114
Pacemaker, 327
Pachauri, Dr Rajendra K, 132
Pacific Ocean, 149, 152, 157–160
Padma awards, 244
Padukone, Prakash, 308, 312
Paes, Leander, 305, 312, 317
Page, Larry, 110, 117
Painters of India, 245–246
Pakistan, 3, 5, 6, 48, 64, 70, 81, 130, 155, 160, 165, 202, 222, 225, 242, 249, 264, 276, 277, 295, 298, 302, 309, 314
Pal, Bipin Chandra, 50, 76
Palace on Wheels, 239
Palau, 202
Paleolithic Period, 1–3
Palm and Hand, 333
Palo Alto Research Centre, 108
Paluskar, Vishnu Digambar, 292
Panama, 23, 151, 159, 160, 202
Panchayati raj, 94, 98
Pandey, Mangal, 50, 75
Panini, 277
Pantulu, Vireshalingam, 88, 290
Papua New Guinea, 203
Paraguay, 203
Param Vir Chakra, 244
Paramhansa, Ramakrishna, 87–88, 89
Pascal, Blaise, 349, 350
Pascal's triangle, 350
Pasteur, Louis, 318, 325
Patel, Vallabhbhai, 51, 76, 90, 242
Pathak, Bindeshwar, 132
Patil, Pratibha Devisingh, 100, 103, 257
Patkar, Medha, 132–133
*Pattachitra* painting, 234
PC with a graphical user interface, 109
PDP-1 (Programmed Data Processor), 108
Pele, 312
Penicillin, 318, 322, 327, 328
Peninsula, 16, 17, 61, 152, 160
Pentagon, 350
Percussion Instrument, 294

Periodic Winds, 154
Permanent winds, 153–154
Personal Computers, 110, 116
Personal Digital Assistants, 111
Pertussis (whooping cough), 342
Peru, 23, 159, 161, 203
Pesticide, 125
Petrarch, 40, 55
Phalke, Dadasaheb, 243, 298
Pharaoh, 4, 5, 10, 14
Photosynthesis, 126
*Phulkari* embroidery, 235
Pictograms, 7
Pillay, Dhanraj, 312
Pir Panjal, 222
Plague, 258, 282, 342
Plain, 67, 151, 162, 165, 221, 223, 225, 226, 260
Planck, Max, 325
Planets, 141–143
Planetary winds, 153, 154
Plankalkul ('Plan Calculus'), 107
Plastic, 126, 137, 139, 294, 327
Plateau, 63, 152, 162, 221, 222, 225, 259, 326
Plato, 54–56
Pneumonia, 121, 317, 338, 342, 343
Poikkal Kudirai Attam, 255
Poland, 10, 20, 21, 96, 139, 204
Polar Easterlies, 154
Poliomyelitis, 342
Polo, 57, 304
Pong video game, 108
Portugal, 40, 204, 313
Postal Index Number (PIN), 237
Prarthana Samaj, 85–86
Prasad, Rajendra, 60, 100, 103, 241, 256
Precipitation, 123, 126, 156–157, 165
Premchand, Munshi, 277, 289
Presidential government, 104
Prime Meridian, 147, 148, 158
Indian Ministers and Presidents, 98–102
   facts on Indian prime ministers 102
Pritam, Amrita, 243, 277
*Prithviraj Rasau*, 63
Prologue, 271

Prose, 60, 89, 270, 271, 273, 276, 281, 284, 288
Protagonist, 271
Ptolemy, 145, 349
Puducherry (Pondicherry), 255
Pulitzer Prize, 276, 288
Punjab, 43, 51, 52, 57, 60, 64–66, 68, 70, 72, 78, 80, 84, 100, 165, 224, 225, 235, 251, 254, 255, 259
Purana Quila 255, 262
Pushkar Fair, 232
Putin, Vladimir, 39
Pythagoras, 349

Qatar, 204
Qutb Minar, 255, 262

Rabies, 325, 342, 343
Radhakrishnan, Sarvepalli, 93, 100, 101, 103, 241, 256
Radioactivity, 327
Rafi, Mohammad, 298–299
Rahman, A.R., 299, 300
Rai, Lala Lajpat, 50, 51, 53, 76, 85
Rain, 6, 7, 16, 121–122, 138, 156, 157, 163–165, 329, 335
Rajagopalachari Chakravarti, 51–52, 90, 241, 256
Rajasthan, 66, 79, 82, 100, 129, 133, 165, 221, 223, 232, 235, 239, 252, 255, 263
Rajdhani Express, 240
Rajiv Gandhi Khel Ratna Award, 304, 306, 308–314
Rajya Sabha, 92–94, 99–101
Ramakrishna mission, 86, 88
Raman, Chandrasekhara Venkata, 241, 256, 325
Ramanujan, Srinivasa (1887–1920), 349
Rani Lakshmibai, 68–69, 260, 274
Rani of Jhansi, 68, 260
Rao, Raja, 277
Rashtrapati Bhavan, 92,105, 255
Ratha Jatra, 232
Rathore, Fateh Singh, 133
Rathore, Rajyavardhan Singh, 313
Ray, Satyajit, 242, 256, 293, 299

Ray, Prafulla Chandra, 325
Raya, Krishna Deva, 69
Recyclable, 126
Red Fort, 69, 255, 257, 263, 292, 329
Reforestation, 126, 128
Reformation, 41–42
Refraction, 330
Renaissance ( in) Europe, 17, 40, 41, 54, 55, 258, 283
Renewable energy, 120
Republic of the Congo, 161, 176
Resource, 126
Revolution of the Earth, 148
Rhine river, 12, 163
Rhyme, 269–271
Rig Veda, 7, 8
Robotics, 337
Rocks, 59, 120, 150, 153, 250, 272
Rohtang Pass, 223
Role-playing Games, 111
Romania, 161, 205
Ronaldo, Cristiano, 313
Roosevelt, Theodore, 32, 106
Roosevelt, Franklin Delano, 31–32, 43
Rotation of the Earth, 148
Rousseau, Jean-Jacques, 41, 56
Rowing, 304
Roy, Arundhati, 277–278
Roy, Jamini, 246
Roy, Raja Ram Mohan, 85, 88–89
Rural India, 94
Rushdie, Salman, 278
Russia, 10–12, 16, 19, 20, 41, 97, 135, 157, 160, 161, 163, 205
Russian Revolution (1917), 19
Rutherford, Ernest, 318
Rwanda, 162, 205

Saccharine, 327
Sadya, 263
SAGE (Semi-Automatic Ground Environment), 107
Saha, Meghnad, 326
Sahara, 157, 164, 331
Sahitya Akademi Award, 244
Sahni, Dayaram, 5
Saint Kitts and Nevis, 205
Saint Lucia, 206

Saint Vincent and the Grenadines, 206
Sama Veda, 7, 8
Samoa, 206
San Marino, 206, 207
Sao Tome and Principe, 207
Satellite, 146
Satpura Range, 222, 226
Saturn, 141, 143, 144
Saudi Arabia, 112, 158, 207
Sauerbronn, Karl D. von, 318
Savarkar, Vinayak Damodar, 52, 75
Schmitt, Harrison, 345
Scientific experiments, 328–329
Scientific principles, 329–330
Scott, Sir Walter, 285
Sea Breeze, 154, 155
Seasons, 149
Sedimentary Rocks, 153
Sehwag, Virender, 313
Senegal, 207
Septic tank, 126
Serbia, 20, 161, 208
Seth, Vikram, 278
Severe Acute Respiratory Syndrome (SARS), 343
Seychelles, 208
Shah Jahan, 59, 65, 69, 257, 261, 263
Shakespeare, William, 143, 269, 270, 271, 284, 285, 289
Shankar, Ravi, 242, 293, 300
Shankar, Uday, 293
Shannon, Claude E., 115
Sharma, Shiv Kumar, 291, 293
Sharma, Vishnu, 278
Shatabdi Express, 240
Shaw, George Bernard, 285
Shelley, Percy Bysshe, 271, 286
Shepard, Alan, 345
Sher-Gil, Amrita, 246
Shi Huangdi, 14
Shinawatra, Yingluck, 39–40
Shiv Ratri, 232
Shiva, Vandana, 133
Shivaji, 69–70
Sholes, Christopher, 319
Short story, 271, 274, 276
Sierra Leone, 208
Sikhism, 84, 275

Sikkim, 222, 223, 252, 265
Simulation Games, 111
Singapore, 161, 208, 209
Singh, Bhagat, 52–53
Singh, Dhyan Chand, 304, 313, 314, 316
Singh, [Dr] Manmohan, 100–103
Singh, Milkha, 314
Singh, Pargat, 314
Singh, Ranjit, 70
Singh, Vijender, 314
Siraj-ud-Daulah, 70
Sleeping sickness, 343
Sleet, 156
Slovakia, 161, 209
Slovenia, 209
Smallpox, 323, 325, 328, 329, 343
Smog (photochemical smog), 126
Snow, 156
Sobers, Gary, 314
Socrates, 55, 56
Soil erosion check, 128
Soil improvement, 128
Soil pollution, 122
Solar eclipse, 148
Solid waste, 127
Solomon Islands, 209
Solstice, 149
Somalia, 210
Sonepur Cattle Fair, 232–233
Sonnet, 55, 271
South Africa, 28, 47, 160, 164, 210, 242, 302, 304
South America, 23, 151, 159, 161, 167, 170, 171, 174, 175, 185, 203, 212, 218, 219, 316
South Korea, 210
South Pole, 147–149
South Sudan, 210
Spain, 19, 23, 40, 41, 159, 160, 211, 215, 302, 307
Spam, 116, 118
Span, 4, 298, 333
Spanish Civil War, 19
Sparse Infectors, 113
Spitzer Space Telescope, 146
Sri Harmandir Sahib, 259
Sri Lanka, 22, 83, 152, 211, 302, 307

Stalin, Joseph, 33, 103
Standard Time, 149
Stanley, William, 319
Stars, 4, 141, 146, 147
State administration of India, 93–94
States of India, 246–253
Stem cells, 336
Stephenson, George, 42, 318,
Stevenson, Robert Louis, 269–271, 286
Stibitz, George, 107, 117
Stone Age, 1, 2
Strait, 152, 161, 307
Strategy Games, 111
Stratosphere, 121, 123, 150
Stringed Instrument, 294
Sturgeon, William, 318
Subbulakshmi, M.S., 242, 293
Sudan, 4, 162, 210, 211, 340
Sulphur dioxide (SO2), 121
Sultan, Raziya, 64, 71
Sultan, Tipu, 58, 71–72, 79, 80, 224,
Sun Temple in Konark, 251, 263
Supreme Court of India, 92, 93
Surajkund Crafts Fair, 233
Suriname, 212
Surkotada, 6
Suspended particulate matter (SPM), 121
Sustainable development, 126, 136
Swaziland, 212
Sweden, 212, 328
Swift, Jonathan, 286
Switzerland, 12, 30, 31, 135, 163, 212
Syria, 213

Tagore, Abanindranath, 246
Taiwan, 213
Taj Mahal, 69, 138, 253, 263
Tajikistan, 213
Takla Makan desert, 164–165
Tamil Nadu, 95, 127, 221, 226, 228, 229, 235, 241, 242, 252, 255, 307, 350
Tanjore art, 235
Tansen Miyan, 58, 294
Tanzania, 131, 158, 161, 162, 214
Tarnetar Mela, 233
Temple of Artemis, 10
Tendulkar, Sachin, 308, 313, 315

Teresa, Mother, 33, 241, 242
Tetragon, 350
Thabal Chongba, 255
Thailand, 39, 160, 162, 214
Thapar, Valmik, 133
Thar desert, 129, 165, 221
Thatcher, Margaret, 34
*The Accidental Billionaires*, 112
The Bahamas, 159, 214
The Bishnois, 129
The Bronte sisters, 286
The first vaccination, 328
The Gambia, 182
The Government of NCT of Delhi, 255
The Great Depression, 31, 42–43
The International Union for the
    Conservation of Nature (IUCN), 135
The Netherlands, 12, 163, 199
The Philippines, 161, 203
The Presidential Palace, Finland, 106
*The Social Network*, 112, 117
The Sun, 5, 120, 121, 141–150,157,
    232, 261, 320, 323, 327, 330, 331,
    332
The Vedas, 7, 8
Theme, 230, 271, 299
Theosophical Society, 45, 86
Thermosphere, 150, 151
Tie and dye, 235
Tilak, Bal Gangadhar, 50, 53–54, 76
Time zones, 148–149
Togo, 214
Tolstoy, Leo, 286–287
Tonga, 215, 220
Trade winds, 154
Trayi Veda, 8
Treaty of Versailles, 20
Triangle, 350
Trinidad and Tobago, 215
Tripura, 252
Trojan Horse, 112, 113
Tropic of Cancer, 148, 158
Tropic of Capricorn, 148, 158
Troposphere, 123, 126, 150
Tuberculosis, 281, 284, 325, 343
Tughlaq, Firuz Shah, 73
Tughlaq, Muhammad Bin, 73

Tulsidas, 279
Tungabhadra dam, 224
Tunisia, 215
Turing, Alan, 107, 117
Turkey, 16, 17, 20, 21, 77, 216
Turkmenistan, 216
Tutankhamen, 4, 14
Tuvalu, 216
Twain, Mark, 287
Twitter, 112
Types of computers, 110–111
Typhoid, 31, 344

Uganda, 162, 216–217
Ukraine, 16, 139, 161, 217, 311
Ultraviolet (UV) radiation, 126
Undecagon, 350
Union Budget of India, 97–98
Union executive, 92
Union territories of India, 253–255
United Arab Emirates, 112, 217
United Kingdom, 35, 217
United Nations Environment Programe
    (UNEP), 134
United States of America, 34, 39, 104,
    218
UNIX programmers, 115
Uranus, 141–144
Urban India, 94
Ursa Minor, 147
Uruguay, 218, 302
US Constitution, 91
Uses of Forests, 128
Usha, PT, 315
Uttar Pradesh, 44, 50, 99, 102, 127,
    129, 222, 226, 241–243, 253, 293
Uttarakhand, 222, 226, 238, 253
Uzbekistan, 218, 305

Vajpayee, Atal Bihari, 101,102, 103
Van Mahotsav, 129
Vanuatu, 218–219
Variable winds, 154, 155
Varma, Mahadevi, 279
Varma, Raja Ravi, 246
Varna, 8
Vatican City, 219

Vedic Age, 7–8
Vehicle simulation games, 111
Venezuela, 23, 159, 161, 219
Venus, 141, 142, 144, 146, 330, 331
Venus Williams, 303
Verne, Jules, 271, 287
Verse, 269–272, 278, 279, 281, 283, 284
Victoria (the Queen), 14–15
Video games, 111
Vidyasagar, Ishwar Chandra, 89
Vietnam, 19–20, 30, 219, 315, 317
Vietnam War, 19, 317
Vindhya Range, 222
Virus, 109, 112–113
Vivekananda, Swami, 86, 87, 89, 90
Volga river, 163
Voltaire, 41, 56
Vulcanized rubber, 327

Walpole, Robert, 105
Warli folk painting, 235
Washington, George, 16, 23, 34–35
Waste water treatment plant, 126, 132
Waste water, 122, 126
Water pollution, 121, 137
Water quality, 122, 126
Waterman, Lewis E., 319
Watson, James, 328
Watt, James (1736–1819), 42, 326
Waugh, Steve, 315
Wazwan, 263
Wearable computers, 111
West Bengal, 45, 88, 99, 224, 228, 231, 238, 241, 242, 253, 255
Westerlies, 154
Western Ghats, 223, 225, 226
Wetlands, 127
Whitaker, Romulus Earl, 134
White Hat Hackers, 114
White House, US, 105
Wilde, Oscar, 269, 287
Wind instrument, 294
Windbreaks and shelter belt, 128
Windows operating system, 109
Winds, 128, 148, 153–155, 165, 332

Woods, Tiger, 315
World War I, 15, 19, 20–21, 26, 30–33, 35, 42, 43, 260, 316
World War II, 20–21, 25, 26, 30, 31, 33, 35, 36, 43, 107, 117, 118, 271, 316
WordStar, 109
Wordsworth, William, 281, 287–288
World Animal Welfare Day, 119
World Environment Day, 119, 266
World Forestry Day, 119, 265
World Habitat Day, 119
World Meteorological Day, 119, 265
World Meteorological Organization (WMO), 134, 135
World Ozone Day, 119
World Population Day, 119, 266
World Water Day, 119
World Wetland Day, 119
World Wide Web (WWW), 109, 116
World Wildlife Week, 119
Worm, 113
Wright Brothers, 326

Xerox, 108

Yahoo, 110
Yajur Veda, 7, 8
Yakshagana, 255
Yamuna, 9, 63, 82, 222, 225, 226, 262, 263
Yangtze Kiang, 3, 163
Yeats, William Butler, 270, 288
Yemen, 220
Yoga, 272
Young Bengal Movement, 86

Zafar, Bahadur Shah II, 61, 261, 274
Zambia, 161, 220
Zanskar (or Zaskar) Range, 223
Zedong, Mao, 35
Zidane, Zinedine, 316
Zimbabwe, 220, 316
Zoji La, 224
Zoroastrianism, 84
Zuckerberg, Mark, 112, 117